Prisoners and the Law

Prisoners and the Law

Second edition

Simon Creighton
Solicitor; partner, Bhatt Murphy

Vicky King
Solicitor, Thanki Novy Taube

Contributor
Hamish Arnott
Solicitor, Prisoners' Advice Service

Butterworths
London, Dublin and Edinburgh
2000

United Kingdom	Butterworths, a Division of Reed Elsevier (UK) Ltd, Halsbury House, 35 Chancery Lane, London WC2A 1EL and 4 Hill Street, Edinburgh EH2 3JZ
Australia	Butterworths, a Division of Reed International Books Australia Pty Ltd, CHATSWOOD, New South Wales
Canada	Butterworths Canada Ltd, MARKHAM, Ontario
Hong Kong	Butterworths Asia (Hong Kong), HONG KONG
India	Butterworths India, NEW DELHI
Ireland	Butterworth (Ireland) Ltd, DUBLIN
Malaysia	Malayan Law Journal Sdn Bhd, KUALA LUMPUR
New Zealand	Butterworths of New Zealand Ltd, WELLINGTON
Singapore	Butterworths Asia, SINGAPORE
South Africa	Butterworths Publishers (Pty) Ltd, DURBAN
USA	Lexis Law Publishing, CHARLOTTESVILLE, Virginia

© Reed Elsevier (UK) Ltd 2000

A CIP Catalogue record for this book is available from the British Library.

ISBN 0 406 91105 3

Printed and bound by Hobbs the Printers Ltd, Totton, Hants

Visit Butterworths LEXIS *direct* at: http://www.butterworths.com

FOREWORD

In his foreword to the first edition of this admirable book, Edward Fitzgerald QC drew attention to its contribution to the process of enlightenment as to how the prison system works. One of my tasks as HM Chief Inspector of Prisons is to inform the public about its prisons, and the work that the Prison Service does with and for prisoners, to prepare them to live law-abiding and useful lives in custody and on release. All this is in line with the aim given to the criminal justice system of protecting the public by preventing crime.

In the course of my inspections I look for what I call 'Healthy Prisons', in which there are four separate attributes. Firstly, a Healthy Prison is one in which the weakest prisoner feels safe. If the weakest feels safe so will everyone else, both those who are confined and those who work with them. Secondly, everyone must be treated with respect as a fellow human being. It is not the role of Prison Officers to be judgmental of committed offences, or to regard prisoners as subordinates. Staff owe prisoners a duty of care.

Thirdly, in a Healthy Prison all prisoners are encouraged to improve themselves, and given the opportunity of doing this through purposeful activity. Hopefully this will be based on individual needs assessments, so that it is aimed at satisfying the best interests of the individual concerned, and so of the community into which he or she will return, with the intention of helping them to find a job, as well as of tackling offending behaviour. Finally, every prisoner is prepared for release, and enabled to maintain family contact while doing so.

Included in the analysis of treating people with respect is making sure that they understand what is going on around them, and are aware of their obligations and rights. As we approach the introduction of the European Convention on Human Rights, this is even more important, not only for the prisoner who is on the receiving end, but on every member of the Prison Service who must be fully aware of what is incumbent on them. What I find so refreshing about *Prisoners and the Law* is that it is designed to help both parties. Prisoners can learn about what are called 'basic legal remedies' for processing any complaints, and staff can learn about the legislation that is binding on them. Thus each should be enlightened about the system of which they are a part, in language that is understandable.

The public is, rightly, suspicious of any organisation that is self-regulated. That is essentially why an independent Inspectorate of Prisons was resumed in 1981, following 104 years of self-regulation since 1877 when the Prison Commission was formed, following barely 42 years of independent inspection since it was introduced in 1835. I mention this because I see *Prisoners and the Law* filling a role in line with my own work. It enables the public to have access to details of procedures affecting issues surrounding prisoners and prisons, about which they often only hear in lurid terms from the media. People feel happier, in a democratic sense, if they know that both they and prisoners have access to laid down procedures to overcome possible miscarriages of justice for example, as well as the ability to complain about treatment and conditions.

It is said that the civilised state of a nation can be judged by the way in which it treats its prisoners. In the case of the United Kingdom that includes the machinery that was described in the first edition of the book, and that which has been added in the second. *Prisoners and the Law* will be in the HM Inspectorate of Prisons library, for the use of inspectors who have a responsibility of seeing that the rights of prisoners are protected. Therefore, in a very positive sense I am as grateful to Simon Creighton, Vicky King and Hamish Arnott, as will be all those who use the book for enlightenment or for practical advice and help.

Sir David Ramsbotham

PREFACE

By coincidence, the second edition of this book has been completed on the tenth anniversary of the Strangeways riots. Depressingly, many of the good intentions that were expressed in the aftermath of those disturbances have fallen by the wayside. The fall in the use of imprisonment that followed the Woolf Report has been reversed and while there have been improvements in the physical structure of prisons, the regimes have become more punitive in many ways with many of the rights prisoners used to enjoy being transformed into privileges which can only be accessed through subjective behavioural assessments carried out by prison officers. As the uncovering of systematic abuse at Wormwood Scrubs has demonstrated, the overall culture of imprisonment with respect to the institutional treatment of prisoners has yet to be addressed.

When we wrote the first edition of *Prisoners and the Law*, there was very little published information on the law relating to prisoners, despite prisons seeming to be endlessly on the public agenda. Prisons remain under very close public scrutiny but the debate no longer seems to address the fundamental issues that have persisted into the twenty-first century. Successive governments have become increasingly reliant on imprisonment as the solution to crime prevention. Despite the lessons of the USA, where the prison population exceeded two million for the first time in February 2000 without any compelling evidence to link this unprecedented use of imprisonment with reductions in crime, the prison population in this country has also risen relentlessly. The United Kingdom is second only to the USA amongst western democracies in terms of its relative prison population and there is no sign that this will abate in the near future.

One of the consequences of the increasing use of imprisonment has been to consolidate the notion of 'prison law' as a distinct area of practice and study. The legal profession has belatedly caught up with the prisoner population in recognising the importance of prisoners' rights as both a legal and philosophical concept. The implementation of the Human Rights Act poses a fresh challenge to the state to examine the purpose and nature of imprisonment. Prisoners have demonstrated a great awareness of the uses to which the European Convention on Human Rights can be put and lawyers will need to ensure that they are as proficient as their clients in this area of law.

Another major challenge for lawyers advising prisoners is the manner in which prisoners' rights work will be publicly funded in the future. Unfortunately, at the time of writing the final proposals for a prisoners' rights franchise and the place this area of work will have in the forthcoming Criminal Defence Service have not been published. We have sought to anticipate the likely developments in the chapter dealing with legal aid. Although it appears the full provision will be made for issues relating to the administrative decisions made about prisoners, such as categorisation, parole and transfers, property claims are likely to be excluded from public funding, and there remains confusion as to how compensation claims for neglect of duty and deliberate abuses of power will be funded.

We would like to acknowledge the help we have received in preparing the second edition of this book. We are indebted to Hamish Arnott, the solicitor at the Prisoners' Advice Service, who has updated and revised large sections of this book. Without his contribution it would not have been possible to prepare this edition. We have also received invaluable assistance from Nicki Rensten, the caseworker at the Prisoners' Advice Service. In addition we wish to thank all members of staff at the Prisoners' Advice Service, both past and present, for their dedication to advancing and promoting the concept of legal rights for prisoners in extremely difficult circumstances.

The section on deaths in custody and suicide prevention has been greatly expanded. Mark Scott of Bhatt Murphy solicitors and Deb Coles of the organisation INQUEST re-wrote this section completely and have produced a comprehensive and unique guide to an often neglected topic. We are grateful to them for writing with such clarity on one of the most emotive and difficult areas of law.

We have also received advice and assistance from a number of other lawyers. We would particularly wish to thank Phillippa Kaufmann, Tim Owen QC and Ed Fitzgerald QC. All three are barristers who have made significant contributions to our work as practitioners and who have a genuine commitment to advancing the rights of those in custody. Kate Akester of JUSTICE, who helped pioneer the development of prisoners' rights in the 1980s, has continued to assist us and many other lawyers with her unique expertise.

Finally, and most importantly, we are fortunate to have this opportunity to thank all of the prisoners who have contacted us over the years, both as clients and to provide us with information about how the prison system actually works in practice. The knowledge they have shared with us has been an integral part of our legal education and we feel privileged to have had access to such invaluable help.

Simon Creighton and Vicky King
4 March 2000

CONTENTS

Contents

SECTION II

Contents

Contents

TABLE OF ABBREVIATIONS

AG	Advice to Governors
ALP	Automatic Lifer Panels
AMBOV	The Association of Members of Boards of Visitors
AUR	Automatic Unconditional Release
CA	Coroners Act (1988)
CDA	Crime and Disorder Act (1998)
CDS	Criminal Defence Service
CI	Circular Instruction
CJA	Criminal Justice Act (both 1991 and 1967)
CJPOA	Criminal Justice and Public Order Act (1994)
CLS	Community Legal Service
CPS	Crown Prosecution Service
CR	Coroners Rules (1984)
CRC	Control Review Committee
CSC	Close Supervision Centre
DCR	Discretionary Release Scheme
DLP	Discretionary Lifer Panel
DSP	Directorate of Services and Programmes
DTO	Detention and Training Orders
E LIST	Escape (risk) list
ECHR	European Convention on Human Rights (*officially* Convention for the Protection of Human Rights and Fundamental Freedoms)
GBH	Grievous Bodily Harm
HCC	High Control Cells
HDC	Home Detention Curfew Scheme
HMCIP	Her Majesty's Chief Inspector of Prisons
HMP	Her Majesty's Prison/Her Majesty's Pleasure
HRA	Human Rights Act 1998
HSU	High Security Unit
ICA	Initial Categorisation and Allocation
IEP	Incentives and Earned Privileges
IG	Instruction to Governors
LAB	Legal Aid Board
LSC	Legal Services Commission
LED	Licence Expiry Date
NGO	Non-governmental Organisation
NPRD	Non-parole Release Date
OCA	Observation, Allocation and Classification
OUP	Oxford University Press

Table of Abbreviations

PED	Parole Eligibility Date
PRRD	Post Recall Release Date
PSI	Prison Service Instruction
PSO	Prison Service Order
ROTL	Release on Temporary Licence
SED	Sentence Expiry Date
SIR	Security Information Report
SO	Standing Order
SSU	Special Security Unit
UAL	Unlawfully at Large
VPU	Vulnerable Prisoners' Unit
YOI	Young Offender Institution

TABLE OF STATUTES

Page numbers in *italic* type refer to the appendices at the end of this book.

TABLE OF STATUTORY INSTRUMENTS

Page numbers in *italic* type refer to the appendices at the end of this book.

TABLE OF CASES

Table of cases

SECTION I

CHAPTER 1
INTRODUCTION

1.1 The law relating to prisons and the rights of prisoners has developed relatively recently, emerging as a distinct area only during the 1980s. In some respects, it remains something of a hybrid area, encompassing aspects of criminal law, administrative law, tort and the developing concept of human rights law. The very nature of closed institutions such as prisons means that the workings of the prison system can appear inscrutable. Despite the ever increasing moves towards openness on the part of government and the willingness of the courts to review the administration of the Prison Service, it can still prove difficult to access the material and information needed to advise prisoners. However, this should not deter lawyers from dealing with enquiries from prisoners as the statutory framework and legal principles upon which the system is based are relatively straightforward.

1.2 The only major piece of prison legislation to address the prison system is the Prison Act 1952 and although it has been subject to amendments, the Act has not substantially changed in the past fifty years. The reason why the statutory framework appears to be so static is that it is primarily enabling legislation. The power to make rules for the running of prisons is devolved upon the Home Secretary, who exercises this power by way of statutory instrument. These rules provide for further devolution of a wide range of discretionary decisions to civil servants and prison governors. The policies and decisions that result are subject to the authority of common law and judicial interpretation.

1.3 The apparent hotchpotch of rules and regulations that results from the interplay between statute, statutory instrument, policy documents and court judgments can appear to be impenetrable. In practice, the rights and remedies which arise will be familiar to lawyers.

1.4 Prisoners will generally resort to the law in two situations: when seeking to enforce public law rights by way of judicial review and when pursuing private law remedies for damages. The distinction between public and private law in this context is not complex. From the time that a person is sentenced to imprisonment until the date of release, a series of administrative decisions will be made. These will encompass issues ranging from the length of time to be served in custody and the prisons in which the sentence will be served, through to the procedures and policies that are adopted for release. The decision maker derives the power to decide upon these matters from public law sources rather than from an agreement or action between private parties (for a full discussion of the distinction between public and private law, see *O'Reilly v Mackman* [1982] 3 All ER 1124 and *Council of Civil Service Unions v Minister for the Civil Service* [1985] AC 374). As such, all of these decisions will be within the realm of public law.

1.5   It is possible to further divide public law decisions into two separate areas. First, there are rights which accrue to people in custody over which there is no discretion by the decision maker. These include, for example, the minimum number of visits a prisoner can receive (Prison Rules 1999, rr 33–39: see section II, chapter 9) or the right to be considered for parole at a certain stage of one's sentence (Criminal Justice Act 1991, ss 32–40: see section II, chapter 12). Second, there are a wide ranging number of situations where a decision maker is obliged to make a decision, but retains an element of discretion. These may include substantive parole decisions (see section II, chapter 12), security categorisation (*R v Secretary of State for the Home Department, ex p Duggan* [1994] 3 All ER 277: see section II, chapter 6) or the exercise of disciplinary and quasi-disciplinary powers (Prison Rules 1999, rr 51–61; *Campbell and Fell v United Kingdom* (1985) 7 EHRR 165 and *Leech v Deputy Governor of Parkhurst Prison* [1988] AC 533 on the exercise of formal disciplinary powers; and *Ex p Ross* (1994) Times, 9 June on the use of the informal disciplinary system). A full discussion of the range of decisions that are amenable to judicial review follows in section I, chapter 3.

1.6   The private law remedies that are relevant to prisoners largely concern the circumstances in which the right to financial compensation will arise. This may be in respect of injuries suffered at work or through dangerous premises (*Ferguson v Home Office* (1977) Times, 8 October), negligent medical treatment (*Knight v Home Office* [1990] 3 All ER 237), assaults by other prisoners or members of staff (there is a range of cases on this topic, see eg, *H v Home Office* (1992) Independent, 6 May, *D'Arcy v Prison Comrs* [1956] Crim LR 56 and *Egerton v Home Office* [1978] Crim LR 494), loss of and damage to property and intolerable conditions of detention (*R v Deputy Governor of Parkhurst, ex p Hague* [1992] 1 AC 58). The tortious principles that apply are discussed in detail in section I, chapter 3 and will be largely familiar to practitioners of civil law.

1.7   The main problem that arises when advising prisoners on matters of both public and private law is to identify the provisions and regulations that guide decision makers and establish the duty of care that is owed to a prisoner. Section II of this book sets out these standards and the sources from which they are derived.

1.8   One of the key difficulties with the manner in which the law is applied to prisoners is that it is susceptible to change at very short notice and with no public explanation of these changes. For example, in 1994 various newspapers began to voice concern at prisoners' entitlement to home leave. As a result, the Home Secretary of the day, Michael Howard, made a policy statement that he intended to tighten these provisions and, in April 1995, a new policy was officially put in place by way of an Instruction to Prison Governors issued by the Prison Service. The new rules were challenged in the High Court and in July 1995, the challenge was dismissed (*R v Secretary of State for the Home Department, ex p Briggs, Green & Hargreaves* [1996] COD 168, and the High Court's decision was later upheld by the Court of Appeal [1997] 1 All ER 397). In the space of a few months, the entire basis on which temporary release from prison is authorised had been changed by the Home Secretary and ratified by the High Court.

1.9 A further problem can arise when new legislation is passed but not implemented or it is implemented in stages. By way of example, the Crime (Sentences) Act 1997 completely re-wrote the legislation for release on parole licence. Although the part of the Act that addressed life sentences was implemented in October 1997, the new parole provisions for prisoners serving determinate sentences have never been implemented and were not formally repealed until the Crime and Disorder Act 1998 was enacted. It is possible to obtain the Home Office circulars, which explain the relevance of new legislation and those parts which are implemented, through the Home Office web site.

1.10 Any book on the law can only be as current as the latest court decision or change to statute, and nowhere is this more apparent than with prison law. Due to the vast extent of discretionary decision-making powers that exist, the interplay between politics and the law is at its most transparent, and speeches made to political party conferences can be implemented as policy within a matter of weeks. A great deal of policy is also to be found in Parliamentary written answers and, for example, virtually the entire policy for the administration of the mandatory life sentence can be found from this source. Lawyers will therefore need to keep abreast of current developments in this field to ensure that they remain up to date. Aside from the normal legal periodicals that cover developments in the law, the Prisoners' Legal Rights Group Bulletin provides a quarterly review of new cases, lists of new Prison Service Instructions and discussions on developments (published by the Prisoners' Advice Service) and the Legal Action Group Bulletin contains a prison law update every six months. The various penal reform agencies, such as the Prison Reform Trust ('Prison Report') and the Howard League ('Criminal Justice'), publish quarterly magazines that provide updates on changes in the law and policy in our prisons.

CHAPTER 2

LEGISLATION

STATUTE AND PRISONS

2.1 There is very little primary legislation that is directly concerned with prisons and imprisonment. Although various Acts of Parliament do, from time to time, contain important provisions for prisoners (eg the Criminal Justice Acts and the Crime (Sentences) Act 1997), the only piece of legislation that deals solely with the prison estate is the Prison Act 1952. Thus, there is no primary source that contains an exhaustive explanation of the rights to which those in custody are entitled and the facilities and privileges which they can expect.

2.2 Much of the Prison Act 1952 is concerned with establishing very basic principles, such as who has legal responsibility for managing prisons and implementing appropriate rules, rather than with the actual rules and regulations themselves. More detail is supplied in the Prison Rules 1999 (consolidating and updating the Prison Rules 1964) which are issued pursuant to the Act but once again, they do not complete the full picture. In many instances, these Rules will make reference to discretionary powers which are to be exercised either by a prison governor or the Secretary of State. It is these discretionary powers that often get to the root of prison life and will in many cases be the matters on which prisoners will need advice and representation. The manner in which these powers are to be exercised and the details of how the Rules are to be implemented are contained in a series of policy documents issued by Prison Service Headquarters. These are currently in the form of Standing Orders and Prison Service Orders ('PSOs') and have previously been issued as Circular Instructions, Advice and Instructions to Governors and Prison Service Instructions.

2.3 The development of prison law has also been greatly affected by common law decision-making and in particular through the jurisdiction of the High Court. One of the reasons why this has been such a fertile area for judicial review is precisely because there is so little statutory material.

2.4 In order to gain an understanding of prison law and to be able to provide effective advice to prisoners, it is necessary to refer to the three different levels of source materials. The starting point is necessarily the Prison Act 1952 as, whilst it does not actually contain detailed information on the day-to-day life of prisoners, it is the primary source of decision-making power and sets the context for the management of the prison estate. There follows a discussion of the Prison Rules 1999, the relevance of changes introduced by the Criminal Justice Acts and then the status of policy documents. Finally, the legal status of 'contracted out' prisons is explored.

THE PRISON ACT 1952

2.5   The main purpose of the Act is not to make detailed provision for the running and management of prisons but to vest authority in those who do hold this power. The corollary of this is that the Act actually says very little about prisoners' rights and the obligations of the state to those in their custody.

2.6   The Home Secretary is charged with the duty of 'general superintendence' over prisons and is empowered to 'make contracts and do acts necessary for the maintenance of prisons and the maintenance of prisoners' (s 4(1)). Section 4(2) goes on to require the Home Secretary to ensure compliance with the Act and the Prison Rules. There is no explanation as to the manner in which compliance should be guaranteed. The section does, however, establish that the Home Secretary is the person ultimately responsible for the manner in which prisons are run and for ensuring that the duties and obligations of the state towards those in custody are properly fulfilled.

2.7   Section 4(2) is important in that it places a clear onus of responsibility on the Secretary of State and it is the Secretary of State who is accountable for any failure to properly comply with this duty. Conversely, this power was often invoked when defending actions brought by prisoners against prison governors' administrative and disciplinary decisions. The argument advanced was that s 4 amounted to an ouster clause whereby the power to ensure compliance with Prison Act and Rules was vested solely in the Secretary of State and it was only if he failed to fulfil this obligation that judicial review could be sought. It was not until 1988 that this interpretation was finally laid to rest following the decision of the House of Lords in *Leech v Deputy Governor of Parkhurst Prison* [1988] AC 533, a challenge to a governor's use of formal disciplinary powers. Lord Bridge perceived this argument as an attempt to undermine the jurisdiction of the court in a manner which was incompatible with the principles of administrative law.

The Chief Inspector and Boards of Visitors

2.8   The Act goes on to make provision for two 'watchdog' bodies: the Chief Inspector of Prisons (s 5A) and the Boards of Visitors (ss 6–9). The Chief Inspector is under a duty to inspect prisons with particular regard to conditions and the treatment of prisoners, to report to the Home Secretary and to submit an annual report that must be laid before Parliament. The Chief Inspector's powers are limited to reporting and it is not possible for binding recommendations to be made. The Chief Inspector will prepare reports on individual prisons throughout each year and will provide a general commentary on prison conditions in the Annual Report. The individual inspections are often highly critical and, despite the fact that they have no formal legal status, they can provide important evidence of particular conditions and policies that are being pursued in a prison at a particular time.

2.9   The Home Secretary is also required to appoint a Board of Visitors for each prison and for these Boards to be allowed to visit the prison and to hear complaints. The right of free access to any part of the prison at any time, and to see any prisoner at any time are protected by the Act (s 6(3)). Originally, Boards also had a disciplinary function in that they acted as adjudicators for disciplinary charges that were considered too serious to be heard by the governor. This power was abolished in 1992 following the Woolf Report when it was considered that their watchdog role was incompatible with that of upholding prison discipline. The confidence of prisoners in the Boards to hear and act upon their complaints was seriously undermined by the fact that they would also be hearing charges against them and awarding punishments of forfeiture of remission. There was a general assumption amongst prisoners that the Boards were too willing to accept the authority of prison staff without question and that it was not possible to have a fair hearing at adjudications. This situation was exacerbated by the fact that the Boards would be hearing the more serious charges and awarding significant punishments.

2.10   Following the removal of this power, all adjudications are now carried out by individual prison governors. There is a certain irony in this solution. Having removed the potential for a conflict of interests from one body, an even greater potential for conflict has been created. It is difficult to see how the dual roles of managing staff, implementing regulations for the running of the prison and acting as an impartial arbiter at disciplinary hearings can be properly reconciled (see chapter 4).

2.11   The Boards do still have one key role to play in the maintenance of discipline in prisons. When a governor authorises the segregation of a prisoner, this can only be done for a period of up to three days in the first instance. Following that three-day period, any decisions to continue segregation must be authorised by the Board of Visitors (Prison Rules, r 45). The fact that there is a direct supervisory body for decisions of this nature is important in principle, but in practice there will be very few occasions when the Board will not accept the governor's decision in such cases.

Prison staff

2.12   Prisons are required to have a governor, a chaplain, a medical officer and such other officers as 'may be necessary' (s 7). The statutory obligation for prisons to have a governor is of importance in assessing the nature of the governor's duties. These powers are distinguishable from those exercised by the Home Secretary and are defined in detail in the Prison Rules. Whilst it is true that the extent of the governor's powers is decided by the Home Secretary, the fact remains that it is the governor who is obliged to carry them out. The governor is empowered, with leave of the Secretary of State, to delegate the powers conferred directly on him/her to another officer at the prison (Prison Rules, r 81).

2.13   It was this point that was considered fundamental in the case of *Leech* [1988] AC 533 when Lord Bridge held that governors' powers were amenable to judicial review in their own right. The court observed that whilst the Prison Rules established the offences against discipline and the punitive powers available, there was no provision for the Home Secretary to direct the governor on how to adjudicate a particular charge, or as to what punishment should be awarded (at 563D).

Location and accommodation

2.14   Section 12(1) states that prisoners may lawfully be confined in any prison, whether on remand or convicted and s 12(2) states that prisoners may be transferred from one prison to another. This power is expressed to rest with the Home Secretary but can be (and in practice, is) delegated to the governor.

2.15   For practical purposes, the importance of s 12(1) is that it establishes that a prisoner has no right to be held in any particular prison. It is a common misunderstanding of prisoners and their families that there is a duty for them to be located in a prison convenient for visits. No such right exists and whilst a whole range of factors are to be taken into account when determining location, any challenges to the allocation decisions can only be made within the confines of administrative law (see section II, chapter 6).

2.16   Whilst in custody, the governor has responsibility (and liability) to each prisoner in his/her prison. This stems from the fact that the governor of the prison is deemed to be the legal custodian (s 13).

2.17   The accommodation available must be certified as being fit for its purpose by the Home Secretary (s 14). The certificate requires inspection of size, heating, lighting, ventilation and fittings. Certification is carried out by officers appointed by the Secretary of State and there is no independent system of certification. The requirements and standards that are to be met are not specified and consequently may be changed depending upon prevailing conditions and the changing requirements of each prison. The Chief Inspector of Prisons will frequently express opinions as to the living conditions in particular prisons and if standards were to fall below a certain level, the conditions of detention may give rise to a cause of action in domestic law or under the European Convention on Human Rights. In general, however, the section is only important in terms of litigation if a prisoner is detained in accommodation that has not been certified.

Disciplinary and miscellaneous provisions

2.18   The Act contains a number of further provisions that are of some importance to prisoners, although the powers created are expanded in far greater detail in the Prison Rules and policy documents. These sections are as follows:

(i)   Section 16A provides the authority for mandatory drugs testing and gives all prison officers the power, on the authority of the governor, to require prisoners to provide a sample of urine (or other non-intimate sample) for the purposes of testing for the presence of controlled drugs;

(ii) Section 25 creates the power to authorise the early release of prisoners. The actual schemes that are put into place for remission of sentence are made under the powers created by s 47 (see below);

(iii) Section 28 creates the power to discharge prisoners temporarily on the grounds of ill health.

(iv) Section 30 allows for discharge payments to be made to prisoners;

(v) Sections 39–42 create offences of assisting prisoners to escape from a prison, bringing alcohol, tobacco or other unauthorised articles into a prison and require notices to be displayed outside of prisons recording these provisions;

(vi) Section 49 states that any time spent unlawfully at large during the currency of a sentence does not count towards that sentence.

The power to make prison rules

2.19   Perhaps the most important section of the Act is s 47 which allows the Secretary of State:

> 'to make rules and regulations for the management of prisons, remand centres, detention centres and youth custody centres, and for the classification, treatment, employment, discipline and control of persons required to be detained therein.'

These rules must be made by statutory instrument. At s 47(2), there is an important safeguard to any rules that are made:

> 'Rules made under this section shall make provision for ensuring that a person who is charged with any offence under the rules shall be given a proper opportunity of presenting his case.'

This section emphasises the duty that exists in common law and under the European Convention on Human Rights to ensure that the rules must follow the principles of natural justice in the administration of prison discipline.

THE PRISON RULES

The legal status

2.20 The Prison Rules were most recently updated in April 1999 when they were redrafted to take account of the 25 amendments that had been introduced since 1964. They contain a mixture of provisions and refer to both general policies, such as the purpose of imprisonment (r 3), and to more specific obligations and duties that are imposed upon the Prison Service. A large number of the Rules confer discretionary powers which are supplemented by documents issued explaining how discretion should be exercised. The remaining rules of importance to prisoners are concerned with the formal disciplinary system that must be adopted.

2.21 The varying nature of the Rules and the fact that they contain a mixture of policy statements, obligations to prisoners and discretionary powers leads to much confusion as to their status. Broadly speaking, the Rules will set out general powers and duties which are to be implemented in the running of prisons. In order to ensure consistency and fairness throughout the system, a series of documents are issued described as Standing Orders and Prison Service Orders and Instructions. These documents are designed to fill in the details of the everyday management of prisons and will deal with everything from the fees to be paid to visiting dentists to the facilities that are to be allowed to prisoners, and to the arrangements for mandatory drugs testing.

2.22 The Prison Rules are not, in themselves, justiciable and were not intended to be so. In 1972, Lord Denning commented that:

> 'If the courts were to entertain actions by disgruntled prisoners, the governor's life would be made intolerable. The discipline of the prison would be undermined. The Prison Rules are regulatory directions only. Even if they are not observed, they do not give rise to a cause of action.'
> (*Becker v Home Office* [1972] 2 QB 407)

2.23 Lord Wilberforce clarified the situation slightly ten years later when he stated that prisoners retain all civil rights that are not taken away, either expressly or by the fact of their imprisonment. However, he went on to say that as there is no contractual relationship between prisoners and the prison authorities that there must be reliance on the normal laws of tort in order for an action to be brought (*Raymond v Honey* [1983] 1 AC 1).

2.24 It was not for another ten years that the present position was fully established by the courts. In *R v Deputy Governor of Parkhurst Prison, ex p Hague, Weldon v Home Office* [1992] 1 AC 58, the House of Lords examined the public and private law rights of prisoners. Although the decision contains dissenting opinion, the Lords agreed that the Prison Rules do not give rise to any specific private law rights. As a result, it is apparent that the Rules are in fact justiciable to the extent that they are amenable to judicial supervision through judicial review. In the private law sphere, whilst prisoners retain the right to bring ordinary private law actions in cases of negligence, there is no right to bring an action for breach of statutory duty in respect of non-compliance with the Rules.

2.25   Thus, the manner in which the Rules are implemented is amenable to judicial review and breaches of them may be evidence in support of negligence actions, but the Rules do not confer any additional right to litigate. However, practitioners do need to be familiar with the Rules in their context as the source of authority from which more detailed regulations are made.

The key provisions

2.26   The Prison Rules 1999 are reproduced in the appendices and each Rule is discussed in the following individual chapters in context (a full and detailed examination of each individual rule and its European equivalent may be found in Loucks and Plotnikoff *Prison Rules – A Working Guide* (1993) Prison Reform Trust. Broadly, they are divided in the following manner:

Part I

Rules 1–11	Statement of intent, maintaining good order and discipline, classification of prisoners, privileges, temporary release, women prisoners and requests and complaints
Rules 13–19	Religion
Rules 20–22	Medical attention
Rules 23–31	Physical welfare and work
Rules 32–33	Education and library
Rules 34–39	Prisoner communications (letters and visits)
Rules 40–44	Property, removal and records
Rules 45–50	Special control, supervision, restraints (including segregation) and drug taking
Rules 51–61	Offences against discipline

Part II

Rules 62–69	Officers of prisons

Part III

Rules 70–73	Persons having access to prisons

Part IV

Rules 74–80	Boards of Visitors
Rules 81–85	Supplemental

2.27   The Rules have been described as falling into five distinct categories. These are comprised of general policy objectives, rules of a discretionary nature (normally concerned with privileges that may be afforded), rules concerning administration and rules of specific individual protection (see Owen and Livingstone *Prison Law* (2nd edn, 1999) OUP, pp 16–20 for a full discussion). Whilst those Rules concerned with discretionary rights such as temporary release (r 6), or correspondence (r 34) are of importance, the classes of prisoners who are allowed to benefit from these privileges and the manner in which that discretion should be exercised are set out in the policy documents issued by Prison Service Headquarters. Many of the Rules therefore do little other than to give a general power or create a general right that is then subject to policy and interpretation as to how it should implemented.

2.28 The key Rules are those that are concerned with the formal and informal disciplinary system (ie those of 'specific individual protection'). In effect this means rr 45–61 which are concerned with maintaining good order and discipline and the formal disciplinary code that is applied to prisoners. These provide a list of the offences against prison discipline (r 51), the procedure to be followed when laying a charge (rr 53–54) and the punishments that can be awarded to prisoners once a charge has been proven (rr 55–60). Where new offences are to be created or the powers of punishment are to be extended, these must be incorporated into the Rules by statutory instrument.

2.29 There have been many calls for a revision of the Rules and for a national set of minimum standards to be approved and incorporated. In the Woolf Report, it was suggested that a set of accredited standards should be prepared and that prisons should be certified once they had reached these standards. Once they had been achieved, Lord Woolf suggested that:

> 'at that stage they would be incorporated in the Prison Rules and so would be legally enforceable by judicial review.' (Cm 1456, para 1.187)

Despite support for a minimum set of standards from many diverse bodies and individuals, the official approach to the Rules remains one of minor revision when considered necessary rather than a complete overhaul.

THE CRIMINAL JUSTICE ACTS AND OTHER LEGISLATION

2.30 The only other legislation which is of direct relevance to prison issues are the various Criminal Justice Acts issued since 1967, the Crime (Sentences) Act 1997 and the Crime and Disorder Act 1998. These Acts contain major legislative provisions for parole, early and compassionate release, recall of prisoners on licence and computation of sentences (CJA 1991, ss 34–48). The Criminal Justice Act 1991 implemented perhaps the most radical overhaul of release and licence provisions since 1967, yet key sections from the older Acts remain in force (eg CJA 1967, s 67 concerning the computation of sentences).

2.31 This raft of legislation is primarily concerned with issues that affect statutory requirements imposed upon the Prison Service rather than simply providing the authority for implementing rules and regulations. The various sections that are of relevance to particular prison issues are not discussed in this chapter but are dealt with in section II. Those parts of the Acts that deal with contracted out prisons are examined below.

STANDING ORDERS AND ADVICE AND PRISON SERVICE ORDERS

2.32 The mechanics of the everyday running of prisons are largely determined by the guidance documents issued by the Prison Service referred to as Standing Orders and Prison Service Orders and Instructions (formerly

Advice and Instructions to Governors and before then, Circular Instructions). Standing Orders are a statement of policy and the exercise of discretion in a particular area. They have been issued to cover topics such as reception to prison, discharge, temporary release, communications and calculation of sentences. Prison Service Instructions and Orders are issued on an ad hoc basis and amend or update information in the Standing Orders. They are also the mechanism by which changes to policy, such as the revisions to home leave criteria, or new Prison Rules are communicated to prison governors.

2.33   These directives, although often made under powers contained in the Prison Rules, do not have any statutory authority. An example of the relationship between statute, statutory instrument and these directives may be found by examining the changes made to Standing Order 5B which deals with prisoners' correspondence.

2.34   Standing Order 5B has been subject to a number of challenges both domestically and in international law. In *Raymond v Honey* [1983] 1 AC 1, it was found that prisoners were being denied the right to have unfettered access to a court as letters being sent by a prisoner were being stopped in accordance with Standing Order 5B. Standing Order 5B had been issued, inter alia, to provide a code of working practice that complied with r 37 of the Prison Rules, which allowed privileged communications to be sent to certain classes of people in certain circumstances. It was held that neither the Prison Act 1952 nor the Prison Rules 1964 contained any provisions that would allow correspondence of this nature to be impeded. Lord Bridge took the view that:

> 'Standing Orders set out an elaborate procedure designed to discourage a prisoner from instituting proceedings in person and impliedly assume that he requires leave of the Secretary of State to do so, which the Secretary of State has an absolute discretion to withhold. The only statutory provision relied on ... is the power in s 47 of the Prison Act 1952 to make rules for the "discipline and control" of prisoners. This rule making power is manifestly insufficient for such a purpose and it follows that the rules, to the extent that would fetter a prisoner's right of access to the courts ... are ultra vires.' ([1983] 1 AC 15C)

The result was that the Standing Order had to be amended to ensure that this right was protected.

2.35   More recently, in *Campbell v United Kingdom* (1992) 15 EHRR 137, Series A no 48, the European Court of Human Rights held that the right afforded to prisoners to privileged correspondence with lawyers was insufficient to comply with the Convention. This decision was then followed by *R v Secretary of State for the Home Department, ex p Leech* [1994] QB 198 which held that the right to unimpeded legal correspondence with solicitors was an integral component of the fundamental right of a prisoner's access to the courts. As a result, r 37 (now rule 39) of the Prison Rules was amended to allow privileged correspondence in a far wider variety of cases and an Instruction to Governors was issued to remedy the defect. The Instruction to Governors declared the new policy and procedures that were to be adopted and these were eventually incorporated into Standing Order 5B. Similarly, in the recent House of Lords decision in *R v Secretary of State for the Home*

Department, ex p Simms and O'Brien [1999] 3 All ER 400, the House found that the application of a policy in Standing Order 5 banning all visits by journalists to prisoners was unlawful, even though the statutory provision under which the policy was formulated was lawful.

2.36 Whilst it is established that these documents are amenable to judicial review when they lead to unlawful administration, it is also arguable that they can establish explicit rights for, and obligations to, those in custody. This arises because they set out particular obligations that the Prison Service undertakes to fulfil vis-à-vis prisoners. Therefore, if the Prison Service decides to adopt a particular procedure or policy in one of these documents and subsequently fails to follow its own procedures, these actions may be reviewable (see eg *R v Deputy Governor of Parkhurst Prison, ex p Hague, Weldon v Home Office* [1992] 1 AC 58).

2.37 It has been argued that these additional rights arise because a legitimate expectation that prisoners can expect a particular type of treatment has been created (see Livingstone and Owen *Prison Law* (1999) pp 22–23). The concept of legitimate expectation for prisoners has not always been well received by the courts and it is certainly the case that legitimate expectations apply primarily to procedural requirements as opposed to creating substantive rights. It is perfectly lawful for the prison authorities to alter the nature of the rights and privileges that prisoners are entitled to during the currency of a prison sentence, providing that the correct procedures are followed. Applications that have sought to argue that a legitimate expectation can arise when a change has been made to a substantive policy decision, such as the criteria for parole or home leave, have been conspicuously less successful (see eg *Re Findlay* [1985] AC 318).

2.38 Since the decision of the House of Lords in *R v Secretary of State for the Home Department, ex p Doody* [1994] 1 AC 531, it may be easier to describe this process as the Prison Service being forced to adopt good administrative practice. An attempt to challenge changes in the policy to home leave on the basis of legitimate expectation was dismissed by Kennedy LJ with the following comments:

> 'So, Mr Beloff [for the Home Secretary] submits, that upon analysis, all that the applicants could legitimately expect was to have their application for home leave decided by reference to the criteria current at the time of the application. We think this is right.' (*R v Secretary of State for the Home Department, ex p Briggs, Green and Hargreaves* [1996] COD 168, a decision upheld by the Court of Appeal [1991] 1 All ER 397).

2.39 The compromise of these two positions appears to be that 'rights' which do not appear in statute or the Prison Rules can be afforded to a prisoner by the Home Secretary voluntarily adopting a particular policy or procedure. If these rights concern the adoption of good administrative practice, then they acquire an independent status which makes it more difficult for them to be subsequently removed. However, if they are concerned with expectations as to discretionary decisions or privileges, it is possible for them to be changed providing that the proper procedures are followed and primary legislation is not infringed.

CONTRACTED OUT PRISONS

The statutory basis

2.40   One of the more contentious statutory changes that has been made in recent years has been to introduce contracted out prisons. These are effectively privatised prisons that operate within the framework of the rest of the Prison Service. The first provision for contracted out prisons was made in the Criminal Justice Act 1991, ss 84–88. These were accompanied by provisions to allow private escorts to be introduced (ss 80–83).

2.41   The Secretary of State was permitted by the Act to introduce contracted out prisons for sentenced prisoners immediately and for remand prisoners by future statutory instrument. The appropriate instruments were subsequently passed in 1992 (CJA 1991 (Contracted Out Prisons) Order 1992 and CJA 1991 (Contracted Out Prisons Order) No 2 1992) and effectively permitted all prisons to be contracted out. The provisions were extended to Scotland by the Criminal Justice and Public Order Act 1994, which also contained various minor modifications to the 1991 Act. The provisions for 'private' prisons in the 1991 Act were then re-written by the Criminal Justice and Public Order Act 1994 which empowers the Secretary of State to enter into contracts for the running of a prison or any part of a prison.

The provisions in detail

2.42   The Prison Act 1952 continues to apply to all contracted out prisons save to the extent that a different set of officers are put in place to run the prisons (CJA 1991, s 84(1)). In place of governors, directors are appointed to run the prison. Directors have the same powers as governors except that they are not allowed to conduct adjudications or to segregate prisoners, apply restraints or to order confinement in a special cell, except in cases of extreme emergency. Controllers are appointed by the Secretary of State, effectively to oversee the running of the prison by the director. The disciplinary powers that are removed from the director are vested in the controller, who is also charged with the responsibility for reviewing the running of the prison and reporting to the Secretary of State (s 85). In an attempt to promote uniformity in the system, area managers are now the direct line mangers for such prisons as they are for state prisons (AG 21/95). Therefore appeals against operational and disciplinary decisions should be directed to the area manager.

2.43   The officers employed to run the prison are known as 'prison custody officers.' The duties of these officers are stated to be to prevent escapes from custody, to detect and prevent the commission of unlawful acts, to ensure good order and discipline and to attend to the well-being of prisoners. Reasonable force may be used in pursuance of these duties (s 86(3)–(4)). These officers have the power to search inmates in accordance with the Prison Rules and to conduct searches of visitors. Searches of visitors do not extend to full body searches and only outer layers of clothing may be removed (s 86(1)).

Provision has also been made for such staff to work in directly managed prisons, those which are not contracted out and vice versa (CJPOA 1994, s 97). The purpose of these provisions is to enable services at directly managed prisons to be contracted out if so desired.

2.44 The Secretary of State is empowered to intervene in the running of the prison in cases where the controller appears to have lost control or where it is necessary to preserve the safety of any person or to prevent serious damage to property (s 88). In such cases, a Crown servant can be appointed to act as governor of the prison and this person then assumes the powers of both the director and the controller.

Private escorts

2.45 The contracting out of prisons was accompanied by a contracting out of the prisoner escort system. This covers the delivery of prisoners to court, to and from police stations and other prisons and for the custody of prisoners outside of prison for temporary purposes (CJA 1991, s 80). The persons who provide escorts are described as prison custody officers and have similar duties and responsibilities to those of prison custody officers in contracted out prisons. Disciplinary breaches by prisoners under such escort are to be treated as if they had been committed in the custody of the governor or controller of the prison (s 83). The charge may be laid by the prison custody officer (CJPOA 1994, s 95).

The contract document

2.46 The standards to be utilised in the running of the prison will be set out in the contract between the contractor and the Secretary of State. The actual contracts are not public documents, although the absurdity of this secrecy was highlighted when the Prison Reform Trust managed to obtain such a contract from the United States as the parent company was obliged to make it public in that jurisdiction (*Prison Report*, Issue 28, Autumn 1994). The tender documents make it clear that the Prison Rules do apply but that policy documents such as Standing Orders may not. The Secretary of State can oblige the contractor to comply with any policy and procedural decisions that are deemed necessary.

2.47 The contract sets out the regime standards that are to be applied in the prison including such matters as time out of cells, association, medical care and suicide prevention. Although it was widely anticipated from tender documents that the contracted out regimes would be designed to produce more positive regimes, the reality may prove to be somewhat different in the long run. In the contract for Doncaster, for example, the certified population was to be 771 but provision was made for up to 1,169 prisoners to be held (*Prison Report*, Issue 28, Autumn 1994). The numerous problems that have been experienced in the running of these prisons, in terms of contract compliance, assaults on staff, poor medical care, escapes from custody and suicides are documented by the Prison Reform Trust in a special section on private prisons in their quarterly publication, *Prison Report*.

The legal implications

2.48 The privatisation of prisons and escort services took place fairly rapidly. By 1995, five contracted out prisons had already been established and the present Labour government, despite opposing private prisons in opposition, has continued to expand the prison estate through the private sector. The majority of escort services have also been contracted out.

2.49 The manner in which prisoners in private prisons should take legal action remains unclear and has not yet been the subject of any court decisions. The basic legal rights afforded to such prisoners remain the same as for those in state prisons and it would indeed be an absurdity if the right to take legal action was circumvented by the nature of the prison in which an individual happened to be held. However, the question of whom the action should be directed against is less clear.

2.50 Applications for judicial review should still be directed against the Secretary of State as the decisions under challenge will either have been made directly by a Crown servant (eg the controller when the use of disciplinary powers is under challenge) or will have been made by the director under delegated powers and will also be subject to approval by the area manager on behalf of the Secretary of State. However, private law challenges are less clear and there has been some debate as to who the proper defendant should be in such cases.

2.51 Livingstone and Owen argue that in the majority of private law claims, such as negligence claims, assaults by other prisoners or members of staff, the proper defendant should be the private contractor unless it is alleged that the Secretary of State has been negligent in appointing a particular contractor (*Prison Law* (1999) OUP, pp 32–33). The Home Office take the view that under the normal principles of agency and vicarious liability, they cannot be held responsible for the actions of independent contractors in a situation where they do not exert direct control over the actions of those contractors' employees. Furthermore, they would argue that as the persons employed in contracted out prisons are not paid out of public funds, they cannot be held liable for their actions (Crown Proceedings Act 1947, s 2(6)).

2.52 Whilst it is not practical to review the law of agency and vicarious liability in detail in this book, the legal situation is complex and, in the absence of decided legal authority, it is difficult to come to firm conclusions about liability. In the case of immigration detention centres, where the statutory authority for contracting out only came into force at the end of 1999, the extent to which the Secretary of State can abrogate responsibility for the custodial function of immigration detention is questionable (see eg the obiter comments of Turner J in *R v Secretary of State for the Home Department, ex p Quaquah* [2000] 03 LS Gaz R 36). In the context of prisons where there is direct statutory authority for contracting out, the issue of whether the Home Office remains liable for the acts or omissions of independent contractors remains open to debate. It has been argued that there is a distinction to be drawn between privatisation, where an entire function of the state is passed into private hands, and contracting out, where the function remains in the public sector but the means of performing it are located in the private sector (Freedland *Public Law Review* (Spring 1994) pp 86–104). The issue for practitioners to identify in advising clients wishing to take private law claims in respect of events in contracted out prisons must be whether there is any purpose or advantage to be gained in seeking to hold the Home Office responsible. If, on the facts of the individual case, there is some purpose to be served by such a course of action, then the issue of liability warrants further examination.

CHAPTER 3

BASIC LEGAL REMEDIES

THE INTERNAL MECHANISMS

3.1 There exists within the prison system a series of structured, internal mechanisms for prisoners to ventilate complaints and make requests. However, prior to utilising the formal structures, prisoners are advised to make use of the informal system that is in operation.

3.2 The informal system is really no more than a suggestion that prisoners should first discuss their problem with a wing officer and make use of wing applications. These are simply one-sheet forms allowing a prisoner the opportunity to write a brief description of the problem. This is known as a 'governor's application' but in practice it will often be replied to by a senior or principal officer. There is no code of practice that requires this to be answered within a specified period of time and although replies are supplied fairly quickly, they do tend to be brief.

3.3 There is no requirement to make use of this process before engaging in the formal requests/complaints system. The main use of this informal method is where the matter is relatively simple and straightforward, and the prisoner feels that it can be resolved without difficulty. It can also be useful for prisoners who have a good relationship with officers on their wing and who do not wish to be perceived as 'troublemakers.'

The formal system

3.4 It is a requirement of the Prison Rules that a mechanism for dealing with prisoners' requests and complaints is in operation. This duty is firstly placed upon the governor (Prison Rules, r 11) and secondly on the Board of Visitors (Prison Rules, rr 11 and 78). Rule 11 states that:

'(1) A request or complaint to the governor or Board of Visitors relating to a prisoner's imprisonment shall be made orally or in writing by the prisoner.
(2) On every day the governor shall hear any requests and complaints that are made to him under paragraph (1).
(3) A written request or complaint under paragraph (1) above may be made in confidence.'

3.5 The present scheme was established in 1990 as a result of the Woolf Report (Cm 1456) and was designed to replace an ad hoc and inefficient system that did not in effect provide any real independent avenue of complaint for prisoners. One of the most frequently voiced criticisms was the lack of any timescale for dealing with enquiries. The actual system that is in operation at the present time bears little resemblance to the outline contained in r 11. For example, the requirement to hear requests and complaints each day may be delegated to another officer of the prison. As such, there is no right for prisoners to see the governor in charge of the prison and in practice, this rarely occurs. However, the consistent and formalised structure that has been implemented does work reasonably well within the obvious constraints of a system that investigates itself.

3.6 The 'Staff Manual on the Requests/Complaints Procedure' issued by the Prison Service envisages that the new system will benefit both prisoners and staff by:

'• preserving and building on the arrangements for resolving requests and complaints informally or by oral applications;
• enabling more decisions to be taken and explained locally;
• inspiring greater confidence in prisoners that their needs and welfare are being looked after;
• reducing tension and anxiety;
• promoting better relationships between prisoners and staff.' (page 1)

3.7 The Manual suggests that prisoners should seek to resolve problems wherever possible through the informal channels but this is not a requirement before the formal procedures can be utilised. The formal process is effectively split into three:

(i)   complaints to be dealt with in the prison;
(ii) requests for the review of decisions; and
(iii) complaints to be dealt with by Prison Service Headquarters.

One of the stated aims of the system is to try and devolve greater decision-making responsibility to the prison. In the first instance, requests/complaints forms will be dealt with at the prison itself. The reply is to be given within seven days and may be dealt with by the governor or referred on to another member of staff.

3.8 Certain subjects cannot be dealt with internally, such as enquiries about parole or matters concerning category A prisoners. These are referred to as 'reserved subjects' and must be forwarded onto the appropriate department at Headquarters (for a full discussion of the operation of the requests/ complaints system and a list of reserved subjects, see section II, chapter 7). Answers to replies sent to Headquarters are required to be dealt with within six weeks of receipt. If a reply cannot be made in that time, then an interim reply should be sent explaining the reasons for the delay and when a full reply can be expected.

3.9 If a prisoner is unhappy with any decision made by the governor, either in response to a requests/complaints form or a disciplinary decision such as an adjudication, the system allows for forms to be sent to the area manager for the prison to be reviewed. The actual investigation of the complaint is dealt with by central casework teams at Prison Service Headquarters who investigate the matter and reply on the area manager's behalf. Again, the time limit for receiving a reply to such enquiries is set at six weeks. There is no right of appeal or review within the Prison Service against decisions made by the area manager or other departments at Headquarters.

Confidential access

3.10   Rule 11(3) of the Prison Rules allows for written complaints to be made confidentially to the governor or the area manager. This is kept within the same overall requests/complaints system on the same forms. In such cases the Manual provides that prisoners should be given an envelope with the form provided to them. It advises that the prisoner writes the reasons why the matter is confidential on the envelope to assist in ensuring that it is passed to the person best placed to deal with the enquiry. Confidential matters for the area manager's attention are supposed to be sent out of the prison unopened (para 3.4.22).

3.11   In practice, the confidential access is not always effective, particularly on matters raised inside the prison. Staff can often be suspicious and obstruct the issue of such forms. There is no guarantee that the envelope will be opened by the most appropriate person and once opened, a unilateral decision is made as to whether confidential access was appropriate and as to whether the allegations/complaints should be passed on to the person against whom they are made. The prisoner has no input into this process. Similarly, the area manager can decide that confidential access is inappropriate and return the complaint to be dealt with by the prison without giving prior notification to the prisoner that this course of action has been taken. For a full discussion of the requests/complaints system, see section II, chapter 7.

Complaints to the Board of Visitors

3.12   Rule 11 authorises the Board of Visitors to hear oral or written complaints from prisoners and this is supplemented by r 78 which directs Boards and their members to 'hear any complaint or request which a prisoner wishes to make to him or them.' This is not a daily requirement but does impose a duty upon the Board to hear these problems when they are in the prison. Arrangements for visits by the Board will vary from prison to prison but as a general rule, visits will take place at least twice a week.

3.13   Complaints to the Board have no formal role to play in the requests/complaints procedure and the Board have no statutory powers to resolve or uphold the complaints that they receive. There is no requirement on prisoners to utilise this procedure before entering the formal disciplinary system and indeed, the Prison Service in fact envisaged that the Boards would become involved once the more formal system has been utilised. In the Staff Manual the advice that staff are recommended to give to prisoners is:

'You may also ask to speak to a member of the Board of Visitors . . . The Board will also consider your written request or complaint if you ask them. But the Board will normally expect you to have already tried to solve the problem by oral application and written request and complaint to the governor.' (p 4, para 8)

3.14   The extent of the Board's powers, or lack of them, is emphasised in the same document. It goes on to explain what might be expected in response to such an enquiry:

'If you have already made a written request or complaint, the Board will look at the reply you were given and any other relevant information. If there is likely to be a delay, you will be told what is happening. The Board will let you know what it has decided to do about your request or complaint. It could, for example, ask the governor to think again about the decision which has been reached, or it could bring it to the attention of the area manager or even the Home Secretary.' (p 4, para 8)

The right to petition

3.15   The right to petition was not removed following the introduction of the present system. Every British citizen has the constitutional right to petition the reigning monarch and this right is extended to citizens of other countries as a matter of courtesy. The right to petition the Secretary of State is extended to all inmates. Standing Order 5C explains that this process enables prisoners to raise matters with Prison Service Headquarters that cannot be dealt with in the prison (para 1).

3.16   Broadly speaking, the purpose of petitioning is now redundant, as the requests/complaints system provides a formal mechanism for problems to be ventilated. This is illustrated by the range of subjects on which it is envisaged that prisoners will present petitions such as parole, adjudications, appeals against conviction, the prerogative of mercy and production at court. In practical terms, all of these matters can now be dealt with by formal procedures and applications that are far more satisfactory. The petitioning procedure therefore has little practical import and is largely an anachronism.

The Prisons Ombudsman

3.17   The Woolf Report (Cm 1456) was strongly in favour of the appointment of a 'Complaints Adjudicator' to ensure that the then new grievance procedure had an independent element. It was envisaged that this adjudicator would have the power to act as a final arbiter in disciplinary decisions and to assess replies made to requests/complaints on both the merits of the individual case and the procedures that were followed. Despite some initial objections, the White Paper *Custody, Care and Justice* broadly accepted the worth of these proposals (Cm 1647, p 93).

3.18   These proposals were finally realised when a Prisons Ombudsman was first appointed in October 1994 (the present Ombudsman, appointed in

September 1999, is Stephen Shaw, former Director of the Prison Reform Trust). The post is slightly different from that envisaged by Lord Woolf in that no primary legislation was put in place for the creation of this office and as such, the Ombudsman's powers are limited to making recommendations and are not binding on the Prison Service or the Secretary of State. The appointment was, however, a great improvement on the previous situation whereby the only Ombudsman with any power to oversee the Prison Service was the Parliamentary Commissioner for Administration. The Commissioner's powers are limited to reviewing administrative errors and delays rather than the merits of decisions, and complaints to the Commissioner must be made through a member of Parliament. These limitations severely curtailed the extent to which prisoners could make use of the Commissioner.

3.19   The Prisons Ombudsman has a fairly broad remit and can receive complaints on most aspects of the prison system from matters as minor as the quality of food to more serious matters such as categorisation and adjudications. Complaints can also be made about the actions of prison staff, including those employed at contracted out prisons, probation officers or members of the Board of Visitors. The matters which are outside his remit are:

(i)   miscarriages of justice and appeals against conviction and sentence;
(ii)   decisions concerning release (eg the merits of parole decisions or the release of lifers);
(iii)   the actions of outside agencies such as the police or the Immigration Department;
(iv)   medical decisions taken by prison doctors. (This limitation remains under review and it is possible that this power will be extended to the Ombudsman in the near future. It appears that it will have to be exercised in conjunction with the Health Services Ombudsman);
(v)   the Ombudsman cannot receive complaints that are already subject to litigation or legal proceedings.

3.20   In order to make a complaint to the Ombudsman, a prisoner must first utilise the formal requests/complaints system. This includes appealing any decisions to the area manager where this right exists. In general, complaints must be made by the prisoner in person and they must be received within one month of the decision which forms the basis of the complaint. The Ombudsman has the power to investigate both the merits of the case and the adequacy of the procedures. The aim is for all complaints to be investigated and a report prepared with the findings of the investigation within 8–12 weeks of receipt.

3.21   If a complaint is upheld, the report is sent to the Director General with a recommendation as to what can be done to rectify the problem. The Director General aims to reply within one month but is not required to do so. If recommendations are not upheld, the prisoner can use the report as the basis for an action for judicial review or to support a claim for negligence but there is no form of redress within the system. In cases where the complaint is rejected, there is no right of appeal, although the Ombudsman has proved amenable to criticism and is not inflexible in reconsidering decisions.

3.22   As with Boards of Visitors, the Ombudsman does not form part of any formal system of complaint. Prisoners cannot be required to make use of this avenue before commencing legal action (ie it is not one of the remedies that have to be exhausted when applying for judicial review). One of the major values of the Ombudsman lies in the fact that an independent body exists which has the power to investigate complaints rather than merely to review decisions made by, or on behalf of, the executive. The ability of the Ombudsman to scrutinise the merits of decisions provides an outlet for problems which are not suitable for judicial review, but where the exercise of discretion may have been unduly harsh or simply unfair.

3.23   The Annual Report of the Ombudsman published for the year 1998–99 (Cm 4369) showed that nearly three quarters of all complaints received in his office were ineligible for investigation, either because of the subject matter or for failing to first utilise internal remedies. Of those that were eligible, a quarter concerned adjudications, 14% property complaints, 12% general conditions with no other category exceeding 10% of complaints investigated. The number of cases where prisoners' complaints were upheld dropped from 44% in 1997–98 to 36% in 1998–99 (p 17). The number of recommendations rejected by the Prison Service increased from 5.9% in 1997 to 6.6% in 1998. The increase in the number of rejections is worrying as it undermines prisoners' confidence in the ability of the Ombudsman to resolve complaints and indicates a reluctance on the part of the Prison Service to accept the legitimacy of outside oversight of their actions.

3.24   The number of recommendations that have been rejected is an indication of some resistance to the work of the Ombudsman. In such cases, the report can form valuable information in support of legal action, whether it is an application for compensation for lost property or for judicial review. Litigation has been commenced by a small number of prisoners in cases where the recommendations have been rejected with the report forming part of the evidence. The High Court appears to be increasingly accepting the importance of the Ombudsman's role in trying to resolve complaints without the need for litigation. In a permission application in December 1999, Sullivan J was particularly scathing of the Prison Service's decision to reject a recommendation on the grounds that the Director General had received legal advice that the governor's decision forming the subject matter of the complaint would be defensible at judicial review (*R v Governor of HM Prison Bullingdon and Secretary of State for the Home Department, ex p Kromer*, permission hearing, 10 December 1999). He felt that the failure to accept recommendations on such narrow grounds undermined the role and remit of the Ombudsman.

JUDICIAL REVIEW

3.25   As such a large part of prison life is concerned with the making of operational and administrative decisions, the most relevant area of litigation for prisoners is that of judicial review. This is unfortunate for prisoners on two counts. First, the nature of judicial review is such that it is not a remedy that can easily be pursued as a litigant in person. Second, solicitors can be reluctant to take on such cases as the actual administrative procedures and guidelines that are in question will often be unfamiliar. When these factors are combined with the traditional reluctance of the courts to interfere with the running of prisons, it may appear that a formidable barrier is in place.

The reality of the situation is somewhat less bleak. Public law remedies are nowadays better utilised than they were in the past and the courts have shown an increasing willingness to intervene in prisoners' cases. The reluctance to disturb security arrangements is still apparent, but in other areas the judiciary have pursued a far more interventionist approach. In particular, the mandatory life sentence system has been the subject of repeated attack and the judiciary have taken it upon themselves to provide strict regulation of a sentence that has attracted strong criticism from all levels. The comments of Steyn LJ in the case of *R v Secretary of State for the Home Department, ex p Pegg* (1994) Times, 11 August, DC, are indicative of this attitude:

> 'Given the essential unfairness of the system in relation to prisoners serving mandatory life sentences the courts have to bear in mind that fundamental rights are at stake. But courts can do no more than to be extra vigilant in the exercise of their powers of judicial review.'

The contrast between the current interventionist approach and the more conservative views of the Court of Appeal in *Payne v Lord Harris of Greenwich* [1981] 1 WLR 754 (where mandatory lifers were refused the right to know of the reasons for the refusal to recommend release) could not be more apparent.

The decisions that can be reviewed

3.26   The problem of whether decisions fall within the ambit of public law and are therefore potentially amenable to judicial review is now fairly clear cut in prisoners' cases. In general, all administrative decisions made in respect of prisoners, be they operational, managerial or disciplinary will fall within the sphere of public law (see *O'Reilly v Mackman* [1983] 2 AC 237).

3.27   The decisions that prisoners seek to review will fall into two broad categories: policy matters, such as the contents of the Prison Rules, and specific decisions made in respect of individuals. The review of policy decisions has never posed a problem on procedural grounds as the decisions clearly fall within the realm of public law. It is a basic principle of administrative law that such decisions are justiciable. As far as decisions made in respect of individuals are concerned, it has long been established that disciplinary decisions made in the prison of a quasi-judicial nature are susceptible to judicial review (*R v Board of Visitors of Hull Prison, ex p St Germain* [1979] QB 425). At the time, this was confined to the powers exercised by the Boards of Visitors but was formally extended to the powers exercised by governors in 1988 following the case of *R v Deputy Governor of Parkhurst Prison, ex p Leech* [1988] 1 AC 533. The courts have also decided that they have the power to exercise jurisdiction over decisions to transfer prisoners *(R v Secretary of State for the Home Department, ex p McAvoy* [1984] 1 WLR 1408), and categorisation procedures (*R v Secretary of State for the Home Department, ex p Duggan* [1994] 3 All ER 277).

Attempts by the Secretary of State to argue that the Prison Act 1952, s 4(2) conferred a unique duty to ensure observance of the Rules on the minister in person and that this ousted the jurisdiction of the court, were rejected by Lord Bridge in the *Leech* case [1988] 1 AC 533.

3.28 The ambit and jurisdiction of the court was fully debated by the House of Lords in 1992 in the case of *R v Deputy Governor of Parkhurst Prison, ex p Hague, Weldon v Home Office* [1992] 1 AC 58. The House of Lords took the view that all operational and managerial decisions affecting prisoners' segregation and transfer were susceptible to judicial review. This effectively removed the last remaining barriers and extended the jurisdiction of the court to all aspects of imprisonment.

3.29 This judgment did not, as the Home Office feared, lead to a flood of applications for judicial review. The House of Lords put many practical barriers in the way by accepting that governors have a wide discretion in their decision-making, particularly when dealing with disciplinary matters. In proceedings under RSC Order 53, the court will rarely become involved in deciding factual disputes and, in any event, it is likely that without powerful evidence to the contrary such disputes would be resolved in favour of the Prison Service. The wide degree of discretion afforded to decision makers and the courts' reluctance to decide upon issues of fact means that challenges as to the reasonableness of a decision alone can be notoriously difficult to win. Some evidence of deficiencies in the procedural elements of a decision is often required in order to provide a sufficient base for an application for judicial review.

The judgment in *Doody*

3.30 The duty that is imposed on the Prison Service in relation to their administrative duties to prisoners was significantly clarified and advanced by the House of Lords in the case of *R v Secretary of State for the Home Department, ex p Doody* [1994] 1 AC 531. This case involved the right of mandatory lifers to know of the level at which their tariff had been set and to make effective representations to the Secretary of State about this decision. Although the right to make representations had always existed, mandatory lifers had no right to be officially told the length of their tariff or the views of the trial judge and Lord Chief Justice that had informed the Secretary of State's decision.

3.31 Lord Mustill took the view that a prisoner was unable to make any effective representations without this information:

> 'To mount an effective attack on the decision given no more material than the facts of the case and the length of the penal element, the prisoner has virtually no means of ascertaining whether this is an instance where the decision-making process has gone astray.'

The relevance of this view lies in the fact that a requirement to make full disclosure is effectively imposed on the Prison Service when making decisions that will affect the length of an individual's detention. As the majority of decisions made about prisoners will have either a direct or indirect impact on the length of time spent in custody, the judgment reaches into all aspects of prison discipline and administration.

3.32   Although Lord Mustill accepted the argument of the Secretary of State that there is no free-standing duty to give reasons for administrative decisions, he identified six principles for openness in the decision-making process. The three most important of these are:

(i)   there is a presumption that administrative powers will be exercised fairly;
(ii)   where a person may be adversely affected by a decision, fairness dictates that the person should have the opportunity to make representations either before it is taken to procure a favourable result or after it is made to have it modified, or both;
(iii) fairness will often dictate that the person is informed of the gist of the case that is to be answered otherwise it is not possible to make effective representations.

3.33   It is arguable that this judgment significantly increased the onus on the Prison Service to be accountable to prisoners in reaching decisions, particularly those which have a direct bearing on their prospects of release. The range of decisions that are affected is potentially vast and can include categorisation, disciplinary transfers, segregation and temporary release amongst others. The impact of the decision was apparent when the court was called upon to consider the procedures for the classification of category A prisoners (*R v Secretary of State for the Home Department, ex p Duggan* [1994] 3 All ER 277). The court, freed from previous authority, was able to conclude that category A prisoners have the right to regular reviews of their categorisation with a review process that included disclosure of the gist of reports prepared upon them, the right to make representations and the right to be informed of the gist of the reasons for the subsequent decision.

3.34   Whilst prisoners face very few inhibitions to the principle of making such an application, the manner in which the courts will receive them will vary depending on the nature of the application. Consequently, the exercise of quasi-judicial powers such as adjudications and decisions as to release will come under very strict scrutiny. Conversely, decisions made in the pursuance of maintaining good order and discipline will attract a weaker level of scrutiny and providing proper procedures are followed, the courts are very reluctant to interfere with a governor's judgment. Thus, in *Ex p Ross* (1994) Times, 9 June the Court of Appeal, in rejecting an application for leave to move for judicial review, decided that a prison governor is best placed to decide upon whether a prisoner is being disruptive. This approach was further apparent when Laws J dismissed a series of challenges to the manner in which the Incentives and Earned Privileges Scheme was operated, reiterating the old proposition that governors are best placed to make assessments on individual cases and not the courts. He indicated that a 'super-*Wednesbury*' test may be applicable on such applications (*R v Secretary of State for the Home Department, ex p Hepworth* [1998] COD 146).

PRIVATE LAW CLAIMS

Actions in negligence

3.35   The view of Lord Wilberforce in *Raymond v Honey* [1983] 1 AC 1 that prisoners retain all civil rights, save for those expressly or impliedly taken away by the fact of their imprisonment, confirms the right of prisoners to commence actions in private law. Whilst the administration of the prison system falls within the realm of public law, there will still be many situations in which a prisoner is seeking to enforce private law rights to compensation arising from the negligence of the prison authorities. In order to plead negligence, it is necessary to establish that there has been a failure to exercise the care which the circumstances demand, and that the resulting loss was a reasonably foreseeable result of those actions. These principles will be familiar to civil practitioners, although the context in which such claims arise for prisoners will be less familiar.

Property claims

3.36   Property belonging to prisoners will fall into two categories, that held in their own possession ('in-possession property') and that which is held as stored property by the prison. The Prison Service take the view that any damage or loss to stored property may be their responsibility, depending upon the circumstances of the loss. However, in-possession property is officially treated as being held at the risk of the individual prisoner and the policy is for no liability to be accepted for any loss or damage.

3.37   This policy is legally unsustainable as there are many circumstances in which a prisoner can no longer exert any control over the property and that any resultant loss or damage must fall within the responsibility of the prison. Examples of this will include when a cell is searched, or when a prisoner is moved to segregation and the cell is supposed to be sealed by staff. The ordinary tortious principles will apply in such cases and providing the loss or damage can be identified to have occurred at a time when the responsibility or control must have reverted to prison officers, then liability will arise (*Winson v Home Office* (18 March 1994, unreported), Central London County Court: a full discussion on how to conduct such claims appears in section III, chapter 14).

Negligent medical treatment

3.38   Whilst a person is serving a sentence of imprisonment, responsibility for medical care rests with the medical officer of the prison in which s/he is located. Medical staff owe a duty of care to prisoners to ensure that they receive adequate treatment whilst in custody. The duty owed by medical staff interacts with the duty owed by the prison authorities to provide access to treatment both in the prison and at outside hospitals (eg by providing escorts). The duty of care that is owed in a custodial context can differ from that which is provided to those at liberty due to the difference in the function of prison hospitals and the constraints that exist when providing medical care (*Knight v Home Office* [1990] 3 All ER 237, a case which was concerned with the standard of care owed to a mentally-ill prisoner detained in a prison hospital).

Dangerous premises and working conditions

3.39   Prison governors are required to ensure compliance with the main statutes that deal with health and safety at work. These include, inter alia, the Factories Act 1961, the Health and Safety at Work Act 1974, the Food Act 1984 and the Offices, Shops and Railway Premises Act 1963 (see Standing Order 14). Prisoners will therefore retain rights provided for in common law and statute in relation to the provision of safe premises and a safe working environment. These duties are limited only to the extent that there is no contractual relationship between a prisoner and the prison authorities and so any rights arising from the existence of a contract (eg employment rights) are inapplicable.

3.40   A range of claims have been brought by prisoners where it has been alleged that the relevant standard of care has not been complied with. These include claims for injuries resulting from defective premises (*Christofi v Home Office* (1975) Times, 31 July where a prisoner fell on a broken step); from being required to work with dangerous equipment; or from working in conditions injurious to health (*Ferguson v Home Office* (1977) Times, 8 October and *Pullen v Prison Comrs* [1957] 1 WLR 1186).

Negligent supervision

3.41   The nature of prison life is such that assaults on inmates by other prisoners is an inevitable fact of life. Claims will lie directly against the assailant for the torts of assault and battery but in the majority of cases, the proposed defendant will not have the funds to meet any damages awarded, rendering such an action futile. In such cases, the main possibility for legal action will be against the Home Office for failing to properly fulfil the duty of care owed to people in their custody.

3.42   The general tortious principle that no person can hold a duty to control another person in order to prevent damage being done to a third party (*Smith v Leurs* [1945] 70 CLR 256) is modified in the custodial context. The speech delivered by Lord Diplock in *Home Office v Dorset Yacht Co Ltd* [1970] 2 All ER 294 sets out the circumstances in which this duty of care would arise. The factors that he considered relevant are:

(i)   that the tortfeasor is in the legal custody of the Home Office;
(ii)   that the Home Office has the legal right to control the proximity of the victim to the assailant;
(iii) that reasonable care in the exercise of the right of custody could have prevented the tortious act; and
(iv)   that the Home Office could reasonably foresee that the victim was likely to suffer loss or injury if reasonable care was not taken.

These principles have long been accepted in the context of a custodial setting (see eg *D'Arcy v Prison Comrs* [1956] Crim LR 56 or *Ellis v Home Office* [1953] 2 QB 135).

3.43 The difficulty in bringing claims in such circumstances is in establishing facts that are strong enough to satisfy the court that the prisons should have been aware that a particular prisoner was in danger of being assaulted and that sufficient steps were not taken to safeguard that person. Each case will have to be considered on its particular merits when assessing whether a claim will be successful. Prisoners that are most likely to be assaulted are those classed as 'vulnerable,' either by virtue of their offences of from an inability to cope with prison life. Damages have been awarded where the negligent disclosure of past convictions for sex offences lead to an assault by other prisoners (*H v Home Office* (1992) Independent, 6 May) and where a prisoner was escorted by an officer from a vulnerable prisoners' unit through a normal wing despite his fears of assault and was duly assaulted by other prisoners (*Burt v Home Office* (27 June 1995, unreported), Norwich County Court). In contrast, the Home Office was not considered to be negligent when a prisoner was assaulted when returning to normal location after a period in segregation, despite the fact that the officers were not aware he had been attacked prior to his segregation. The court accepted the argument that an experienced officer could not have foreseen the actual attack that took place (*Egerton v Home Office* [1978] Crim LR 494).

3.44 Prisoners who are not considered 'vulnerable' at the time of an assault will face even more difficulties in satisfying the court that the prison should have been aware of the danger to them and failed to take all reasonable steps to ensure their safety. In one case a prisoner was stabbed by another prisoner who was considered to be highly dangerous but nevertheless, had been allowed to work in a tailor's workshop with access to scissors. Although it was accepted that he was highly dangerous, Neill LJ took the view that it was not possible to keep a prisoner permanently segregated, except in very extreme cases and it was also desirable to provide work where possible and in balancing these considerations, the governor had not been negligent (*Palmer v Home Office* (1988) Guardian, 31 March, CA). In a similar vein, a prisoner who had been attacked previously and had informed prison staff was attacked two weeks later in the television room. The court accepted the governor's view that he did not consider the prisoner to be at serious risk and that he had discharged his duty by instructing staff to keep a closer eye on him (*Porterfield v Home Office* (1988) Independent, 9 March).

3.45 The case law highlights the difficulty in assessing how extensive the duty of care is in such cases. In order for the duty of care to arise in the first place, the prison staff will normally have to be aware either that a particular prisoner is a serious danger to other inmates or that an individual is in particular danger of being assaulted. The steps taken to ensure safety have to be balanced against the operational needs of the prison as a whole and the duty of the governor to allow reasonable facilities to inmates. Although it appeared for many years that the parameters of such claims had been set, interestingly, the Court of Appeal upheld a successful claim by a prisoner based on an argument that the overall management of a prison was negligent and that this negligence directly resulted in him being assaulted and injured by other prisoners (*Hartshorn v Home Office* (21 January 1999, unreported), CA). In that case, it was normal practice for a gate between two landings to be closed and guarded by prison officers due to a high incidence of unauthorised prisoner movement and assaults. A failure to locate staff on the gate was held to be negligent against that background and liability established for a resultant assault. Although both the County Court and Court of Appeal emphasised that the case was decided on its own particular facts, the decision does extend the scope of negligence claims to encompass more general management decisions rather than to simply deal with decisions made on individual cases.

The decision in *Hague*

3.46   Two cases brought by prisoners concerning their alleged mistreatment by the prison authorities were heard together by the House of Lords (*R v Deputy Governor of Parkhurst Prison, ex p Hague, Weldon v Home Office* [1992] 1 AC 58). The decision established important principles which define and limit the extent of tortious claims that may be brought by prisoners. Hague sought judicial review of a decision to segregate and transfer him and damages for false imprisonment. Weldon commenced a private law claim for assault and false imprisonment following an assault by prison staff and his detention in a strip cell.

Breach of statutory duty

3.47   The House of Lords rejected the idea that claims could be brought by prisoners solely for breach of statutory duty, a decision reached with particular consideration of the provisions of the Prison Rules 1964, r 43, which provides the authority for segregation. Lord Jauncey considered that the mere fact that the statutory provision was designed to protect prisoners did not in itself confer a private law right of action. In order for this right to arise, it was necessary for the statute to contain enabling regulations providing for enforcement. Lord Bridge took the view that as the Prison Rules were concerned with the management and administration of prisons and prisoners, rather than solely being designed to protect prisoners from personal injury, it gave no right to a private law claim for breach of the Rules in isolation.

False imprisonment

3.48   The House of Lords also rejected the possibility of prisoners bringing claims for false imprisonment. Previous decisions had indicated that a right to commence claims in such circumstances did not arise (eg *Williams v Home Office (No 2)* [1981] 1 All ER 1211). In *Hague*, the House of Lords also rejected the concept that prisoners retain an element of residual liberty that can be denied by their detention in more onerous conditions. Lord Bridge took the view that false imprisonment required freedom of movement to be denied and that if a prisoner was lawfully detained in the first place, the complaint was merely that another form of restraint had been applied rather than his freedom being infringed

([1992] 1 AC 130 at 139D). Lord Jauncey commented in a similar vein that:

'a prisoner at any time has no liberty to be in any place other than where the regime permits . . . An alteration of his conditions therefore deprives him of no liberty because he has none already.' ([1992] 1 AC 130 at 177E)

It should be noted that claims for false imprisonment can still be brought against prisoners who hold other prisoners hostage. The legal foundation that prevents the claim being pursued against prison governors, namely that the prisoner is already lawfully detained, does not apply to the actions of another prisoner who has no such authority. It is also arguable that unlawful acts by prison officers which inhibit a prisoner's liberty could give rise to such claims (see eg *Toumia v Evans* (1999) Times, 1 April, CA), although it is difficult to envisage facts on which such a case could be successfully mounted.

3.49 Whilst the *Hague* decision places limitations on the types of claims that prisoners are entitled to bring, it does provide clear guidance as to the private law claims that are possible. In addition to general claims in negligence as detailed above, prisoners may look to commence actions for assault and battery resulting from the actions of prison staff, and in exceptional circumstances, for misfeasance in public office. Public law remedies will, however, continue to be the main method of seeking to challenge the conditions of detention.

Assault and battery

3.50 The right of prisoners to bring claims for assault and battery is an important safeguard over the actions of the authorities, particularly as claims for false imprisonment are unavailable. These torts have been long established, with an assault defined as an action which causes a person to fear the unlawful infliction of force (*Stephens v Myers* [1830] 4 C & P 349) while a battery involves the actual application of force during an assault (*Cole v Turner* (1704) 6 Mod Rep 149 where Holt CJ commented that, 'the least touching of another in anger is a battery').

3.51 In a prison context, prison officers will routinely be required to apply force in a lawful context. The question that will normally arise therefore, is whether it was necessary for force to be applied and whether the extent and duration of the force were reasonable. The most likely scenarios in which such a claim will arise are:

(i)   a deliberate attack by a prison officer (also, see misfeasance in public office below);
(ii) when a restraint continues to be imposed after a prisoner has ceased to be a danger, either to others or to him/herself *(Rodrigues v Home Office* [1989] Legal Action 14);
(iii) where excessive force is used to carry out a lawful order;
(iv) where force is used to execute an unlawful order.

3.52 In order to make an assessment as to whether the actions of prison staff constitute an assault, it is necessary to look at the scope of their powers in a particular situation. Therefore, if a prisoner is placed in a mechanical restraint or placed in a strip cell without the proper procedures being followed and the proper authority being sought from an officer of suitable rank, this can constitute an assault. In cases where officers are alleged to have acted outside, or in excess of, their powers, it is also necessary to look at the tort of misfeasance in public office.

Misfeasance in public office

3.53   In *Hague*, the House of Lords made express reference to the tort of misfeasance in public office as an appropriate remedy where it is alleged that prison officers have deliberately abused their powers. The elements of the tort are onerous and aside from establishing that damage to the person has been caused, it must be established that the tortfeasor is the holder of a public office, that the damage was caused to a foreseeable plaintiff and that the actions were malicious or taken with the knowledge that they were outside of lawful powers (*Jones v Swansea City Council* [1990] 1 WLR 54). The evidential problems in establishing malice or actions undertaken deliberately outside of lawful powers are formidable.

3.54   In the prison context, the prevailing view had been that if a prison officer acted outside of his/her powers, then the Home Office could not be vicariously liable for these actions. In *Hague*, Lord Bridge commented that:

> '... if the officer deliberately acts outside the scope of his authority, he cannot render the governor or the Home Office vicariously liable for his tortious conduct.' ([1992] 1 AC 58 at 164D)

3.55 In the case of *Racz v Home Office* [1994] 2 AC 45, the House of Lords had the opportunity to consider the issues of vicarious liability that arise from this tort. The Court of Appeal had accepted the Home Office argument that misfeasance, by its nature, was a cause of action to which vicarious liability could not attach. This was because it is an element of the tort that the perpetrator was acting in a deliberate abuse of authority. This was rejected by the House of Lords which held that the issue of vicarious liability for misfeasance in public office must be determined by the individual facts of each case. The ambit of this tort in the prison context will be further examined by the spate of claims arising from the allegations of deliberate brutality made against prison officers at Wormwood Scrubs.

CHAPTER 4
STATUTORY AGENCIES AND NON-GOVERNMENTAL ORGANISATIONS

BOARDS OF VISITORS

4.1 The Prison Act 1952, s 6(2), states that 'the Secretary of State shall appoint for every prison a Board of Visitors of whom not less than two shall be justices of the peace.' Members of the Board of Visitors for a prison 'may at any time enter the prison and shall have free access to every part of it and to every prisoner' (s 6(3)). Whilst the Boards do not retain any role in the formal disciplinary process (see chapter 2), they retain responsibility for authorising the continued segregation of prisoners under the Prison Rules 1999, r 45 beyond three days. Boards of Visitors celebrated their centenary in 1998.

4.2 Boards of Visitors also have a statutory duty under the Prison Rules to receive complaints from prisoners (rr 11 and 78—see chapter 2). The quality and willingness to intervene varies greatly from prison to prison. The Rules require the Boards to meet at the prison once a month (r 76). Their other general duties are set out in r 77, which include satisfying themselves as to the state of the prison premises, its administration and the treatment of prisoners. As well as hearing complaints, other specific duties include examining food at frequent intervals, and inquiring into any report that a prisoner's health is likely to be 'injuriously affected by the conditions of his imprisonment' (r 78).

4.3 Rule 80 requires Boards to make an annual report to the Secretary of State. Few Boards publish their reports openly although this is clearly desirable, and it has also not been the policy to disclose the names of Board members, although this is to change. There is a national organisation of members of Boards (AMBoV) which produces a quarterly bulletin.

THE CHIEF INSPECTOR OF PRISONS

4.4 The Chief Inspector is also a statutory post, created by the Prison Act 1952, s 5A, which imposes duties to inspect prisons and report to the Secretary of State 'on the treatment of prisoners and conditions in prisons.' The Secretary of State can also refer specific issues to the Chief Inspector for a report and he is to submit an annual report to the Secretary of State which is laid before Parliament (s 5A(5)). He does not investigate individual complaints from prisoners.

4.5 The current Chief Inspector is Sir David Ramsbotham. He has consistently issued damning reports on the conditions in local prisons, most notably into Wormwood Scrubs and Wandsworth. In his 1997/98 Annual Report he stated 'Of all the parts of the prison system, it is the local prisons that cause my inspectors and me the greatest anxiety.' The Chief Inspector issues two forms of report on prisons, either following a full inspection or a short, unannounced, inspection. His team carries out approximately twenty of each type of inspection a year.

THE PRISONS OMBUDSMAN

4.6 The Prisons Ombudsman is not a creation of statute, but was appointed following a recommendation in the Woolf report (see chapter 2). Full details of the procedures for making complaints to the Ombudsman are contained in section II, chapter 7. The remit of the Ombudsman has varied slightly since the inception of the office in 1994. Whilst the previous Ombudsman, Sir Peter Woodhead, continually canvassed for the remit to include investigations into clinical decisions of healthcare staff and deaths in custody, these remain outside the remit. Another area where the Ombudsman and the Prison Service have disagreed over the remit is decisions affecting mandatory lifers. The position now is that the Ombudsman can review all decisions made by the Prison Service affecting lifers up to and including the advice given to ministers on release and other issues. Ministers' personal decisions are excluded.

4.7 Although the Ombudsman does not have any statutory authority and there is no requirement on prisoners to make complaints to his office, it is likely that he will have an increasingly important role to play in dispute resolution. The Funding Code issued by the Legal Services Commission will place a greater onus on prisoners to explain why they have not utilised the Ombudsman before seeking public funding for legal action. The Ombudsman is discussed in greater detail in chapter 3.

THE PAROLE BOARD

4.8 The Parole Board was created by the Criminal Justice Act 1967. It makes decisions on the early release of determinate sentence prisoners serving up to 15 years, and recommendations to the Secretary of State for early release of those serving 15 years or over (see chapter 12). It also decides on the release of most life sentence prisoners after expiry of the tariff, such decisions being made following oral hearings in front of specially convened panels. In relation to adult mandatory lifers it can only make recommendations for release, following paper reviews, to the Secretary of State who makes the final decision (see chapter 11).

4.9 The membership of the Parole Board includes judges, psychiatrists, probation officers and others. The Board maintains a register of members' interests which is open to inspection. In 1998/99 the Board considered the cases of 6078 determinate sentence prisoners and recommended parole in 2383, some 39% of cases (10% lower than in 1994). The Board considered 753 lifer cases of all types in 1998/99, with release recommended or directed in 127 cases.

LOCAL AUTHORITIES AND OTHER ENFORCEMENT AGENCIES

4.10   Local authorities maintain a limited role in enforcement of standards in prison. Enforcement of food hygiene issues is dealt with by local authority environmental health officers (EHOs), and food standards issues by trading standards officers (TSOs) under the Food Safety Act 1990. If an investigating EHO is satisfied that there has been a contravention of any food hygiene or processing regulation s/he can issue an improvement notice, or where there is an imminent risk of injury to health, an emergency prohibition notice. It is theoretically possible for a prisoner to complain to local TSOs to investigate the sale of goods in the prison canteen other than food under the sale of goods legislation.

4.11   The Health and Safety Executive inspects prisons to ensure compliance with the Health and Safety at Work Act 1974. Inspections can cover all parts of the prison (as wings as well as workshops are work places for staff) although it would presumably be difficult to persuade the HSE to investigate matters that are more obviously within the Chief Inspector's remit. HSE officers have powers to issue Crown Enforcement Notices on governors of prisons for breaches of the legislation.

PRISON REFORM GROUPS

4.12   There are a wide range of charities and other NGOs working in the area of penal reform. The Howard League aims to develop national policy for prisons and offenders based on impartial and informed research, to demonstrate practical alternatives to prisons and to educate the public about good practice in the penal system. The organisation has been active in recent years in the areas of young and pregnant women in prison (providing expert evidence in the *Flood* case—see chapter 6), and in the area of youth justice. It also produces *Criminal Justice* magazine.

4.13   The Prison Reform Trust aims to create 'a just, humane and effective penal system' by inquiring into the system, informing prisoners, staff and the public, and influencing government and Parliament towards reform. It produces original research papers and other briefings and produces a quarterly magazine *Prison Report*. Jointly with the Prison Service it produces a series of Prisoner Information Books which should be given to all prisoners (although this does not always happen), to provide basic information on prison regimes and the Prison Rules. It also provides advice to prisoners.

4.14   Other smaller organisations include Women in Prison, Prisoners' Families and Friends Service (which maintains a free helpline 0808 808 3444), Black Prisoners' Support Groups, the Detention Advice Service (for immigration detainees in prisons) and the Prison Education Trust (which can fund courses). INQUEST provides advice and advocacy in cases involving deaths in custody (see chapter 10), and the Prisoners' Advice Service is an organisation that provides legal advice on prison law issues both to prisoners and to other practitioners and support agencies on a second tier basis. The National Association for the Care and Resettlement of Offenders (NACRO) and Unlock, the National Association for Ex-Offenders, provide information, advice and support for prisoners when they have been released.

UNITED NATIONS AND EUROPEAN COMMITTEES FOR THE PREVENTION OF TORTURE

4.15   Article 17 of the UN Convention against Torture provides for the establishment of a Committee against Torture consisting of 'ten experts of high moral standing and recognised competence in the field of human rights, who shall serve in their personal capacity.' The Committee is authorised to receive reports from states parties and to consider them on a quadrennial basis and can also request other reports to be submitted. The Committee does not carry out visits and officially can only report on the basis of the state's own report, but unofficially NGOs can make information available to Committee members, and it can obtain information from other UN sources in order to assess the information provided by the state. The committee makes 'general comments' on states' reports which are forwarded to the relevant state concerned. There is a procedure to deal with interstate complaints and individual complaints, although very few complaints have reached the Committee (for further information see Rodley *The Treatment of Prisoners under International Law* (1999) OUP, pp 152–161).

4.16   The European Convention for the Prevention of Torture and Inhuman and Degrading Treatment was opened for signature in 1987. Article 1 of the Convention provides for the setting up of the Committee for the Prevention of Torture (CPT) composed of one person from each of the states which are party to the Convention. The Committee pays periodic visits to each of these states. The reports of the visits will be published with the state's consent, or the Committee can make a public statement where states do not consent if a state has failed to co-operate with a visit or refused to improve the situation in light of the Committee's recommendations. The Committee last visited the UK in 1997 and its report in relation to prison dealt with conditions on the ship HMP The Weare, and focused on prison overcrowding. Whilst not making any findings of inhuman and degrading treatment in relation to prison conditions it did state:

> 'For so long as overcrowding persists, the risk of prisoners being held in inhuman and degrading conditions of detention will remain. To return to the example of HMP Dorchester, even if conditions there are "safe" according to Prison Service criteria, in the view of the CPT they can hardly be qualified as decent.'

This strongly echoes the criticisms of the Chief Inspector in relation to local prisons.

SECTION II

CHAPTER 5

THE VARIOUS TYPES OF PRISON

MEN'S PRISONS

Local prisons

5.1   Local prisons are so called because they tend to be located in towns or cities. They are where prisoners are held on remand and when first convicted. Local prisons are almost always old buildings, some still do not have integral sanitation, and due to the general state of the buildings they are more likely to be infested with vermin and cockroaches than the other newer prisons. In his Annual Report for 1997–98, the Chief Inspector of Prisons, Sir David Ramsbotham, wrote:

> 'Of all of the parts of the prison system, it is local prisons that cause my inspectors and me the greatest anxiety.'

5.2   Prisoners are generally held on remand in the local prison nearest to the court where their case will eventually be heard and so there is a constant turnover of prisoners as newly arrested prisoners are remanded into custody, and others are released or transferred following trial. Local prisons are the first point of entry to the prison system and, because receptions of new prisoners are initiated by the courts rather than managed by the Prison Service, they are particularly susceptible to overcrowding.

5.3   In addition to remand prisoners, local prisons contain short-term convicted prisoners and newly convicted long-term prisoners awaiting initial allocation. Some long-term prisoners will return to local conditions from time to time for reallocation or when they are transferred under IG 28/93, in the interests of good order and discipline (see chapter 8).

5.4   Regimes at local prisons are the most deprived in the system and prisoners often complain that they are locked up for 23 hours a day.

5.5   The Chief Inspector of Prisons inspected HMP Birmingham 7–9 September 1998. He found that the prison was 32% overcrowded at the time of his inspection and that the treatment and conditions of prisoners fell far below what was acceptable. HMCIP noted that between six and seven hundred prisoners were unemployed and that they spent the majority of the day locked in their cells. Some prisoners only had the opportunity to shower three times a week. Prisoners did not get one hour a day of exercise, and evening association was sometimes limited to twice a month. In concluding the preface to his report, HMCIP said that the negative aspect of local prisons was the 'impoverished nature of their facilities and thus their inability to replicate conditions and treatment in training prisons.'

5.6   One of the most damning reports ever published by HMCIP followed his unannounced full inspection of HMP Wormwood Scrubs, 8–12 March 1999, following numerous allegations of violent assaults on prisoners at the hands of prison officers. His previous report had described the prison as a 'flagship dead in the water' and drawn attention to the impoverished regimes for prisoners and the allegations of prisoners' mistreatment at the hands of prison staff. Far from returning to find an improvement in prison conditions the Chief Inspector reported that the:

> 'overall treatment of prisoners was profoundly unsatisfactory ... we learned that, until the crop of allegations, which led to the police investigation and the referral of over 40 cases to the CPS, no improvements appeared to have been made to the running of the segregation unit, nor was there any evidence that managers had investigated rumours of the illicit use of force, to which we had drawn attention ... we found treatment and conditions for prisoners had declined yet further.'

5.7   After conviction prisoners are categorised and allocated to other types of establishment. The exceptions to this are where someone is serving such a short sentence that there is not enough time to allocate them elsewhere, or where they elect to stay behind as 'retained' labour at the local prison.

High security prisons

5.8   Until the early 1960s there were no especially secure prisons in the English prison estate. However, following highly publicised escapes of prisoners considered to be particularly dangerous, Lord Mountbatten was asked to conduct an inquiry into security within the prison system. Broadly speaking, Mountbatten recommended that prisoners should be categorised according to the level of security needed in order to prevent their escape; that prisoners who were afforded the highest level of security categorisation, A, should be held together in a maximum security prison on the Isle of Wight, and that within high security prisons the regime should be made more constructive and liberal in order that the desire to escape would be reduced and that good order within the prisons would be more likely to be attained.

5.9   The Home Secretary accepted Mountbatten's recommendations with regard to categorisation, however the Advisory Council on the Penal System were asked to give further consideration as to the regimes in which long-term prisoners should be held. The subsequent report 'The Regime for Long-Term Prisoners in Conditions of Maximum Security' did not agree with Mountbatten that all category A prisoners should be held together in one prison, and recommended that they should be 'dispersed' amongst category B prisoners in several prisons whose physical security would be upgraded in preparation.

5.10   This heralded the start of the dispersal prison system, which is still in use today. However, the terminology has recently been changed so that the prisons formerly known as dispersal prisons are now known simply as high security prisons. Some remand facilities have also been included in this part of the prison estate. At the present time, there are nine high security prisons. Five—Full Sutton, Frankland, Long Lartin, Whitemoor, and Wakefield— hold long-term convicted adult male prisoners. The remaining four—Durham, Woodhill, Belmarsh and Doncaster—are primarily local prisons. Woodhill and Durham also contain close supervision centres (see further below) and Doncaster and Belmarsh provide maximum security remand facilities.

5.11   All of the high security prisons take standard and high risk category A prisoners. Exceptional risk category A prisoners are held in special security units within the confines of the high security prisons (see below). Each high security prison will only take a specific quota of category A prisoners, and the rest of their populations are largely made up of category B prisoners and the occasional category C or D prisoner whom the prison have not been able to transfer to conditions of lesser security (eg because the prisoner requires full-time medical treatment).

5.12   Prisoners held in high security conditions are generally those serving the longest sentences. In a full inspection of HMP Frankland, which took place 5– 13 January 1998, the Chief Inspector of Prisons found that of the 445 prisoners held there 169 were serving between 4 years and 10 years, 176 were serving determinate sentences of over 10 years and 100 were serving life.

5.13   Because of the length of time that the majority of prisoners in high security conditions are serving, they are likely to receive a much better regime than that offered in other prisons. There are more educational facilities and there should be work for every prisoner. High security prisons for convicted prisoners have facilities for prisoners to purchase and cook their own food. It is also common practice for prisoners to be able to wear their own clothing and to have the facilities to wash and dry their clothes.

5.14   The list of items that high security prisoners are allowed to keep in their possession is extensive and covers far more items than those allowed for prisoners in other parts of the system. However, prisoners' ability to hold property has been affected by the system of volumetric control which was introduced following the Woodcock and Learmont Inquiries into security in the high security prison system. The Inquiries recommended that prisoners' property allowances should be severely restricted as excessive amounts of property hinder effective searching. The introduction of the Earned Privileges and Incentives Scheme over recent years has also adversely affected prisoners' ability to purchase items, or have property sent into prison.

Special security units and high security units

5.15   Special security units (SSUs) were conceived in the 1960s as a result of the recognition that there were a group of prisoners for whom escape should be made impossible. Initially special security wings were established at HMPs Durham and Leicester. However, it was considered that these did not provide secure enough accommodation as they were housed in local prisons. Furthermore, their regimes were limited and oppressive. By the late 1970s the Prison Service had decided to build SSUs at dispersal prisons.

5.16   Special security units are effectively prisons within a prison. They are fully self-contained and facilities include an exercise yard (which is fully enclosed), a gym, facilities for association including television, hobbies room etc, and their own visits room and segregation cells.

5.17   Special security units have their own perimeter security overlooked by closed circuit television cameras. The perimeter security of the dispersal prison where the SSU is housed surrounds both the prison itself and the walls of the SSU. Until 1994 when six prisoners escaped from Whitemoor SSU, it was thought that escape from an SSU would be impossible.

5.18   There are two SSU/HSUs in operation at the present time. Whitemoor SSU holds convicted exceptional risk category A prisoners, and Belmarsh High Security Unit holds remand prisoners provisionally categorised as high or exceptional risk category A and a small number of similarly categorised convicted prisoners who are on temporary transfer.

5.19   Security procedures dominate the SSUs, which are physically claustrophobic and which have been thought to have a detrimental effect on prisoners' health and well being. When such concerns were raised in judicial review proceedings the government asked its Chief Medical Officer, Sir Donald Acheson, to conduct research as to the long-term health of SSU prisoners (*Review on the Effects on Health in the Special Secure Units at Full Sutton, Whitemoor, and Belmarsh Prisons* (unpublished)). Known as the 'Acheson Report,' this review found that:

> 'the lack of natural light and the limited view from the cells ... all gave the team particular cause for concern. It was felt that [this] might, over time, lead prisoners to suffer from mental health problems ... the most likely symptoms would be anxiety related, such as irritability, poor concentration and poor sleep. In addition, particularly vulnerable prisoners might develop more severe symptomatology' (Acheson Report, para 4.6).

5.20   In view of this, the report recommended that the general health of SSU prisoners should be reviewed at regular intervals, taking into account their degree of susceptibility to psychological symptoms.

5.21   HMCIP's report of an unannounced inspection of HMP Whitemoor on 16–17 September 1996 commented on the SSU's regime. It was noted that 'there was no work, little education and far too much boredom for prisoners in the SSU.' Similarly, an HMCIP report of a full inspection at HMP Belmarsh found that the regime for prisoners was restricted. There was limited education, a small selection of books which provided 'one of the poorest choice of books we have ever seen' and the only work available was cleaning duties around the unit (report of an inspection 11–20 May 1998).

Close supervision centres

5.22 From 1969 to 1983 there were ten major disturbances and riots in the prison estate. In response to this a Home Office working party was established to:

'review the maintenance of control in the prison system including the implications for physical security, with particular reference to the dispersal system, and to make recommendations.'

This working party became known as the Control Review Committee (CRC), and published its report 'Managing the Long-Term Prison System' in 1984.

5.23 In considering how prisoners who presented particular control problems should be dealt with, the CRC said that the existing facilities of transfers in the interest of good order and discipline and segregation were not long-term solutions. They recommended that:

'a number of small units should be established for prisoners in this group (ie prisoners presenting control problems which cannot be dealt with in normal prison conditions).'

This provides the basis of the Close Supervision Centre (CSC) estate.

5.24 Close Supervision Centres operate as part of a national management strategy which aims to 'secure the return of problematic or disruptive prisoners to a settled and acceptable pattern of institutional behaviour.' The functions of the CSCs are said to be:

'(a) to remove the most seriously disruptive prisoners from mainstream high security or training prisons;
(b) to contain highly dangerous or disruptive individuals in small, highly supervised units with safety for staff and prisoners;
(c) to provide the opportunity for individuals to address their anti-social disruptive behaviour in a controlled environment;
(d) to stabilise behaviour and prepare for a return to the mainstream with minimum disruption, wherever possible; and
(e) to contain for as long as necessary any prisoner presenting so great a threat to the safety of staff and prisoners that long-term containment is the only option available (Operating Standards for Close Supervision Centres, Statement of Purpose).'

5.25 Detailed guidance on allocation to CSCs is laid out in chapter 8.

5.26 Prisoners who are selected to the CSC system will go to units at either Woodhill or Durham prisons. The Woodhill CSC contains prisoners who are not considered to have mental illness; the Durham CSC is meant primarily for disruptive prisoners with psychiatric problems, but also has a unit for prisoners who have progressed through the Woodhill unit and which aims to prepare people for a return to normal prison locations.

5.27 The Close Supervision Centres operate differential regimes. At Woodhill CSC the prisoners who are assessed as exhibiting the most challenging behaviour are held in conditions akin to segregation or cellular confinement in the 'Restricted Regime Centre.' Such prisoners will have no association with others (except exercise if they earn this as a privilege), will not be allowed to participate in the running of the regime and will only get basic regime privileges. Time out of cell is limited to the statutory period of exercise and contact with the outside world is limited to two social calls mid week, one at the weekend and two 30 minute visits each month. All furniture is cardboard and prisoners sleep on concrete plinths rather than conventional beds.

5.28   Prisoners are expected to commence their imprisonment in the CSC at Woodhill in the 'Structured Regime Centre.' This is supposed to have been set up in order to 'encourage a settled pattern of acceptable behaviour' (Operating Standards 5S.2). Prisoners participating in this regime will also be subjected to basic regime privileges, but will get a minimum of 17 hours per week out of cell for daily exercise, cleaning activities, one session of evening association and regime-based activities. Prisoners will be expected to participate in psychological assessment and testing and behavioural therapy. Outside contact is less limited, with prisoners able to make telephone calls when they are unlocked and able to receive two one-hour visits per month. Cell furnishings are the same as for Restricted Regime prisoners.

5.29   The final stage of the CSC at Woodhill is the Programmes Intervention Centre. Prisoners must progress to this level before they can be transferred out of Woodhill on a permanent basis. Conditions are rather better than in the other Centres but prisoners are still subjected to a very regimented regime. They must participate in psychological assessment and testing, casework officer interviews, group therapy, education, cleaning and food preparation. Visits are limited to three one-and-a-half hour sessions a month and prisoners may make telephone calls during association periods. Privileges are akin to standard level under the Incentives and Earned Privileges Scheme.

5.30   Woodhill CSC also holds a segregation unit. The regime is not dissimilar to that operated in the Restricted Regime Centre, although access to telephones is even more limited. Prisoners are not allowed a radio and very few possessions are allowed in the cells.

5.31   Prisoners can be removed from CSCs to 'high control cells' in Wakefield, Belmarsh, Frankland, Full Sutton, Whitemoor and Long Lartin if they are presenting 'exceptionally difficult control problems' (Operating Standards 1.26). The maximum period of segregation in a high control cell is 56 days.

5.32   In practice, the high control cells are perfectly ordinary segregation cells at high security prisons. Most CSC prisoners who have been transferred out of Woodhill under this provision find that the conditions are far more favourable than the ones which they have become used to.

5.33   There is no flexibility in the CSC system. If prisoners choose not to co-operate then the Prison Service says that they will stay on the Restricted Regime Centre at Woodhill CSC until they are released from prison. A number of prisoners have put this theory to the test by refusing to engage with the regime. All have remained at Woodhill, although most have also had periods where they have been transferred out to high control cells. Thus, the Prison Service has created an entirely confrontational system from which there would appear to be no way out.

5.34   The governor of Woodhill has publicly recognised that 'some of those in the CSC are not capable of changing their behaviour,' and is reportedly 'uneasy' about locking prisoners up 23 hours a day (*Economist* 15 May 1999, p 36). However, it would seem that the Prison Service has no intention of accepting that it cannot coerce prisoners into following a system imposed upon them.

5.35   The Boards of Visitors have privately expressed concerns about the health and well being of prisoners:

> 'it seems to me that sleeping on a mattress on a stone plinth (as well as being degrading) is also unhealthy ... I anticipate the imminent appearance of mould (or mushrooms!). It would be too much, I suppose, to request beds ... The effects of inactivity on health are well known—bone density loss, impaired heart and lung function, muscle wastage etc...Would there be any value in suggesting a regular check up by the Health Care Centre—always assuming you're allowed to examine them? The effects of lack of stimulation on mental health, I can only guess at ... I am no bleeding heart liberal ... however, it might only be a matter of time before a man falls very ill and we have a duty to care.' (Letter from BOV member to the SMO at Woodhill (unpublished))

Category B training prisons

5.36   There are ten category B training prisons at Albany, Blundeston, Dartmoor, Garth, Gartree, Grendon, Kingston, Lowdham Grange, Maidstone, Parkhurst and Swaleside.

5.37   Category B training prisons tend to have a secure perimeter and relatively high levels of staffing. However, they offer a more relaxed regime than in high security prisons and there is less internal security. Opportunities for work and education should be available.

5.38   Each category B training prison has different criteria that operate in its allocations criteria, and this inevitably affects the type of regime offered and the type of prisoners received. All of these prisons take life sentence prisoners—Gartree is a main lifer centre taking prisoners who are in the first three years of their sentence, and Kingston only takes life sentence prisoners. Maidstone and Albany are particularly noted for running sex offender treatment programmes and assessments for the programme.

5.39   Levels of physical security at category B prisons differ dramatically. Swaleside's security is not dissimilar to a high security prison and it is generally considered to be the highest security category B training prison. Conversely, Maidstone is considered to be low security and will not take prisoners who have recently been on the escape list. Albany, Parkhurst and Gartree are former dispersal prisons which have changed their role in recent years.

5.40   Category B, C and D prisoners may be held in category B training prisons, although those of lower security categories will almost certainly be applying for transfers elsewhere.

Category C prisons

5.41   Category C prisons make up one of the largest parts of the prison estate, and there are 32 such establishments. Like category B training prisons, they vary enormously from prison to prison.

5.42   In general, category C prisons have lower levels of staff supervision and less perimeter security. Until recent years they tended to have a younger population serving shorter sentences. However, following disturbances at HMP Wymott in the summer of 1994, the Prison Service reviewed the population of category C prisoners and identified prisoners aged under 25 at conviction, those sentenced to less than four years, and those serving sentences for robbery or burglary as the most likely to pose control problems. Quotas were set on the numbers of such prisoners that each category C prison should take (see chapter 5).

5.43   Many category C prisons have dormitory accommodation rather than or as well as cellular accommodation, and many long-term prisoners find this difficult to cope with. Because there is less staff supervision, there will often be more rules in operation. Prisoners found to be in breach of the rules will be more likely to be charged with breaches of r 51 of the Prison Rules than they would be in conditions of higher security. In general prisoners are expected to be more accountable for their actions and to take more responsibility for their behaviour.

5.44   Category C and D prisoners are held in these prisons.

Category D/open prisons

5.45   There is very little security in category D prisons, and prisoners tend not to be locked up, and often retain their own keys to their rooms. Perimeter security often consists of little more than a fence, and some governors at open prisons have remarked that this serves more to keep the media out than the prisoners in.

5.46   Prisoners are only transferred to open conditions if the Prison Service is satisfied that they can be trusted not to abscond. Because of the ease with which prisoners could abscond, and in response to local feeling in the community, some open prisons will not take prisoners convicted of sexual offences.

5.47   Prisoners may be engaged in work at the prison or alternatively may be released from prison every day to do community work (often with the elderly or at schools for children with special needs).

5.48   Prisoners in open conditions are likely to be released from prison regularly in order to work, take town visits and temporary releases on resettlement or facility licence. Open prisons do not have full-time medical staff, and so prisoners will be released to attend local hospitals, dentists and opticians rather than being treated by Prison Health Care staff. Prisoners with serious medical problems which require constant attention or monitoring will often not be allocated to open conditions and will remain in prisons where there is full-time medical care.

Resettlement prisons

5.49   The first resettlement prison to open was at HMP Latchmere House in 1991. Since then several smaller units have opened at local and category C and D prisons.

5.50   Long-term prisoners are transferred to resettlement prisons towards the end of their sentences in order that they might re-establish their links with their families and the wider community and obtain paid employment. It is hoped that this will significantly diminish rates of recidivism.

5.51   Because much of prisoners' time will be spent outside the prison, the facilities at resettlement prisons are generally poorer than at other prisons. Prisoners found guilty of breaches of prison discipline are often transferred out to higher security establishments as are those who are suspected of being involved in any subversive behaviour.

5.52   Mandatory life sentenced prisoners of working age are usually required to spend the last few months of their sentence in resettlement prison conditions.

Vulnerable prisoners' units

5.53   Historically, prisoners convicted of sexual offences and others who would not be acceptable to the mainstream prison population (because they are informers, in debt to other prisoners or former police or prison officers), have asked to be segregated for their own protection under the provisions of r 43 of the Prison Rules (now r 45). Whilst this removed the immediate threat of violence from other prisoners, it meant that the most vulnerable prisoners in the system were often held in the very worst conditions in the prison system.

5.54   In response to an increase in the number of prisoners segregated for their own protection, the Prison Service set up a number of vulnerable prisoners' units (VPUs) which were intended for:

'... a relatively small number of medium and long sentence prisoners—mainly sex offenders and child abusers—who will fail all attempts to survive on normal location and who will need to remain in a protected environment until their discharge, whilst having the benefit of the facilities available to other medium and long term prisoners.' (Report of the Prison Department Working Group on the Management of Vulnerable Prisoners (1989))

5.55   The Programmes Department in DSP 2 at Prison Service Headquarters carried out a review of VPUs in 1995. This found that the numbers of prisoners held separately has significantly increased. They considered that the population of VPUs tended to rise in proportion to the number of available spaces, and that many of these prisoners should be able to survive on normal location. Governors were asked not to create new VPUs without permission from Headquarters and to be more flexible about accepting prisoners for normal location despite them having been held in a VPU or on segregation in the past. Routine transfers of vulnerable prisoners are to be seen as an opportunity to integrate prisoners onto normal location (IG 82/95).

WOMEN'S PRISONS

5.56   There are 16 prisons in the female prison system. Unlike men's prisons, women's prisons are simply categorised as either open, closed or local prisons. Female young offenders are held in prisons with adult prisoners which will have certain areas designated as young offender institutions (see chapter 6).

5.57   Five prisons operate as local prisons (Brockhill, Eastwood Park, Low Newton, Holloway and New Hall) and women will be held in one of these prisons whilst they are on remand, until they are allocated to another establishment after conviction or where they are serving short sentences. Female category A remand prisoners are held at Holloway prison, as are women who are in need of psychiatric care.

5.58   The closed women's prisons are Styal, Durham, Cookham Wood, Foston Hall, Bullwood Hall, Send, Highpoint and Winchester (annex). These operate similar regimes as category B and C prisons in the men's prison estate. Holloway keeps some long-term prisoners for significant parts of their sentences, although its primary function is as a remand prison. Convicted category A women are held in a discrete wing at Durham (whose other functions are a local prison for male prisoners, and a close supervision centre). This is the highest security prison in the women's prison estate.

5.59   There are three open women's prisons—Askham Grange, Drake Hall and East Sutton Park.

5.60   In addition to the above there are four mother and baby units in the women's prison estate. They have a total of 64 places and are found at Styal, Holloway, New Hall and Askham Grange prisons. The purpose of mother and baby units is to:

'allow the mother/baby relationship to develop whilst safeguarding the child's welfare.' (PSO 4801)

The 'culture and ethos' of the units is described as follows:

'It is policy that babies are not locked in rooms. When mothers on the units are required to remain in their rooms, room doors will not be locked. The ethos of mother and baby units is that they are fair and open ... all documents relating to babies will be disclosed to the mother. The whole application process must be conducted openly, with the mother involved at all stages.' (PSO 4801, p 1)

5.61 Holloway and New Hall have facilities for women to keep their babies with them up until they are nine months old, and the other units will allow mothers to keep their babies until they are 18 months old. In considering women's applications to go to a mother and baby unit, the following criteria are considered by the Admissions Board:

'It is in the best interests of the child/children to be placed in a mother and baby unit.

The mother is able to demonstrate behaviour and attitude which is not detrimental to the safety and well-being of other unit residents (or the good order and discipline of the unit).

The mother has provided a urine sample which tests negative for drugs.

The mother is willing to remain drug free.

The mother is willing to sign a standard compact, which may be tailored to her identified individual needs.

The mother's ability and eligibility to care for a child is not impaired by health or legal reasons.' (PSO 4801, p 5)

5.62 The Admissions Board is normally made up of an independent chairperson, the mother, an operational officer of the mother and baby unit, a probation officer, a social services representative, a nursery nurse, a health visitor and any other appropriate professionals. The Board will have access to a dossier of information from Social Services, security reports, medical reports, a wing conduct report, and information from the Probation Service.

MALE YOUNG OFFENDER INSTITUTIONS

5.63 Prisoners between the ages of 15 and 21 are held in young offender institutions (YOIs), although in exceptional situations they can be transferred into adult prisons. Those who turn 21 during their sentence are generally transferred into the adult prison system at that stage, although if they are due for release shortly afterwards, they may remain in a YOI.

5.64 The male YOI estate is similar to the women's prison system in that the only distinctions between prisons is whether they are open or closed. At the present time there are 15 closed YOIs and two open YOIs (Hatfield and Thorn Cross). Young offenders may also be held on remand in a wing of a male local prison or in the juvenile prison estate.

5.65 Young offender institutions are governed by the Young Offender Institution Rules 1988 rather than the Prison Rules 1999, although they are very similar in effect.

5.66 The main difference between the regimes at YOIs and those at adult prisons are that prisoners under the compulsory school leaving age should be provided with at least 15 hours of education each week. In their report *Banged Up, Beaten Up, Cutting Up* (1995), the Howard League for Penal Reform found that school age children in prison are not offered the national curriculum, and that although 'most establishments try to encourage all young people to attend classes ... the quality of facilities is often more of a deterrent than an incentive' (p 25).

5.67   The physical conditions in YOIs can be very impoverished. The Howard League found that teenage prisoners were often accommodated in cellular accommodation on wings of up to 60 people, that integral sanitation was not available throughout the YOI estate, and that overcrowding was 'endemic' in virtually all of the establishments they visited. The newer YOIs gave the impression of being maximum security prisons, whereas young offenders held in male local prisons had 'no proper communal eating or recreation space' and the cells were 'cramped and bare' (*Banged Up, Beaten Up, Cutting Up*, p 25). Following a visit to the young offender's wing at Hull prison, one of the Howard League's Commissioners wrote:

'I find it hard to describe exactly how awful I found it. The building lacks natural light almost completely. Landings are narrow, separated by flights of stairs and suicide nets ... The building is quiet but sounds echo. Furniture and furnishings are of poor standard, and often piled into inappropriate rooms. The atmosphere is of "making the most of it," while facilities are poor and damaged. To me, the young people looked confused and aimless.'

5.68   In terms of regimes, the YOI estate tends to mirror that of the adult prison system, with sentenced prisoners being offered better facilities and having more opportunity for constructive employment, and remand prisoners merely being contained until their cases are dealt with by the courts.

5.69   In 1997, the Chief Inspector of Prisons conducted a thematic review of the conditions for and treatment of young prisoners (*Young Prisoners: A Thematic Review by HM Chief Inspector of Prisons for England and Wales*). The Chief Inspector was so concerned at the lack of a coherent structure within the YOI estate that he reported:

'The chaos which surrounds the treatment of children and young adults in Prison Service custody leads me to the conclusion that separate arrangements for dealing with young prisoners are essential.'

5.70   Thus, HMCIP recommended that all children under the age of 18 should be removed from prison and into a separate youth justice framework, that the Prison Service should appoint a Director of Young Prisoners to ensure consistent regimes for young people held within the prison system, and that the Director of Young Prisoners should conduct an urgent examination of the operating standards for young people in custody.

5.71   In response to the Thematic Review, the Crime and Disorder Act 1998, s 73, established a new custodial sentence—Detention and Training Orders (DTO). This will be imposed on children and young people under the age of 18. The Prison Service has issued PSO 4950, which sets out regimes for young offenders, remand and convicted, who are under 18 years of age.

5.72   Whilst governors are given discretion as to how these regimes are to be delivered, the PSO defines the principles upon which they should be based.

This says:

'It is important at the outset to make clear that regimes for under 18 year olds are different because under 18 year olds are, as adolescents, different. In order for the regimes to be appropriate to the needs, abilities and aptitudes of the individuals and focused upon preventing offending, they must take into account the characteristics of adolescent behaviour:

(i)   the importance of peers and peer pressure on behaviour;
(ii) their impulsiveness and inclination not to think ahead but to gratify immediate needs;
(iii) emotional immaturity even when cloaked in physical maturity;
(iv) their capacity for being cruel to one another—hence the importance both of the staffs' and peers' role modelling and promoting good behaviour and of clearly defining and maintaining the boundaries of bad behaviour;
(v)   the prevalence of impoverished upbringing in their backgrounds and a history of low achievement;
(vi) their potential to mature and grow out of crime.

Underpinning the entire PSO is the belief that custody cannot just be about containment. However, if it is to have a positive influence we must provide regimes which recognise that:

(i)   adolescents do change
(ii) that adults matter to adolescents
(iii) that adolescents need care and control.' (PSO 4950, paras 1.5–1.6)

5.73 The main differences in the way that young offenders are treated in relation to adult prisoners are highlighted throughout the text of this book.

CHAPTER 6

CATEGORISATION, ALLOCATION AND SENTENCE PLANNING

THE DEFINITION OF CATEGORIES

The authority to categorise

6.1 The Prison Rules 1999, r 7, requires the Secretary of State to classify prisoners. The power is expressed broadly to take account of:

'age, temperament and record and with a view to maintaining good order and facilitating training and, in the case of convicted prisoners of furthering the purpose of their training and treatment ...' (r 7(1))

The arrangements for the separation of inmates should not 'unduly deprive a prisoner of the society of other persons' (r 7(4)).

6.2 Rule 7 goes on to state that unconvicted prisoners should be kept out of contact with convicted prisoners to the extent that the governor considers that this can reasonably be done. An unconvicted prisoner may never be required to share a cell with a convicted prisoner. This relaxes the previous provisions that forbade mixing in living areas under any circumstances.

6.3 Women prisoners and young offenders are not assigned to formal categories, other than those who are deemed to be category A (see below). These prisoners are therefore only assigned to either closed or open conditions and so the process is more tightly bound to allocation (see below). Broadly speaking, if a woman prisoner or young offender would normally meet the equivalent criteria for category D, they can expect to located in an open prison.

The Mountbatten criteria

6.4 The broad power that is created once again leaves a great deal of detail to be filled in by the policy documents issued by the Home Office. The present categories were first established following a report of the Inquiry into Prison Escapes and Security by Lord Mountbatten in 1976. This established four security categories ranging from A, reserved for the most dangerous prisoners, to D, the lowest category. These criteria are now contained in PSO 2200, the Prison Service Manual that deals with Sentence Management and Planning. Further guidance on categorisation is also provided in PSO 1000, the Security Manual.

6.5 All prisoners can be made category A, whether unconvicted, female or juveniles. A full discussion of the procedures and implication for category A prisoners appears below. The remaining three categories of B, C and D are reserved for convicted, adult male prisoners. Part 7 of PSO 2200 deals with 'Categorisation, Classification and Allocation.' The primary criteria for categorisation are:

> '*Category A*: Prisoners whose escape would be highly dangerous to the public, the police or the security of the state, no matter how unlikely that escape might be; and for whom the aim must be to make escape impossible.
>
> *Category B*: Prisoners for whom the very highest conditions of security are not necessary but for whom escape must be made very difficult.
>
> *Category C*: Prisoners who cannot be trusted in open conditions but who do not have the resources or will to make a determined escape attempt.
>
> *Category D*: Prisoners who can be reasonably trusted in open conditions.' (para 7.1.2)

Unconvicted prisoners are placed in category U (unclassified) and are normally assumed to require accommodation appropriate to category B. However, PSO 2200 does state that in principle unconvicted prisoners could be considered for category C conditions if there is enough information available to show that category B conditions are not necessary and the decision is approved by the area manager (para 7.1.6).

Escape list prisoners

6.6 It is also possible for a prisoner to be identified as an 'escape risk' and placed on the 'Escape' or 'E List.' This is not a security category as such, but a security decision relevant to the matter of category. The decision to place a prisoner on the escape list must be given by a governor grade or equivalent at the relevant prison (Security Manual, para 9.17). The person making the decision must consider whether there is 'reasonable intelligence that the prisoner is planning to escape,' which would be enough to warrant E List status in itself. Otherwise what must be considered is whether the prisoner has recently escaped or tried to escape and whether any such attempt was credible; whether the prisoner has escaped or tried to escape before and whether there are now similar circumstances and finally; whether the prison's 'physical and procedural security' is sufficient to deal with the threat of escape without putting the prisoner on the E List (Security Manual, para 9.18).

6.7 If a prisoner is to be placed on the E List, the governor must ensure that s/he is re-categorised to B and if located in a lower security prison, that an immediate transfer to a prison of the appropriate security is effected. The prisoner must be notified orally and in writing of the reasons for the decision, although the reasons will be drafted to ensure that security is not compromised.

Reviews of the decision should be made at least every 28 days and the prisoner should be removed from the list 'as soon as he or she no longer presents a high risk of escape' (Security Manual, para 9.19).

6.8   Escape list prisoners are subject to stringent security measures set out in an appendix to the Security Manual that require them to be located in the same cells as category A prisoners, with a low-wattage night light for observation at night. Amongst a large array of measures they will be subject to (paras 34.31–34.50) are hourly checks of their cells and changing of cells at least once a month without notice. In addition E List prisoners must wear 'distinctive E List clothing,' normally jackets and trousers with distinctive yellow markings, known to prisoners as 'patches.'

The initial categorisation decision

6.9   The decision to allocate a prisoner to a security category, save for category A prisoners, rests with the governor of the prison. PSO 2200, section 7, provides guidance on the exercise of this power to ensure there is consistency throughout the system. Perhaps the most important part of this guidance in relation to the initial decision is:

> 'Prisoners must be categorised objectively according to the likelihood that they will seek to escape and the risk that they would pose should an escape succeed. The security category must take account of these considerations alone.' (para 7.1.3(1))

The considerations of factors such as control, good order and discipline, likely conduct (other than that relevant to escape risk), ability to mix with other prisoners, educational or medical needs may be relevant to allocation but not categorisation. The PSO further states that all 'must be placed in the lowest category consistent with the needs of security' (para 7.1.3(4)). This is an ongoing duty as 'every prisoner, at each stage of their sentence, should be in the lowest category that meets the security risk' (Security Manual, para 9.11).

6.10   These guidelines are of extreme importance as security category determines the type of prison to which prisoners are allocated, and also affects other decisions such as entitlement to temporary release on licence. Parole decisions are also affected by the security category of the applicant.

6.11   PSO 2200 also provides further detailed guidance on the initial categorisation decision. The starting point is that:

> 'All prisoners must be regarded as suitable for Category D on first categorisation unless they:
> (a) are sentenced to over 12 months for any offence of violence; or
> (b) are convicted of any but the most minor sex offence; or
> (c) have a previous sentence of over 12 months for any violent or sexual offence and did not serve part of that sentence in an open prison; or
> (d) have current or previous convictions for arson or any drugs offence involving importation or dealing; or
> (e) have a recent history of escapes or absconds.' (para 7.1.4(1))

After applying these criteria prisoners should be regarded as 'probably suitable' for Category C unless they:

'(a) are sentenced to over 7 years for any violent or sexual offence; or
(b) have a previous sentence of over 7 years for any violent or sexual offence and did not successfully serve part of that sentence in a Category C prison; or
(c) have a current sentence exceeding 10 years; or
(d) have a recent history of escape from closed conditions, or have significant external resources which they might use to assist an escape attempt.' (para 7.1.4(2))

The Order makes it clear that the above criteria 'must not be seen as either exhaustive or inflexible' (para 7.1.4(4)) and a refusal to consider departing from them in the appropriate case would accordingly render a decision unlawful.

6.12 Generally the Order anticipates that those convicted of non-violent offences or serving short to medium sentences will normally be category C, whilst those convicted of a serious, violent, sexual or drug related offence will normally be category B. However the Security Manual states that 'no prisoner should be in category B unless he really needs to be held in highly secure conditions' (para 9.11). Civil prisoners and fine defaulters will normally be category D, as will those who have successfully served a previous sentence in an open prison unless the new offence is clearly more serious (PSO 2200, para 7.1.4(3)).

6.13 The process of initial categorisation should be in two stages and will be carried out by the 'Observation, Allocation and Classification' (OCA) unit in the prison. The first stage is a provisional assessment on paper using form ICA 1 which directs the documents that should be collected to inform the decision, and contains an algorithm to determine the provisional categorisation. This is followed by an interview with the prisoner.

Subsequent decisions and challenges

6.14 As prisoners have to be in the lowest appropriate category at any given stage in their sentence, prisons must have procedures for reviewing security category as prisoners may become less likely to escape or re-offend. Similarly it is possible for prisoners to be moved to a higher security category. PSO 2200 states that recategorisation 'should be based on a clear change in risk factor' (para 7.3.2). However a wider range of factors may be taken into account when considering risk than at initial categorisation. The Order states that 'Account should be taken of risk to the public, likelihood to escape, positions of trust held, progress in addressing offence related concerns, and attitude' (para 7.3.2). A prisoner who successfully completes a period on temporary licence must be considered for category D. With regard to timing of reviews 'All prisoners other than those serving less than 12 months must have their security category reviewed at regular intervals or whenever there is a significant change in their circumstances' (para 7.3.2(3)). More particularly, those serving between 12 months and four years should have a review at least every six months, while those serving four years and over should have one at least every 12 months (para 7.3.2).

6.15   The procedure for reviewing a prisoner's security category should be broadly similar as for the initial decision. Most governors now delegate their duties to boards, which will review security category following sentence planning reviews. The sentence planning reviews should involve an interview with the prisoner (para 7.3.2(5)) which in turn should inform the categorisation decision. The decision will also take account of reports and comments from prison officers and others, and reports relating to the prisoner's level on the incentives scheme. In one case (*R v Governor of HM Prison Latchmere House, ex p Jarvis* (20 July 1999, unreported), HC) the court held that a transfer from an open to a category B prison for reasons of good order and discipline was unlawful for failure to follow the recategorisation procedures contained in PSO 2200, especially as there did not appear to be any urgent circumstances warranting a by-pass of normal procedures.

6.16   Given the sources of information used in these decisions it is difficult to ensure that considerations which are not strictly relevant to category do not inform the decision. For example, a prisoner who is considered to be 'difficult' may not in fact present an escape risk or a danger to the public. There is in any event a duty to give reasons for all decisions relating to security category (*R v Governor of HM Prison Maidstone, ex p Peries* (1997) Times, 30 July). The extent to which a decision may be challenged will depend on the precise reasons given. It is in the nature of administrative decisions such as these that if carefully worded reasons are given for a decision, a challenge can be extremely difficult to mount.

6.17   Prisons may have their own local criteria for recategorisation which are too rigidly applied. A common example of this is a requirement that a prisoner serve a certain proportion of their sentence before being eligible for recategorisation. Whilst prisons may have their own criteria, these must not be inflexible as otherwise they will be vulnerable to challenge on the basis that the criteria defeat the requirement that every prisoner is required to be in the lowest category possible at each stage of their sentence and that this will depend upon a proper assessment of risk, not length of time served.

Category A status

6.18   This is the only category that can apply to all prisoners, whether male, female, juvenile or remand. The decision to so classify a prisoner is made by the category A Committee which is comprised of various senior Prison Service officials. The Committee can order that remand prisoners are 'provisionally' category A until the time of their trial and if convicted, categorisation is reviewed at that time. The reality for a 'provisional' category A prisoner is that s/he will be subject to the same security restrictions as a convicted category A prisoner.

6.19   There are further subdivisions within category A, relating to the escape risk of an individual. The definition of this category is to make escape impossible for prisoners, 'no matter how unlikely such an escape may be.' The corollary of this definition is that a wide range of prisoners will fall within this definition despite the fact that it is accepted that many will never have the potential or resources to mount a serious escape attempt. Therefore, such prisoners can be made an exceptional, high or standard escape risk. For those with a high or exceptional escape risk, even more restrictions will be placed upon them whilst in custody.

6.20   Guidance on escape risk category is contained in the Security Manual. Standard risk prisoners 'are not considered to have the determination and skill to overcome the range of security measures which apply to the custody and movement of Category A prisoners.' High risk are those prisoners 'that have a history and background which suggest that they have the ability and determination' to overcome the same range of security measures and where there may be 'current information to suggest that they have associates or resources' to carry out an escape attempt. Exceptional risk prisoners are those that have the same features as high risk, but where 'the nature and extent of the external resources which could be called upon to mount an escape attempt are such that the level of threat posed requires that the prisoner be held in the most secure accommodation and conditions available to the Prison Service' (Security Manual, para 9.8).

6.21   The implications for a prisoner classified as category A are far-reaching. Only a small number of prisons are designated to hold prisoners of this category on a permanent basis, by and large the nine high security prisons and HMP Highdown and Doncaster. However, even within the high security system, some prisons are not deemed secure enough to hold high or exceptional escape risk prisoners. Only certain of the high security prisons are deemed secure enough for high and exceptional risk category A prisoners who are kept in SSUs.

6.22   The restrictions that are faced by such prisoners fall into two levels. Firstly, there are the straightforward restrictions on contact with people outside of prison. Visits can only be received from official visitors (eg solicitors, probation officers) or friends and family members who have been approved centrally through the Approved Visitors Scheme (annex 23A to the Security Manual). The procedure for obtaining approval is for a list of the proposed visitors, who must also provide two photographs, to be given to the prison who will then contact the police for a security check. All exceptional risk category A prisoners will have closed visits, even for visits of legal advisers, and the Security Manual states that the Director of High Security Prisons at Headquarters must agree before such prisoners can have open visits (para 23.64). A challenge arguing for the removal of these restrictions for legal visits on the basis that the right to confidential legal advice was breached failed (*R v Secretary of State for the Home Department, ex p O'Dhuibhir* [1997] COD 315 CA), although the basis upon which the court made its decision was questionable.

6.23   The second level of restrictions relate to the regimes which are in operation within the prison itself. A summary of the special procedures applicable to category A prisoners is contained in an appendix to the Security Manual. Category A prisoners are liable to be moved more often that other prisoners, both from cell to cell within a prison and between prisons. No notification is given before moves are made to ensure that security is not compromised. This makes it extremely difficult to maintain effective communications with family members and places an additional stress on visitors. It is not uncommon for visitors to complain that the person they were seeking to visit had been moved and that no notification was given before they arrived at the prison. In view of the often inaccessible locations of the high security prisons, this is a source of particular concern and conflict. The only manner in which such moves can be challenged in domestic law is if a decision to move is taken unreasonably. The courts are extremely reluctant to interfere in what they see as the disciplinary and security functions of prison governors when reaching such decisions and challenges can be very difficult to sustain. In the case of *Ex p Ross* (1994) Times, 9 June, CA, Waite LJ considered that the governor of a prison was best placed to decide whether a category A prisoner posed a threat to discipline and providing general reasons were given, the court would not interfere.

6.24   Attempts to challenge the apparently random movement of high security prisoners through the European Convention on Human Rights would also appear to be difficult following the finding of the Commission in *Roelofs v Netherlands* (1 July 1992, No 1943592: see LAG, January 1993). This Dutch prisoner had been held in isolation and moved continually following allegations from an informer that he was to escape from custody. The Commission found the case to be inadmissible on the grounds that administrative decisions such as these were imposed for security reasons and not as a sanction and could not therefore be regarded as a determination of the person's rights.

6.25   The facilities available to category A prisoners, both educational and rehabilitative will depend very much on the resources of the particular prison in which they are located. In the period following the Woolf Report, the emphasis slowly moved towards rehabilitation but after the Woodcock report prepared following the escapes from Whitemoor prison in September 1994 there was a shift, in dispersal prisons in particular, towards an emphasis on security. In general, the courses designed to address offending behaviour that are available to category A prisoners are very limited and there is little uniformity between the facilities and courses available in the various high security prisons. This can create a vicious circle whereby prisoners are kept category A on the basis that the risk they pose has not been reduced because of the failure to complete courses that are unavailable to them.

The judgment in *Duggan*

6.26   The enormous impact of category A status was finally recognised by the Divisional Court in December 1993 in the case of *R v Secretary of State for the Home Department, ex p Duggan* [1994] 3 All ER 277. Historically, the position had been that category A prisoners were not entitled to know of the reasons for their categorisation following the case of *Payne v Home Office* (2 May 1977, unreported). Cantley J took the view that the provision of sufficient information to allow prisoners to fully understand the reasons for their categorisation could seriously hamper and frustrate the proper management of prisoners!

6.27 The antiquity of such views was exposed by the House of Lords in *R v Secretary of State for the Home Department, ex p Doody* [1994] 1 AC 531. The Woolf Report had already recommended that reasons be given for decisions as a matter of good administration and management. In *Doody*, Lord Mustill set out six principles of good administrative practice that included the right to know of the reasons why a decision has been made:

> 'Fairness will very often require that a person who may be adversely affected by a decision will have the opportunity to make representations on his own behalf either before the decision is taken with a view to expressly procuring a favourable result, or after it is taken, with a view to procuring its modification: or both.'

6.28 Lord Justice Rose was freed from earlier constraints by this judgment and in *Duggan*, he was able to approve his own comments from the earlier case of *R v Secretary of State for the Home Department, ex p Creamer and Scholey* [1993] COD 162 where he had still been bound by the case of *Payne*. His view was that:

> 'A prisoner's right to make representations is largely valueless unless he knows the case against him and secret, unchallengeable reports which may contain damaging inaccuracies and which result in the loss of liberty are, or should be, anathema in a civilised, democratic society.'

6.29 It was accepted by the court that the criteria for placing a prisoner on category A meant that release on parole became practically an impossibility. Therefore as the decision had a direct impact on the liberty of the subject, it was held that procedural fairness entitles prisoners to know of the gist of the reports that have been prepared, to make representations and to be informed of the reasons to maintain them as category A. This was subject to any exemptions that may arise from public interest immunity.

The implementation of the judgment in *Duggan*

6.30 Following the judgment in *Duggan*, if a prisoner is made category A the first review by the Category A Review Committee at Prison Service Headquarters will take place as soon as is practicable after conviction and sentence. The Committee meets every two months and is made up of senior Prison Service personnel and is assisted by a police adviser. Reports and information to be considered by the Committee are distilled into a gist that is disclosed to the prisoner. This gist tends to be very limited and will often amount to no more than 50–100 words, comprising of a recital of the convictions and sentence, recent custodial behaviour and work that has been undertaken into offending behaviour if any. The recommendations in the gist are often contradictory with some reporters recommending downgrading whereas others will express reservations, often based on the nature of the original offences. It is not clear from the gist who has made what recommendation if there is a conflict between reporters.

6.31 After this has been disclosed, representations can be made by the prisoner and the case will be referred to the Committee. Decisions are notified some two to three months after the Committee sits. The whole process can take up to six months and this leads to problems in keeping the gist up to date, particularly when a prisoner has been moved, and in disclosing all of the information that has been considered by the Committee. Decision letters tend to be as cursory as the gist and will on occasion make reference to material that has never been seen by the prisoner. If the decision is that the prisoner should remain category A then there will be an annual review. Such annual reviews are only referred to the Committee if there is a recommendation for downgrading from the governor or head of custody of the prison, or if the case has not been reviewed by the Committee in the past five years.

6.32 Although *Duggan* was an extremely important case for prisoners, the gist procedure looks increasingly anomalous now that in most contexts (such as parole, tariff setting, sentence planning and categorisation for other prisoners, and prison discipline) full disclosure is the norm. However further challenges to the level of disclosure in category A reviews have not met with success. In *R v Secretary of State for the Home Department, ex p McAvoy* [1998] 1 WLR 790 it was argued that fairness required full disclosure of reports relied on, subject to public interest immunity, by analogy with the open reporting of the parole process. The Court of Appeal rejected the argument by stating that a gist was all that was required by the principles in *Doody* and *Duggan*, and that the procedure was fair as long as there was consideration of whether additional information should be made available in individual cases. An attempt to argue that there was a right to see more of the police information than appeared in the gist where that information was contested and prejudicial also failed (*R v Secretary of State for the Home Department, ex p Arif* (29 November 1996, unreported), HC). The initial sentence planning document for category A prisoners, ICA 4, which should be completed at the start of a sentence can, however, be disclosed to the prisoner (PSO 2200, para 7.3.12) and some category A prisoners have successfully argued for disclosure of police information under the Data Protection Act 1984, directly from the relevant police force.

Remand prisoners and category A

6.33 The judgment in *Duggan* did not extend to remand prisoners. The court was specifically concerned with the bearing that categorisation has on release and accepted the need for speedy categorisation decisions to be made in the public interest. As a consequence, the initial decision was not subject to the review procedures, but only the formal annual review. Following this decision, the Prison Service took a stringent line and refused to extend the requirements imposed upon it to remand prisoners.

6.34 The view of the Prison Service remains that it is not bound to give reasons for decisions made to make remand prisoners category A. The slightly absurd position whereby unconvicted prisoners are deemed to have less rights in respect of the conditions of their detention is likely to be less well received by the courts. Perhaps in recognition of this, the Prison Service will, in most cases, provide written reasons for such decisions on request. Any refusal to do so should be made the subject of judicial review. On a practical level, however, once the reasons have been disclosed the possibility of a successful challenge to the decision is likely to be limited. The Prison Service will undoubtedly have reached the decision on the basis of information supplied by the police. Unless compelling evidence can be put forward to counter the allegations, a court is unlikely to be persuaded that it is wrong to rely on this information.

THE BASIS OF ALLOCATION

Adult male prisoners

6.35 In the minds of prisoners, security categorisation and allocation are often inextricably linked. However, PSO 2200 warns that while the two procedures will be completed by the same OCA unit allocation 'will form a process distinct from that of categorisation' (para 7.1.10).

6.36 The Order also sets out the criteria and priorities used in the allocation process. The four priorities, which are not always compatible are:

'(a) the needs of security
 (b) the needs of control
 (c) the need to make the maximum use of available spaces in training prisons and
 (d) the needs of the individual prisoner.' (PSO 2200, para 7.1.11(1))

6.37 Staff who work in OCA units are advised that while the main factor in considering where a prisoner should be transferred to after conviction is the security category, account must also be taken of:

'(a) His likely conduct, ie will he present an unacceptable control problem in that establishment?
 (b) His suitability for particular types of accommodation (factors such as vulnerability, age, etc).
 (c) His medical and/or psychiatric needs that may require a particular type or level of care.
 (d) Need for identified offence-related behavioural programmes to confront assessed risk.
 (e) His home area, or that of his likely visitors.
 (f) His educational or training needs or potential.
 (g) Any restrictions on allocation criteria agreed with local authorities.' (PSO 2200, para 7.1.11(2))

6.38 Thus whilst a prisoner should be given the lowest possible security categorisation at all stages in his sentence, other factors may come into play and cause a prisoner to be allocated to a prison which is of a higher security category than his categorisation would appear to merit. This may be because of the type of offence that he has been found guilty of—open prisons may have an agreement with the local authority that sex offenders will not be allocated there—or it could be because the only places available in an open prison are in a dormitory and a particular prisoner may be considered too much of a 'loner' to be able to cope there. The Order makes it clear that prisons should never modify the categorisation process in order to match prisoners to available places (PSO 2200, para 7.1.12(3)).

6.39   Where a prisoner is allocated to a prison of a higher security category than he is, this should be confirmed by a senior officer and reasons recorded on the prisoner's Initial Categorisation and Allocation Form (ICA 1)(para 7.1.11(3)). These forms can be disclosed to the prisoner (para 7.2.2). A prisoner should only be allocated to a prison of a higher security category 'on the grounds that no available space is available in prisons of the correct category' (para 7.1.12(4)). The Order also makes clear that a prisoner must never be allocated to a prison of a lower security than their own category (para 7.1.12(2)). Where a prisoner is serving a sentence of less than 28 days the presumption is that they will either be suitable for category C or D establishments and so due to the need to make maximum use of places in lower security prisons they should, if practical, be allocated and transferred accordingly (PSO 2200, para 7.1.12(6)).

6.40   The procedure for initial allocation is for the OCA department to complete form ICA 1 which indicates the sources of information that may be necessary. As with categorisation, a provisional assessment will normally be followed by an interview (PSO 2200, para 7.1.13(8)) and the prisoner's comments should be recorded. On completion of the process the officer making the decision will decide which kind of establishment is suitable for the prisoner, giving reasons (para 7.1.13(10)).

Reallocation

6.41   Many prisoners will serve their sentences in a number of different prisons. For example, a prisoner serving more than ten years could be initially allocated to a category B high security prison, and then 'progress' through to a category B training prison, category C conditions and finally an open prison. Given the terms of the Prison Act 1952, s 12(1), that prisoners 'may lawfully be confined in any prison' it is clear that prisoners do not have a right to be in any particular prison. However there is guidance on the circumstances that prisoners might be moved. PSO 2200 recognises that reallocation:

'(a) Precedes the transfer of a prisoner to another establishment of the same category, as a result of an assessment that he is unsuitable to remain at his present establishment, or could appropriately be moved to another of a different type to fulfil needs identified during the sentence planning process, *or*

 (b) Follows the process of recategorisation.' (para 7.3.3)

The Order states that a prisoner considered for reallocation should be treated in virtually the same way as one being allocated for the first time with reference to the ICA 1. If the change in category is due to a review and this has resulted in a lowering of category, the prison will make arrangements with a prison of a lower security category for the prisoner's transfer there.

6.42   The requirement to follow these procedures even where a governor wishes to transfer a prisoner for reasons of good order and discipline would appear to make a transfer consequent to a failure to do so unlawful (see *R v Governor of HM Prison Latchmere House, ex p Jarvis* above). There are special provisions for the transfer of prisoners deemed disruptive in category B prisons and above in IG 28/1993 (see chapter 8).

6.43   Standing Order 1H, which deals with some of the administrative matters surrounding transfers, anticipates that transfers may need to be made to relieve overcrowding, although prisoners whose 'domestic circumstances would be gravely prejudiced' should not be transferred for this reason (para 5). Standing Order 1H also states that prisoners other than those in category A should be able to inform their family or other intending visitors of an impending transfer, and should be provided with a letter with first class postage for this purpose (para 7). The medical officer should certify that prisoners are fit for travel before transfer (para 3).

6.44   Life sentence prisoners are allocated by the Lifer Management Unit at Prison Service Headquarters rather than being considered under the above criteria (see chapter 11 for details).

6.45   Category A prisoners are allocated by the Directorate of High Security Prisons at Prison Service Headquarters. For the most part they will be held in high security prisons unless they are 'exceptional' or 'high' risk in which case they will be held in Special Secure Units (see chapter 5).

Particular considerations for allocation to category C prisons

6.46   In September 1994, instructions came into effect changing the allocation criteria to category C prisons (Instruction to Governors 55/94). Following serious disturbances at HMP Wymott, research was conducted into the 'effects of population make up on the risk to good order in category C prisons.' This guidance is still in force (see PSO 2200, para 7.1.13(6)).

6.47   The research drew three main conclusions:

(i)   that those prisoners who were under 25 years old when convicted, serving sentences of less than four years, and convicted of burglary and robbery offences were more likely to be guilty of disciplinary offences, and that where a high proportion of them are held together there is a greater risk of riots taking place;

(ii)   that the design of a prison was an important factor in maintaining good order. In particular, secure buildings with cellular accommodation, good sight lines and secure internal gates were considered aids to the maintenance of control;

(iii) that where there was a rising number of new receptions to the prison, and a rising number of disciplinary hearings against prisoners, there would be an increasing potential for disturbances.

6.48   In view of the research findings, category C prisons were divided into the following four groups depending upon whether their control capability is deemed 'very good,' 'good,' 'medium' or 'poor.' The aim was to regulate the number of prisoners meeting the high risk criteria outlined above by awarding one point for being under 25 at the date of conviction, one point for serving less than four years, and one point for serving a sentence for burglary or robbery. A category C prisoner who meets all three of the above is defined as a 'score 3' inmate. Each group of prisons is allowed to take a certain percentage of score 3 prisoners. Where control is deemed to be 'very good' the population may comprise 18% score 3 inmates, where control is 'poor' a maximum of 8% of the population may be score 3.

Allocation of male young offenders

6.49   Male young offenders are allocated to either open or closed conditions, and the decision is taken primarily on the basis of risk. Subordinate to this is the need to place the prisoner as near as possible to his home. There is a general provision that young male offenders should be held in young offender institutions (Criminal Justice Act 1988, s 123(4)), although the Secretary of State retains the discretion to direct that a young offender over the age of 17 may serve his sentence in an adult prison (s 123(4)). The Crime and Disorder Act 1998, s 73, introduced in April 2000 the Detention and Training Order (DTO), a unified custodial sentence to replace the previous secure training orders (for 12–14 year olds) and detention in a young offender institution (for 15–17 year olds). The Prison Service has issued guidance on regimes for under 18s in PSO 4950 to coincide with the introduction of DTOs which includes guidance on allocation (generally those aged 15–17 will serve their sentence in YOIs, and those aged 12–14 in secure local authority accommodation).

6.50   Information relevant to the allocation decision for other young offenders is collated before the decision is made. This includes the prisoner's:

(i)   age;
(ii)   home area;
(iii)   current offence and sentence;
(iv)   time spent in the care of a local authority;
(v)   medical requirements;
(vi)   nature of any outstanding charges;
(vii)   whether the prisoner is appealing against conviction or sentence;
(viii)   social enquiry reports;
(ix)   previous prison reports (CI 37/1988).

6.51   Staff working in the OCA unit use a standard assessment form (ICA 2) in determining whether someone is suitable for open or closed conditions. The assessment is largely based upon a risk assessment involving the prisoner's current and past offences. Prisoners serving over three years or who have been convicted of murder, manslaughter, wounding, GBH, robbery, aggravated burglary, rape, buggery, sexual offences attracting sentences of over 12 months, arson, and importation or dealing in drugs will be allocated to closed conditions initially.

6.52 Prisoners whose current offence is for death by dangerous driving, possession of an offensive weapon, affray, ABH, assault on the police, malicious or wilful damage, threatening behaviour, other minor violence, unlawful sexual intercourse, incest, indecency between males, and minor sex offences will be allocated to closed conditions if as well as the current conviction they have a previous conviction for one of the offences outlined above.

6.53 Prisoners who do not fall into any of the above categories will be allocated to open conditions unless they fall into two or more of the following three groups; those who have a current conviction for motor theft, three or more previous convictions for motor thefts or have absconded from local authority care—if so they will go to closed conditions. These last criteria were set after research was conducted into the characteristics of young male prisoners who had absconded from open conditions (CI 37/1988).

Allocation of female adult prisoners

6.54 The allocation of women prisoners is considerably less complex than the allocation of men. Women are allocated to Durham if they are category A prisoners, and otherwise they are simply allocated to 'open' or 'closed' conditions.

6.55 In deciding whether a woman is suitable to be allocated to open or closed conditions, a risk assessment is conducted (on form ICA 3) and this takes into account the need for security and control. The following factors are relevant to the allocation decision:

(i)   age;
(ii)   home area;
(iii)   current offence and sentence;
(iv)   previous custodial sentences;
(v)   whether time has been spent in local authority care;
(vi)   the nature of any outstanding charges;
(vii)   any medical requirements;
(viii) time left to serve;
(ix)   any outstanding appeal against sentence or conviction;
(x)   whether there is information indicating that the prisoner is an escape or an abscond risk;
(xi)   if the prisoner is liable to be detained under the Immigration Act 1971 (CI 2/1991).

6.56 Prisoners who are serving sentences of over three years, or who are serving sentences for offences of attempted murder, manslaughter, causing death by dangerous driving in the course of committing a crime, wounding, grievous bodily harm, aggravated burglary, sexual offences, arson, drug smuggling, drug trafficking, or who are liable to be detained under the Immigration Act should be initially allocated to closed conditions. Staff are advised that a decision to deviate from this policy should be 'capable of justification as truly exceptional and a decision to allocate such an offender to open conditions should be confirmed by a more senior officer' (CI 2/1991, para 10).

6.57   Aside from the above, some other factors may be relevant to a woman's allocation, and these are whether she is a young offender, is in need of full-time medical care, is due to be released within 14 days, has a further court appearance within 14 days, is pregnant and likely to have her baby during her period of imprisonment, or has a baby and has applied to be allocated to a mother and baby unit. The Prison Service amended allocation procedures to mother and baby units following a Review into Mothers and Babies/Children in Prison in 1999. The current guidance on applications to enter mother and baby units is contained in PSO 4801. The Order, whilst stating that the Children Act 1989 does not directly apply to Prison Service decisions made under the Prison Act 1952, states that the underlying principle of giving primacy to the welfare and best interests of the child should be followed where possible (para 2.3.2). The Order explicitly refers to the corresponding duty on states contained in art 2, para 1 of the United Nations Convention on the Rights of the Child. The Order also recognises that art 8 of the ECHR will be relevant to decisions involving mother and baby units.

6.58   All women (whether sentenced or not) who are pregnant or have a child under 18 months old can apply for a place in a mother and baby unit (para 3.2.1). Applications must be considered by an admissions board, and 'temporary admission' pending consideration may be granted by the governor in exceptional circumstances (paras 3.3–3.4). The admissions board must be a multi-disciplinary group and may include representatives from probation, social services, a health visitor, a nursery nurse and an independent chairperson. The mother should attend, unless unable to because of a medical condition or due to being located in a prison without a unit. If not able to attend she must be invited to make a full written submission. If she can attend she can invite a friend (who may be another prisoner or member of staff) to provide support (para 4.1.2). Each case must be considered on an individual basis and the criteria considered by the board will be whether:

'•   It is in the best interest of the child/children to be placed in a mother and baby unit.
•   The mother is able to demonstrate behaviour and attitude which is not detrimental to the safety and well-being of other unit residents (or the good order and discipline of the unit).
•   The mother has provided a urine sample which tests negative for drugs.
•   The mother is willing to remain drug-free.
•   The mother is willing to sign a standard compact, which may be tailored to her identified individual needs.
•   The mother's ability and eligibility to care for a child is not impaired by health or legal reasons.' (para 3.5.1)

An applicant will be refused if she fails to meet any of the criteria (para 3.7.1) and reasons must be given for the decision. If the mother was not present at the board hearing she can appeal by requesting that the board be reconvened in her presence. If present at the board hearing she may only appeal through the requests/complaints procedure (see chapter 7).

6.59   There are only 16 prisons in the women's prison estate. Brockhill, Eastwood Park, Holloway, Low Newton, New Hall and Styal are closed establishments and hold both remand and convicted prisoners. Durham, Cookham Wood, Foston Hall, Highpoint, Send, Winchester and Bullwood Hall are closed prisons solely for convicted prisoners, and Askham Grange, Drake Hall and East Sutton Park are open prisons for convicted prisoners. Holloway, Askham Grange, Styal and New Hall have mother and baby units.

6.60 Once a woman has been deemed to be suitable for either open or closed conditions she should be allocated to the prison establishment of that status nearest to her home.

The allocation of female young offenders

6.61 There is no female equivalent to a young offender institution which holds only people under 21. Thus young women are allocated to 'partly designated young offender institutions,' ie an adult women's prison with spaces made available for young offenders. Young women will be allocated to open or closed conditions on the principles outlined above (also on form ICA 3). In each 'partly designated young offender institution' particular areas will be deemed to be YOIs and other areas will be deemed to be an adult prison. The application of the Prison or Young Offender Institution Rules will depend on which area in the prison a woman sleeps rather than upon her age.

6.62 Whilst it is possible to locate an adult woman in a young offender institution designated area (Prison Act 1952, s 43(2)(a) as substituted by Criminal Justice Act 1982, s 11(2)), and a young woman aged 17 or more in a prison (Criminal Justice Act 1982, s 12(5)) there are guidelines which state when this might not be appropriate. Adult women who are to be 'mixed' with young women should be selected on the basis that they are a 'good influence,' they should not have been convicted of offences against children, serious violent offences or drugs offences (unless they have given up drugs and are thought likely to be influential in dissuading young women from involvement with drugs) (CI 31/1988).

6.63 A policy of routinely detaining young offenders in adult prisons for allocation purposes following sentence was declared unlawful in the case of *R v Secretary of State for the Home Department, ex p Flood* [1998] 2 All ER 313, as such a general policy was inconsistent with the statutory authority to place young offenders on an individual basis. This was of most importance to female young offenders because of the lack of young offender institutions for them. There is separate guidance for regimes for women under 18 in PSO 4950 who are subject to DTOs from April 2000. Following the *Flood* case the Prison Service response was to designate young offender accommodation in more prisons. As of February 2000 there were 10 prisons with such designated accommodation (Askham Grange, Brockhill, Bullwood Hall, Drake Hall, East Sutton Park, Eastwood Park, Holloway, Low Newton, New Hall and Styal).

SENTENCE PLANNING

6.64   Sentence planning is assuming a more important role in decisions that prisoners may seek to challenge legally. The perceived need for sentence planning gained impetus, like many changes over the last decade, from the Woolf report into prison disturbances which proposed that all prisoners serving over 12 months should have a sentence plan (para 14.75). The Prison Service responded to these proposals in the white paper *Custody, Care and Justice* and developed the current system following a joint review with the Probation Service in 1994–95. The current procedures, like the bulk of those on categorisation, are contained in PSO 2200, the manual on sentence management and planning.

6.65   The joint review led the Prison Service to place the assessment of risk at the heart of sentence planning, with emphasis on integrating this into all aspects of sentence management as described in PSO 2200:

> 'The sentence management process begins by drawing on information available prior to sentence and initially focuses on ensuring appropriate categorisation and allocation. This maximises its contribution to the safety of the public.
>
> Sentence planning builds on the initial assessment and widens its scope. By drawing on information from both within and outside prison, risk can be predicted and assessed, and regimes and programmes developed, which can contribute to reducing the risk:
> —to the public when the prisoner is released;
> —of re-offending;
> —to staff and other prisoners in establishments.' (para 2.1)

Whilst the Order states that the aims of both sentence management and planning include enabling prisoners to make the best use of their time it is also clear that the assessments made in sentence planning are expected to 'have a bearing on all the assessments and decisions made about the prisoner' including work allocation, education and training (para 2.1). In practical terms this raises the possibility of prisoners being refused access to facilities, in one example to study in his own time through an Open University course, if this is not seen as sufficiently addressing risk.

6.66   Whilst the stated priorities of sentence planning, namely 'to prepare for safer release' and 'to make best use of the prisoner's time' (para 3.2) are positive, the practicalities of applying the risk assessment to all aspects of a prisoner's life can on occasion defeat meeting those priorities. For example the most important way that prisoners can demonstrate a reduction in risk is to attend offending behaviour courses. Due to lack of resources these are often unavailable or have huge waiting lists. Prisoners are on occasion given a target to attend a certain course and then transferred to a prison that does not run it, so that year after year the same target remains on their sentence planning documents. This in turn can affect their progress to lower category prisons and eligibility for parole. This, together with the very formulaic nature of the sentence planning documents themselves can lead prisoners to have little faith in these processes. Another example is the fact that prisons are required to take into account not only institutional behaviour, but also 'attitudes to and involvement in sentence planning' in setting the level of privileges prisoners have access to, and this can lead to frustration if prisoners feel they are effectively being punished when downgraded because they cannot undertake offending behaviour work. It can also lead to strange results such as the wording of the introduction to PSO 4250 on Physical Education which states 'The purpose of physical education in Prison Regimes is to address the offending behaviour of inmates, tackle their criminogenic factors and reduce the likelihood of re-offending' with no mention at all of keeping healthy.

6.67 PSO 2200 introduced a national scheme for sentence management and planning with standard documents. It made sentence planning a requirement for:

'—All young offenders with at least 4 weeks to serve.
—ACR prisoners (12 months and over, but less than 4 years) with at least 6 months left to serve.
—All DCR prisoners (4 years and over).' (para 3.4)

Lifers are subject to separate sentence planning arrangements. The initial sentence planning documents are ACR 1 (for young offenders and adults serving under four years) and DCR 1 (for young offenders and adults serving four years and over). The purposes of these forms are to provide a risk assessment, to inform decisions concerning the prisoner, and to identify targets for the time the prisoner is both in custody and on licence. All sentence planning documents can be disclosed to the prisoner (see para 5.2). The initial sentence plans must be completed no later than eight weeks after sentence for ACR 1, and three months for DCR 1 (para 5.3.1).

6.68 The Order states that prisoners should have the central role and be interviewed during the sentence planning process, and makes clear that it should be an open process (see section 6). The sentence plan should be reviewed at regular intervals using form ACR 2 (for young offenders and adults serving under four years) and DCR 2 (for young offenders and adults serving four years and over). Young offenders should be reviewed at least every three months, ACR prisoners at least every six months, and DCR prisoners within three months of arrival at a new prison and at least every 12 months (para 5.2.8). These reviews may inform decisions on categorisation, and so obtaining the relevant sentence planning documentation will be useful if a prisoner is seeking to challenge their category.

TRANSFERS BETWEEN JURISDICTIONS

Transfers between prisons in England and Wales, and other UK jurisdictions

6.69 Transfer between the different UK jurisdictions is dealt with in the Crime (Sentences) Act 1997, Sch 1, brought into force on 1 October 1997. The way in which applications under this legislation will be dealt with was outlined by the Home Secretary in a written answer on 28 October 1997. The statement provides a comprehensive explanation of the policy and procedures currently in force:

'The Government attach considerable importance to enabling prisoners to maintain family ties while serving their sentences. As part of a number of measures to facilitate family contact, there is provision for prisoners to transfer to another United Kingdom jurisdiction, or to one of the islands, where they have close family members...

The new provisions provide for prisoners to be transferred to another jurisdiction on either an unrestricted or a restricted basis. In the case of an unrestricted transfer, the administration of the prisoner's sentence will become a matter entirely for the receiving jurisdiction. A restricted transfer will be subject to conditions whereby the sending jurisdiction will continue to administer certain specified aspects of the sentence.

Transfers will continue to require the consent of the Secretary of State of both the sending and receiving jurisdictions. Normally, transfer requests will be approved only where the prisoner has at least six months left to serve in the receiving jurisdiction before his or her release date at the time of making the request, and where the prisoner has no outstanding appeal against conviction or sentence, is not charged with further criminal proceedings, and is not liable to any further period of imprisonment in lieu of payment of any outstanding monetary orders made by a court.

Each application will be assessed on its individual merits, taking into consideration:

(i)   the purpose for which the transfer is requested;
(ii)   whether the prisoner was ordinarily resident in the jurisdiction to which transfer is sought prior to the imposition of the current sentence; or whether members of the prisoner's close family are resident in that jurisdiction and there are reasonable grounds for believing that the prisoner will receive regular visits from them; or whether the prisoner has demonstrated through preparations that he has made for his life following release from prison that he intends to reside in the receiving jurisdiction upon release and he is in the later stages of his sentence;
(iii) whether there are grounds for believing that the prisoner may disrupt or attempt to disrupt any prison establishment, or pose an unacceptable risk to security; and
(iv)   any compelling or compassionate circumstances.

When considering whether to make an unrestricted or a restricted transfer, the Secretary of State of the sending jurisdiction will take into account the period and terms of transfer requested by the prisoner, and whether, as a consequence of an unrestricted transfer, there would be likely to be any effect on the length of time which the prisoner would be required to serve, or on any post release supervision requirement.

Where an unrestricted transfer is granted, the prisoner will serve the remainder of his or her sentence in the receiving jurisdiction as if that sentence had been passed there, and will be subject for all purposes to the statutory and other provisions applying to prisoners within the receiving jurisdiction. A prisoner granted a restricted transfer will automatically remain, for the duration of his or her transfer, subject to the law governing release on licence, automatic release, post release supervision and recall applicable in the sending jurisdiction. In addition, any other condition relating to the terms of a prisoner's detention as the Secretary of State of the sending jurisdiction may deem appropriate in any particular case or class of case may be attached to the transfer. A prisoner transferred on a restricted basis will normally become subject for all purposes, other than those specified in any conditions attached to the transfer, to the statutory and other provisions applying to prisoners in the receiving jurisdiction (including, for example, such matters as categorisation).'

6.70 Whether the provisions on temporary release of the sending or receiving jurisdiction apply to those granted restricted transfers depends on whether or not the transfer is time limited (eg for accumulated visits). If so the temporary release provisions of the sending jurisdiction will apply, otherwise it will be those of the receiving jurisdiction.

6.71 Prisoners held in England and Wales should apply for a transfer under these arrangements through the requests/complaints procedure. The governor will collate all relevant documents and forward them to Prison Service Headquarters for consideration. This process will include consultation with the Home Department of the other jurisdiction.

6.72 Prisoners who are granted a restricted transfer to another jurisdiction may be returned to England or Wales if the purpose for which the transfer was granted no longer applies, or at the request of the receiving jurisdiction (eg as a result of disruptive behaviour).

The Repatriation of Prisoners Act 1984

6.73 The Repatriation of Prisoners Act 1984 came into effect on 15 April 1985, and facilitated ratification of the Council of Europe Convention on the Transfer of Sentenced Persons.

6.74 The Convention enables foreign nationals convicted and sentenced to terms of imprisonment to be transferred back to the country of which they are a national and to serve their sentence there (so long as the crime of which they are convicted also constitutes a criminal offence in their country of origin). Sentenced prisoners from countries which are signatories to the Convention are eligible to apply for repatriation so long as they have at least six months of their sentence left to serve until their earliest date of release and are not appealing against their sentence or conviction.

6.75 The Convention requires the government to inform all foreign prisoners who may be eligible for transfer of the substance of its provisions, and thus all prisoners whose country of citizenship has signed the Convention should be aware that they may ask to be repatriated. Each time a country ratifies the Convention, Prison Service Headquarters sends a notice to all prison governors and a list of the names of the prisoners who should be informed of their eligibility to apply for repatriation.

6.76 A prisoner who wishes to be considered for repatriation should make his or her application to the governor of the prison where s/he is held. This is done through the requests/complaints procedure, and the prisoner should give details including their full name, date of birth, address in their home country, passport number and the place and date of issue (IG 101/95).

6.77 When the governor has received the prisoner's request, this should be forwarded to the Directorate of Security and Programmes at Prison Service Headquarters, and the following documents should be attached by the prison:

(i)   copies of indictment, warrants and court orders relating to the period of imprisonment;
(ii)   notice of recommendation for deportation (if relevant);
(iii)   an assessment of the security and control risks which the prisoner is thought to pose;
(iv)   the prisoner's disciplinary record;
(v)   an assessment of the prisoner's medical condition including any recommendations for future treatment;
(vi)   copies of social inquiry reports and probation reports;
(vii)   details of previous convictions;
(viii)   two recent photographs of the prisoner;
(ix)   police and/or customs and excise reports on the offence (IG 101/95, annex C).

6.78   After receipt of the application, Prison Service Headquarters consults with the Secretary of State and the government of the country of which the prisoner is a national to decide whether repatriation is considered appropriate by all parties. The main bone of contention at this stage is the length of sentence which the prisoner will have to serve if s/he is repatriated.

6.79   The 1984 Act specifies two separate procedures under which sentences to be served after repatriation may be calculated—the continued enforcement procedure, and the conversion of sentence procedure.

6.80   The continued enforcement procedure essentially means that the maximum sentence which the prisoner would serve if s/he were repatriated would remain the same as it would be were s/he to serve the sentence in this country. The period of time which has been served here prior to repatriation is taken into account, and the prisoner takes with them any remission earned in this country. If the sentence given in this country is longer than a sentence which could be imposed for the same offence in their home country, it can be changed to the nearest equivalent sentence lawfully imposed in that country, although this could not be longer than the original sentence (IG 101/95, annex B). If this method of calculation is used, the prisoner is informed of the exact length of sentence that has to be served prior to transfer and is given an opportunity to accept or reject this.

6.81   If the conversion of sentence procedure is used, then a prisoner will not know exactly how long they will have to serve after repatriation until that event has occurred. This is because after transfer a court in the prisoner's home country will convert the sentence into one which would have been given if the offence had been committed in that country. Thus when the application for transfer is being considered the prisoner can only be given rough details of how long a sentence such an offence would be likely to attract. Again, the sentence cannot be longer than the original sentence and will take into account the period of time that the prisoner has already spent in custody, and the prisoner will be asked to consent to repatriation in view of the information given by the government of their home country (IG 101/95, annex B).

6.82   The main problem that prisoners experience in applying for repatriation appears to be where the sentence that they would have to serve in their home country is significantly shorter than the sentence that they are serving in this country. In these circumstances the British government is likely to refuse to repatriate on the basis that for the sentence to be so reduced would undermine the British criminal justice system and reduce the deterrent effect to other foreign nationals.

6.83   If a prisoner is repatriated, his/her sentence will be enforced according to the law of the country in which they are then serving their sentence. However, if the prisoner subsequently decides to appeal against sentence or conviction, they would have to do so through the courts in this country and their home country would have no jurisdiction.

6.84   A prisoner who is accepted for repatriation may be required to pay his/her own fare home at the discretion of the other country concerned.

6.85   At 11 February 2000, the following countries other than the UK had ratified treaty agreements under the Convention:

> Andorra, Austria, Bahamas, Belgium, Bulgaria, Canada, Chile, Costa Rica, Croatia, Cyprus, Czech Republic, Denmark, Finland, France, Germany, Greece, Hungary, Italy, Iceland, Ireland, Israel, Latvia, Liechtenstein, Lithuania, Luxembourg, Malta, Netherlands, Norway, Nigeria, Malawi, Panama, Poland, Portugal, Romania, Former Yugoslav Republic of Macedonia, Slovakia, Slovenia, Spain, Sweden, Switzerland, Trinidad and Tobago, Turkey, Ukraine, United States of America, Zimbabwe.

SENTENCE CALCULATION

6.86   Following sentencing, all prisoners will be notified of their relevant release dates. These are calculated in the prison in which the individual prisoner is held by the Discipline Department under the guidance contained in Standing Order 3C, a document which is regularly amended to take account of new judgments and statutory amendments. The Prison Service accepts that, to a prisoner, notification of the correct release date is of great importance and necessary to allow him/her to prepare for the sentence. It is somewhat unfortunate that in light of the importance of this to prisoners, that sentence calculation is one of the most difficult areas of law. It is the subject of some of the most obtuse statutory wording to be found, leading to numerous challenges providing conflicting legal authorities. It is an area of law that is subject to constant change and requires extra vigilance in looking at new statutory provisions and law reports.

6.87   The dates that will be calculated will depend on the length of sentence that is received:

(i)   Prisoners serving under four years will be informed of the automatic release date that applies, being one half of the sentence as well as the date on which they are eligible for release under the Home Detention Curfew scheme;

(ii)   Prisoners serving four years or more will be notified of their parole eligibility date (PED) and non-parole release date (NPRD). The PED is at one-half of the sentence and the NPRD at two-thirds. In addition, they will be informed of the licence expiry date (LED) and sentence expiry date (SED). These are explained further in chapter 12;

(iii)   Prisoners who were sentenced before 1 October 1992 continue to be treated under the terms of their original sentence (calculated under the Criminal Justice Act 1967) and will be notified of their PED (one-third of the total sentence), NPRD (two-thirds of sentence) and SED (see chapter 12 on parole and release from prison).

The single term prior to the Crime and Disorder Act 1998

6.88   The first principle of sentence calculation is the concept of the single term. The concept appears relatively straightforward and makes provision for sentences which are imposed to be served consecutively or which are concurrent and partly overlapping, to be calculated as if they are one overall sentence (CJA 1967, s 104(2) and CJA 1991, s 51(2)). However, the deceptive simplicity of this concept is undermined by difficulties in the precise definition of when a sentence ends, thereby affecting the circumstances in which sentences can overlap, and the effect of the Crime and Disorder Act 1998, ss 101–102.

6.89   For prisoners sentenced before the enactment of the Crime and Disorder Act 1998, the single term applies to any sentence which is imposed on a prisoner who is serving another custodial sentence—the sentences shall be calculated into a single term (*R v Secretary of State for the Home Department, ex p François* [1999] AC 43). The only difficulty in this definition is in determining the circumstances in which a prisoner is serving another custodial sentence. The concept of serving a custodial sentence has been interpreted by the Prison Service as only applying to prisoners who are in custody when the subsequent sentence is imposed. This means that a prisoner who has been released and is not in custody before the subsequent sentence is passed, but who has not yet reached the sentence expiry date, will not have the sentence calculated into a single term. The correctness of this approach was called into question by some obiter dicta observations of the Divisional Court (*R v Governor of HM Prison Haverigg, ex p McMahon* [1997] 37 LS Gaz R 41, DC). Both Sedley J and Astill J seemed to be of the view that a sentence subsisted right up until the sentence expiry date, but their comments were a side issue to the case and have never been followed in any subsequent arguments or decision.

6.90   The calculation of consecutive sentences is relatively straightforward. The second sentence is simply added to the first one that has been imposed. The appropriate release scheme is then calculated on the basis of the resulting single term. If a prisoner is serving a sentence of three years and then receives a second, consecutive sentence of two years, the relevant release scheme is based on the single term of five years. Thus the prisoner would be eligible for parole after serving one-half of the sentence and would be automatically released after serving two-thirds. It is *not* the case that one-half of each sentence will be served (see *ex p François* above and CJA 1991, s 33(5)). Prisoners in this situation will therefore be significantly disadvantaged and ideally, the sentencing court should be made aware of the effect of imposing a consecutive sentence that extends the total term of imprisonment beyond four years. In cases where remand time has been served on any of the consecutive sentences, it will reduce the total time to be served.

6.91 The calculation of concurrent sentences is slightly more complex. A concurrent sentence takes effect from the day on which it is imposed and so the only method of calculating the single term is to make two separate calculations as to the length of time to be served. Remand time should be excluded at this stage. When the two sentences have been calculated, the latest sentence expiry date must be taken. If the two concurrent sentences were imposed on the same day, it is the longer sentence which provides the basis for calculating the single term (as the shorter sentence is wholly subsumed within it). Remand time relating to either sentence is then deducted from that single term (paras 6.94–6.97 below).

6.92 If the sentences were imposed on different days, the single term will run from the date on which the first sentence was imposed to the latest sentence expiry date of the sentences. It is this single term which defines whether a prisoner is a short or long term prisoner and allows the relevant release scheme to be identified. Again, remand time relevant to any of the sentences comprising the single term will count towards the time to be served.

The Crime and Disorder Act 1998 and the single term

6.93 The Crime and Disorder Act 1998 introduced two important new provisions into the single term calculations which take effect on any prisoner sentenced after the implementation date of the Act. Section 101(1) amends CJA 1991, s 51(2) for prisoners who have been released from custody under the terms of the CJA 1991 at any time, even if the prisoner has been returned to prison pursuant to that sentence. For any such prisoners who have been released under the terms of the CJA 1991, any subsequent concurrent sentences shall not be treated as a single term. Section 102(1) of the CDA 1998 prohibits the sentencing court from imposing a consecutive sentence on a prisoner who has been released from custody at any time. These amendments should make the construction of the single term far easier in future and will avoid the necessity for the *McMahon* issues to be re-ventilated (see para 6.89 above).

Remand time

6.94 The general principle is that remand time and time in police custody, in respect of an offence for which a prisoner is subsequently convicted, counts towards the length of a sentence (CJA 1967, s 67 as amended and CJA 1991, s 41). It is important to note at the outset that time spent in prison custody is only treated as remand time if it is the sole reason for that person's detention (CJA 1967, s 1A(b)(i) and (ii)). Thus, a prisoner who is serving both a prison sentence and is on remand for further offences cannot have this period of time treated as 'remand time' towards any subsequent conviction as the authority for the detention is the custodial sentence. However, once the automatic release date for the sentence has been reached, the prisoner will then fall to be a remand prisoner again (see para 6.97 below).

6.95   On a simple calculation, if a prisoner spent exactly six months on remand and then received a sentence of four years, the prisoner's release date would be reduced by six months. Remand time also reduces the dates on which a prisoner is eligible for parole and all other release dates. Time spent in police custody on matters relating to the offence for which the prisoner was convicted will also count as remand time. Any part of a day in such custody, however brief, falls to reduce the length of a sentence. The Crime (Sentences) Act 1997 contained a number of provisions relating to remand time and earned parole but these have not been implemented and the Home Office has indicated that they are unlikely to ever be implemented (Home Office circulars 54/1997 and 55/1999).

6.96   The difficulties in assessing whether remand time falls to reduce the length of a custodial sentence arise when looking at how much remand time falls to be counted against concurrent or consecutive sentences calculated into a single term. For many years, the courts had applied a very restrictive interpretation of statute whereby complex assessments were made as to what periods of remand were relevant. Eventually, the situation was clarified by the successive judgments in *R v Home Secretary, ex p Naughton* [1997] 1 WLR 118 and *R v Governor of HM Prison Brockhill, ex p Evans* [1997] QB 443. Lord Bingham CJ explained in the *Evans* case that the problem to be assessed is as follows:

> 'where a defendant spends time in custody awaiting trial for more than one offence, and is on conviction sentenced to concurrent or overlapping terms of custody. To what extent is account to be taken, in assessing the term of custody to be served ... of time spent in custody ... before the sentences were imposed.'

6.97   In answer to this question, the court held that any time which is counted as remand time pursuant to the CJA 1967, s 67 should count towards the total term of imprisonment to be served (the single term). This means when calculating the relevant remand time, the periods to be counted should include all time on remand relating to any of the offences for which the prisoner subsequently received a prison sentence. It has also been held that in situations where a prisoner is remanded in custody for several charges, but sentenced on different occasions, as soon as the prisoner reaches his automatic release date on any one of those sentences, he becomes a remand prisoner again and that this remand time will fall to reduce any subsequent sentences imposed (*R v Governor of HM Prison Haverigg, ex p McMahon* [1997] 37 LS Gaz R 41, DC). This situation most commonly arises in cases where prisoners receive a number of short sentences for separate offences on different occasions. The long line of authorities which contended against this construction and put in place a far more complex method of calculation were expressly overturned by the *Evans* judgment. Any judgment referring to sentence calculation which pre-dates *Evans* should therefore be read in the light of this ruling.

6.98   One-day appearances at court to answer to bail and the time spent at court attending a trial, where bail has been granted, do not count as days in custody. However, if the judge or magistrate orders that the person be confined to the court cells during any recesses, this will normally count as relevant remand time (*R v Governor of Kirkham Prison, ex p Burke* (18 March 1994, unreported), DC). Damages for false imprisonment have been awarded in a case where the Home Office refused to deduct these days from a prisoner's sentence in circumstances where the prisoner was required to surrender to custody on each morning of his trial at 9.30 am and was not released until 30 minutes after the court had finished sitting each day (*Burgess v Home Office* (22 February 2000, unreported), Maidstone County Court). The Home Office indicated that they consider *Burke* to have been wrongly decided and were granted permission to appeal the judgment.

Juveniles and remand time

6.99   Juveniles will often be remanded into the care of the local authority prior to conviction. Remands to secure accommodation which is certified as being provided for the purpose of restricting liberty will always count to reduce sentences. It is also possible for time spent in non-secure accommodation to be counted, but the circumstances will be limited. The Prison Service has issued the following guidance, stating that time will count as remand time in non-secure accommodation if the following criteria are met:

(i)   the accommodation was a children's home;
(ii)   s/he was not permitted to live at home with parents;
(iii) s/he was not permitted to leave;
(iv)   education was provided on the premises (IG 51/95).

6.100   This approach was confirmed by the House of Lords in *R v Secretary of State for the Home Department, ex p A* [2000] 1 All ER 651. The Lords stated that in order for such time to count under CJA 1967, s 67(1), the place to which the person had been remanded must restrict liberty to the extent that it amounts to a form of custody.

Time spent unlawfully at large

6.101   Any time that a prisoner spends unlawfully at large (UAL) does not count towards the length of the sentence to be served (Prison Act 1952, s 49(2)). The effect for prisoners who spend time UAL is that their release dates are simply delayed by the relevant period of time by adding this period to the sentence. Whilst this seems straightforward, problems can arise with prisoners who went UAL, then committed further offences and received consecutive and overlapping sentences.

6.102   The manner in which such sentences used to be calculated was to start the calculation from the date of the first sentence, then to count the number of days to the end of the second sentence. This calculation included the time spent UAL. The UAL period was then added onto the total length of time to be served. The effect of this calculation was that prisoners were effectively having the period UAL added into their sentence twice, firstly in the overall length and then by delaying the final release date. As a result of the prejudicial effect on the prisoners involved, the policy was amended so that the number of days in the length of sentence was calculated ignoring the period UAL and this is then added onto the end (AG 19/95).

Time spent awaiting extradition

6.103   Time spent in a foreign jurisdiction awaiting extradition does not automatically count to reduce sentence (CJA 1991, s 47). Case law on the subject indicates that this time should be considered by the sentencing judge when passing sentence and it should be stated whether any allowance is being made for this time. Relevant considerations will include the general conduct of the prisoner and whether extradition was resisted (see eg *R v Scalise and Rachel* (1985) 7 Cr App Rep (S) 395; *R v Stone* (1988) 10 Cr App Rep (S) 322). A failure by the sentencing judge to take account of such time or to take enough account of this time can be subject to appeal.

Returns to custody

6.104   One area of sentence calculation that has been the subject of a great deal of litigation has been the meaning and effect of CJA 1991, s 40. This section makes provision for prisoners who are released from custody and then commit a further offence before the sentence expiry date to receive a further custodial sentence. Although the statute refers to the power of the court to 'return' such a person to prison, it has been held that any penalty imposed pursuant to this section is in fact a term of imprisonment in its own right (*R v Secretary of State for the Home Department, ex p Probyn* [1998] 1 WLR 809; *R v Worthing Justices, ex p Varley* [1998] 1 WLR 819n; *R v Taylor* [1998] 1 All ER 357). The consequence of this interpretation is that any such sentence can be imposed to run consecutively to a further term of imprisonment that is imposed for the actual criminal offence that has been committed. The order of imprisonment is a new sentence and not a reactivation of the original sentence, and so the imposition of a consecutive sentence is not precluded by the CDA 1998 (*R v Lowe; R v Leask* [2000] 1 WLR 153). If consecutive sentences are imposed in this manner, the overall term imposed must not be excessive and must accord with any limitations on the powers of the sentencing courts, a matter which is particularly relevant to magistrates and youth courts (*R v F* [2000] 1 WLR 266).

6.105   There is one aspect to such sentences which remains unclear, and that is whether it is appropriate for a s 40 sentence to be imposed in circumstances where a long-term prisoner has been released on parole and has already been returned to custody, the parole licence having been revoked. In *R v Governor of HM Prison Elmley, ex p Moorton* [1999] 2 Cr App Rep (S) 165, DC, the Divisional Court stated that s 40 orders should not be made in such circumstances as the prisoner has already been returned to custody. The Court felt that the purpose of the s 40 order was to deal with those prisoners whose licences had not been revoked and who would therefore not face any further punishment for breaching their parole licence. Lord Bingham CJ disagreed with this interpretation in *R v Sharkey* [2000] 1 WLR 160. He felt that the provisions authorising the revocation of licences are administrative and should not oust the punitive powers of s 40. His judgment did rely, however, on an interpretation of a case concerning detention under the Mental Health Acts (*Dlodlo v Mental Health Review Tribunal for South Thames* (1996) 36 BMLR 145, CA). The same case was raised in the *Moorton* judgment and it is arguable that it may not be readily transferable to the administrative functions of the Criminal Justice Acts.

Default and civil sentences

6.106   Sentences imposed under civil powers or confiscation orders imposed to run consecutively to the criminal penalty must not be calculated into the single term. Civil sentences that attract early release will be treated as follows:

(i)   Sentences of 12 months or less will have an automatic release date set at one-half of the sentence;

(ii)   Sentences of 12 months and over will have an automatic release date set at two-thirds of the sentence (CJA 1991, s 45);

(iii) Sentences of imprisonment to be served in default and consecutive to a criminal sentence will be treated separately. The sentence will be calculated to run from the time that the criminal sentence has expired. Such prisoners will still be eligible for parole on the original sentence and if parole is granted, the default sentence takes effect from that date.

6.107   The following civil sentences are subject to early release provisions:

(i)   Contempt of court, unless the court has fixed the date for release on the warrant of committal;

(ii)   Persons committed under the Magistrates' Court Act 1980, s 63(3) for the non-compliance of an order of the court, other than for the payment of a sum of money;

(iii) A parent or guardian committed in default of payment of a fine or damages to be paid in respect of a young person under the provisions of the Criminal Justice Act 1982, s 26 (but *not* sums due under CJA 1991, s 58(3));

(iv)   Persons committed in default of entering into a recognizance with or without a surety.

6.108   Certain civil sentences do not attract early release and must be served in full, ie imprisonment for breaches of/related to:

(i)   An affiliation order;

(ii)   A maintenance order;

(iii) National Insurance contributions;

(iv)   Income tax;

(v)   Any other duty or tax collected by the Inland Revenue or Customs and Excise;
(vi) A legal aid contribution;
(vii) The Community charge.

In addition, prisoners remanded under the Family Law Act provisions cannot have this period reflected in their release date.

CHAPTER 7

THE REQUESTS/COMPLAINTS PROCEDURE

AN OVERVIEW OF THE PROCEDURE

7.1 The Prison Rules 1999 impose a duty to deal with prisoners' complaints. This duty is firstly placed upon the governor (Rule 11—who may delegate this duty under r 81) and secondly on the Board of Visitors (rr 11 and 78). The current requests/complaints procedure developed to meet this duty was established in 1990. The procedure had the stated aim of improving the management and control of prisons by 'inspiring greater confidence in prisoners that their needs and welfare are being looked after; promoting better relations between inmates and staff; and reducing tensions and anxieties' (Prisoners' Requests/Complaints Procedures Staff Manual, para 1.2).

7.2 The system was designed to enable prisoners to make complaints about their treatment within the prison system, and for the first time provision was made for a complaint to be kept confidential from staff at the prison where the prisoner is held. Responses to written applications were to be made in writing, and a right of appeal to more senior prison officials was built into the system.

7.3 The importance of giving reasoned replies to the prisoner is highlighted, and staff with responsibility for providing written replies were told that they have a particular responsibility to ensure that they bear the principles of the requests/complaints procedure in mind when doing so.

7.4 The principles of the system are stated to:
'• protect the prisoner's rights to make requests or complaints;
• provide—in line with the European Prison Rule 42(3)—confidential access to an authority outside the establishment;
• ensure that requests and complaints are fully and fairly considered— both from the inmates' and staff's viewpoints—and that well-founded complaints can be remedied;
• allow appeals to higher management levels;
• produce timely and reasoned replies.' (para 1.2)

7.5 In practice, in some establishments reasons given in rejecting a complaint are sparse, and replies can take much longer than the specified period. In addition, prisoners who submit numerous written requests/complaints may find that staff consider that they are a management problem in terms of the amount of time that is occupied in dealing with their complaints and providing written answers. Further, a very few prisoners who have been transferred in the interests of good order and discipline have attributed this to the fact that as well as submitting their own requests/complaints they encouraged other inmates to make written complaints about their treatment or made many complaints on behalf of others.

7.6   The Staff Manual lays down the stages of the requests/complaints procedure as follows:

'•   Daily oral applications to wing staff.
•   Oral applications to designated members of the establishment's senior management team.
•   The first step—the establishment stage—of the formal procedure where a prisoner's written request or complaint receives a written reasoned reply.
•   The second stage—the Headquarters stage—of the formal procedure where a prisoner's written appeal against a decision by the establishment receives a written reasoned reply. Headquarters also deals with requests or complaints on reserved subjects.

As a safeguard:

•   Confidential access, where a prisoner may write using a sealed envelope to the:
    —Governor of the establishment;
    —The Chair of the Board of Visitors;
    —The Area Manager at Prison Service Headquarters.
•   Oral or written applications to the Board of Visitors.' (para 2.2)

7.7   Where the problem is not resolved after following these stages, further avenues of complaint are suggested by the Manual. These include MPs, MEPs, the police, petitioning the Queen or Parliament, the Commission for Racial Equality, the Criminal Injuries Compensation Authority, the European Commission for Human Rights, legal advisers and organisations in the voluntary sector.

7.8   Since 1994, the Prisons' Ombudsman has been investigating prisoners' complaints, and although he is only able to make recommendations to the Prison Service, his thorough investigations often provide a more effective remedy than many of the above.

HOW THE PROCEDURE WORKS WITHIN PRISON ESTABLISHMENTS

7.9   The Prisoners' Requests/Complaints Procedures Staff Manual does not lay down in detail how the system should operate within each prison and this responsibility is delegated to governors. However, all governors are asked to ensure that they provide clear guidance on who has responsibility for considering complaints and should seek to ensure that as a complaint progresses it is considered by progressively more senior staff (para 2.4–5).

Oral applications

7.10 Oral applications are the first stage in the requests/complaints procedure. A prisoner may raise such an application informally with a personal officer (an officer allocated to deal with an individual prisoner and his/her grievances), or formally by making a wing or landing application. Wing and landing applications should be heard every day in a private office and out of the hearing of other prisoners. The member of staff dealing with the application should consider the query given by the prisoner and advise as to how it may be resolved.

7.11 Governors' applications should be heard every day except Sundays and bank holidays. Thus if the problem is not resolved by wing or landing staff, the prisoner may make an application to see a governor. Prisoners do not have any right to see the governing governor (often known as the number one governor), who is able to delegate the duty to hear oral applications (Prison Rules 1999, r 81).

7.12 Brief records of all oral applications should be kept in an applications book that is held at the prison.

Formal requests/complaints

7.13 Formal requests and complaints are submitted on a requests/complaints form that is available by oral application or from a member of staff. Requests/complaints forms are A4 size and prisoners complete them by providing the names of the members of staff that they have raised the matter with previously and giving full details of the problem. Guidance given on the form tells prisoners that they should confine themselves to raising only one problem on each form that they submit. If a prisoner does not wish to raise a complaint orally the guidance notes to staff in the Manual make it clear that 'prisoners do not have to raise a request or complaint orally before putting it in writing' by submitting a form. Prisoners often complain that they are denied requests/complaints forms on the basis that they must make an oral or wing application first. Such a requirement breaches the procedures set out in the Manual and also the requirements of Prison Rule 11.

7.14 A time limit for the submission of requests/complaints forms was introduced on 2 June 1997 by guidance to governors in PSI 30/1997. This stated that prisoners should submit a requests/complaints form within three months of the matter under complaint coming to light. Complaints will only be eligible for consideration outside that time limit 'if there are exceptional circumstances, or the prisoner can show good cause why the complaint was submitted out of time' (para 2). The PSI confirms that prisoners cannot be denied requests/complaints forms even if the complaint appears to be time-barred.

7.15 For the most part the requests/complaints will be dealt with by designated staff within the prison. However, there are two scenarios where this will not occur. Firstly, if the complaint is about a 'reserved subject' it will be sent to the relevant department at Prison Service Headquarters. Reserved subjects are those where the governor at the establishment has no power to make a decision. The reserved subjects include appeals against adjudications, allegations against the governing governor, early release to take up employment, litigation against the Prison Service, lifer issues (change of name, temporary release from prison, release on licence, transfer and allocation), category A prisoner issues (approved visitors, categorisation, change of name, marriage, 'supergrass casework,' transfer and allocation), artificial insemination, repatriation, transfer to Scotland or Northern Ireland, mother and baby units, allocation of s 53 young offenders, and parole for determinate sentenced prisoners. Although the response is made by staff at Headquarters, the views of staff at the prison will often be sought before any decision is made. Thus, if a life sentence prisoner submits a request to be temporarily released, staff dealing with lifers at that prison will be asked to give their views as to whether the lifer will comply with licence conditions, the reason for the temporary release etc. Therefore, although the final decision rests with Headquarters staff, prison staff will have a large input into the decision-making process.

7.16 Secondly, if the prisoner has asked for a complaint to be submitted to either the governor, chairperson of the Board of Visitors or the area manager, then the form should be handed in a sealed envelope marked 'confidential access' and delivered to the relevant person unopened. Confidential access does not mean that the contents of the form will be kept confidential, it merely aims to provide an 'unfettered channel of communication between the prisoner, and the governor, area manager or chair of the Board of Visitors.' Once the form has been delivered, its recipient may decide that they are not the most appropriate person to deal with the complaint and refer it elsewhere for a reply to be made or involve other staff in investigating issues raised in the form. It is therefore important that prisoners who use the confidential access scheme should make out their reasons for doing so on the form and specify in relation to whom the matter should be kept confidential. Although this will not ensure secrecy, it is hoped that the person in receipt of the form will respect the prisoner's reasons and act with discretion.

7.17 Where the requests/complaints form is to be dealt with inside the prison itself, staff are reminded that prisoners may ultimately take judicial review of any adverse decision. Thus replies should be reasoned and 'decisions should not be taken arbitrarily or give the impression that they were taken arbitrarily' (para 3.2.5). If a prisoner's requests/complaints is governed by clear rules and regulations, staff are advised that it is good practice to explain these so that the decision is more likely to be respected by the prisoner. It is not enough for a governor simply to say that a previous decision is correct, and an explanation of why this is the case should be provided.

7.18 If, however, an adverse decision is taken as a result of an exercise of discretion, replies to queries should 'avoid being abrupt or adversarial' (para 3.2.11). Instead, staff should focus upon the factors that were taken into account in reaching the decision and why that particular decision was reached.

7.19 Prisoners should generally receive a substantive response to their requests/complaints within seven days of submission of a form which is answered at establishment level. If this is not possible because further investigation is needed, then an interim reply should be sent within seven days, and this should explain the reason for the delay (para 3.2.25).

Role of the Board of Visitors

7.20 Prisoners may apply to see a member of the Board of Visitors at any time, and staff should ensure that the application is referred to the Board without undue delay. Boards of Visitors have a statutory duty to satisfy themselves that prisoners are being treated properly and to hear any requests or complaints that they have.

7.21 The procedures followed by the Boards of Visitors will vary from prison to prison. However, in general, a Board member will hear a prisoner's complaint and advise the prisoner as to the best avenue of redress. Some Board members will actively take up prisoners' complaints by pursuing them with a governor. It is also relatively common for Board members to refer prisoners to outside organisations. Members of Boards of Visitors have no powers to overturn governors' decisions.

7.22 Requests/complaints may be sent to the chairperson of a Board of Visitors under 'confidential access.' However, although the Boards of Visitors are independent of the prison authorities, a chairperson may still pass the reply back to Prison Service staff for a response if s/he considers that this is appropriate.

7.23 Boards of Visitors are also given the responsibility of monitoring the operation of the requests/complaints system at their establishments. If they discover that there are problems or delays in providing responses, these should be drawn to the governor's attention.

THE CONSIDERATION OF REQUESTS AND COMPLAINTS AT PRISON SERVICE HEADQUARTERS

7.24 If prisoners are not happy with the answer to a request/complaint which was dealt with in the prison establishment, they have the right to appeal to Prison Service Headquarters. Such appeals are usually dealt with by the cumbersomely titled Deputy Director General's Briefing and Casework Unit on behalf of the area manager for the prison at which the complaint arose, regardless of where the prisoner is located or the initial request/complaint was lodged. However, reserved subjects will be dealt with by the department with overall responsibility for the issue raised, and complaints which raise substantive policy issues will be dealt with by the department that deals with the relevant policy area.

Appeals against the governor's decision

7.25   Appeals to the area manager's office are submitted on a blue requests/complaints appeal form which is in the same format as the first requests/complaints form. The prison will append the original request/complaint containing the decision being appealed against, and will also give any other information that was relevant to the decision-making process, including information that has not been disclosed to the prisoner.

7.26   In considering appeals, staff in the Briefing and Casework Unit should familiarise themselves with all of the facts of the case, check the relevant rules and regulations, and consider whether the governor's decision was fair and reasonable, and whether adequate reasons for the decision were given to the prisoner. Consideration should also be given to whether the circumstances of the case would allow an exception to be made to any relevant rules. The Briefing and Casework Unit should reply within six weeks (para 3.2.25), although there are severe delays in dealing with complaints at Headquarters, and a wait of several months is not uncommon.

7.27   The Staff Manual advises caseworkers that the point of the review is to 'consider whether in the light of all of the available information, there is any reason to think that the decision was other than fair and reasonable' (para 4.1.5). Responses upholding the governor's response can be extremely terse demonstrating little evidence of an active review process. If fault is found with the decision made at the prison then caseworkers draft a reply to the prisoner, and a memo to the governor explaining the reasons for the decision to depart from the prison's decision and asking the governor to take any necessary action. Such drafts are approved by the area manager personally before being sent out to the prison.

Reserved subjects

7.28   The following issues cannot be dealt with at establishment level, and any requests and complaints submitted by prisoners will be referred to the relevant department within Prison Service Headquarters or the Home Office.

7.29   Category A prisoners   Requests/complaints submitted by category A prisoners can be dealt with by the prison unless the prisoner's category A status is relevant to the issues raised in the request/complaint. Queries about their security categorisation, Headquarters' decisions refusing to downgrade them and issues relating to their transfer, allocation and production at court will all need to be considered at the Directorate of High Security Prisons at Headquarters rather than at the establishment.

7.30   Life sentence prisoners   Lifers' requests/complaints will be reserved subjects if they relate to transfer and allocation, temporary release, life sentence reviews, the Parole Board's refusal to recommend their release on life licence, revocation of life licence, delays in their Parole Board reviews, or a request to change their names.

7.31 Parole Requests and complaints relating to any aspect of the parole process for determinate sentenced prisoners will be dealt with by the Sentence Management Group at Headquarters. There is no formal right of appeal against a Parole Board refusal, and although prisoners may submit requests/complaints this will not lead to their papers being put back in front of the Parole Board unless there have been major changes in the prisoner's circumstances which were not considered when the parole decision was made, or where there has been procedural impropriety. The Staff Manual states that if a complaint does not raise one of the above factors or is not about delay in the parole process, then the prisoner will simply receive a standard reply saying that there is no right of appeal against the decision.

7.32 Adjudications If a prisoner complains about a finding of guilt at adjudication, the Briefing and Casework Unit will conduct a full paper review. The transcript of the adjudication and any other documentation should be forwarded by the prison, and the adjudicator should also provide a memo containing their comments on the issues raised in the prisoner's complaint. Adjudications for category A prisoners are reviewed at the Directorate of High Security Prisons.

7.33 Deportation Prisoners liable to deportation are able to submit requests/complaints relating to this. However, these will be forwarded to the Immigration and Nationality Department rather than within the Prison Service. Prisoners who want to appeal against a decision to deport them or to make representations asking to be given further leave to remain in the UK should seek advice and representation from a solicitor or an organisation specialising in immigration issues such as the Joint Council for the Welfare of Immigrants, Immigration Advisory Service or the Refugee Legal Centre.

7.34 Release on compassionate grounds Requests/complaints asking for compassionate release should be dealt with by the Sentence Management Group at Prison Service Headquarters. The prison will be asked to give detailed supporting evidence or obtain this from other agencies (eg hospitals, social workers etc). See chapter 12 for further details.

7.35 Special remission Prisoners may apply for early release from prison on the basis that they have rendered 'some commendable service to the prison authorities or to the community at large that merits some tangible recognition' (Staff Manual, annex M, para 1). Such applications are made via the requests/complaints system and the governor will need to provide supporting evidence. Applications are considered by the area manager's office initially, and a decision is taken as to whether early release should be effected by Royal Prerogative of Mercy or whether additional days awarded at adjudication could be restored with the effect of releasing the prisoner earlier than would otherwise have been the case. The minimum number of days remitted from a sentence is usually seven days.

7.36 Examples of conduct meriting early release from prison and the longest periods of time remitted from their sentences at the time of publication of the Staff Manual are:

(i)   assisting staff in danger of death or injury—eight months;
(ii)   supplying information to the prison authorities—56 days;
(iii) firefighting—35 days;
(iv)   assisting staff in a prison context (eg providing interpretation service, unblocking a sewer)—seven days;
(v)   assisting a prisoner in danger of death or injury—42 days;
(vi)   assisting the public—28 days.

7.37   The other kind of special remission is where there has been a 'Pledge of Public Faith' (annex M2) which can be applied for where a prisoner has either been misled into thinking that he or she will be released before the correct release date, or where the prisoner has been released before it is realised that the full sentence has not been served. Factors to take into account will be the length of time the prisoner was under a misapprehension, the extent to which the prisoner has made plans for his or her release on the incorrect date, whether he or she has purposely withheld knowledge of the error, and the amount of time or proportion of the sentence that would not be served. The decision should be made by the area manager and ministerial involvement is needed if release is to be brought forward by more than one month. As special remission is an exercise of the Royal Prerogative of Mercy the Queen must sign a royal warrant, although in cases involving remission of four days or less the Palace has agreed that a warrant will not be required for signature and remission can be granted by the area manager.

7.38   **Allocation of young offenders sentenced under the Children and Young Persons Act 1933**   Such young offenders are centrally managed at Prison Service Headquarters. Governors will be asked to give their views.

7.39   **Mother and baby units**   Prisoners' complaints relating only to the refusal to admit them to a mother and baby unit, a decision to separate them from their child, or any aspect of their treatment whilst in a mother and baby unit are dealt with by staff at Prison Service Headquarters.

7.40   **Artificial insemination**   Applications for artificial insemination are dealt with at Prison Service Headquarters, and will only be granted where there 'are exceptionally strong reasons for doing so' (para 3.4.17). Applications are only considered if the couple are married, but aside from that no set criteria apply and each application is considered on its own merits. Although the Prison Service has refused applications in the past, as far as is known, it has always reversed its decisions where legal action has been initiated.

7.41   **Wrongful conviction or sentence**   Request/complaints about conviction and sentence used to be referred to the Home Office, although given the creation of the Criminal Cases Review Commission which now has the role of referring cases back to the Court of Appeal prisoners who have exhausted appeal procedures should contact the Commission.

Confidential access to the area manager

7.42   Requests and complaints sent to the area manager's office under confidential access should not be opened before they leave the prison. When they are received at the area manager's office, they will be read and consideration will be given as to whether they should have been sent under confidential access or not. If the complaint should have been raised at the prison first, the area manager should consider the reasons given by the prisoner for using the confidential access system and decide whether to simply forward the requests/complaints form to the prison for a response, or to write to the prisoner advising that the matter is raised in a fresh request/complaint to the governor. In making this decision, the area manager should have regard to the urgency and seriousness of the complaint and whether it would make sense for the matter to be referred directly to the governor (para 4.1.7).

7.43   Allegations against the governor or a senior member of staff at any prison should not be referred back to the establishment and should be dealt with by the area manager's office. Aside from that, most other requests and complaints sent to the area manager's office under confidential access are liable to be referred back to the prison unless they raise reserved subjects, in which case they will be referred to the appropriate department within Prison Service Headquarters.

7.44   Prisoners should receive a response to requests and complaints forms dealt with at Prison Service Headquarters within six weeks of the date of submission (para 3.2.25). If this is not possible, an interim reply should be sent detailing the reasons for the delay.

THE PRISONS OMBUDSMAN

7.45   The Prisons Ombudsman was created in 1994 following recommendations in the Woolf Report. The post does not have a statutory basis and if complaints are upheld the Ombudsman can only make recommendations to the Director General of the Prison Service or the Home Secretary. In the vast majority of cases recommendations are followed, although a significant minority are rejected (6.6% according to the Ombudsman's 1998–99 annual report). A fuller discussion of the background to the Ombudsman is contained in chapter 4.

7.46   The Ombudsman's remit has varied slightly since the creation of the office. The current remit is covered in the Terms of Reference in force from 1 May 1999 (enclosed in annex A to the Ombudsman's annual report, and as appendix 1 to the current guidance to prisons on the Ombudsman contained in PSO 2520) which states the 'Prisons Ombudsman will investigate complaints which are submitted by individual prisoners who have failed to obtain satisfaction from the Prison Service requests and complaints system.' The Ombudsman can investigate complaints about all decisions affecting prisoners made by Prison Service staff and those working in prisons if not employed by the Prison Service (eg prison probation officers, staff in privately run prisons, prison teachers, and members of Boards of Visitors) with the exception of decisions involving the clinical judgement of doctors. He cannot investigate:

> '—policy decisions taken by a minister and the official advice to ministers upon which such decisions are based.
>
> —the merits of decisions taken personally by a minister save in cases which have been approved by ministers for consideration.
>
> —the personal exercise by ministers of their function in the setting and review of tariff and the release of mandatory life sentenced prisoners.
>
> —actions and decisions outside the responsibility of the Prison Service such as issues about conviction and sentence; cases currently the subject of civil litigation or criminal proceedings; and the decisions and recommendations of outside bodies including the judiciary, the policy, the CPS, the Immigration Service, the Parole Board and its Secretariat.'
> (Ombudsman's Terms of Reference, para 5)

Complaints about the Prison Service's administrative role in any of these areas may be investigated by the Ombudsman (eg delay in referring applications to the Parole Board). In relation to decisions of ministers the most recent Terms of Reference make it clear that although the final decisions in relation to, for example, tariff setting or release for mandatory lifers, complaints about the administrative processes up to and including provision of official advice on individual cases will be eligible. Further if there has been a response to an MP's letter (which by convention will be a ministerial response) this technical involvement by the minister will not take a complaint out of eligibility (PSI 77/1999, para 8, which introduced PSO 2520).

7.47   Before a complaint is eligible for consideration by the Ombudsman, prisoners must first follow the internal requests and complaints procedure by submitting forms to the governor and area manager or other relevant department at Prison Service Headquarters. Complaints must be submitted to the Ombudsman's office within one calendar month of the response from Headquarters. However, complaints will not normally be accepted if there is a delay of more than 12 months from the prisoner becoming aware of the relevant facts and submitting a complaint unless this delay is the Prison Service's fault (para 7). In fact because of the delays in dealing with requests/complaint forms both at prison level and at the Briefing and Casework Unit, it is not unusual for complaints to reach the Ombudsman well over a year after the incident in question. The Ombudsman will consider complaints outside the time limit 'where there is good reason for the delay, or where the issues raised are so serious as to override the time factor' (para 8).

7.48   If a complaint to Headquarters remains unanswered after six weeks (the time limit for dealing with complaints under the requests/complaints procedure) then it will be eligible for consideration by the Ombudsman at that stage (para 6). In practice if there has been a delay of more than six weeks at Headquarters the Ombudsman will only commence an investigation in these circumstances if the matter is urgent.

7.49   A complaint to the Ombudsman does not have to be made on any specific form and can be made by letter. The current remit states that complaints must be 'submitted by individual prisoners' (para 2) and so prisoners should either write themselves or if a complaint is drafted on their behalf sign the complaint before it is sent. In practice however the Ombudsman will accept complaints from legal representatives and MPs as long as they have permission from the prisoner. This can be important if the deadline for the complaint's submission is imminent.

7.50   Prisoners' letters to the Ombudsman may be sent at the prison's expense (PSO 2520, para 6.1.1) under confidential access, although of course this does not mean that the nature of the complaint will not be disclosed to prison staff (as the Ombudsman may need to discuss the complaint with prison officials in the course of investigating it). Prison staff must not prevent the submission of complaints nor judge their eligibility (eg on time grounds) (para 6.1.3). Letters sent to the Ombudsman can be handed in sealed as long as they are marked 'confidential access' and the address is correct, and can only be opened if there is reasonable cause to believe they contain an illicit enclosure and then only in front of the prisoner (para 6.2.1). Correspondence from the Ombudsman to prisoners should be clearly identified as such on the envelope and marked as confidential. They should not be opened by prison staff unless there is reason to believe that they did not originate from the Ombudsman's office and in such a case, they should be passed to the governor who should check with the Ombudsman's office that an inquiry is ongoing. If there is any remaining doubt, a letter purporting to be from the Ombudsman should only be opened in the presence of the prisoner concerned (para 6.2.2).

7.51   The Director General is to ensure that the Ombudsman has 'unfettered access to Prison Service documents, including classified material' (Terms of Reference, para 11) and Prison Service staff 'must co-operate fully with all requests from the Prisons Ombudsman or his/her staff for information, material or access to establishments and prisoners' (PSO 2520, para 7.2). The consent of the prisoner is needed if medical records are to be disclosed to the Ombudsman. The Ombudsman will not disclose 'sensitive information' to the complainant or the public, that is where disclosure is:

'—against the interests of security;
—likely to prejudice security measures designed to prevent the escape of particular prisoners or classes of prisoners;
—likely to put at risk a third party source of information;
—likely to be detrimental on medical or psychiatric grounds to the mental or physical health of a prisoner;
—likely to prejudice the administration of justice including legal proceedings;
—of papers capable of attracting legal professional privilege.'
(Terms of Reference, para 14)

Prison Service staff should identify information they believe comes within the above grounds and also check the Ombudsman's draft reports (Terms of Reference, para 15).

7.52   The access to information normally withheld from prisoners is one of his most important powers for prisoners. It means for example that the Ombudsman will be able to see the Security Information Reports (SIRs) upon which a prisoner's segregation or transfer may have been based, enabling him to come to his own view on the merits of the prison's action. This is very different to the court's role in judicial review where such documents would not normally be disclosed and where the review is largely of procedural rather than substantive fairness.

7.53   Staff from the Prison Ombudsman's office may visit any prison establishment in the course of an investigation and may interview prison staff (who can take a colleague or trade union representative with them—PSO 2520, para 7.3.5) or prisoners who consent to an interview. Visits with prisoners should be in the sight but out of the hearing of prison staff, and do not count against a prisoner's allowance of visiting orders.

7.54   A new development in the most recent Terms of Reference is the power of the Ombudsman to seek to 'resolve the matter by local settlement' (Terms of Reference, para 11). This process of local resolution is designed to deal with matters which are not 'reserved subjects' under the requests/complaints procedure (see above) and where the Ombudsman anticipates that the complaint will be upheld. The consent of both prisoner and the governor of the relevant prison must consent to the procedure (PSO 2520, para 8.1.1). Governors have authority to agree such settlements (para 8.1.2) and the idea is that this procedure will provide a speedier resolution for relatively minor complaints that can be dealt with at a local level where the investigation throws up new evidence or factual errors in the decision-making process so reaching 'agreement on justified complaints at an earlier stage' (para 8.1.5). If the procedure is followed the Ombudsman will not produce a full report. The local resolution procedure became available for complaints eligible on or after 1 December 1999.

7.55   The Ombudsman's office aims to complete investigations within 12 weeks of receiving the complaint (Terms of Reference, para 19). A draft report is firstly prepared which is sent to the Director General and the prisoner to allow for factual corrections and for criticised staff to make representations and then the Ombudsman will issue a final report. If the prisoner's complaint is upheld then the Ombudsman will send a copy of his report to the Director General of the Prison Service or the Home Secretary making recommendations as to the remedy that should be offered to the prisoner. The Prison Service has a target of four weeks for either accepting or refusing the recommendation. Even if a complaint is not upheld the Ombudsman has a discretion to make recommendations.

7.56   If the Prison Service rejects a recommendation, then the Ombudsman's office may enter into further correspondence with the Prison Service. The Prisons minister will sometimes adjudicate between the Director General and the Ombudsman in these circumstances. The Director General has informed the Ombudsman that recommendations will not be refused unless there are 'compelling reasons to do so' (1998–99 annual report, p 23). However, ultimately, the prisoner would be best advised to seek legal advice promptly, with a view to pursuing a judicial review of the refusal to follow the recommendation.

CHAPTER 8
PRISON DISCIPLINE

THE FORMAL DISCIPLINARY SYSTEM

Offences against prison discipline

8.1 The power to discipline prisoners for misconduct whilst they are in prison is contained in the Prison Act 1952, s 47(1). This provides for rules to be made for the discipline and control of prisoners, and gives prisoners the right to have a proper opportunity to present their case if charged with an offence. An offence against prison discipline may be treated as having been committed in the prison at which the prisoner is held (Criminal Justice Act 1961, s 23(1)), and thus a prisoner who commits an offence at one establishment may be charged and adjudicated upon at another prison. Unless a contrary indication is made, all references in this section relate to paragraphs of the 1995 edition of the Discipline Manual. The Prison Service proposes to introduce a new Discipline Manual to reflect the amendments made by the Prison Rules 1999 but no date has been set for publication.

8.2 The list of offences against prison discipline with which a prisoner may be charged are contained in r 51 of the Prison Rules 1999, r 51, the full text of which follows:

'51. A prisoner is guilty of an offence against discipline if he:
(1) commits any assault;
(2) detains any person against his will;
(3) denies access to any part of the prison to any officer or any person (other than a prisoner) who is in the prison for the purpose of working there;
(4) fights with any person;
(5) intentionally endangers the health or personal safety of others or, by his conduct is reckless whether such health or personal safety is endangered;
(6) intentionally obstructs an officer in the execution of his duty, or any person (other than a prisoner) who is at the prison for the purpose of working there, in the performance of his work;
(7) escapes or absconds from prison or from legal custody;
(8) fails to comply with any condition upon which he is temporarily released under Rule 9;
(9) administers a controlled drug to himself or fails to prevent the administration of a controlled drug to him by another person (but subject to Rule 52);

(10) is intoxicated as a consequence of knowingly consuming any alcoholic beverage;

(11) knowingly consumes any alcoholic beverage other than that provided to him pursuant to a written order under rule 25(1);

(12) has in his possession:
(a) any unauthorised article, or
(b) a greater quantity of any article than he is authorised to have;

(13) sells or delivers to any person any unauthorised article;

(14) sells or, without permission, delivers to any person any article which he is allowed to have only for his own use;

(15) takes improperly any article belonging to another person or to a prison;

(16) intentionally or recklessly sets fire to any part of a prison or any other property, whether or not his own;

(17) destroys or damages any part of a prison or any other property, other than his own;

(18) absents himself from any place he is required to be or is present at any place where he is not authorised to be;

(19) is disrespectful to any officer, or any person (other than a prisoner) who is at the prison for the purpose of working there, or any person visiting a prison;

(20) uses threatening, abusive or insulting words or behaviour;

(21) intentionally fails to work properly or, being required to work, refuses to do so;

(22) disobeys any lawful order;

(23) disobeys or fails to comply with any rule or regulation applying to him;

(24) receives any controlled drug, or, without the consent of an officer, any other article, during the course of a visit (not being an interview such as is mentioned in rule 38);

(25) (a) attempts to commit,
(b) incites another prisoner to commit, or
(c) assists another prisoner to commit or to attempt to commit, any of the foregoing offences.'

Charging

8.3   Prisoners are generally charged with a disciplinary offence by any officer who witnessed the breach of the Rules. Alternatively the charge can be laid by an officer who discovers that the offence has been committed. The Prison Rules 1999, r 53(1) requires that a prisoner should be charged as soon as possible, and at the latest within 48 hours of the offence being discovered. If the charge is not laid within 48 hours then a finding of guilt at adjudication will be void unless there are 'exceptional circumstances'. A charge is laid when a form F1127 ('Notice of Report') is handed to the prisoner. F1127 contains details of the time, date and place of commission of the offence, the paragraph of r 51 under which the prisoner has been charged, details of the allegations made against the prisoner, and the time of the hearing. The charge must be laid out in sufficient detail for the prisoner to have a full understanding of the allegation made (para 2.11). Prisoners are advised that they may write out their defence to the charge on the back of the form, and state whether they wish to call any witnesses. At the same time as being handed the F1127, prisoners may also be given an information sheet, F1145 ('Explanation of Procedures at Disciplinary Charge Hearings') which provides a brief explanation of the stages that the adjudication will follow. Prisoners should be allowed time to prepare their defence, and thus they must be charged at least two hours before the adjudication takes place.

8.4   A charge cannot be reduced during the adjudication, and therefore if it is not clear which of two charges a prisoner may be guilty of, staff are advised to lay two separate charges, one or both of which may be dropped at adjudication if it transpires that there is not enough evidence against the prisoner to support it (para 2.6).

8.5   Although prisoners can be charged with several separate offences which arise from the same incident (eg a prisoner who breaks a window whilst fighting with another prisoner could be charged under r 51(4) for fighting and under r 51(17) for damaging prison property), they cannot be charged twice for what is essentially the same offence. Therefore a prisoner who refuses to go to work cannot be charged under r 47(18) for refusing to work, and r 47(19) for disobeying an officer's order that he should go to work. Prisoners may not be charged with continuing offences, and so a prisoner who refuses an order to clean the toilets and is charged with that offence may not be charged again if he refuses the same order a couple of hours later (para 2.12).

8.6   If, in the course of an adjudication, the adjudicator considers that a prisoner is not guilty of the offence with which he has been charged, but may be guilty of a different offence, the original charge may be dropped and a new charge laid so long as this is still within 48 hours of the discovery of the alleged offence. In this case, the proceedings must be started afresh and a different governor should hear the newly laid charge (para 2.5).

8.7   Before the adjudication a prisoner should be examined by the medical officer who is asked to certify whether the s/he is fit enough to attend the adjudication and to undergo cellular confinement, and to inform the adjudicator of anything in the prisoner's physical or mental health which may be relevant to the adjudication process. Where, exceptionally, the prisoner is not examined by a doctor before the hearing, they should be examined as soon as possible afterwards, normally within 24 hours. In the meantime, a punishment of cellular confinement should not be imposed (para 2.18(b)). In the case of *R v Governor of HM Prison Long Lartin, ex p Pewter* (18 January 1999, unreported), the High Court upheld a decision made by a governor to continue an adjudication against a prisoner where the medical officer had certified him as fit for adjudication, despite there being evidence to the contrary. This conflicting evidence came from an outside hospital which had treated the prisoner earlier that day and representations advanced by the applicant's solicitors calling into question the medical officer's assessment and decision. The court confirmed that the decision was one within the adjudicator's discretion.

8.8   In order to adequately prepare their defence, prisoners are allowed to request copies of any statements that will be used in evidence against them, and they should not be charged any photocopying fees. Prisoners should also be afforded the facilities in which to interview any witnesses who may be able to give evidence at the hearing, although whether such interviews take place within or out of the hearing of prison staff is at the discretion of the governor. However, if witnesses are only to be interviewed in the presence of staff, the supervising officer should be someone who is unconnected with the hearing.

Legal representation

8.9 Prisoners who are charged with an offence against prison discipline should be allowed to consult a solicitor if they so wish. Adjudicators are advised to adjourn the proceedings if a prisoner has not had enough time to contact a solicitor between the charge being laid and the adjudication starting.

8.10 At the beginning of an adjudication, the adjudicator should ask the prisoner if s/he requires any assistance in putting forward a defence. This could be either a solicitor or a McKenzie friend. A McKenzie friend only has a limited role in the proceedings, and may attend the hearing, take notes, and offer advice and support to the prisoner (para 3.4). Prisoners may choose their own McKenzie friend, but the adjudicator can remove the McKenzie friend from the hearing if it is considered that s/he is interfering with the proceedings or participating without the adjudicator's permission.

8.11 The adjudicator has discretion as to whether to allow a solicitor to represent, or a McKenzie friend to attend the hearing. In considering whether to grant a request for assistance the adjudicator should comply with the judgment in *R v Secretary of State for the Home Department, ex p Tarrant* [1984] 1 All ER 799. This held that there was no right for a prisoner to be legally represented at an adjudication, but that in deciding whether a request for representation should be granted, the adjudicator should have regard to the following factors:

(a) the seriousness of the charge and the potential penalty;
(b) whether any points of law are likely to arise;
(c) the capacity of the prisoner to present his own case;
(d) whether or not there are likely to be any procedural difficulties;
(e) the need for reasonable speed in hearing the charge;
(f) the need for fairness as between prisoners and between prisoners and prison staff.

8.12 If legal representation is granted then the hearing will be adjourned for the prisoner either to instruct a solicitor or find a McKenzie friend. If the request is denied, then the request will be noted on the record of the proceedings together with the reasons for refusal. The adjudication will then go ahead.

8.13 Where, in the course of explaining why they need legal representation, the prisoner incriminates himself by disclosing something which would make it impossible for the adjudicator to be unprejudiced in hearing the charge, the adjudication should be adjourned and heard by another adjudicator at a later date.

8.14   If legal representation is granted for the prisoner, then the Prison Service will also instruct solicitors to act for him/her. A solicitor acting for a prisoner may ask for access to the prison or to prison staff prior to the hearing in order to interview potential witnesses or to look at the place where the incident took place. Such requests should be dealt with by a member of prison staff who is not involved in the adjudication process.

8.15   Solicitors may advise prisoners about their adjudications under the Legal Advice and Assistance scheme, and may claim for preparation. However, where a prisoner is in a contracted out prison, the Legal Aid Regulations allow their solicitors to claim for representation under the ABWOR scheme. The question of the likely impact of the Human Rights Act on legal representation at adjudications is discussed at para 8.100 below.

An in-depth look at the charges

8.16   The Prison Discipline Manual contains detailed guidance to adjudicators on the elements of each charge under r 51. In order to find a prisoner guilty of a charge, the governor must be satisfied beyond reasonable doubt that the prisoner is guilty, regardless of how the prisoner has pleaded (para 7.1).

8.17   **(1) Commits any assault.** A prisoner is guilty of assault if s/he intentionally or recklessly applies unlawful force to another person, or causes another person to fear the immediate application of unlawful force (although adjudicators are advised that a charge under para 17 is preferable in this instance). In order to find a prisoner guilty of assault, the adjudicator must be satisfied that:

(a)   the prisoner applied force to another or committed an act which put the other person in fear of immediate application of force;
(b)   the prisoner intended to do so or was reckless as to whether this would happen;
(c)   the force was unlawful, ie was not applied in self-defence or in order to prevent the commission of a serious crime (paras 6.3–6.5).

8.18   **(2) Detains any person against his will.** This relates to situations where a prisoner takes a hostage. Adjudicators are advised to consider whether the hostage and the hostage taker were acting together, and if so to consider whether a charge may more appropriately be brought under para 3 (if staff have been denied access to part of the prison where the incident took place).

8.19   In order to find a prisoner guilty of this offence, the adjudicator must be satisfied that:

(a)   the hostage's freedom of movement was inhibited by force or by the threat of force;
(b)   the hostage was detained against their will. If the accused can show that the victim collaborated, then this will be a complete defence, although the adjudicator should establish whether the incident started out as a joint venture, and then turned into a situation whereby the

victim was prevented from withdrawing against their will. In such circumstances a prisoner may be found guilty;

(c)   the prisoner intended the victim to be detained against their will, or was reckless as to whether this would happen (paras 6.6–6.8).

8.20   (3) Denies access to any part of the prison to any officer or any person (other than a prisoner) who is at the prison for the purpose of working there.   Prisoners who erect barricades or deny access to a part of the prison are liable to be found guilty of this offence. In order to find a prisoner guilty, the adjudicator must be satisfied that the following elements of the charge are present:

(a)   someone working at the prison was denied access to any part of it;
(b)   the prisoner intended that this should be so, or was reckless as to whether it would happen (paras 6.9–6.11).

8.21   (4) Fights with any person.   In order to find a prisoner guilty under this paragraph, the adjudicator must be satisfied that:

(a)   the prisoner intentionally committed an assault by inflicting unlawful force on another prisoner in the context of a fight;
(b)   the fight must involve at least one other person and constitute more than one blow. It should have continued for 'a sufficient time to amount to a fight in the ordinary sense of the word';
(c)   self defence is a complete defence, and so where two prisoners are charged with fighting each other, one may be found guilty of fighting and the other found not guilty on the basis of self defence (paras 6.12–6.13).

8.22   (5) Intentionally endangers the health or personal safety of others, or, by his conduct, is reckless as to whether such health or personal safety is endangered.   The elements of this charge are that:

(a)   there was a 'definite and serious' risk of harm to the safety of at least one person other than the prisoner;
(b)   this danger was caused by the prisoner's behaviour;
(c)   the prisoner intended to cause the danger, or was reckless as to whether it would occur (paras 6.14–6.16).

8.23   (6) Intentionally obstructs an officer in the execution of his duty, or any person (other than a prisoner) who is at the prison for the purpose of working there, in the performance of his work.   This charge covers both physical obstruction of an officer and situations whereby a prisoner might provide false information to an officer. The elements of the charge are as follows:

(a)   there was some sort of obstruction;
(b)   the person who was obstructed was working at the prison, and was attempting to perform his or her work;
(c)   the prisoner intended that the person should be obstructed (paras 6.17–6.19).

8.24   **(7) Escapes or absconds from prison or from legal custody.**   This charge is aimed at prisoners who actually get away from the prison and are not caught as they are attempting to escape or abscond. An adjudicator may only be satisfied to the guilt of a prisoner when the following elements of the charge are made out:

(a)   the prisoner was held in legal custody, including on escort to or from a prison or whilst working outside the prison;
(b)   the prisoner escaped or absconded;
(c)   the prisoner had no authority to do so;
(d)   the prisoner intended to escape or abscond (ie s/he knew that s/he was leaving lawful custody without authority);
(e)   it is a complete defence for the prisoner to plead that s/he believed that s/he had authority to leave (paras 6.20–6.22).

8.25   **(8) Fails to comply with any condition upon which he is temporarily released under r 9.**   When a prisoner is temporarily released s/he will be issued with a licence which lists the conditions which should be complied with. An offence under this paragraph could range from failing to return to prison on time to drinking alcohol whilst temporarily released.

8.26   Many prisoners who fail to return to prison on time use the defence that they were too ill to travel and licences should include a statement which should be signed by a doctor if the prisoner is unfit to return. If this statement is signed by a doctor then the prisoner has a complete defence to the charge. If the prisoner produces any other medical evidence, the adjudicator should consider whether or not this amounts to certification that the prisoner was unable to travel back to the prison on time.

8.27   For a finding of guilt to be made, the adjudicator must be satisfied of the following:

(a)   the prisoner was released on a temporary release licence containing clear conditions of which the prisoner was aware. The licence was signed by a governor with authority to do so;
(b)   the prisoner intentionally or recklessly did not comply with one or more of the conditions;
(c)   there was no justification for the prisoner's failure to comply with the condition(s).

8.28   A prisoner who did not return on time will have a defence to the charge if they can show that they were genuinely unable to get back to the prison because of circumstances beyond their control. Prisoners who are charged with a criminal offence committed on temporary release may be charged with an offence against prison discipline if they have also breached their licence conditions.

8.29   The Prisoners (Return to Custody) Act 1995 makes it a criminal offence to be unlawfully at large without reasonable excuse following a period of temporary release on licence, or whilst knowing or believing that an order has been made for their recall to prison and failing to take all necessary steps to comply with it as soon as is reasonably practicable without reasonable excuse. Prisoners convicted of this criminal offence may be sentenced by a magistrates' court to up to six months' imprisonment and/or a fine not exceeding level 5 on the standard scale (see chapter 9 for further details).

8.30   (9) Administers a controlled drug to himself or fails to prevent the administration of a controlled drug to him by another person (but subject to r 52). Prisoners may be required to give a urine sample that will be tested to check for the presence of controlled drugs (Prison Act 1952, s 16A as amended by the Criminal Justice and Public Order Act 1994, s 151). Samples of sweat and non pubic hair may also be requested for this purpose, however samples of blood and semen may not.

8.31   All categories of prisoner are liable to be tested for drugs, and will be selected on a random basis, although if officers have a reasonable suspicion that a particular prisoner is involved in misusing drugs, that person may be tested more frequently than others ('The Introduction of a Mandatory Drug Testing Programme for Prisoners in England and Wales: a guide to the main issues', IG 15/95, paras 7–8). Very detailed guidance on mandatory drug testing is to be found in PSO 3601.

8.32   Governors may make their own provisions for the collection of urine samples within their establishments, although the following provisions should be a common feature in establishments:

(a)   prisoners will not be given prior warning that they will be required to give a sample;

(b)   prisoners should be given precise instructions, asked to remove bulky outer clothing, and be searched thoroughly;

(c)   prisoners will be given 'as much privacy as is consistent with the need to prevent adulteration or substitution of false samples . . . a greater invasion of privacy may be necessary of those individual prisoners caught cheating';

(d)   samples will be divided, and one-half will be kept in case of appeal. Samples will be sealed and the seals signed by the prisoner (IG 15/95, para 17).

8.33   Prisoners who refuse to provide a sample can be charged under the Prison Rules 1999, r 51(22), for disobeying a lawful order, and where prisoners cannot provide a sample they may be segregated for up to five hours and provided with controlled amounts of water (r 50(7)).

8.34   If the prisoner tests positive then so long as the sample was taken under the provision of r 50, the prisoner may be charged with an offence under r 51(9). Rule 52 provides statutory defences and these are:

(a)   that the controlled drug was lawfully in the prisoner's possession for their own use;

(b)   that the controlled drug was administered in the lawful supply of the drug by another person;

(c)   the controlled drug was administered by or to him in circumstances which he did not know and had no reason to suspect that such a drug was being administered; or

(d) that the drug was administered under duress or without consent in circumstances where it was unreasonable to resist.

8.35 (10) Is intoxicated as a consequence of knowingly consuming any alcoholic beverage. This charge is meant to deal with prisoners who are clearly intoxicated rather than those who have taken a small amount of alcohol.

8.36 In order to find a prisoner guilty of this offence the adjudicator must be satisfied beyond reasonable doubt that:

(a) The accused was intoxicated. If a prisoner is found to have been 'elated beyond the point of self control' then it is said that this will 'satisfy the test of intoxication'. However, 'skylarking' or 'an excess of high spirits' are not sufficient;

(b) The intoxication was caused, either wholly or in part, by the consumption of alcohol. The adjudicator must enquire into the possible causes of reported behaviour such as slurred speech, instability, or the smell of alcohol on a prisoner's breath;

(c) The accused knowingly consumed the alcohol. Therefore, the prisoner may advance in his/her defence that they were given a spiked drink (paras 6.30–6.33).

8.37 (11) Knowingly consumes any alcoholic beverage other than any prescribed to him pursuant to a written order of the medical officer under Prison Rule 20. This offence is less serious than (10) above. It deals with situations where a prisoner is not intoxicated but has knowingly consumed alcohol which was not prescribed to him or her.

8.38 In order to find a prisoner guilty of the offence, the adjudicator must be satisfied beyond reasonable doubt that:

(a) The prisoner's behaviour was as a result of consuming alcohol. 'The evidence should be such as would lead a reasonable and right thinking person to conclude that the accused had consumed alcohol' (para 6.36 (a));

(b) The accused knowingly consumed the alcohol (as for (10) above);

(c) It is a complete defence to the charge that the alcohol was prescribed by a medical officer (paras 6.34–6.36).

8.39 (12) Has in his possession (a) any unauthorised article, or (b) a greater quantity of any article than he is authorised to have. Paragraph (a) of this charge covers situations where the prisoner had something in possession which is unauthorised (eg drugs, firearms) or an article which is authorised in itself but is not authorised in this instance (eg because it was issued to another prisoner). Paragraph (b) aims to deal with prisoners who have more of an article in their possession than they are allowed to have (eg tobacco or telephone cards).

8.40   Before a prisoner can be found guilty under this paragraph, the adjudicator should be satisfied that the following three elements of the charge have been made out:

(a)   Presence—that the article exists, that it is what it is alleged to be, and that it was found where alleged;

(b)   Knowledge—that the prisoner knows what the article is, and knew that it was present;

(c)   Control—that the accused had either sole or joint control over the article (para 6.32).

(See also *R v Board of Visitors of Camp Hill, ex p King* [1984] 3 All ER 897.)

8.41   Thus, if two prisoners are sharing a cell and one has a tin containing cocaine, the other should not be convicted if he believed it was milk powder, or if he knew the substance was cocaine but exercised no control over it.

8.42   In respect of charges under both (a) and (b) above, the governor must be satisfied that the prisoner was aware that an article was unauthorised or was restricted in terms of quantity allowed in possession. A genuine belief that the article was allowed or that there were no restrictions on quantity will be a defence (para 6.40).

8.43   **(13) Sells or delivers to any person any unauthorised article.** This charge covers articles which are unauthorised in themselves or are not authorised to a particular prisoner. Before finding a prisoner guilty the adjudicator must be satisfied that the following are established:

(a)   the article was sold or delivered by the accused to another person (who does not have to be a prisoner);

(b)   the article was not authorised;

(c)   the prisoner intended to sell or deliver the article or was reckless as to whether they were selling or delivering it. It would be a defence for the prisoner to plead that they believed they were authorised to pass on the article in that way.

8.44   **(14) Sells, or without permission, delivers to any person any article which he is allowed to have only for his own use.** In finding a prisoner guilty, the adjudicator does not have to establish whether the article was sold or delivered, however the following elements of the charge must be made out:

(a)   the article was sold or delivered to someone;

(b)   it was authorised only for the prisoner's own use;

(c)   the prisoner did not have permission to pass the article to someone else (para 6.47).

8.45   **(15) Takes improperly any article belonging to another person or to a prison (or young offender institution).** This is essentially theft, and in order for a prisoner to be found guilty at adjudication, the adjudicator must be satisfied of the presence of the following elements of the charge:

(a)   there was an article which belonged to another person or to a prison;

(b)   the prisoner took physical control of the article without permission;
(c)   the prisoner intended to take the article without permission, or was reckless as to whether s/he did so (para 6.50).

8.46   It is a defence for the prisoner to plead that they thought that they had permission to take the article or that they believed that it belonged to them (para 6.50(e)).

8.47   (16) Intentionally or recklessly sets fire to any part of a prison (or young offender institution) or any other property whether or not his own.   In order to be satisfied of the guilt of a prisoner charged with this offence, the adjudicator should establish the following:

(a)   the prisoner set fire to part of the prison or some other property of a tangible nature;
(b)   the prisoner acted with intent or was reckless as to whether they set fire to the property.

8.48   (17) Destroys or damages any part of a prison (or young offender institution) or any other property, other than his own.   This is similar to the charge of criminal damage in criminal law. It is not sufficient to show merely that the prisoner was in possession of a damaged article, and before a finding of guilt can be made, the adjudicator must be satisfied that:

(a)   part of a prison or some other property of a tangible nature was damaged;
(b)   the property belonged to someone other than the prisoner;
(c)   there was no lawful excuse for the damage to the property;
(d)   the prisoner intended that the property should be destroyed or damaged or was reckless as to whether this should occur.

8.49   It is a defence for the prisoner to plead that they thought that the property belonged to them.

8.50   (18) Absents himself from any place where he is required to be or is present at any place where he is not authorised to be. This charge can apply to situations which occur both inside or outside a prison. For example if a prisoner leaves an open prison to go and meet someone in the locality but has every intention of returning to the prison, then this would be appropriate rather than a charge of absconding. Likewise, if a prisoner in a closed prison leaves the workshop and decides to go to the gym, they could be charged under this paragraph.

8.51   For a finding of guilt to be made, the adjudicator must be satisfied that the following elements of the offence are made out:

(a)   the prisoner was required to be in a particular place or did not have permission to be in the place that they were found;
(b)   the prisoner was in fact absent from the place where they were required to be or was in fact present at the place that they did not have permission to be in;
(c)   the prisoner was not able to justify their actions;
(d)   the prisoner intended to commit the offence or was reckless as to whether it was committed.

8.52   A prisoner who pleads a genuine belief that they had permission to be somewhere, or was not required to be in a particular place will have a defence (paras 6.56–6.58).

8.53   **(19) Is disrespectful to any officer, or any person (other than a prisoner) who is at the prison for the purpose of working there, or any person visiting a prison.**   For the purposes of this charge, disrespect can be shown by both verbal and physical behaviour. To be satisfied that the prisoner is guilty of the offence the adjudicator should ensure that the following elements are present:

(a)   there was an act which was directed towards a specific person or group of people;
(b)   the act was disrespectful in the ordinary meaning of the word and in the particular circumstances;
(c)   the person at which the act was aimed was either an officer, visitor to the prison, or a person working at the prison;
(d)   the prisoner intended to be disrespectful or was reckless as to whether s/he was being so.

8.54   If a prisoner pleads a genuine belief that s/he did not consider the act to be disrespectful, this would be a defence (paras 6.59–6.61).

8.55   **(20) Uses threatening, abusive or insulting words or behaviour.**   An adjudicator hearing a charge under this paragraph should be satisfied that the following elements are present before finding a prisoner guilty:

(a)   the prisoner did a specific act, adopted a general pattern of behaviour or said specific words;
(b)   the above conduct was either threatening, abusive, or insulting (in the ordinary senses of these words) rather than annoying or rude;
(c)   the prisoner intended to be threatening abusive or insulting or was reckless as to whether he was so (paras 6.62–6.64).

8.56   **(21) Intentionally fails to work properly or, being required to work, refuses to do so.**   In laying a charge under this paragraph, an officer must specify which of the two separate offences it is alleged that the prisoner has committed. Where a prisoner is charged with intentionally failing to work properly, a finding of guilt can only be made if the adjudicator is satisfied that:

(a) the prisoner was lawfully required to work at the time and in the circumstances specified;
(b) the prisoner failed to work properly (this is measured against a standard of work expected);
(c) the prisoner intended not to work properly or was reckless as to whether s/he was doing so.

8.57   Thus, to be found guilty a prisoner must know that his work was not or may not be up to the required standard. A prisoner who pleads that s/he thought that s/he was working hard enough would have a defence to the charge (paras 6.65–6.67).

8.58   Where a prisoner is charged with refusing to work, the adjudicator must establish that the following elements of the offence are made out before making a finding of guilt:

(a)   the prisoner was lawfully required to work at the time and in the circumstances specified;
(b)   the prisoner refused to work, either by act or omission;
(c)   the prisoner intended to refuse to work or was reckless as to whether s/he was doing so.

8.59   In order to find a prisoner guilty the adjudicator must be satisfied that the prisoner knew that he was required to work or was aware that he may have been so required. If the prisoner genuinely believes that s/he did not have to work then they would have a defence. Prisoners charged with this offence often say that they were medically unfit to work, and in such circumstances the adjudicator should investigate the assertion and seek evidence as to the prisoner's state of health (paras 6.68–6.70).

8.60   (22) Disobeys any lawful order.   A lawful order is defined as 'one which a member of staff has authority to give in the execution of his or her duties' (para 6.72). When hearing a charge under this paragraph the adjudicator must ensure that the following are established before finding the prisoner guilty:

(a)   the action of the member of staff was an order. An order is 'a clear indication by word and/or action given in the course of his or her duties by a member of staff requiring a specific prisoner to do or refrain from doing something'(para 6.73(a));
(b)   the order was lawful;
(c)   the prisoner did not obey the order within a reasonable period of time;
(d)   the prisoner intended not to comply with the order or was reckless as to whether it was complied with.

8.61   In defence, a prisoner may plead that they did not understand what was being asked of them (paras 6.71–6.73).

8.62   (23) Disobeys or fails to comply with any rule or regulation applying to him.   Many prisons have local rules which are not contained in the Prison Rules, and this charge aims to discipline prisoners who are alleged to have acted in breach of such rules.

8.63   Before a prisoner can be found guilty of this offence, the adjudicator must be satisfied that the following are established:

(a)   the rule/regulation applied to the prisoner who must have been aware of its existence, or reasonable steps must have been taken to draw it to his/her attention;
(b)   the rule or regulation was lawful in respect of the particular prisoner concerned;
(c)   the prisoner did not obey the rule/regulation, either intentionally or recklessly (6.74–6.75).

8.64 **(24) Receives any controlled drug, or, without the consent of an officer, any other article, during the course of a visit (not being an interview such as is mentioned in rule 38).** This new offence against prison discipline was introduced in the Prison Rules 1999 and no detailed guidance has been given to adjudicators as to how they should investigate the charge. It is likely that video evidence from CCTV cameras in visits rooms will play a large part in any adjudication proceedings.

8.65 In addition to the usual punishments awarded, visitors who are discovered bringing drugs into prison will normally be banned from the prison under the Prison Rules 1999, r 73 for a period of at least three months. Prisoners who are believed to be smuggling drugs through visits will be targeted for mandatory drug testing.

8.66 **(25) (a) Attempts to commit, (b) incites other prisoners to commit, or (c) assists another prisoner to commit or attempt to commit any of the foregoing offences.** This charge must specify whether (a), (b) or (c) above is relevant and must also specify the relevant paragraph of the Prison Rules 1999, r 51.

8.67 Where a prisoner is charged with an attempt, the adjudicator should be satisfied of the following:

(a) the prisoner did an act which was more than merely preparatory to the commission of the offence;
(b) the prisoner intended to commit the full offence (paras 6.79–6.81).

8.68 Incitement is defined as 'seeking to persuade another prisoner to commit a disciplinary offence' (para 6.83(b)). If the charge is one of inciting, the following elements should be made out before the prisoner is found guilty:

(a) the prisoner's action was communicated to other prisoners who were near enough to be able to respond to the incitement;
(b) the act was capable of inciting other prisoners to commit the full offence;
(c) the full offence was the consequence or the subject of the incitement;
(d) the prisoner intended or was reckless as to whether they incited other prisoners to commit the offence (paras 6.82–6.83).

8.69 If a prisoner is charged with assisting the commission of an offence, the adjudicator must make out the following elements:

(a) another prisoner committed an offence (including an attempt);
(b) the prisoner on the current charge actively assisted in the commission of the offence and intended to do so (para 6.85).

8.70 Being aware that the offence being committed is not sufficient for a finding of guilt. In *R v Board of Visitors of Highpoint Prison, ex p McConkey* (1982) Times, 23 September, the Divisional Court held that a prisoner's presence whilst knowing that an offence was being committed by other prisoners is not an offence against prison discipline.

The conduct of adjudications

8.71   Section 10 of the Discipline Manual describes a model procedure for the conduct of an adjudication. The main points of this are as follows.

8.72   Proceedings must always start afresh without reference to any previous hearings of the same charge. This enables the adjudicator to determine the case only on the evidence presented at the hearing (para 10.1).

8.73   At the start of the hearing, the adjudicator should not have access to the prisoner's prison record or record of previous findings of guilt at adjudication (para 10.2).

8.74   The adjudicator should check:

(a)   that the charge has been laid properly;
(b)   that the preliminary parts of the Record of Hearing and Adjudication Form (F256) have been completed with the same information as that contained in the charge sheets;
(c)   that each charge is outlined in enough detail for the prisoner to know its 'precise nature';
(d)   that the 'Explanation of the Procedure at a hearing of a Disciplinary Charge by a Governor' form was given to the prisoner in sufficient time for him/her to read and understand it. This is normally deemed to be at least two hours before the hearing;
(e)   that the medical officer has certified that the prisoner is fit to appear on adjudication, and is fit to be subjected to the punishment of cellular confinement, and that any further report made by the medical officer is available to the adjudicator (para 10.4).

8.75   At the beginning of the adjudication, the adjudicator must:

(a)   identify the prisoner;
(b)   check that the prisoner has received the charge sheet, the explanatory information, and that they understand the procedure;
(c)   read out the charge;
(d)   check that the prisoner understands the charge;
(e)   ask the prisoner if s/he has had time to prepare her/his defence and whether s/he has made a written answer;
(f)   ask the prisoner whether s/he wishes to apply for legal representation;
(g)   ask the prisoner if s/he is pleading guilty or not guilty to the charge. If the prisoner pleads guilty the adjudicator should still hear evidence to be sure that the prisoner fully understands the charge. If the adjudicator believes that the prisoner is pleading guilty as a result of misunderstanding the charge, then the prisoner should be advised to change his/her plea to not guilty. Whether or not the prisoner consents to this, an adjudicator may proceed on the basis of a not guilty plea and dismiss the charge;
(h)   ask the prisoner if s/he wants to call any witnesses (para 10.7).

8.76   If the adjudicator believes that the prisoner needs more time to prepare a defence, or to prepare a request for legal representation or needs more information about the charge or the procedure, then the adjudication should be adjourned (para 10.9).

8.77   In investigating the charge, the adjudicator should first hear the evidence of the reporting officer and then ask the prisoner if s/he wishes to cross-examine the officer. The adjudicator may also ask further questions (para 10.12). The prisoner should be asked whether s/he has any defence to the charge, or if s/he wants to give any explanation or evidence (para 10.14).

8.78   Where the prisoner wants to call witnesses, the adjudicator may ask what their evidence will show. Unless it is considered that their evidence is irrelevant, the witnesses named should be called. If the adjudicator refuses to allow the witnesses to be called, then s/he must note the reason for refusal on the written record of the adjudication. The prisoner must be told the reason and allowed to comment upon it. Where witnesses are produced, they should be invited to say all that they know of the incident. The adjudicator, prisoner and the reporting officer will be allowed to cross-examine them (paras 10.15–10.20).

8.79   When all of the evidence has been heard, the adjudicator should ask the prisoner whether s/he wishes to say anything further before considering the question of guilt. The adjudicator should only find the prisoner guilty if satisfied that all of the essential elements of the charge are present (see above) (para 10.22). The adjudicator may not reduce or change the charge during the hearing, and thus if it is thought that the prisoner is guilty of a lesser charge the current charge must be dismissed and a new one laid so long as it is still within 48 hours of the discovery of the alleged offence. Any new hearing should be before a different adjudicator (para 10.23).

8.80   The adjudicator must announce whether the prisoner has been found guilty or not guilty, and record the finding on the written record. A prisoner who is found guilty of a charge should be asked whether they want to put forward any mitigating evidence, and may also call witnesses in support of the mitigation (paras 10.24–10.25).

8.81   Before the adjudicator decides on an appropriate punishment, an officer will be called to give a report as to the prisoner's custodial behaviour, including previous findings of guilt at adjudication. The prisoner should be given an opportunity to question the officer on the information contained in the conduct report (paras 10.24–10.26). Unless the adjudicator decides to adjourn the hearing to consider the matter of the punishment to be awarded, the prisoner should be told what the punishment is to be, and if the prisoner has been found guilty of more than one offence whether the punishments are to be consecutive or concurrent. If a suspended punishment imposed at a previous hearing is to be activated the adjudicator must inform the prisoner of this and explain it (paras 10.27–10.29).

Evidential matters and the standard of proof

8.82   Adjudications are considered to be administrative acts in English law, however, they operate to the same standard of proof as criminal proceedings.

Before entering a finding of guilt, the adjudicator must be satisfied of guilt beyond reasonable doubt (*R v Secretary of State for the Home Department, ex p Tarrant* [1984] 1 All ER 799).

8.83 Although the standard of proof is beyond reasonable doubt, it was stated in the *Tarrant* case that adjudicators are, 'the masters of their own procedure' and as such, the strict rules of evidence do not automatically apply at such hearings. At paragraph 5.7 of the Discipline Manual, there is a general prohibition against adjudicators relying on disputed hearsay evidence. A finding of guilt based solely on disputed hearsay evidence is considered to be unsafe. In the case of *R v Governor of HM Prison Swaleside, ex p Wynter* (1998) Times, 2 June, the Divisional Court held that the hearsay rule did not need to be strictly applied to expert scientific evidence. The case concerned the mandatory drugs testing procedures whereby the sole evidence against a prisoner consists of a written report from a laboratory scientist. Although this report was acknowledged to be hearsay evidence, it was held that a fair hearing could be achieved by relying upon the written report and cross examination of the scientist would only be necessary if the prisoner could establish some reason why it would be unreasonable for the adjudicator to rely upon the evidence in written form.

Punishments

8.84 An adjudicator may only award those punishments that are listed in the Prison Rules 1999, r 55 or the Young Offender Institution Rules 1988, rr 53 and 60. The power to award additional days to a sentence of imprisonment derives from the CJA 1991, ss 41–42. Punishments should take into account the circumstances and seriousness of the offence; the previous custodial behaviour of the prisoner; the type of prison establishment in which the offence took place; the prisoner's circumstances; whether the commission of the offence had any effect upon the regime; order and discipline within the prison; and the need to have a deterrent effect on the offender and other prisoners (Discipline Manual, para 7.6).

8.85 The Prison Service does not provide any central guidance to adjudicators on the appropriate punishments for particular offences. However, punishments handed down within any establishment should be consistent and to achieve this governors may set up a local tariff system. Adjudicators should be able to consult a list of recent offences and punishments awarded so that the chance of significant variation is diminished (para 7.7).

8.86 An adjudicator can suspend punishments for up to six months (para 7.33) or impose them to run concurrently to other punishments imposed at the same time. Suspended punishments may be ignored, activated in full, activated in part (in which case the remainder will lapse), or an adjudicator may change the suspension period by suspending the punishment for a further six months from the date of the current adjudication if the prisoner commits another breach of prison discipline within the original period of suspension (paras 7.33–7.34).

8.87   Otherwise, all punishments other than the award of additional days of imprisonment to be served will take effect immediately they are handed down (paras 7.11–7.12). Pregnant women should not normally be given punishments whereby they will be segregated, and if an adjudicator thinks that someone is unfit to be punished, then no punishment should be imposed (paras 7.13 and 7.10).

8.88   The punishments contained in the Prison and Young Offender Institution Rules are listed below together with a brief explanation of what they entail:

(a)   Caution—a warning not to repeat the offending behaviour;

(b)   Forfeiture of facilities—the withdrawal of privileges listed in the Prison Rules 1999, r 8 for up to 42 days for adult prisoners and up to 21 days for young offenders;

(c)   Exclusion from associated work or activities—this punishment is usually served on normal location in the prison and is for a maximum of 21 days for adult prisoners. The equivalent punishment for young offenders is that they may be excluded from any activity taking place in the YOI other than training courses, work, education or physical education;

(d)   Stoppage of earnings—all or part of a prisoner's pay may be stopped for up to the equivalent of 42 days full pay for adults or 21 days for young offenders. This punishment may be spread over 84 days and 42 days respectively;

(e)   Cellular confinement—may be imposed for up to 14 days for adult prisoners and seven days for young offenders aged 18 or over so long as the medical officer certifies that the prisoner is fit to undergo this punishment. Cells should be set aside in which prisoners serving a period of cellular confinement are located. These should contain a bed, bedding, table, chair and access to sanitary facilities. The bedding and mattress may be taken from the cell during the daytime for up to the first three days of the punishment if the adjudicator so specifies at adjudication. Otherwise, prisoners should be allowed all facilities other than those which are 'incompatible with cellular confinement' such as use of the canteen, use of private cash, and association with other prisoners (para 7.22). Prisoners who are serving periods in cellular confinement should be checked on by an officer at least once every hour, and visited every day by the chaplain and the medical officer (para 7.24). Prisoners should be allowed to receive visits and have access to the telephone unless their 'behaviour and attitude made removal from cellular confinement impracticable or undesirable' (para 7.23). In practice it is rare for prisoners to be refused visits, and any visitor turned away from an establishment should make enquiries of the governor as to the reasons for the refusal and contact a legal adviser if they are worried;

(f)   Additional days—adult prisoners may be awarded up to 42 additional days of imprisonment in respect of any one offence (or offences arising from a single incident) if they are serving a determinate sentence. Lifers cannot be given additional days as a punishment. Additional days affect the prisoner's sentence by pushing back the parole eligibility date of prisoners sentenced before 1 October 1992 and the non-parole release date of prisoners serving sentences of four years and over. Remand and unsentenced prisoners may be given the prospective punishment of additional days and this will only take effect if they are sentenced to a period of imprisonment. This punishment cannot be awarded to young prisoners serving a Detention and Training Order;

(g)   Extra work—is only available as a punishment for young offenders, who may be required to work for up to two extra hours a day for up to 21 days;

(h)   Removal from a wing or living unit—may only be used to punish young offenders for up to 21 days. Young offenders undergoing this punishment will be held in a cell or a room away from their normal wing but will otherwise be able to participate in the full regime of the YOI;

(i)   Possessions of unconvicted or unsentenced prisoners—the right to have books, writing materials and 'other means of occupation' can be forfeited for any period. If found guilty of escaping or attempting to escape they may forfeit their right to wear their own clothing (paras 7.15–7.32).

Appealing against findings of guilt

8.89   Prisoners may apply for a finding of guilt at adjudication to be reviewed through the requests/complaints procedure by submitting a requests/complaint appeal form to the Prisoner Casework Unit or Directorate of High Security Prisons Support Unit at Prison Service Headquarters. The prisoner or legal adviser may ask for a transcript of the adjudication in order to prepare their appeal, and they should not be charged any photocopying fees in connection with this (para 9.5).

8.90   The appropriate team at Prison Service Headquarters will conduct a paper review of the case and will recommend to the area manager or the director of high security prisons whether to quash the finding of guilt and remit any punishments awarded.

8.91   Guidance in the Prisoners' Requests/Complaints Procedures Staff Manual states that where a solicitor writes to Prison Service Headquarters asking for a transcript of the adjudication, the adjudication should be reviewed and the transcript sent out only if the guilty verdict is not quashed (annex N, para 3.3).

8.92   If, after considering representations from a solicitor or a request/complaint from the prisoner the area manager upholds the finding of guilt, the prisoner may ask the Prisons Ombudsman to review the decision so long as the request is made within one month of the final reply from the Prison Service.

8.93   Applications for judicial review may be lodged either against the adjudicator's finding of guilt, the area manager's decision to uphold that finding, or the Prison Service's refusal to act upon a recommendation from the Ombudsman that the finding of guilt should be quashed. As a matter of good practice, it is generally advisable to use the internal review process through an application to Prison Service Headquarters before applying for judicial review. In cases where this line of 'appeal' is not followed, the permission hearing will often be adjourned to allow the Prison Service to conduct its own review potentially causing further delays to the application.

8.94   The question of whether a governor's finding of guilt can be directly reviewed has been the subject of much litigation. However, in *Leech v Deputy Governor of Parkhurst Prison* [1988] 1 All ER 485 the matter was finally settled. The House of Lords confirmed that although governors are servants of the Home Secretary in general terms, they are not acting as such when they are fulfilling their disciplinary roles. In those circumstances governors are exercising 'the independent power conferred...by the Rules' and thus the Home Secretary has no authority to direct the governor. Therefore, judicial review proceedings may be taken directly against a governor's decision.

Applying for remission of additional days

8.95   The Prison Rules 1999, r 61(2) allows prisoners who have been awarded additional days of imprisonment at adjudication to apply to have them remitted. In order to be eligible to have an application considered, a prisoner must have been awarded no further additional days for a period of six months if an adult or four months if a young offender (para 8.5). The prisoner need not have been in prison custody throughout that period, and may have been in a special hospital, community home, in police custody, or temporarily released under the Prison Rules 1999, r 9 (para 8.6).

8.96   The application process starts when a prisoner completes form F2129A and submits it for consideration. A prison officer will complete form F2129B which details the offences which led to the award of additional days, and also gives information about the prisoner's behaviour since. Where the prisoner has been held in another prison for at least half of the qualifying period, staff there should also be asked to submit a report. Reports from prison staff should be accurate and unbiased and should not include unsubstantiated information (paras 8.9–8.12).

8.97   The application is considered by a governor within one month of being submitted by the prisoner. Prisoners are allowed to appear before the governor and give information about the application orally if they wish to do so. In such cases all reports considered by the governor should also be read to the prisoner so that s/he has an opportunity to comment on them. The report writers should also be present so that the prisoner may ask questions of them or they can give further information if necessary (para 8.13).

8.98   In making a decision as to whether to remit the additional days awarded, paragraph 8.15 advises that the governor should take the following factors into account:

(a)   whether the prisoner has a constructive approach to their imprisonment, makes the most of opportunities to participate in the regime and respects any trust placed in them;

(b)   whether there has been any genuine change of attitude on the prisoner's part;

(c)   the nature of the original breach of prison discipline for which the additional days were awarded and whether it is appropriate to remit days in recognition of a constructive approach and a change of attitude.

8.99   If a governor decides to remit additional days that were awarded at a governor's adjudication, the number of days remitted should not normally amount to more than half of the days awarded for any one offence unless it is considered that the offence was not serious, there are exceptional circumstances, or the additional days date back to an adjudication conducted by the Board of Visitors (para 8.15(c)).

8.100   Prisoners are informed of the outcome of the application immediately and they should also be given a written decision on form F2129C within seven days of consideration of the application. This form should give details of the reasons for the decision, when they may apply again for the remission of additional days, and where appropriate any amendments to their sentence dates (para 8.17).

The Human Rights Act and prison discipline

8.101   The Human Rights Act 1998 could have potentially far reaching effects on prison discipline. The view of the English courts has always been that prison disciplinary hearings do not amount to criminal proceedings but are administrative tribunals and as such, adjudicators are given a wide degree of discretion as to how to conduct the disciplinary hearings. However, it is arguable that the prison disciplinary system should attract, at least in part, the safeguards of the criminal trial process as protected by art 6 and, to a lesser extent, art 5.

8.102   The European Court has not been called upon to examine the prison disciplinary system in its current form. The only cases which have looked at prison discipline in this country were in respect of the system that pertained prior to the CJA 1991 when the more serious charges were dealt with by the Boards of Visitors who had far more extensive powers of punishment. However, the principles that derive from those cases do have some application to the current system and provide an indication of how prison discipline may come to be dealt with domestically under the Human Rights Act.

8.103   The leading case on prison discipline is *Campbell and Fell v United Kingdom* (1982) 5 EHRR 207. In *Campbell*, the European Court held that prison discipline must be looked at autonomously from the domestic law when assessing whether the proceedings were civil or criminal (as per the decision in *Engels v Netherlands* (1976) 1 EHRR 647. Therefore, it becomes necessary to examine the nature of the charge to assess whether it can be properly characterised as 'criminal' and the nature and severity of the punishments available if a finding of guilt is made. On the first test, there are clearly some charges which have no parallel with the criminal law and which make it impossible to characterise a charge as criminal (eg refuses to work) whereas some charges have direct parallels in the criminal law (eg commits any assault). On the second test, the Court overruled an earlier decision of the Commission which had held that the loss of remission following a prison disciplinary hearing did not affect the liberty of the subject as it was effectively the loss of a privilege—the early release from a prison sentence—rather than a direct loss of liberty (*Kiss v United Kingdom* (1976) 7 D & R 55). The Court in *Campbell and Fell* formed the opinion that the early release provisions were implemented uniformly and as of right for all prisoners and that it was immaterial whether they were seen as a privilege or a right, as the practical effect was the deprivation of liberty.

8.104   Since the decision in *Campbell and Fell* there have been three key changes to the prison disciplinary system: all adjudications are now dealt with by governors (or controllers at contracted out prisons); the punishments available are limited to 42 additional days; and the early release provisions and the description of disciplinary awards as 'additional days' on the prison sentence are statutory (CJA 1991, ss 32 and 41). The statutory recognition of the right to 'early release' from a prison sentence and the recognition that punishments are additional days on that sentence considerably strengthen the argument that the nature of punishments available mean that the proceedings should properly be characterised as criminal. The key issue is whether a penalty of 42 days is sufficiently serious to meet this criterion.

8.105   The answer to this question might lie in the Court's decision in *Benham v United Kingdom* (1996) 22 EHRR 293. In *Benham*, the European Court found a breach of art 6 through the failure to afford legal representation to persons facing imprisonment for failing to pay the community charge. One of the factors that persuaded the Court that the proceedings were criminal and afforded the protection of art 6 was the actual punishment imposed of 30 days' imprisonment against a maximum available punishment of three months' imprisonment. Given that imprisonment for default in such cases attracts the automatic early release provisions at one-half, the actual and potential punishments are almost identical to those available at adjudications. This provides powerful arguments to suggest that the current prison disciplinary system could be considered to be in breach of the Convention.

8.106   The possible implications for the prison disciplinary system are vast. Although it will never be the case that all prison disciplinary charges can be classified as 'criminal' proceedings, there is a powerful argument that the more serious charges will be, and for particular classes of prisoner, such as young offenders and remand prisoners, the arguments are even more powerful. On average, over 120,000 adjudications are conducted in prison each year and of these there is legal representation at approximately 20. If only a small proportion of these hearings attract art 6 safeguards, there will be a huge increase in legal representation. The role of the prison governor as the adjudicator will also be called into question as it is difficult to envisage how the governor's role as prison manger and administrator can be properly reconciled with the requirement for such cases to be heard before an impartial tribunal. The Woolf report considered the possibility of visiting magistrates hearing the more serious charges which are akin to criminal charges, with the governor being confined to dealing with charges for which the only punishment would be the loss of privileges (Cm 1546, paras 14.398–14.418). Although Woolf was equivocal on the answer, the report having been prepared in advance of the current disciplinary system being implemented, this may well prove to be the long-term solution to the problem.

THE INFORMAL DISCIPLINARY SYSTEM

Rule 45   Good order and discipline

8.107   The Prison Rules 1999, r 45, provides for the removal of prisoners from normal location to the segregation block of an establishment. This may be for the prisoner's own protection (most commonly for sex offenders, prisoners who are in debt to other prisoners, or informants), or as a solution to the problem of managing prisoners whose presence on the wing is thought to pose a threat to the good order and discipline of the wing.

8.108   Governors have a power to segregate prisoners for up to three days (r 45(2)). Segregation for a longer period requires the approval of a member of the Board of Visitors or the Home Secretary. PSO 1701 states that members of the Board of Visitors are expected to see and speak to segregated prisoners in every case where continued authority for segregation has been requested (para 3.31). In exceptional circumstances the Secretary of State may authorise continued segregation for the same period as can be authorised by the Board of Visitors. This power can be exercised by the area manager for the prison.

8.109   When segregation has been approved by a member of the Board of Visitors or the Secretary of State prisoners may be segregated for up to one month (r 45(3)). However, the Board of Visitors may authorise a shorter period of segregation if they believe it appropriate in the circumstances (PSO 1701, para 2.1.4). Although segregation may have been authorised for one month it should not necessarily follow that a prisoner has to be segregated throughout that whole time and they may be returned to normal location at the governor's discretion (r 45(3)). In practice such a move would not take place unless it were considered that the prisoner's return to the wing would not undermine the good order and discipline of the establishment.

8.110   The chaplain and a medical officer should visit a prisoner at least once every three days throughout the period of segregation (PSO 1701, para 3.1.1). If at any time the medical officer recommends that the prisoner is unfit for segregation, then s/he must be returned to normal location (r 45(3)).

8.111   Although PSO 1701 states that:

> 'the regime for each prisoner for the purpose of good order and discipline must be no less than the level of privileges provided for under the Prison Rules' (para 2.3.3)

the reality for most prisoners is that they will be subjected to an impoverished regime held in a cell in the segregation block for 23 hours per day, with the other hour being spent on exercise. Segregation blocks have their own exercise yards and these are usually extremely small and often have a cage-like appearance. In some segregation blocks prisoners are required to exercise completely alone, in others more than one prisoner is allowed out at a time.

8.112   PSO 1701 draws governors' attention to the need to provide access to religious services, time in the open air, toiletries and washing facilities,

117

work, access to telephones, education and library facilities to segregated prisoners. However, in assessing prisoners' suitability to receive these basic aspects of the regime, the governor is expected to:

'make a judgement on the balance between the needs of the individual and the maintenance of order or the safety of staff or prisoners.' (para 2.3.3)

8.113   A governor should visit each prisoner held on r 45 every day.

8.114   Prisoners must be given oral reasons for their segregation at the time that they are removed from normal location and these should be followed by written reasons within 24 hours. The written reasons should be given on form F1299D, which should be signed by a governor grade. Reasons given on form F1299D should be exactly the same as those reasons given on the Governor's Authority for Segregation for up to 72 hours (F1299B) and the Continued Authorisation by Board of Visitors Member (F1299C), both of which are retained by the prison. However, exceptions arise where it is considered that to disclose those detailed reasons to the prisoner:

'is considered likely to endanger the safety of others or the security of the establishment.'

In such cases the prisoner should be given reasons for their segregation which remove all references which may pose a threat.

8.115   Whilst on paper the requirement to give reasons appears satisfactory, in practice this is often not the case. Prisoners are often told that they are being held in segregation because their behaviour on normal location threatened the smooth running of the establishment, however such assertions do not often give detailed examples of the particular behaviour complained of.

8.116   A period of segregation under r 45 can be extended at the end of each month for an indefinite period so long as the governor and the Board of Visitors/ Home Secretary authorise segregation, and the medical officer does not object.

8.117   Prisoners may query their segregation by submitting a request/ complaint to the governor asking for the reasons to be amplified and the decision to be reviewed. Many prisoners will also want to apply for a transfer to a different prison where they will be able to start afresh. Appeals against the governor's reply may be submitted to the area manager, and the Prisons Ombudsman may be asked to review the area manager's decisions.

8.118   The litigation on the use of and conditions of segregation has produced disappointing results. In the conjoined appeals *R v Deputy Governor of Parkhurst Prison, ex p Hague; Weldon v Home Office* [1992] 1 AC 58, prisoners argued that their segregation and detention in a strip cell constituted breach of statutory duty and false imprisonment by depriving them of their residual liberty. The House of Lords held that no prisoner could bring an action for breach of the Prison Rules as they were merely regulatory and not designed to protect a prisoner against loss, injury or damage. Furthermore, no right of action lay in false imprisonment as the prisoners were lawfully committed to prison and had no right to do what they wanted, when they wanted, as their lives were governed by the prison regime. Detention could not become unlawful when the conditions became intolerable.

8.119 However, the House of Lords confirmed that a person who is held lawfully in prison and who is subjected to intolerable conditions does have remedies. These would be an action in negligence where the intolerable conditions caused the prisoner to suffer injury to his health, an action for assault where appropriate, an action for misfeasance in public office if malice could be established, and the termination of such conditions by judicial review.

Instruction to Governors 28/93

8.120 Instruction to Governors 28/93 provides a 'Management Strategy for Disruptive Inmates' which gives staff at Prison Service Headquarters the power to compel prison governors to accept 'disruptive' prisoners at their establishments. Governors do have a right to appeal against the allocation of a prisoner whom they do not want to accept.

8.121 All convicted prisoners held in category B prisons are liable to be dealt with under the strategy if they are deemed to pose '*serious* control problems.' The aim is to 'secure the return of a disruptive inmate to a settled pattern of behaviour on normal location'.

8.122 The instruction introduced a five stage management strategy for dealing with disruptive prisoners. However, only the first three of those stages are still in use. The fourth stage has been overtaken by the introduction of the close supervision centre system, which replaced the special unit system which was the fourth stage of the strategy.

8.123 Following recommendations contained in the Woolf Report, safeguards were introduced to protect prisoners who were being 'ghosted' (transferred in the interests of the good order and discipline of an establishment). These safeguards are incorporated into IG 28/93:

'(a) no inmate should be transferred as a form of punishment;
 (b) the reasoned grounds for transfer must be recorded and noted on an inmate's record;
 (c) inmates must be advised in writing of the reasons for their transfer or segregation within 24 hours of such actions;
 (d) all appropriate security measures must be taken over the transfer of category A inmates, including the prior approval of the Population Management Section in the case of exceptional and high risk inmates;
 (e) requests/complaints about a transfer must be replied to within seven days by the governor of the establishment where the transfer decision is taken;
 (f) intending visitors should be notified of an inmates transfer including, where appropriate, by the inmate himself;
 (g) decisions on segregating inmates under r 45 are matters for the governor, and subsequently the Board of Visitors, in the establishment in which the inmate is then being held.' (para 9)

8.124   The Management Programme: Stage 1—Internal action at the parent establishment. In the first instance governors are advised that when a disruptive or subversive prisoner comes to their attention, they should consider whether there is cause to lay a disciplinary charge against that prisoner for breach of r 51, try to ascertain the reasons for disruptive behaviour, and try to persuade the prisoner to change that behaviour. Consideration should be given to moving the prisoner within the prison, either to another prison wing or to the segregation block under r 45. If this approach does not cause the prisoner to settle, or there are other 'exceptional' (undefined) circumstances, the prisoner will move on to stage 2.

8.125   Stage 2—Temporary transfer from the parent establishment. If the governor considers that the temporary transfer of a 'seriously disruptive inmate is unavoidable', then transfer to a local prison may be arranged. This transfer is arranged in consultation with Prison Service Headquarters who advises as to the availability of vacant cells, which are always in the segregation blocks of local prisons. The prisoner is then transferred for a period of up to one month, and at this time the expectation will be that the prisoner will return to the parent establishment when the month expires. Prisoners and prison staff refer to this period as a 'lay down' and the idea is that it will provide a suitable cooling off period for the prisoner who will then be prepared to settle.

8.126   If, however, the governor of the parent establishment does not want to take the prisoner back, then s/he may apply to the relevant department of Prison Service Headquarters explaining the reasons why a return to the establishment is thought to be unsuitable. If Headquarters accepts the governor's representations it will arrange for the prisoner to be allocated to another prison (stage 3). Alternatively it will reject the representations and order the governor to take the prisoner back.

8.127   Stage 3—Centrally managed transfers to training and local establishments. If it is decided that the prisoner will not return to the parent establishment then Prison Service Headquarters will arrange reallocation to either a high security prison, a local prison or a category B training prison. Governors are compelled to accept prisoners who are allocated to their establishments under stage 3, although they are able to 'appeal' to their area managers who liaise with Headquarters in an attempt to reach a solution.

8.128   Decisions to move prisoners through the stages of the Management Strategy are judicially reviewable, although a successful challenge is unlikely. Whilst prisoners are entitled to be informed in writing of the reasons for their transfer under IG 28/93, such reasons will often be vague. In *Ex p Ross* (1994) Times, 9 June, CA, a prisoner was transferred on the basis that he was a 'disruptive prisoner who is doing his best to destabilise the wing'. No specific incidents were alluded to, and when pressed the governor did not provide any evidence against the prisoner in question. In a renewed application for leave to move for judicial review, the Court of Appeal found that the governor was under no requirement to give 'chapter and verse' of the reasons why the prisoner was transferred, and said that a governor could make such a decision if he thought the prisoner's behaviour might in any way threaten the smooth running of the prison.

8.129 Transfer to a Close Supervision Centre. Close supervision centres (CSCs) have replaced special units, transfer to which was stage four of the Management Strategy for Disruptive Inmates. The CSC system was first introduced in February 1998 following the insertion of a new Rule 43A into the Prison Rules 1964. The provision for CSCs is now contained in the Prison Rules 1999, r 46, which empowers the Secretary of State to direct a prisoner's removal from association and to confine him in a close supervision centre. The authority to remove a prisoner from normal location should not exceed one month, but this can be renewed at the end of each one month period (r 46(2)).

8.130 In practice prisoners are allocated to CSCs by the CSC Selection Committee which meets monthly to select prisoners for the CSC system, to review assessment reports prepared on unit prisoners, to authorise movement between units and to authorise movement of prisoners back into the mainstream system. Detailed Operating Standards were first published by the Prison Service in September 1998 (and updated in May 1999) and these should be made available to prisoners held in the CSC. It is essential to obtain the Operating Standards from the Prison Service when advising prisoners detained in a CSC.

8.131 To enter the CSC system, prisoners must meet one or more of the allocation criteria. They must have:

(a)   been violent to staff and/or prisoners;
(b)   regularly incurred disciplinary reports;
(c)   caused serious damage to property in prison;
(d)   shown dangerous behaviour (such as roof top protests or hostage taking);
(e)   failed to respond to earlier measures to improve control; or
(f)   been on continuous segregation under r 45 for a period of three months or more (Close Supervision Centre Operating Standards, annex 1).

8.132 Within 48 hours of arriving in the CSC each prisoner should receive an allocation letter which clearly sets out the reasons for their selection. This should contain reference to specific instances of disruptive behaviour. The prisoner will be given the opportunity to make written representations against his transfer (Operating Standards, para 1.8). These representations will then be considered at the next monthly meeting of the CSC Selection Committee.

8.133 Prisoners will be deselected from the unit if:

(a)   there is evidence from assessment by a forensic psychologist/psychiatrist that the prisoner is suffering from symptoms of florid mental illness;
(b)   the prisoner's behaviour can be dealt with more appropriately elsewhere in the prison system (Operating Standards, annex 1).

8.134 It was originally envisaged that the purpose of the CSCs would be to address and stabilise disruptive and dangerous behaviour to prepare for a return to the mainstream prison population. However, since May 1999, a new function was ascribed to the CSCs which enables prisoners to be detained there indefinitely if the prisoner continues to pose a threat to the safety of staff or other prisoners so that long-term containment is the only option (Operating Standards, Statement of Purpose, para 2(v)).

8.135   The CSC system operates two units, at Woodhill and Durham prisons. Woodhill is normally the first stage of entry to the CSC and places at Durham are designed for prisoners with psychiatric needs and those who have successfully completed the programme at Woodhill who are being prepared for a return to the mainstream high security prisons. Selection for the psychiatric unit at Durham (I wing) is dependent upon staff from Durham interviewing the prisoner and a psychiatric assessment confirming that the prisoner does not have an active mental illness warranting in-patient treatment at a secure hospital (Operating Standards, para 1.7).

8.136   For prisoners who are not transferred to the psychiatric unit at Durham, the first CSC placement will be in Woodhill. Woodhill is divided into a number of wings, with prisoners first being placed on an assessment wing (B wing), also termed the 'Structured Regime Centre'. Prisoners who fail to comply with the regime can be moved to a basic wing (A wing) or segregated within the CSC (D wing). Those who comply with targets are moved to a more open regime (C wing), known as the 'Programmes Intervention Centre'.

8.137   Prisoners who continue to be considered disruptive within the CSC can be moved to one of seven high control cells (HCCs) located in segregation units in the high security prisons for a period of 56 days (Operating Standards, para 1.26). Although the prisoner is not in one of the two CSC units, he will still come to be managed under the auspices of the Prison Rules, r 46, and the prison governor and Board of Visitors will have no jurisdiction over his segregation or the privileges whilst in the HCC. The lack of any statutory definition of a CSC or designation procedure for parts of the prison estate to be classified as CSCs raises some concerns over the source of the authority for such transfers. It is also surprising that such transfers have had to be built into a system which was intended to replace the old system of constantly moving disruptive prisoners (often referred to as the 'ghost train'). The Secretary of State is expected to amend r 46 to provide clearer designation procedures for both CSCs and HCCs.

8.138   Prisoners who progress through the system at Woodhill satisfactorily will normally be moved to Durham G wing before being returned to the mainstream prison system (Operating Standards, para 5G). The purpose of the wing is:

'(i)   to manage prisoners in a positive activity based small centre environment providing counselling and cognitive behaviour programmes to individual inmates;

(ii)   to prepare prisoners for a return to normal location, liaising directly with mainstream prisons and developing specific re-entry programmes for individual inmates.' (Operating Standards, para 5G.1)

8.139   The philosophy behind the unit is to provide a more punitive environment for prisoners who refuse to comply with the regimes in place, and the conditions on the restricted regime and the segregation unit are the most spartan within the prison system. In segregation, for example prisoners have no physical contact with other prisoners at all, have no radios, receive the minimum number of visits and only two telephone calls per week. These conditions were strongly criticised following inspections by the Prison Reform Trust and the Chief Inspector of Prisons. The long-term impact of such conditions on prisoners is worrying, particularly as there is no limit of time for which they can be detained there.

8.140   Two of the first prisoners to be selected for the CSC at Woodhill commenced proceedings against the failure to provide them with adequate reasons for their selection. During the course of the proceedings, the Prison Service published the Operating Standards and the applications ultimately failed. Turner J was very critical of the manner in which the Prison Service had introduced the CSCs but, as a matter of law, he found that the decision to allocate a prisoner to a CSC was not 'adverse' and thus there was no common law requirement of procedural fairness in the process (*R v Secretary of State for the Home Department, ex p Mehmet and O'Connor* (1999) 11 Admin LR 529, HC). Since that decision, a number of further legal challenges have been commenced pertaining to both the general conditions in Woodhill and the treatment of particular prisoners although these have not concluded at the time of writing.

Prisoner informants

8.141   Governors will often run into problems in providing prisoners with the reasons for their segregation under r 45 or their transfer under IG 28/93 because of the need to protect the identity of other prisoners. It is relatively common for one prisoner to provide information about the activities of another by having a private conversation with staff or by placing a 'note in the box'. Each prison wing has a box on it where prisoners post the correspondence that they wish to send out of the prison. Sometimes, a prisoner will also post an anonymous note informing the authorities of the activities of another prisoner, for example that an escape attempt is being planned, drugs are being sold, or someone is planning to take a hostage. The notes will be referred to the Security Department within the prison, and if information is thought to be reliable, the suspected prisoner will be segregated or transferred.

8.142   There is also a more formal Inmate Informant System, the mechanics of which are laid out in the Prison Service's Security Manual. The Inmate Informant System recognises that prisoners are one of the best sources of security intelligence, and that the best informants are 'prisoners who have the respect of other prisoners and who are regarded as above suspicion' (Security Manual, para 15.1). Prison governors do not have to adopt the Inmate Informant System, although they are advised that to do so will maximise security intelligence and ensure that staff dealing with informants behave properly.

8.143   Each prison which adopts the Inmate Informant System should appoint a manager who is responsible for staff dealing with informants, available to advise and brief staff, and who ensures that all information received is processed and assessed for reliability. The manager also identifies likely informers, records rewards given to them and maintains secure records of the names of informants.

8.144   Seven particular types of prisoner are identified as being most likely to be willing to provide information:

(a)   those who are well settled in prison and unlikely to welcome disruption to their life styles from other prisoners;
(b)   those who relate easily to staff;
(c)   those anxious to change their life style and distance themselves from other more criminal prisoners;

(d)   those whose offences suggest that their criminality is not well established;

(e)   those who are known to have provided information to prison or police authorities in the past;

(f)   those due for release in the near future (para 15.13).

8.145   Prisoners who pass information to the prison authorities can expect to be rewarded for their trouble. Rewards given are supposed to relate to the usefulness of the information that they have provided. The following rewards are suggested:

(a)   a commitment to report directly on the informant's work to third parties (including the Parole Board);

(b)   acknowledgement that a prisoner's approach to criminal behaviour has changed, justifying progress to better regimes or lower security categorisation;

(c)   the sympathetic consideration of transfer requests where security factors permit;

(d)   additional facilities, for example longer visits, favourable job allocations, and access to other discretionary facilities available within the establishment;

(e)   payments of incentive bonuses within the provisions of the prisoners' pay scheme;

(f)   in particularly worthy cases, a recommendation may be made that the use of the Royal Prerogative of Mercy be considered to remit part of a sentence as a reward for meritorious acts (para 15.14).

8.146   Staff dealing with informants are warned that they should only offer the above rewards; that they must only reward a prisoner when information has been delivered and after they have received any necessary authority; that rewards may be visible to other prisoners and this may place the informant at risk. The risk of informers using the system for their own means and providing fabricated information in order to receive a reward is recognised.

8.147   Staff who 'handle' informants may be selected for their skills in developing relationships, their post within the prison or their experience of working within prisons. In particular, staff who frequently deal with prisoners in privacy whilst they are conducting cell searches, acting in a personal officer role, or dealing with prisoners' applications are the best placed to extract good quality information without arousing the suspicion of other prisoners and thus putting the informant at risk.

CHAPTER 9

RIGHTS AND PRIVILEGES

INTRODUCTION

9.1 The question of what prisoners are entitled to in terms of contact with the outside world, with each other, their possessions and other facilities is a complicated one. The position has changed drastically over the last decade, and will be affected by the coming into force of the Human Rights Act 1998. The Prison Act 1952 and Prison Rules do contain minimum entitlements in some areas (eg to a minimum number of social visits in the Prison Rules 1999, r 35) but what prisoners should expect on top of these, or where the statutory framework is silent, has been a matter of debate. The Woolf Report following the prison riots in 1990 recommended that Standing Order 4, which deals with facilities for prisoners, should be amended to:

> 'make clear the facilities which should normally be provided for prisoners. The amendments should recognise that these facilities should no longer be provided as privileges, but as a prisoner's normal expectation.' (para 14.35)

This was suggested to ensure consistency between prisons, the lack of which had fed prisoners' grievances. The report suggested that facilities that were not part of the prisoner's 'basic standard of life' could be forfeited only as a result of disciplinary proceedings. Despite the huge effect of the Woolf report in other areas no such amendments were made.

9.2 By contrast, the Woodcock Enquiry into the Whitemoor escapes in 1994 recommended that the Prison Service should quickly resolve the issue and that:

> 'the underlying premise should be that all allowances are "privileges," to be earned by good behaviour and work performance, with sanctions for bad behaviour.' (recommendation 50)

Accordingly in the following year the Prison Rules were amended (see now the Prison Rules 1999, r 8) to allow for the introduction of 'Incentives and Earned Privileges' (IEP) schemes on the Woodcock model, which now effectively govern prisoner entitlements beyond the basic level. Because the rule allows each prison to have their own scheme (as long as it meets the requirements of a national framework), the very mischief identified by the Woolf report, of arbitrary differences between prisons fostering resentment, has been perpetuated. A fuller discussion of IEP schemes follows below.

9.3   Another problem for prisoners is that those areas that are not governed by statute are subject to policy changes throughout a prisoner's sentence. One example of this was when the Secretary of State significantly reduced entitlement to temporary release in respect of both newly sentenced and existing prisoners (in IG 36/1995). Prisoners who had signed compacts on the basis that they would benefit from the old entitlements argued they had a legitimate expectation to not be affected by the changes. The Court of Appeal rejected this argument holding that the only legitimate expectation the prisoners had was to the benefit of any lawful policy promulgated by the Secretary of State from time to time (*R v Secretary of State for the Home Department, ex p Hargreaves* [1997] 1 All ER 397). This leaves prisoners vulnerable to rapid changes to very important entitlements relating to the quality of their living conditions, and contact with the outside world.

9.4   There are many areas where the control of prisoners' rights and privileges by the prison authorities will engage fundamental rights. An example that has formed the basis of substantial litigation is the right of prisoners to privileged correspondence with legal advisers which engages the fundamental right of access to the court. Whilst this has always been protected to some degree, the precise extent has been subject to numerous actions both domestically and before the European Court of Human Rights. It is therefore important to bear in mind that fundamental rights may be at stake and that this will limit the level of interference permitted, and that a given policy, rule, or even statute may be vulnerable to legal challenge. When the Human Rights Act 1998 is in force prisoners will be able to argue in domestic courts that restrictions on them breach their right to enjoy the rights contained in the ECHR (see chapter 18).

9.5   The rest of this chapter will look at basic entitlements in each of the key areas in turn and then examine the implications of the introduction of IEP schemes under r 8 and the manner in which privileges beyond the basic entitlement are now linked to custodial behaviour.

VISITS

Social visits

9.6   The Prison Rules 1999, r 35(2) states that prisoners are entitled to receive, as of right, two visits in every four-week period, but this may be reduced to one visit in each four-week period if so directed by the Secretary of State. This allowance of visits is known as 'statutory visits.' The Rules make allowance for the right to a visit to be deferred by the governor whilst a prisoner is subject to cellular confinement (r 35(5)).

9.7   In addition to statutory visits, the Rules make provision for 'privilege visits' to be allowed. These may be conferred by the governor (r 35(3)) or the Board of Visitors (r 35(6)). The Secretary of State also has the power to authorise additional visits for individual or particular classes of prisoners (r 35(7)). Governor's privilege visits are to be allowed where necessary for the welfare of the prisoner's family or as part of IEP schemes, but there is no express guidance as to when the Board of Visitors should utilise its power to authorise extra visits or to allow a statutory visit to last for longer than normal.

9.8   Prisoners are also entitled to special visits from legal advisers and other people visiting in a professional capacity such as probation staff, priests and consular officials. Privilege and special visits do not count against the number of statutory visits to which a prisoner is entitled.

Remand prisoners

9.9   Unconvicted prisoners are entitled to receive as many visits as they wish, 'within such limits and subject to such conditions as the Secretary of State may direct, either generally or in a particular case' (r 35(1)). At the present time, the entitlement is to at least 90 minutes per week but it is up to the governor of each prison as to how these visits will be structured. In most prisons, it is arranged for remand prisoners to have a visit each day (except Sunday) of at least 15 minutes duration. However, it is becoming more common for as few as three visits a week to be allowed, but each visit will last longer than 15 minutes. Visitors do not need a visiting order to enter the prison, although many prisons are now asking remand prisoners' visitors to telephone in advance in an attempt to make visiting arrangements better structured. Once on a visit, the same rules apply as for convicted inmates.

Standing Order 5A

9.10   The policy document that sets out how the visits system should be administered is Standing Order 5A. This document was last consolidated in 1997 but is still in urgent need of updating, and is the only public source of policy on this topic. The main purpose of visits is to enable prisoners to maintain meaningful contact with the outside world during their time in custody. Consequently, the normal class of persons entitled to visit is defined as close relatives. These include, spouses (including 'common law' partners), parents, siblings (including half and step brothers and sisters), fiancees and people who have been in loco parentis for the prisoner or for whom the prisoner has been in loco parentis (para 30). Social visits are also allowed from other persons but are more vulnerable to be stopped by the governor if he feels that good order and discipline or security may be threatened.

9.11   All visitors must be in possession of a valid visiting order to enable admittance to the prison. Visiting orders are issued to the individual prisoner who then sends them out to the proposed visitor. They should be issued in sufficient time to enable the visit to take place as soon as it becomes due (paras 22–23). The conditions for social visits are loosely defined so as to take place in 'the most humane conditions possible' (para 24). They are to be taken in the sight of a prison officer and are liable to take place within hearing of an officer if it is deemed necessary in the interests of security (para 25). In general, up to three visitors (not including children under 10) are permitted at any one time and they should take place in a visiting room with a table. Prisoners and visitors should be allowed to embrace each other. No tape recordings or photographs may be taken and if camera or tape recorders are found, visitors will be asked to surrender them for return at the end of the visit. The film or tape is liable to confiscation and their contents should be checked. Any recording or photographs taken within the prison will be wiped and the film or tape returned to the visitor (para 28). Visits may be conducted in any language but there are provisions for visits to be conducted in English, or monitored by a person who speaks the language used or tape recorded for later translation, if it is felt necessary in the interests on prison or national security or the prevention of crime (para 29).

9.12   Special allowances are made for prisoners to accumulate visits and to visit other prisoners. If a prisoner is located in a prison where s/he is unable to receive visits, it is possible to accumulate between 3 and 26 visiting orders. The prisoner can then apply for a temporary transfer to a prison where it is possible to receive these visits. Normally, such transfers are for one month and should not be allowed more frequently that every six months (paras 11–18). Visits are also allowed between two prisoners at different prisons who fit the definition of close relatives. Arrangements can be made, subject to security and the availability of transport and accommodation, for the prisoners to be transferred to a prison where they can have a visit with each other. This privilege is to be permitted once every three months and each prisoner must surrender one visiting order (paras 20–21).

Restrictions on social visits

9.13   Closed visits may be ordered whereby prisoners and their visitors will be afforded no, or limited contact (para 24). These can be imposed 'where security or control considerations so require' and are commonly used when prisoners are suspected of receiving unauthorised articles during visits (although in cases where drugs are involved see below) or where behaviour in the visits room has breached standards of good order and discipline. There is no limitation on the time for which closed visits may be enforced under this provision although they are commonly used for periods of one to two months in the first instance. Closed visits do not form part of the punishment available following an adjudication and the decision must be made on its own merits. It therefore follows that this decision can be made even when there has been no formal disciplinary charge made against a prisoner.

9.14   The Prison Rules 1999, r 34(1) contains a catch-all provision allowing restrictions to be placed upon visits in the interests of good order and discipline or the prevention of crime. The power to exclude visitors should only be used in exceptional circumstances for close relatives but is more widely available for other classes of persons. In general, it is more appropriate to consider the use of closed visits before a decision to exclude a visitor is made. The governor is also empowered to exclude visits to or from persons under 18 years of age where it is felt that this would not be in the best interests of the visitor or the inmate.

9.15   PSO 4400, chapter 1 introduced child protection measures in November 1998 designed to 'minimise the risks that certain prisoners, particularly those convicted of, or charged with, sexual offences against children may present to children whilst in prison.' The Order introduced a new provision into Standing Order 5A by replacing para 33(3) which now states that convicted prisoners:

> 'identified as presenting a risk to children should be permitted to receive visits only from their own children and their siblings, unless exceptionally the governor believes that it is in the best interests of a child not in this category to visit.'

'Own children' for this purpose is defined to include stepchildren, adopted children and children of a prisoner's partner if they were living together before sentence. Guidance on the exercise of this power, including how prisoners should be identified as a risk to children, is given in PSO 4400 which makes it clear that its primary purpose is to prevent the 'grooming' of children for exploitation by paedophiles (para 1.1.2). The Order also introduced para 33(4) into Standing Order 5A which states that unaccompanied children should not normally be allowed to visit prisoners who present a risk to children.

9.16 When the Prison Rules 1999 came into force in April 1999, a new rule 73 was included that states:

> '(1) Without prejudice to any other powers to prohibit or restrict entry to prisons, and to his powers under rules 34 and 35, the Secretary of State may, with a view to securing discipline and good order or the prevention of crime or in the interests of any persons, impose prohibitions on visits by a person to a prison or to a prisoner for such periods of time as he considers necessary.'

This power is not to be used to prohibit visits from members of Boards of Visitors or to stop legal visits. The specific purpose of the new rule was to facilitate the issuing of guidance to governors on measures to be taken against visitors found to be smuggling drugs into prisons. Such guidance is found in PSO 3610 which states that visitors found to be smuggling drugs into prisons should normally be banned from visiting for at least three months, followed by a period of closed visits for three months (para 3(ii)–(xiii)). The Order states that the power can only be used if a visitor 'is found to be engaging in this activity' and not on the basis of intelligence alone, or on the indication of a drugs dog (paras 6–7).

9.17 The order states that a ban must be the normal response unless there are 'exceptional reasons' for not imposing one (para 3(ii)). Circumstances where the governor should exercise his discretion not to impose a ban are detailed in para 9:

- '• If a ban would cause disproportionate harm to the prisoner's or visitor's right to a family life (protected by the European Convention on Human Rights, art 8).
- If a ban would cause disproportionate harm to the rights of the prisoner's child or children to access to a parent (UN Convention on the Rights of the Child, art 9(3)).
- If the prisoner is a juvenile and a ban would cause disproportionate harm to his or her right of access to a parent.
- For exceptional compassionate or other grounds.'

Notwithstanding the Order's requirements for governors to make decisions based on proper evidence, and even where drugs are found to consider a proportionate response taking into account the prisoner's and visitor's rights, in practice decisions are often clearly made with no proper consideration of the guidance. The Order states that prisoners should appeal decisions made under this rule through the normal requests/complaints procedure (para 26), and that visitors can write to the governor to appeal, who should refer the matter to the area manager if he does not wish to amend the decision (para 27). Clearly where the right to family life under art 8 is in issue, decisions where governors have not properly applied Convention standards in relation to visits in all contexts can be challenged domestically once the Human Rights Act is in force.

9.18   Visits by journalists are subject to special provisions. The general guidance is that if these are made in a professional capacity, they should not be allowed. The governor has authority to exclude these without reference to any higher authority. If the visit is in a personal capacity, the governor can require that an undertaking is given by the prospective visitor that any material obtained will not be used for publication or other professional purposes (Standing Order 5A, para 37). Standing Order 5A, para 37A allows governors to exceptionally allow journalists to visit in their professional capacity on giving a:

> 'written undertaking that no inmate will be interviewed except with the express permission in each case of the governor and the inmate concerned, that interviews will be conducted in accordance with such other conditions as the governor considers necessary, and that any material obtained at the interview will not be used for professional purposes except as permitted by the governor.'

9.19   The Prison Service's contention that these provisions did not permit interviews with journalists unless the prisoner was incapable of communicating in another way, was the subject of the case of *R v Secretary of State for the Home Department, ex p Simms and O'Brien* [1999] 3 All ER 400, HL. The House of Lords held that although the provisions of the Standing Order itself were not ultra vires the Prison Act or the Rules, there was a fundamental right for prisoners to seek through oral interviews to persuade a journalist to investigate the safety of their conviction and to publicise the findings in an effort to gain access to justice for the prisoner (an amalgam of the right to free expression with that of access to the court). This right was not inconsistent with the need to maintain order and discipline in prisons. Therefore the Secretary of State's interpretation of the Standing Order was unlawful, as such a blanket ban as he contended for could not be justified.

9.20   Although conjugal visits are allowed in some European countries, attempts to challenge the refusal of the prison authorities to allow such visits in any circumstances on the basis that such a policy breaches the prisoner's right to family life have failed. The most recent application to be considered by the Commission in Strasbourg was found to be inadmissible, notwithstanding the fact that the applicants were strict catholics who had religious objections to having artificial insemination (that is allowed), on the basis that it was still within the UK's margin of appreciation to maintain such a blanket ban (*ELH and PBH v United Kingdom* [1998] EHRLR 231).

Searching

9.21 Both prisoners and their visitors are liable to be searched. Governors have a general power to search prisoners in their custody as they deem necessary and it appears to be increasingly common for searches to take place both before and after visits. The power to search visitors must be exercised more circumspectly and it is arguable that a greater level of suspicion is required. In general, visitors to prisons will be subject to perfunctory 'pat down' searches on arrival and will be screened by the use of metal detecting equipment. The visitor cannot be required to submit to such a search, but access to the prison may be denied in that situation. More stringent searches can only be carried out with the consent of the visitor or by calling the police to carry out such procedures in accordance with PACE (see chapter 10 for a detailed discussion of searching provisions). Visits may be terminated if an officer believes it is necessary to prevent violence, where an unauthorised article has been passed, where it is suspected that the rules concerning correspondence are being contravened (eg by passing out a letter) or where a conversation is overheard that indicates an escape attempt, or a plan to commit criminal offences or pervert the course of justice (para 25).

Visits to category A prisoners

9.22 Category A prisoners are subject to special provisions. All visitors to prisoners in this category must be authorised by Prison Service Headquarters. The procedure is for category A prisoners to submit details of their proposed visitors to the prison concerned who then make arrangements for them to be vetted by the police. It is only once this approval has been obtained that the visitor is authorised to visit the establishment. Visitors to category A prisoners are more likely to be asked to submit to a search and the Woodcock Report has led to more frequent strip searches of these prisoners before and after visits. The Security Manual requires exceptional high risk category A prisoners to have closed visits unless the Director of High Security Prisons consents to open visits.

Visits by legal advisers

9.23 The Prison Rules 1999, r 38(1) requires facilities to be made available to legal advisers who are acting for prisoners in connection with legal proceedings to which the prisoner is a party. These facilities should allow the prisoner to be interviewed in sight of, but out of the hearing of, a prison officer. Rule 38(2) authorises this facility to be extended for the purposes of any other legal business but makes the authority subject to any further directions that the Secretary of State may issue.

9.24 The phrasing of this rule has been designed to take account of numerous problems that had arisen over the construction of being party to legal proceedings. Many applications had been made, both to the domestic and European Courts (see eg *Guilfoyle v Home Office* [1981] QB 309 and *R v Secretary of State for the Home Department, ex p Anderson* [1984] QB 778) in which the precise meaning of these words was debated. The Rules had previously not extended access to legal advisers for 'other legal business' and the new phrasing is clearly designed to circumvent such problems.

9.25   Various new security arrangements for legal visits with high security category A prisoners, such as observation cameras mounted above the tables at Belmarsh and 'closed visits' at Whitemoor were brought in following the Woodcock report. The use of such security measures raises problems as to how confidential advice may be given and one solicitor describes having to get on to her knees to shout through a glass partition whilst at Whitemoor. However, a challenge arguing for the removal of these restrictions for legal visits on the basis that the right to confidential legal advice was breached failed (*R v Secretary of State for the Home Department, ex p O'Dhuibhir* [1997] COD 315, CA). The court strangely adopted an analysis that the *Leech* test did not apply when fundamental rights were raised (see chapter 3 and below) and subordinate policy guidance was being considered, rather than the Prison Rules. Such an analysis cannot survive the judgment of *Simms and O'Brien* (see above, where the court considered the vires of a policy document applying the *Leech* test) and will be redundant in relation to Convention rights once the Human Rights Act 1998 has come into force.

LETTERS

9.26   The provisions for correspondence are also contained in the Prison Rules 1999, rr 34 and 35, and are closely linked to visits. Rule 35(2)(a) allows convicted prisoners to send one letter a week at public expense. Provisions are also made for prisoners to receive privilege and special letters and to exchange visiting orders for letters, at the discretion of the governor or as a privilege under IEP schemes. It is necessary to look to the Standing Orders for a more detailed explanation of what is actually permitted in practice.

9.27   Standing Order 5B commences with the following statement of principle:

> 'The policy of the Prison Service is to encourage inmates to keep in touch
> with the outside world through regular letter writing, to respect the privacy
> of correspondence to and from inmates as far as possible and to ensure that
> it is transmitted as speedily as possible.' (para 1)

9.28   Standing Order 5B authorises prisoners to send as many privilege letters as they wish each week, save at establishments where routine reading is in force (see below). The cost of sending such letters is met from prisoners' own funds. Where routine reading is in force, the governor has a discretion to set the number of privilege letters that may be sent, subject to a minimum of one a week for adults and two a week for young offenders, although prisoners should be able to send as many privilege letters as are practicable bearing in mind the staff resources available for reading correspondence (para 6A).

9.29   Special letters are issued according to need. The general guidance is that they should be issued in the following circumstances:

(i)   when they are about to be transferred to another establishment; or, if the prisoner is not given a special letter before transfer, on reception at the new establishment. The number of letters should correspond to the number of visiting orders the inmate has outstanding;

(ii)   immediately after conviction if he or she needs to settle business affairs;

(iii) where necessary for the welfare of the prisoner or his or her family;

(iv)   in connection with legal proceedings to which the prisoner is a party (but see legal correspondence below);

(v)   if necessary to enable a prisoner to write to a probation officer or to an agency arranging accommodation or employment on release;

(vi)   to write to the Parliamentary Commissioner for Administration (or the Prisons Ombudsman);

(vii) at Christmas, subject to the discretion of the governor (para 7).

The cost of special letters will normally be met from prisoners' own funds, save in the case of transfers when they should be sent at public expense.

Restrictions on correspondence

9.30   The Prison Rules 1999, r 34 contains a number of provisions that authorise restrictions on correspondence. These include the right to prevent correspondence in the interest of good order and discipline or preventing crime, or in the interests of other persons, to read and examine all letters save where forbidden by the Rules and to withdraw the right to communicate with any person where such communication is a privilege rather than a right. These provisions are implemented so as to provide for a number of restrictions on the manner in which prisoners can correspond with the outside world.

9.31   Letters must be in a particular format that includes the name of the sender and the address of the prison. Anonymous letters are forbidden and the address of the prison can only be omitted on request to the governor (para 18). On the same basis, letters sent to the prison must normally show the sender's name and address. In general, letters may be sent to any person, though recipients can request that letters are not sent and restrictions are placed on the following classes of people:

(i)   correspondence to minors may be stopped if the person having parental responsibility makes such a request (para 21(a)). Similarly, the person with parental responsibility of a minor in custody can request the stopping of correspondence between that minor and any other person except the minor's spouse (para 21(b));

(ii)   the governor may prevent correspondence between a minor in custody and any person whom it is thought it would not be in that minor's interests to communicate with. In reaching this decision, the views of the minor's parents or guardian should be sought (para 22);

(iii) convicted inmates may write to each other if they are close relatives, or if they were co-defendants and the correspondence relates to their conviction or sentence. In all other cases, the approval of both governors must be obtained (para 23);

(iv)   correspondence with ex-prisoners is permitted unless the governor considers that this would impede the rehabilitation of either party or that there would be a threat to good order or security (para 24);

133

(v)   if a prisoner wishes to write to the victim of their offences, an application must be made to the governor who will consider whether it would cause undue distress. This provision does not apply to unconvicted prisoners, or where the victim is a close family member or has already written to the prisoner (para 25);

(vi)   correspondence with any person or organisation can be stopped if the governor has reason to believe that the correspondent is engaged in activities or planning which present a genuine and serious threat to the security or good order of that prison or the prison estate (para 26);

(vii) prisoners are only able to advertise for penfriends with approval of the governor and after submitting the text of the advertisement (para 28).

9.32   Correspondence may also be prohibited on the grounds of its contents (para 34). The following is a list of prohibited material:

(i)   material which is threatening, indecent or grossly offensive, or which is known to be false;

(ii)   plans or material which would tend to assist in the commission of a criminal or disciplinary offence;

(iii) escape plans or material which jeopardises the security of the prison;

(iv)   material that would jeopardise national security;

(v)   descriptions of the making or use of any weapon, explosive, poison or other destructive device;

(vi)   obscure or coded messages which are not decipherable;

(vii) material which is indecent and obscene under the Post Office Act 1953;

(viii) material which, if sent to, or received from, a child might place his or her welfare at risk. This provision was introduced as part of the child protection measures in PSO 4400 (see above);

(ix)   material which would create a clear threat or present danger of violence or physical harm to any person, including incitement to racial hatred;

(x)   material intended for publication or broadcast which is in return for payment, and concerns the prisoner's own crime or criminal history (unless it forms part of serious representations about conviction, sentence or comment on the criminal justice system), or identifies individual members of staff or other prisoners, or which contravenes the other restrictions on correspondence;

(xi)   in the case of convicted prisoners, material constituting the conduct of business activity unless it relates to a power of attorney, the winding up of a business following conviction or the sale or transfer of personal funds, or other personal financial transactions within set limits.

9.33   In general, there is no restriction on the length of letters but the governor can set a limit of not less than four sides of A5 if routine reading is in force (para 9). Routine reading is the method by which these regulations are policed. Routine reading is reserved effectively for all prisoners in maximum security prisons, all prisoners who are normally in maximum security prisons but are temporarily in another prison, all category A prisoners and those being considered for such categorisation, whether convicted or unconvicted, all prisoners in category A units whatever their category and all prisoners on the escape list (para 32). The list also covers all prisoners on remand or convicted of making or attempting to make obscene telephone calls or sending obscene letters. In such cases, routine reading should continue as long as the governor considers necessary.

9.34 Other prisoners may also be subject to routine reading in exceptional circumstances. These will normally include the prevention or detection of a criminal offence, a threat to good order or the security of the prison. It will also be used if there is reason to believe that a prisoner may seek to infringe any of the general restrictions on correspondence or if it is in the prisoner's own interest (eg in the case of severe depression) although reading in these circumstances should be for no longer than is strictly necessary (para 32(2)).

9.35 Governors have the power to copy and disclose prisoners' letters in limited circumstances (paras 38–39). This power exists only if it is necessary to prevent an escape from prison, to prevent or reveal a miscarriage of justice, to help in the recovery of the proceeds of crime or where national security or public safety is affected. Controversially, this power can also be used to help prevent and detect crime or to convict an offender. The agencies to whom this may be disclosed include the police, the Immigration Department, Customs and Excise, MI5 and the Serious Fraud Office. The police or other investigating bodies can also make such requests to the governor but the governor must be sure that the information sought is specific and that s/he is not being asked to conduct a 'fishing expedition.' Legal correspondence is excluded from these provisions.

Unconvicted prisoners

9.36 The Prison Rules 1999, r 35(1) allows unconvicted prisoners to send and receive as many letters as they wish, but within such limits and subject to such conditions as the Secretary of State may direct. It is unusual for any restrictions to be placed on the number of letters sent and received. Incoming mail will be examined for unauthorised articles but will not normally be read and outgoing letters will not generally be subject to routine reading. Category A remand prisoners will find that their letters are read and in exceptional circumstances, the governor may direct that ordinary remand prisoners' letters are read in order to prevent the planning of escapes.

Legal correspondence

9.37 Prisoners have fought a series of cases challenging the extent to which the prison authorities can interfere with legal mail (as in *Silver v United Kingdom* (1983) 5 EHRR 347 and *R v Secretary of State for the Home Department, ex p Leech* [1993] 4 All ER 539). The succession of such cases culminated with *Campbell v United Kingdom* (1992) 15 EHRR 137, in which the European Court of Human Rights decided that routine reading of a Scottish prisoner's correspondence with his lawyer breached art 8. This lead to a comprehensive revision of the Prison Rule governing legal correspondence.

9.38   Rule 39 now provides that a prisoner may correspond with his/her legal adviser and the court (the definition of a court includes the European Commission and Court of Human Rights and the European Court of Justice). Prisoners must be provided with writing materials on request for the purpose of sending such correspondence. There is no restriction imposed on this right, such as being party to legal proceedings. The governor can only open, examine and read such correspondence if there is reasonable cause to believe that it contains an illicit enclosure or that there is reasonable cause to believe that its contents may endanger prison security, the safety of others or are otherwise of a criminal nature. A prisoner whose legal correspondence is to be dealt with under these provisions has the right to be present when it is opened.

9.39   Standing Order 5B, para 35 confirms that the rule allows legal mail to be handed in sealed and provides that it should not be read or examined except in accordance with instructions to prisons. Instructions were provided in IG 113/95 that provided comprehensive guidance to prisons on how to comply with rule 39 (which was rule 37A before the Prison Rules 1999 came into force). Letters from prisoners to legal advisers should be marked 'Rule 39' (or 'Rule 14' for young offenders) and as long as the recipient is legal adviser or court (and prisons are advised to check the adviser's status) then the letter will be protected by the rule. The position with incoming post is slightly different. As long as an incoming letter is marked 'Rule 39' and is identifiably from a legal adviser (eg by a stamp on the back) then similarly it should be covered by the rule. Unfortunately IG 113/95 also describes a procedure agreed with the Law Society and Bar Council whereby it is suggested that advisers should send the sealed letter inside a covering letter to the governor asking him/her to pass it unopened to the prisoner. If in doubt this procedure should be used. Notwithstanding the clear guidance given in the rule, and in IG 113/1995, prisoners continually complain about breaches of r 39 procedures.

9.40   The ambit of the Prison Rules 1999, r 39 has also been challenged by the Prison Service in relation to prisoners in the close supervision centre at Woodhill. There a practice has been introduced of checking all incoming and outgoing legal correspondence for illicit enclosures on a blanket basis without individual suspicion of illicit enclosures. The rationale appears to be that the prisoners in the CSC are of such a class that justifies such routine checking, although even accepting this rationale it is hard to see how it would apply to incoming letters from solicitors. At the time of writing these measures are subject to legal challenge.

TELEPHONE CALLS

9.41   All prisons now have card phones installed, but the Prison Service is introducing a new PIN system. The introduction of phone cards led to major changes in prisoners' use of telephones. Prison card phones will only accept cards issued by the Prison Service. These may be purchased from the prison canteen from wages or private cash. Governors are entitled to impose restrictions on the purchase of such cards and the possession of cards above a specified number can be grounds for a disciplinary charge (see CI 21/92). These regulations are designed to prevent 'racketeering' in the prison.

9.42   All card phones are monitored and can be recorded by prison staff. Calls can be stopped on the same grounds as for stopping correspondence. Prisoners are not permitted to consult a telephone directory but can be given access to STD codes. Calls to the operator and emergency services are barred. The procedures for recording conversations are subject to the Data Protection Act 1984 and access may be obtained to such records under the Act.

9.43   Category A prisoners and those on the escape list are not permitted to retain phone cards (Security Manual, para 36.35). Whilst such prisoners are entitled to purchase the same number of cards as other prisoners, they will be held and calls logged in the wing office. All calls made by such prisoners must be pre-booked and to certain pre-approved telephone numbers. These calls will be simultaneously monitored and recorded. The guidelines state that they must be conducted in English unless prior approval is obtained to use another language in which case the recording may be kept for translation. This level of monitoring was held to be justified by the courts in *R v Secretary of State for the Home Department, ex p Kaniogulari* [1994] COD 526, although the legality of charging prisoners for interpreting beyond a single short call per month is the subject of further challenges.

9.44   Calls to legal advisers are liable to be monitored as part of the general surveillance system. Although confidentiality cannot be guaranteed, governors are advised to notify their staff to turn off monitoring equipment as soon as they realise a genuine call of this nature is being made. Details of the conversation cannot be disclosed and if a tape recording had inadvertently been made, this should not be listened to or played back (CI 21/92, paras 40–43).

9.45   Telephone calls to the media are expressly forbidden following an incident where one of the Parkhurst escapees telephoned and participated in a radio chat show. Any unauthorised call to the media is now to be treated as a disciplinary offence (IG 73/95). Prisoners can make applications to use official telephones, either for urgent family circumstances, to speak to legal advisers or to contact the media. However, governors are strongly discouraged from allowing such applications and are asked to recover the costs of such calls from prisoners.

9.46   The new PIN phone system began to be piloted in 1999 and the Prison Service hope to bring it in for all prisons during 2000. The prisoners are given a Personal Identification Number to use when using phones which will automatically deduct amounts from their credited accounts and so the use of phone cards will disappear. It will only be possible for prisoners to call pre-approved numbers and any 'globally' approved numbers (that is approved for all prisoners) which will include freephone numbers for help and advice agencies. Some legal challenges to the PIN system have been started, for example to the limited amount of approved numbers allowed and to the fact that an outgoing message confirms that the call is from a prison.

TEMPORARY RELEASE

9.47   The Prison Rules 1999, r 9, which provides the authority for release on temporary licence (ROTL), was substantially redrafted in 1995. The purpose of this redrafting was to enable the Secretary of State to introduce more stringent measures in respect of temporary release and to provide punitive sanctions for those who failed to comply with the terms of their licence. The move was in response to a series of press stories about prisoners who had re-offended whilst on release but has been severely criticised for impeding the rehabilitative programmes that are available to prisoners.

9.48   Rule 9 provides authority for prisoners to be released temporarily from prison for the following reasons:

(i)   on compassionate grounds;
(ii)   to engage in employment or voluntary work;
(iii)   to receive instruction or training not generally available in prison;
(iv)   to participate in proceedings before any court or tribunal;
(v)   to consult with a legal adviser where the consultation cannot take place in the prison;
(vi)   to assist the police in their enquiries;
(vii)   to facilitate a transfer between prisons;
(viii) to assist in the maintenance of family ties or the transition from prison life to freedom;
(ix)   to visit the locality of the prison as one of the privileges under r 8 (r 9(3)).

9.49   The rule provides that before release can take place, the Secretary of State must be satisfied that the person will not present an unacceptable risk of committing further offences (r 9(4)), or that the length of sentence and the frequency of release will not undermine public confidence in the administration of justice (r 9(5)). This duty is expressed in even more severe terms for prisoners who have committed further offences whilst released on licence (r 9(6)). Prisoners may be recalled to prison at any time during a period of temporary release, whether or not their licence conditions have been broken (r 9(7)).

9.50   The manner in which the rule is operated is contained in IG 36/95. This establishes that the following classes of prisoners are not entitled to temporary release in any circumstances: category A and escape list prisoners, unconvicted and convicted unsentenced prisoners, those subject to extradition proceedings, and prisoners who are remanded on further charges or who are awaiting sentence following further convictions (para 2.3).

Risk assessment

9.51   There are three forms of temporary release; compassionate licence, facility licence and resettlement licence. Although eligibility differs for each form of release, in all cases a risk assessment must be completed before the release can be authorised. The main factors to be considered in completing this assessment are the risk that is posed to the public, whether the licence will be adhered to, the availability of suitable accommodation and whether the purpose of release is likely to be acceptable to reasonable public opinion.

9.52 The assessment is carried out in the prison but is subject to approval by the Lifer Management Unit for life sentenced prisoners and the Home Office Controller for contracted out prisons. Instruction to Governors 36/95 contains a ten-page appendix setting out the main areas to be investigated. These include some obvious areas for assessment, such as a prisoner's previous response to temporary release, custodial behaviour and home circumstances. However, other considerations are less easy to assess, such as the position and views of known victims or an offence analysis to see whether a prisoner may be prone to recidivism. It is difficult to see how prison staff will have either the information or resources to accurately assess this aspect of offending.

9.53 Prisoners serving less than 12 months are not subject to sentence planning and as such less information is available on them. As a minimum, the prison must obtain details of the offence, sentence and previous record, and probation reports (pre or post-sentence), any police post-sentence reports and records of any previous custodial sentences. The application will be considered by a board at the prison who can either make a recommendation or defer a decision for further information. Any decision to authorise temporary release must be made by a governor above grade 4 and if such a governor is not available, the application must be referred to the area manager for a decision.

9.54 Prisoners serving 12 months or more have more stringent arrangements in place. Within 12 weeks of sentence, a preliminary assessment must be prepared based on the same documents as listed for prisoners serving less than a year and attached to sentence planning documents. Once an application for a temporary licence is made, a request is sent to the outside probation office for a home circumstances report. The papers will then be considered by a board in the prison (unless it is less than six months since the last grant of temporary release and there has been no significant change in circumstances). This board will contain a governor, a prison officer, a seconded probation officer and for lifers, the lifer liaison officer. The prisoner can be invited to attend but there is no requirement for this to take place.

9.55 The board will obtain, in addition to the preliminary reports, a probation report dealing with previous offending, the present offence and whether any areas of concern arise such as child protection issues. A report from the wing detailing prison behaviour, an assessment of what has been done to address offending behaviour and other relevant information must also be prepared. The medical officer can be asked to provide a report if considered relevant. In borderline cases, enquiries can be made of the police and the probation services if information on the victim is deemed necessary. The police must be asked to provide factual information only and not an opinion as to the suitability of release on licence. A recommendation can then be made to the governor, and if it is thought necessary, additional licence conditions may be imposed.

Compassionate licence

9.56   This is reserved for prisoners with exceptional personal circumstances that may include visits to dying relatives or funerals, marriage or religious ceremonies, medical appointments or for primary carers to resolve problems with their children. The two most common applications are to see ill relatives/ attend funerals or to attend medical appointments. In the case of prisoners who have terminally ill relatives or who wish to attend funerals, this will usually only be authorised for 'close relatives.' Medical evidence or proof of the funeral is required to allow an application to proceed. Close relative does not normally include 'in-laws' but may be extended beyond immediate relatives in certain circumstances, usually on the advice of the chaplain or a minister of the prisoner's religion. Release is normally for a very short period of time, for example, to attend a funeral and a brief period of family mourning but not attendance at a wake. Young offenders can be released on temporary licence to visit parents where the parents are unable to visit due to disability or serious illness. Those in open or resettlement prisons can also apply for compassionate licence to attend a weekly religious service.

9.57   Prisoners may be allowed licence to attend medical appointments only once the full risk assessment has been carried out. Given the cumbersome process, this will often mean that compassionate release is unavailable in these circumstances and is only appropriate for prisoners who have to attend a series of outside appointments. The governor will seek the advice of the medical officer on the nature of the treatment and whether the prisoner is fit enough to attend unaccompanied. Lifers must have spent a minimum of six months in open conditions and have the application approved by Lifer Section to be eligible.

Facility licence

9.58   In addition to those prisoners not eligible for any form of temporary release, category B prisoners may not be considered for facility licence. The general principles of this licence are to enable prisoners to participate in regime related activities (such as work experience, community service projects, educational courses) and for official purposes such as attending civil court hearings. In order to be eligible, prisoners must have served at least one-quarter of their sentence, including any time spent on remand.

9.59   Facility licence cannot be granted for social or recreational purposes but must have a 'clear and substantive purpose which will allow reparation or help prisoners to lead law abiding and useful lives' (para 4.2). The duration of such a licence must not be for more than five consecutive days unless the needs of the work require longer, although this can be granted each week and the governor must be satisfied that excessive grants of such a licence do not undermine the punitive element of a sentence. PSI 46/1998 removed the restrictions on paid work in the community for prisoners under facility licence.

9.60   Meetings with legal advisers do fall within the scope of facility licence, but only in exceptional circumstances. This usually means cases where the volume of paperwork is such that it cannot be brought to the prison or where the prisoner needs to attend a legal conference where parties other than his/ her legal advisers are present. Attendance for the purpose of attending court hearings will normally be allowed if the risk assessment is positive and the court requires the prisoner's attendance or if attendance will further resettlement into the community. However, due to the possibility of adverse reactions if the outcome is unfavourable, governors are required to seek approval from the area manager for all category C prisoners who have more than six months until their release date.

Resettlement licence

9.61   Eligibility to apply for resettlement licence is determined by length of sentence:

(i)   Adult prisoners serving less than 12 months are ineligible.
(ii)   Young offenders serving less than 12 months may apply after three months from the date of sentence or four weeks before their release date, whichever is the earlier.
(iii)   Prisoners serving four years or more who were sentenced after 1 October 1992 are eligible after one-half of the sentence has been served (ie at the time of parole eligibility). The parole decision must have been made and if it is unfavourable, the prisoner must wait for a period of six months from the refusal or the parole eligibility date, whichever is the earlier. At subsequent parole reviews, the delay is two months from the refusal. If a prisoner in this group has served one-third of their sentence and has had previous home leaves, applications can be made within 12 months of the parole eligibility date.
(iv)   Prisoners serving 12 months but less than four years may apply after having served one-third of the sentence or after four months, whichever is the longer period.
(v)   Prisoners sentenced before 1 October 1992 to sentences of four years or more may apply after having served one-third of their sentence (ie the parole eligibility date). Adverse parole decisions defer the timing of the application as above.

Lifers

9.62   Life sentenced prisoners are entitled to apply for all forms of temporary release. In order to be eligible, such prisoners must either have been in custody for a period of four months after having been notified of a provisional release date, or have been in an open prison for six months for compassionate and facility licence or nine months for resettlement licence. All decisions to grant temporary release must be approved by Prison Service Headquarters.

9.63   The purpose of release on resettlement licence is expressed to be to enable prisoners to maintain family ties and links with the community and to make suitable arrangements for accommodation, work and training on release. Licences may be granted for between one and five days at a time. Unless the prisoner is at a resettlement prison, there must be a gap of eight weeks between each grant of a licence. Prisoners must also be in custody for at least seven days before final release from prison. For prisoners at resettlement prisons, more frequent grants of resettlement licence can be made providing they have worked outside of the prison for at least two weeks.

Breach of licence conditions

9.64   Governors are required to make spot checks on prisoners on temporary release to ensure, for example, that the prisoner is at the correct address or has not gone to the pub. The most common breaches of such licences are failing to return to prison on time, failing to return at all or the commission of further offences whilst on licence. In all cases, this constitutes an offence against prison discipline and on return to prison, charges should be laid against the prisoner immediately. If any criminal charges have also been brought or if the police are mounting their own investigation, the disciplinary proceedings will be adjourned pending their outcome. The governor must notify the local police force in any case where a prisoner has failed to return and inform the supervising probation officer. Where a licence has been breached, governors are instructed not to make any further grants of temporary licence, save for exceptional cases, until the prisoner is four weeks from release on parole or automatic release.

9.65   The Prisoners (Return to Custody) Act 1995 makes it a criminal offence for prisoners to be unlawfully at large. The offence is committed either:

(i)   by failing to return from a period of temporary release from prison within the time specified on the licence, without reasonable excuse; or

(ii)   by knowing or believing that an order has been made recalling him/her to prison and failing to take all necessary steps to comply with this, without reasonable excuse.

9.66   Prisoners who are convicted of the offence will be tried in a magistrates' court who may impose a sentence of up to six months' imprisonment, and/or a fine not exceeding level 5 on the standard scale.

AUTHORISED POSSESSIONS

9.67   Standing Order 4 on 'Facilities' is the document that was issued to provide a framework for prisoners' possessions and other facilities under the version of prison rule that was in force prior to the introduction of IEP schemes (it is due to be replaced by a new chapter of PSO 4000). Many of its provisions have been replaced with IEP schemes and other measures. Standing Order 4 requires prisons to publish a 'statement of their facilities (including a list of items that prisoners may normally retain in their possession).' This will now cross over with entitlements under IEP schemes as PSO 4000, chapter 1, appendix 3, which sets out acceptable privileges that prisons may include in schemes, and includes 'Possessions (including all previously [in] Standing Order 4 and establishment facility list items).'

RETAINING PERSONAL POSSESSIONS

9.68   The statement of principle is for prisoners to be allowed to retain sufficient property to enable them to live as normal and individual an existence as possible within the constraints of custody (Standing Order 4, para 7). Property held by a prisoner in possession is for the use of that prisoner alone. It is only possible to lend, sell or give property to another prisoner with the permission of the governor, a measure designed to prevent racketeering (para 6).

9.69   Standing Order 4 lists those possessions that prisoners are generally entitled to retain as:

(i)   a minimum of six newspapers or periodicals;
(ii)   a minimum of three books;
(iii)   a combined music system, or a radio and either a record, cassette or compact disc player;
(iv)   records/cassettes/compact discs in an amount that is reasonable;
(v)   smoking material (convicted prisoners may have 80 cigarettes or 62.5 grams of tobacco, unconvicted prisoners 180 cigarettes or 137.5 grams of tobacco);
(vi)   writing and drawing materials;
(vii)   a watch;
(viii)   a manual typewriter;
(xi)   a battery shaver;
(x)   batteries for personal possessions;
(xi)   personal toiletries;
(xii)   one plain ring;
(xiii)   a medallion or locket;
(xiv)   a calendar;
(xv)   religious articles at the discretion of the governor;
(xvi)   photographs, pictures and greeting cards;
(xvii)   a diary, an address book, postage stamps and phonecards (Standing Order 4, para 9).

The Prison Service Order on Race Relations (PSO 2800) states that 'subject to normal restrictions on the possession of personal items...prisoners may have in their possession any items which are important in the practice of their faith' (para 5.6.7).

9.70   The Woodcock report into the Whitemoor escapes made a recommendation, in the light of security concerns about the amount of property prisoners in the dispersal prisons could accumulate, that:

'A volumetric control of all prisoners' possessions should be introduced forthwith to reduce dramatically the amount of property in possession/ storage and facilitate effective searching.' (recommendation 6)

It was also a recommendation that this should apply to all prisoners notwithstanding their category.

9.71   In response to this recommendation the Prison Service introduced volumetric control of property for all prisoners in IG 104/1995. This states that 'the standard limit for all prisoners is that property held in possession will be limited to that which fits into 2 of the new volumetric control boxes' (para 2.2). The boxes measure 0.7 m x 0.55 m x 0.25 m. In addition prisoners may have in possession 'one sound system *or* one outsize item,' that is one that will not fit into the boxes and 'one birdcage' where birds are permitted (para 2.3). Exemptions in respect of all prisoners are made for legal papers, bedding and one set of clothes (para 2.6). Further exceptions are made for unconvicted prisoners in respect of property needed to carry on their occupation, and for women in mother and baby units (paras 2.7–2.8). Governors must consider whether in individual cases exceptions should be made (para 2.9). Property in excess of the limits can be handed out to relatives or friends and in exceptional circumstances property will be kept by the Prison Service at the central store in Branston.

9.72   With regard to computers (which prisoners often need to be able to prepare their own appeals) the Security Manual states that category A prisoners should not be allowed them in possession unless the governor decides to make an exception. If he does, or where prisoners of other categories are allowed computers, the Manual requires controls to be in place to monitor what is being processed on them. These measures should ensure that:

(i)   the computer does not have a modem so that it can access systems outside the prison;

(ii)   there is a competent member of staff who can check that only licensed copies of software are being used, and can check files to ensure that pornography, 'drug-related material,' racist 'and other illegal or undesirable material is not present';

(iii)   a watch is kept so that the computer is only used for the purpose for which it was allowed in possession;

(iv)   on searches, floppy disks must be treated as documents and their contents scanned (although legally privileged material should by extension only be scanned to the extent necessary to confirm that it is bona fide);

(v)   floppy disks must be carefully controlled (para 34.25).

In practice there is no consistency between prisons as to whether and in which circumstances computers will be allowed. This situation has been criticised in successive annual reports by the Prison Ombudsman but the above guidance from the Security Manual remains the only centrally issued policy. Prisoners have successfully challenged refusals to allow computers on an individual basis, and such challenges will be strongest where the need for a computer is tied to the fundamental right of access to the courts, or the Convention right to a fair hearing under art 6.

9.73   PSO 4000, chapter 1, appendix 3 sets out the 'acceptable privileges' for IEP schemes and includes 'Possessions (including all previously in Standing Order 4 and establishment facility list items). Subject to new security and volumetric controls.' Accordingly the property that prisoners may have in possession will be linked closely to their level on the incentives scheme (see below).

Prisoners' money

9.74   The majority of purchases a prisoner can make are from the prison shop or 'canteen.' Following the introduction of IEP schemes, new guidance was given to governors on the amounts of private cash prisoners could spend in prison. The most recent guidance is contained in PSI 79/1997 (although this is soon to be replaced by a new chapter of PSO 4000). This confirmed the position under the Prison Rules 1999, r 43(3) that prisoners are not to be allowed to keep cash on them and that accounts are maintained for them whilst in prison (para 6). The basic position is that:

> 'prisoners will be allowed to spend whatever they can earn from purposeful activity but access to private cash [cash, cheques or postal orders credited to prisoners' accounts] will be capped according to the weekly limits set by the level of the incentive scheme they are on.' (para 7)

The three levels of basic, standard and enhanced have weekly private cash allowances of £2.50, £10.00 and £15.00 respectively (£15.00 for unconvicted prisoners on basic, £30.00 for those on standard and enhanced).

9.75   The amount of private cash a prisoner may accumulate in his 'spend' account is set at a maximum of 10 times the weekly private cash allowance (para 8). However the governor does have a discretion to override these limits in individual or exceptional circumstances, for example for purchases of expensive items (para 14). Exceptions to the limits are also made for resettlement prisons, mother and baby units, overseas phone calls for specified prisoners, legal proceedings, business activities for unconvicted prisoners where permitted, and items for unconvicted prisoners in exceptional circumstances (para 12).

9.76   Although prisoners' purchases are mainly confined to the canteen, it is possible to buy items by mail order but these must be purchased from companies belonging to the Mail Order Protection Scheme (Standing Order 4, para 22 SO4) and must be sent to the prison direct. It is increasingly common for prisons to severely limit the number of suppliers that prisoners can obtain goods from and often this means that they have a restricted choice of goods at high prices. Access to mail order goods is also listed in the list of acceptable privileges that can be included in IEP schemes in PSO 4000, chapter 1, appendix 3.

Forfeiture of personal possessions

9.77   The governor has the power to remove possessions and to arrange for them to be placed in stored property or handed out to relatives if it is felt that the volume of personal possessions may be such as to make effective searching unduly difficult or if there is a risk to health and safety or good order and discipline. Magazines, newspapers and books can also be withdrawn if it is felt that they constitute a threat to good order and discipline, national security or the interests of the prison (Standing Order 4, para 35). This power has sometimes been invoked by governors to prevent access to political publications, or gay publications, although when challenged such items are normally allowed. As the right to free expression in art 10 of the ECHR includes the right to 'receive and impart information,' specific instances of withholding such material may be challenged under the Human Rights Act.

9.78   In addition to these discretionary powers, the governor has the power to order the forfeiture of items on disciplinary grounds. The Prison Rules 1999, r 55(1)(b) empowers governors to order the forfeiture of privileges as part of a punishment at an adjudication for a period of up to 42 days (21 days for young offenders). Forfeiture of educational notebooks, radios, writing materials and postage stamps should not normally be ordered.

INCENTIVES AND PRIVILEGES

The basis of the scheme

9.79   The system of privileges and facilities afforded to prisoners has been the matter of some discussion within the Prison Service. In 1995 following an amendment to the Prison Rules (see now the Prison Rules 1999, r 8) a framework document was issued to try and establish regimes that will link these to custodial behaviour. This has recently been revised and guidance on the operation of IEP schemes is now included as PSO 4000, chapter 1, appendix 3. All prisons are now required to operate a local incentives scheme intended to motivate prisoners to good behaviour and performance. Accordingly r 8 states:

> 'Systems of privileges approved under paragraph (1) may include arrangements under which privileges may be granted to prisoners only in so far as they have met, and for so long as they continue to meet, specified standards in their behaviour and their performance in work or other activities.'

9.80   PSO 4000, chapter 1 includes the National Framework for Incentives and Earned Privileges (IEP). This is a document setting out the basic requirements for prisons' individual schemes. Individual schemes must have aims that are consistent with those set out in the National Framework. Prisons' individual schemes and amendments to them must be approved by the appropriate area manager (para 1.2.1). The seven privileges that are identified as the 'key earnable privileges' are:

(i)   access to private cash;
(ii)   extra and improved visits;
(iii)   eligibility to participate in higher rates of pay schemes;
(iv)   community visits for category D prisoners, adult females and young offenders (subject to normal risk assessment procedures);
(iv)   access to in-cell television for standard and enhanced prisoners;
(v)   the ability to wear own clothes;
(vi)   time out of cells for association (para 1.5.2).

Whilst individual prisons can consider which privileges to include in their schemes, where the key earnable privileges are available, they must be included. In addition appendix 3 of the Order sets out other acceptable privileges that may be included in schemes. The list includes the best jobs available, cooking facilities, additional access to the gym and library, mail order facilities, own bedding, extra cell furniture and possessions.

9.81 The first point to note from this framework document is that it relates to privileges and cannot affect prisoners' rights to statutory entitlements such as the right to two visits every four weeks. Similarly, time out of cell is linked to this scheme but it is not possible to undermine the right of prisoners to time in the open air under the Prison Rules 1999, r 30.

9.82 IEP schemes are to be operated on a three tier system of basic, standard and enhanced regimes (PSO 4000, para 1.8.1). This can either by based on location (entire wings of prisoners on the same level) or simply on individual prisoners. The crucial difference is between basic and standard regimes, whereas the enhanced regime may only be slightly more favourable than standard, depending on the nature of the prison and the privileges available. On entry to the system prisoners should be placed on standard level. On transfer from other prisons, prisoners should be placed at least on standard even if they were on basic at their previous prison (para 1.8.5). Prisons can allow enhanced prisoners from other prisons entry on the enhanced level but if not there should be provision for 'quick reassessments on arrival' so that enhanced status can be achieved (para 1.8.6).

9.83 For the key earnable privileges, appendices 1 and 2 of PS0 4000, chapter 1, set out tables which determine entitlement by privilege level for convicted and unconvicted prisoners respectively. The private cash limits have been discussed above. Convicted prisoners on basic are essentially restricted to minimum entitlements (two social visits a month, minimum association and no entitlement to in-cell television, ability to wear own clothes, community visits, or earned community visits). Subject to availability, standard prisoners are entitled to all the key earnable privileges, and the difference between standard and basic is one of degree. For example the table recommends that standard prisoners should have at least three visits per 28 days, and enhanced prisoners four or five one-hour visits every 28 days. Prisoners should be allowed some association time with other prisoners (see para 1.5.17), although there is no statutory minimum in the Rules and the amount will therefore be hugely variable between prisons. Prisoners can only be denied association if segregated for good order and discipline under r 45, or as a punishment of cellular confinement following a disciplinary finding of guilt. IEP schemes apply to womens' prisons although all women prisoners can wear their own clothes.

Unconvicted prisoners

9.84 Unconvicted prisoners are also subject to IEP schemes (para 1.10.1), although these will have to take account of their particular status. This means that certain behavioural indicators such as work performance should not be used as remand prisoners cannot be required to work. Private cash limits are set out above. Unconvicted prisoners retain the right to wear their own clothes at all levels, and at basic level are entitled to a one-and-a-half hour visit each week. Entry will be to the standard regime in the first instance.

The assessment of behaviour

9.85   The only guide as to how behaviour will be assessed appears in PSO 4000, chapter 1, appendix 5. This sets out the following principles:

'(a)   standards of behaviour and performance must clearly demonstrate the criteria for movements to higher or lower privilege levels;

(b)   the emphasis must be on *patterns* of behaviour and performance and not generally on individual incidents;

(c)   prisoners as well as staff must be aware of the expected standards, and prisoners' points of view about their own behaviour and performance must be taken into account when assessments are made.' (para 3)

The appendix then sets out the factors that should be taken into account. Firstly 'institutional behaviour,' which incorporates compliance with rules, formal disciplinary offences (a single offence should only trigger a review of level if 'serious,' and para 1.7.8 states that if a prisoner is found not guilty the evidence should not be used in IEP assessments), and more subjective assessments as to how a prisoner relates to other prisoners and staff. Secondly, 'attitudes to sentence planning' including the use made of the personal officer scheme, the approach to the sentence and the willingness to make effective use of time in custody. Finally, the 'attitudes to relationships outside prison' including family members and victims must be assessed.

9.86   The appendix also sets out suggested criteria as to how behaviour should be assessed, although if such criteria are to be included in schemes they should be expressed so that it is 'clear what prisoners have to do, or not to do, to fulfil criteria for gaining and retaining each privilege level or particular privilege.' The criteria are non-violence, non-discrimination, civility, mutual respect, treating others with justice and fairness, respect for establishment rules and routines, due regard for personal hygiene and health, due regard for others' health and safety and effort and achievement in work and other constructive activities. Whilst prisons can introduce compacts setting out the facilities to be expected and the behaviour required for the various levels, prisoners cannot be required to sign compacts and refusal to do so in itself should not affect privilege level (see PSO 4000, chapter 5, para 5.3.1).

Decision making and reviews

9.87   The basic standard that the Order requires that schemes should meet is that taking into account the criteria in appendix 5. Governors should be able to state:

'prisoners here earn and retain privileges above the basic level through good and responsible behaviour and, where appropriate, through their performance in work and other constructive activities.' (appendix 5, para 2)

Accordingly 'decisions must be taken on general, objective and specified grounds, and seen to be following from a particular pattern of performance and behaviour.' Perhaps the main criticism of schemes by prisoners since their introduction in 1995 has been that officers are able to make negative reports without the prisoner having any realistic method of challenging them, and without the procedural safeguards of the formal disciplinary system. In response to this the new guidance in PSO 4000 that was introduced by PSI 90/1999 stresses that systems are not to be designed as 'secondary disciplinary' systems and must be determined by 'an open and fair process.'

9.88   The Order encourages prisons to use boards or panels to make decisions, and whether they do or not, more than one officer must be involved in the decision-making process, and decisions to place prisoners on basic must be taken by at least a Principal Officer grade (unless derogation is agreed by the area manager) (para 1.7.4). Decisions must be based on 'correct information' and take into account 'the prisoner's perspective' and so schemes 'must seek to build in verbal and/or written warnings, and reports to boards must seek to reflect prisoner responses to these and any other relevant comments.' Clearly given the more serious impact of being placed on basic, the requirements of fairness will be more stringent. In an application for permission to bring an application for judicial review the Court of Appeal accepted that there was an arguable case that prisoners should have a proper chance to make representations before being downgraded to basic (*R v Governor of HM Prison Featherstone, ex p Bowen* (26 January 1998, unreported)).

9.89   The Prison Rules 1999, r 8(4) requires schemes to 'include a requirement that the prisoner be given reasons for any decision adverse to him together with a statement of the means by which he may appeal against it.' PSO 4000, para 1.7.6 states that reasons need not be lengthy but sufficient to enable the prisoner to understand which criteria s/he has failed to meet and on what grounds. Where the decision is counter to representations made by the prisoner, it must indicate why a different view has been taken. In giving decisions the avenues of appeal must be stated beginning with any local remedy and reference to the requests/complaints procedure.

9.90   Schemes must have a mechanism for reviews of prisoners' privilege levels. Although the Order does not specify minimum review periods for prisoners except those on basic, reviews will partly be dependent on time left to serve, and anticipates that some schemes will depend on prisoner application. Downward reviews may be triggered by single incidents such as findings of guilt at adjudication (although appendix 5 states that single breaches of discipline would have to be 'serious' to warrant a review of privilege level). Prisoners on basic schemes must have reviews at least monthly, or every 14 days for young offenders (para 1.8.8).

9.91   The courts have proved reluctant to intervene in IEP schemes. In *R v Secretary of State for the Home Department, ex p Hepworth* [1998] COD 146 a number of prisoners serving sentences for sex offences that they denied, challenged the prisons' policy that barred them from the enhanced level as participation in the Sex Offender Treatment was required before they were eligible. Though this was a blanket policy with no discretion for consideration of individual cases the judge stated:

'there are plain dangers and disadvantages in the court's maintaining an intrusive supervision over the internal administrative arrangements by which

149

the prisons are run, including any schemes to provide incentives for good behaviour, of which the system in question is plainly an example. I think that something of the nature of bad faith or what I may call crude irrationality would have to be shown, which is not suggested here.'

This apparent return to an approach of judicial non-intervention in prisoners' cases was justified by comparison with cases involving categorisation, where the 'prisoner's aspiration to liberty' was much more clearly in issue.

9.92   In practice alleged misbehaviour can result either in a formal disciplinary charge being laid, or impact on a prisoner's incentive level. Often the impact on a prisoner's quality of life will be greater and last for longer if action is taken within the IEP scheme, yet the procedural safeguards involved are much weaker. Another problem is that the linking of incentive level with sentence planning can impact unfairly on those challenging their convictions (as in *Hepworth*). Despite the recent amendments to the guidance given to prisons on their schemes many prisoners will continue to feel that IEP schemes constitute 'informal' disciplinary systems. Further the fact that the National Framework gives governors wide discretion as to what may be included in schemes means that the problems of inconsistency in what prisoners may expect as identified in the Woolf Report will continue.

PRODUCTION AT COURT IN CIVIL CASES

The right to be produced

9.93   Prisoners who are engaged in civil litigation, be it against the Secretary of State, the Home Office, the Prison Service or any of its employees, or simply in other civil matters unrelated to their imprisonment such as child care, will often face difficulties when their action reaches the stage where their attendance at court is necessary. There has been a great deal of resistance to production in those circumstances and where attendance is authorised, the prisoner has been asked to pay a contribution towards the costs of production. These contributions are often set at a level which is impossible for the prisoner to pay.

9.94   The principle that a prisoner may be taken to court for these purposes arises from the Crime (Sentences) Act 1997, Sch 1, para 3. This gives authority for the Secretary of State to authorise any person detained in the UK to attend any other place in the UK where it is desirable in the 'interests of justice or for the purposes of attending any public inquiry.' Any person who is produced under this section, remains in custody throughout the time they are outside of prison (Sch 1, para 3(3)).

9.95   This section does not actually create any rights, being merely an enabling section to permit attendance at court. The power granted to the Secretary of State is to decide whether it is 'desirable' in the interests of justice for a prisoner to be so produced. There is no explanation as to when this power should be exercised in either the Prison Act 1952, or in the Prison

Rules 1999. Similarly, there is no explanation as to who should be responsible for the costs of production.

9.96   The judiciary has never developed a consistent approach to this matter (for earlier discussions on this point see *Becker v Home Office* [1972] 2 QB 407 and *R v Governor of Brixton Prison, ex p Walsh* [1985] AC 154) although detailed guidance can be obtained from the case of *R v Secretary of State for the Home Department, ex p Wynne* [1992] QB 406, CA. The Court of Appeal looked at these provisions in some detail on behalf of a category A prisoner who was seeking to attend a judicial review hearing that he was conducting in person. The application was actually dismissed because the prisoner had failed to make a formal application to the prison governor to be produced and prisoners must be made aware that this is an essential step to take when attendance at court is necessary. Nevertheless, the court, who consisted of Lord Donaldson MR, Staughton and McGowan LJJ, looked at the provisions for production in some detail. Whilst the judgments did not concur on the precise extent of a prisoner's rights to be produced, Lord Donaldson gave the most detailed ruling and it is submitted that his views should prevail. The case did go to the House of Lords (*R v Secretary of State for the Home Department, ex p Wynne* [1993] 1 All ER 574), but as the prisoner had not applied to the governor, the issue was not clarified. Certainly, the Prison Service has accepted these arguments in all applications for production and there have been no further applications for judicial review on this subject. The law in this section is therefore extrapolated from Lord Donaldson's views, but it may be the case that if applications made on this basis are refused in the future, further guidance from the court will be necessary.

9.97   Lord Donaldson was unable to think of any circumstances in which it would not be desirable for a prisoner to attend court when it was adjudicating on his rights. This was seen as a basic human right, consistent with art 6 of the European Convention on Human Rights. The question of whether it would cause administrative difficulty was not strictly speaking relevant to the issue of whether production is desirable. The dissenting view was that where the Secretary of State considered a case to be hopeless, as there is still a discretion to be exercised, production may not be desirable in the interests of justice. It seems unthinkable that this view could now prevail, particularly when it involves the exercise of an essentially judicial power by the Secretary of State, rather than the exercise of executive discretion. It would be impossible for this power to be utilised in cases where the action was against the Prison Service, the minister or an employee as this would effectively amount to the Secretary of State being 'judge in his own cause.'

9.98   The approach of Lord Donaldson in *Wynne* has also been strengthened by the decision in the case of *R v Immigration Officer, ex p Quahquah* [2000] 03 LS Gaz R 36, 20 January, HC. Here a Ghanaian national, who was liable to removal as a failed asylum seeker, sought judicial review of a decision to enforce his removal pending his claim for malicious prosecution against the Home Office and Group 4 (arising out of the riot at the Campsfield detention centre). The application succeeded on the facts, the judge holding that once it was established that the right to fair trial under art 6 was in issue, it was for the respondent to identify countervailing circumstances that would compellingly outweigh the applicant's rights. Given that the Home Office was a defendant in the civil proceedings:

'any fresh decision would also have to address the manner in which the Secretary of State approaches the discharge of his duty to demonstrate that his decision does not create the appearance of bias.'

Once article 6 is directly enforceable in judicial review proceedings the position will be accordingly stronger for applicants. The courts have also held that the Prison Act 1952, s 12(2) that states prisoners 'shall be committed to such prisons as the Secretary of State may from time to time direct,' was not authority to interfere with the right to a fair trial which is as much of a fundamental right as access to the courts (*R v Secretary of State for the Home Department, ex p Quinn* [1999] 21 LS Gaz R 40).

The costs of production

9.99 The second, and more difficult point addressed by the court was the question of what direction should be made as to the costs of production. Whilst it was accepted that it is not unlawful or unreasonable for a charge to be made to the prisoner, the court took the view that the Secretary of State was under a duty to ensure that this charge was reasonable in light of the ability of the prisoner to pay. As the statutory power was concerned with the interests of justice, it cannot be the position that a prisoner who is able to afford the costs should be in a better position than one who cannot.

9.100 The basis for the calculation of the costs must be made on production from the prison nearest to the court. Prisoners have no right to be detained in a prison of their choice and if this were not provided for in the judgment, it would have been susceptible to abuse simply by transferring the applicant to a prison as far away from the court as possible. Prisoners may not be required to contribute to the costs of the escort as this would amount to them contributing to the cost of their own imprisonment.

9.101 The question of legal representation is a relevant one when determining decisions of this nature and the amount of costs to be requested. If a prisoner is in receipt of legal aid, then the costs can be set closer to their true level rather than at a level commensurate with the prisoner's own ability to pay as these costs can properly be claimed as a disbursement. A prisoner who refuses to apply for legal aid will be in a difficult position as the disadvantage would be seen to be self-inflicted and the state could not be construed to have prevented the right to justice. Lawyers should still argue for the costs in such cases to be set at the lowest possible level so as to discharge their duty to the Legal Services Commission.

Conclusion

9.102 The dissenting views on production, and the costs of production, appear to have been made with a view to the possibility that prisoners would commence unmeritorious litigation in the hope of obtaining a free day out of prison. In cases of doubt, the dissenting view was that the judge hearing the matter would have the power to direct the attendance of the prisoner if it was felt necessary and to make an assessment as to what costs should be recovered. This view seems somewhat antiquated in the present climate and it is certainly the case that Lord Donaldson's opinions have been accepted in arguments for production. If the policy were to change it would almost certainly lead to a breach of art 6 of the European Convention on Human Rights.

CHAPTER 10

PRISON CONDITIONS

SEARCHING

10.1 Rule 41 of the Prison Rules requires that every prisoner will be searched when first taken into prison custody, upon being received at any prison, and at any other time that the governor believes a search to be necessary. Searches should be conducted 'in as seemly a manner as is consistent with discovering anything concealed' (r 41(2)). Prisoners may not be strip searched in the sight of another prisoner, and strip searches must not be conducted in the sight of a person who is not of the same sex (r 41(3)).

10.2 Comprehensive guidance on searching is given in the Prison Service's Security Manual (PSO 1000). Searching policy is dealt with in chapter 17 and procedures in chapter 18. Paragraph 17.1 requires prisons to have 'systems to detect and deter the hiding of objects, persons or activities that may threaten security or good order in the prison' and local searching strategies must be agreed with the Area Manager.

Searches of the person

10.3 Rule 47 states that force must not be used unnecessarily, and that no more force than is necessary should be used. Whilst a wide range of staff may conduct pat-down or rub-down scans, only Prison Officers or Prison Custody Officers may take part in a strip search (Security Manual, para 17.21). There is no power to conduct intimate searches of those in prison custody. Strip searches must only be carried out by officers of the prisoner's own sex, and other searches of women must be carried out by female members of staff (para 17.26). Otherwise prisoners with a genuine cultural or religious objection to being searched by a member of the opposite sex should be searched by members of their own sex. Prisoners who refuse to co-operate when informed that they will be searched, may be charged with the disciplinary offence of disobeying a lawful order (see chapter 8). Prisoners who are subjected to excessive or unreasonable force may have claims for assault or misfeasance in public office, although this will depend upon the circumstances of each case (see chapter 3). Searches which are more intrusive than the legitimate security concerns of the prison authorities justify will also be likely to breach the prisoner's right to private life under art 8 of the ECHR.

10.4 Chapter 18 of the Security Manual details the authorised procedures for searching including pat-down, rub-down and strip searches, which 'must be followed by staff during a search' (para 17.14). A common problem for prisoners is that they are routinely asked to squat during strip searches, which makes the process even more degrading than it already is. The Security Manual provides that prisoners should only be asked to squat or bend over if there is a reasonable suspicion of something concealed in the anal or genital area (para 18.15). Accordingly it should not be part of the searching routine and an order to squat in the absence of such an individual suspicion will not be 'lawful' for the purposes of any disciplinary charge against the prisoner.

Strip searches and intimate searches

10.5 Strip searches of prisoners may only be conducted by officers of the same sex (r 41(3)), and unless there are exceptional circumstances (for example where a search has to be conducted using control and restraint techniques) only two officers should carry out a strip search (Security Manual, para 18.9). The current Security Manual does not give specific guidance to governors on when prisoners should be strip searched beyond the requirement to agree a searching policy with the area manager which will include frequency targets, that is 'how often, in each context, routine, or random searches will be conducted' (para 17.11). This frequency will depend upon the security level of the prison. However prisoners will be strip searched at certain times, such as before MDTs or cell searches.

10.6 The Security Manual procedure for a strip search is a visual search of the prisoner only, and that other than when checking the head, there should be no need to touch a prisoner at all (para 18.15). A step-by-step guide for strip searching a male (which is the same procedure for visitors and staff when they are searched) is produced in the Security Manual which sets out the authorised steps as follows:

(i)   Officer 1 asks the subject whether he has any unauthorised items, and to empty his pockets, remove jewellery and hand over any other items; Officer 2 searches the contents of the pockets and other items handed over.
(ii)   Officer 1 asks him to remove headgear; Officer 2 searches headgear.
(iii)   Officer 1 searches his head by either running fingers through the hair to the back of the ears, or by asking him to shake his hair out and run his fingers through it.
(iv)   Officer 1 looks in and around ears, nose and mouth and can ask him to raise his tongue.
(v)   Officer 1 asks him to remove the clothing from the top half of his body and pass it to Officer 2 who searches it.
(vi)   Officer 1 asks him to hold his arms up and turn around and observes the upper body; Officer 2 returns the clothing.
(vii)   He is allowed time to put his clothes back on.
(viii) Officer 1 asks him to remove shoes and socks and pass them to Officer 2 who searches them and places them to one side.
ix)   Officer 1 asks him to lift each foot so that the soles can be checked.
(x)   Officer 1 asks him to remove his trousers and underpants and pass them to Officer 2, who searches them and places them to one side.
(xi)   Officer 1 then asks him to lift the upper body clothing to waist level to observe the lower half of the body.
(xii)   He must stand with his legs apart while the lower half is observed.
(xiii) If Officer 1 suspects there is anything concealed in the anal or genital area, he asks him to bend over or squat.

(xiv) Officer 1 looks at the area around him to see if he has dropped anything before or during the search.

(xv) Officer 1 asks him to step to one side to ensure he is not standing on anything; Officer 2 returns clothing.

(xvi) He is allowed time to put on clothing.

10.7   The strip searching procedure for women prisoners is essentially the same as above (see paras 18.32–18.41). However when the top half of her body has been searched, a woman should be given a dressing gown to wear for the rest of the search and she will be asked to lift this so that officers may visually examine the bottom half of her body (para 18.41(vii)). The procedure for women does not allow for asking women to bend over or squat, and whilst externally applied sanitary towels can be removed (and a replacement supplied), staff must not ask women to remove tampons (para 18.41(xii)).

10.8   Intimate searches (of body orifices) cannot be carried out by prison officers. Healthcare professionals may conduct internal examinations for clinical reasons only and may only do so with the prisoner's consent, except where there is a common law power to treat without consent (para 17.22).

Rub-down searches

10.9   The Prison Rules were amended in 1992 to allow for searches other than strip searches to be carried out by officers who are not the same sex as the prisoner. However, Prison Service policy is that rub-down searches of male prisoners may be conducted by either male or female officers, whereas female prisoners may only be searched in this way by officers of their own sex (Security Manual, para 17.26). However, male prisoners who have 'genuine religious or cultural objections' to being searched by a female officer should not be (para 17.27).

10.10   Rub-down searches are generally carried out by one officer, and the procedure that they should follow for a male is laid down in paras 18.16–18.25 of the Security Manual. There is a level A search for prisoners and their visitors, and a level B search for professional and official visitors (except that the level A search must be used for all visitors to Special Secure Units). The level B search is the same as level A but without the search of feet, shoes and head. This states that the officer should stand facing the prisoner and ask the prisoner to empty his pockets. The contents of the pockets should be searched together with any items that the prisoner is carrying. Any headgear that the prisoner is wearing should be handed over by the prisoner to be searched and the officer should then run his or her fingers through the prisoner's hair or ask the prisoner to do so. The officer should then look around and inside the prisoner's ears, nose, and mouth and feel behind and around the prisoner's collar and across the top of his shoulders. The prisoner should then be asked to raise his arms so that they are level with his shoulders with his fingers apart and his palms facing downwards whilst the officer runs both of his hands along the prisoner's arms. Following this, the officer should check in between the prisoner's fingers and look at his arms and the backs of his hands. The officer should then run his hands down the front of the prisoner's body from the neck to waist, down the sides of the body from armpits to waist, the front of the waistband, the prisoner's back from collar to waist, the rear of the waistband and then the seat of the trousers. The back and side of each leg should be checked separately from the prisoner's crotch to his ankle, and the prisoner should then be asked to lift up each foot so that the soles of his shoes can be checked. The prisoner should then be asked to remove his shoes and socks so that these can be scrutinised together with the soles of his feet. The front and sides of each leg should be checked, as should the prisoner's abdomen. Finally, the officer should look around the room to ensure that the prisoner did not drop anything either before or during the search.

10.11   The procedure for conducting a rub-down search of a female prisoner is essentially the same as for a male (see paras 18.42–18.49). However, staff are reminded that they must check around and under 'but at no time touch the breasts' (para 18.49(xi)). Although it is recognised that it may be difficult to check around the top of a woman's legs if she is wearing a skirt, the searching officer should nevertheless run her hands over the woman's legs outside her skirt.

10.12   During rub-down searches headgear worn for religious or medical reasons should be searched by a hand-held metal detector and should only be removed on suspicion or because of an unaccounted-for alarm. If it is necessary to search such headgear, privacy should be offered and the person being searched should be allowed to remove it him or herself (para 18.23 for men and 18.47 for women).

10.13   The third kind of search of the person for which there are detailed procedures in the Security Manual is the pat-down search. This is a more cursory search than the rub-down search, although if there is suspicion that the person being searched is concealing something the searching officer will proceed to the more thorough search. The Security Manual also details procedures for searching babies both in mother and baby units and for babies visiting prison (paras 18.54–18.67), and special procedures for rub-down searches of wheelchair users (paras 18.68–18.81).

Searches of visitors

10.14   In relation to visitors, Prison Rule 71(1) provides that a person seeking to enter or leave a prison may be searched and that such a search 'shall be carried out in as seemly a manner as is consistent with discovering anything concealed'. Searches on entry can only be by consent (as a visitor may decline to enter the prison). If consent is refused a visitor should be informed that the visit may be held in closed conditions or refused (para 17.36). Prison officers can search on the visitor leaving without consent but should not use force if the person resists, unless they have power to search without consent under other legislation (see below). In relation to private prisons, prison custody officers may search on leaving without consent and using reasonable force, but no more than an outer coat, jacket and gloves may be removed without consent (the Criminal Justice Act 1991, s 86). Visitors will never be strip searched under the Prison Rules, but only where other legislation provides for searching without consent and only where a full rub-down search has failed to reveal the suspected item.

10.15   A separate chapter of the Security Manual (chapter 23) deals with security procedures on visits. Prisons should display a list of items that visitors may not bring into the prison (para 23.21). Visitors will be searched in accordance with the local searching strategy but the Manual sets down minimum percentages of visitors to be searched depending on the category of the prison. The most common type of searching procedure that visitors will be subjected to are pat-down or rub-down searches, which may involve the use of a metal detector when searching the person and/or an x-ray machine when searching luggage. In prisons holding category A prisoners 100% of visitors must be subject to a metal scan, a rub-down search and an X-ray of property. Category B prisons 20% of visitors must be subject to rub-down searches if the prison does not have a metal detector portal, 10% if the prison does. Category C prisons must conduct rub-down searches of at least 10% of visitors (para 23.24). Annex 23F sets out acceptable forms of identification for visitors to closed prisons. For legal advisers this includes an identity card from the firm/chambers or an introductory letter on headed paper.

10.16   Professional visitors should be able to retain documents and briefcases containing documents needed for the visit. Other visitors should leave all property except personal clothing, some money for refreshments, items needed for medical reasons and babies' dummies and bottles, and, unless provided by the prison, baby food and nappies (para 23.25). Visitors under 16 can only be searched with the consent of the accompanying adult having care and control, though if unaccompanied may give their own consent (para 17.35).

10.17   The Manual requires all E List prisoners to be strip searched following visits, and for prisoners to be strip searched if there is reason to believe they are smuggling contraband, and for a percentage of other prisoners to be strip searched randomly at a level to be agreed with the area manager (para 23.52). A policy to strip search all prisoners whose visitors leave early without individual consideration of whether there were concerns about smuggling unauthorised items would clearly not be authorised and susceptible to legal challenge.

10.18   If prison staff have a reasonable suspicion that a visitor is trying to smuggle in items which are legal outside prison (eg alcohol or tobacco) they may decide to allow the visit but maintain close supervision, conduct a rub-down search, allow only a closed visit, or refuse the visit (para 17.51). If the visit is allowed then it is possible that the prisoner will be strip-searched afterwards on suspicion.

10.19   If it is suspected that a visitor is attempting to smuggle explosives, any weapons other than firearms, or items for use in an escape attempt, the police should be informed and asked to come to the prison. Where the police are not able to attend, or cannot do so promptly, the visit may be refused or the visitor asked to consent to waiting for the arrival of the police. In some circumstances the prison officer's power of arrest may apply (see below) (para 17.52).

10.20   Searches of visitors without consent up to and including strip searches can be carried out by prison officers (but not prison custody officers) only where firearms and drugs legislation or PACE allows. The circumstances are:

(i)   if there is reasonable cause to suspect the subject is carrying a firearm (with or without ammunition) in a public place, or (in public or private) for the purpose of committing an indictable offence;

(ii) if there is reasonable cause to suspect the subject is carrying a class A, B or C controlled drug;

(iii) if the prison officer has arrested the subject (see below) if there is reasonable cause to suspect he or she is a danger to self or others, or to search for anything which might be used to escape from arrest, or which might be evidence relating to an offence. They must not be required to remove more than a coat, jacket or gloves in public and the search must only be to the extent that is reasonably required to find the object (para 17.43).

10.21   In *Bayliss and Barton v Home Secretary and Governor of HM Prison Frankland* [1993] *Legal Action* February p 16, HHJ Marshall Evans ruled that the power to strip search a visitor to a prisoner would be unlawfully exercised if more than reasonable force was used, if the decision to search was perverse, and/or if the search was not conducted in a reasonably seemly and decent manner. The plaintiffs were awarded compensation following the judge's ruling that they had been unlawfully induced to strip, and that they had not been searched in a reasonably seemly and decent manner.

10.22   Section 8 of the Prison Act 1952 gives prison officers the power of a constable, including the power of arrest, but only in circumstances relating to the prison and their duties. Section 24(6) and (7) of the Police and Criminal Evidence Act 1984 (PACE) states that a prison officer may arrest a person if there are reasonable grounds to suspect that they are guilty of, or are about to commit an arrestable offence. The following offences are highlighted as being relevant to prisons in the Security Manual (para 18.182):

(i)   possession of a class A or B controlled drug, or class C with intent to supply (Misuse of Drugs Act 1971, s 5);

(ii)   possession of a weapon prohibited by Firearms Act 1968, s 5;

(iii) possession of any firearm or ammunition with intent to endanger life;

(iv)   possession of any firearm, or imitation firearm, with intent to cause any person to believe unlawful violence is to be used;

(v)   possession in a public place of a loaded shotgun, loaded air weapon, or any other firearm together with ammunition suitable for use in it;

(vi)   possession of an explosive in suspicious circumstances (Explosive Substances Act 1883);

(vii) conveying a thing into a prison with intent to facilitate the escape of a prisoner (Prison Act 1952, s 39);

(viii) unauthorised disclosure of information under Official Secrets Act 1989, ss 4 or 5;

(ix)   riot or violent disorder under the Public Order Act 1986.

10.23   Furthermore, PACE, s 25 gives prison officers the power to arrest anyone where there are reasonable grounds for suspecting that they are committing, attempting to commit, or have committed or attempted to commit any offence including:

(i)   bringing alcohol or tobacco into a prison contrary to regulations (Prison Act 1952, s 40);

(ii)   conveying anything into or out of a prison contrary to prison regulations (Prison Act 1952, s 41).

To effect an arrest on this basis one of the general arrest conditions must be fulfilled (ie the name of the person is unknown and cannot be readily ascertained; there are reasonable grounds for doubting that the person has given his real name or a satisfactory address; there are reasonable grounds for believing that arrest is necessary to prevent physical injury or damage to property; there are reasonable grounds for believing that arrest is necessary to protect a child or other vulnerable person from the person who is to be arrested) (paras 18.178 and 18.183).

10.24   A prison officer exercising the power of arrest should fulfil the requirements of PACE by telling the person that he is being arrested, the reasons why, and cautioning him. Until the police arrive, an arrested visitor should be supervised by a member of prison staff who will note anything that the visitor says voluntarily as prison staff should not question them. Reasonable force may be used to detain the person until the police arrive.

Searches of prisoners' accommodation

10.25   The rules on cell searching changed in May 1995 to reflect the recommendations in the Woodcock Report (*Report of the Inquiry into the Escape of Six Prisoners from the Special Security Unit at Whitemoor Prison, Cambridgeshire, on Friday 9 September 1994* Cm 2741). Instruction to Governors 53/95 introduced the changes, which are now included in the Security Manual: it contains a step-by-step guide on the searches of prisoners' living accommodation (paras 18.97–18.104).

10.26   The procedure states that unless a prisoner is 'not available' s/he should be informed that his or her cell will be searched and that this procedure will include a strip search. The prisoner should be taken to the cell, strip searched and then be taken to another part of the prison from where s/he should not be able to see the cell being searched. The rationale for ensuring the prisoner is not present at the search is to 'avoid intimidation' by the prisoner (Woodcock recommendation 8). Before the search starts, the prisoner should be asked if s/he has have any unauthorised articles and given the opportunity to give these in. Although s/he may still be charged with possession of such articles, it is possible that any punishment received at adjudication would be lesser so as to take account of this.

10.27   The cell should then be thoroughly searched including 'all known voids, ventilators, ceilings, floors, walls, doors, windows (inside and, where possible, out), grilles, pipes and fixed furniture and fittings' (Security Manual, para 18.104(vi)). The officers conducting the search have the discretion to remove items from the cell to another area of the prison and search them thoroughly. This provision is designed to cover situations where for example, it is thought necessary to take electrical equipment and x-ray or dismantle it to see whether there is something concealed inside. If any unauthorised articles are found during the cell search, and these could constitute the basis for disciplinary proceedings to be taken against the prisoner, then they must be bagged up, sealed, and labelled to be used as evidence in the adjudication or in any court hearing if there is the possibility of prosecution through the criminal courts (paras 18.152–18.173). If a prisoner has been allowed a computer in possession, the contents of any floppy discs should be scanned (para 34.25).

10.28   When the search has been completed, the staff who have been involved must tell the prisoner whether any articles have been removed from the cell, even if they are to be returned at a later date (para 18.104 (ix)). If any damage has been caused to any of the prisoner's property he should be advised of this and told of the procedures to follow in order to claim compensation (para 18.104(xii)).

10.29   These cell searching procedures have caused great concern amongst prisoners and prison reformers, primarily on the basis that under the previous procedures it was advised that prisoners should be present during a cell search so as to ensure that no allegation that articles had been planted could take place. Also, it has been argued that damage to prisoners' possessions is less likely to occur if the prisoner is on hand to point out fragile items and that officers may exercise a greater degree of care when handling property if its owner is present.

10.30   If a prisoner charged with possession of an unauthorised item complains that the item was planted in his absence, then at adjudication he should plead this as a defence. If he is found guilty of the offence an 'appeal' may be made to the area manager and an application may be made to the Ombudsman if the finding of guilt is upheld. Judicial review proceedings may be commenced at any stage in the process (see chapter 8).

10.31   A further concern for prisoners has been the extent to which legal papers can be examined during a cell search. Paragraph 17.73 of the Security Manual states that:

> 'during a cell search staff must examine legal correspondence thoroughly in the absence of the prisoner. Staff must examine the correspondence only so far as it is necessary to ensure that it is bona fide correspondence between the prisoner and a legal adviser and does not conceal anything else'.

As the search takes place in the prisoner's absence there is no way for the prisoner to ensure that officers do not examine legal papers to a greater degree. The legality of the policy of searching legal papers in the prisoner's absence was considered in the case of *R v Secretary of State for the Home Department, ex p Main, Simms and O'Brien* [1998] 2 All ER 491) in which the Court of Appeal held that in the light of security concerns raised by the Woodcock report there was a self evident and pressing need for the level of searching permitted by the policy. A subsequent challenge in which the prisoner argued that Prison Rule 39 provided a comprehensive code to cover legally privileged correspondence (not limited to the initial opening) also failed in the Court of Appeal (*R v Secretary of State for the Home Department, ex p Daly* [1999] COD 388). Kennedy LJ, who had also given judgment in the case of *Main,* held that the argument had been dealt with by the earlier case. The prisoner is to appeal to the House of Lords.

WORK AND PAY

10.32   Rule 31(1) of the Prison Rules requires adult convicted prisoners to do 'useful work' whilst they are in prison, but limits the requirement to a maximum of 10 hours per day. Work required to be done in the 'ordinary course of detention' does not count as 'forced or compulsory labour' for the purposes of art 4 of the ECHR (see art 4(3)). Unconvicted prisoners are not required to work, but if they wish to do so, they should be able to work as if they were convicted (r 31(5)). The policy guidance on work and pay contained in Standing Order 6A and the Pay Manual issued in 1992 is very out of date and the Prison Service are in the process of preparing a new PSO on this area. In practice, unconvicted prisoners often find that there is no work available for them to do in local prisons. If an unconvicted prisoner asks to work, but turns down a subsequent job offer for 'no valid reason', the governor does not have to offer further employment (SO 6A, para 22).

10.33   The Prison and Young Offender Institute Rules provide that prisoners who are practising Christians should not be required to do any 'unnecessary' work on Sunday, Christmas Day or Good Friday, and that prisoners of other religions should not be required to do unnecessary work on their days of religious observance (rr 18 and 32 respectively). Prison Service Headquarters advise governors of the relevant days each year though Prison Service Instructions.

10.34   In order to allocate prisoners to suitable types of employment, the governor and the medical officer have responsibility for classifying them as No 1 (heavy), No 2 (medium) and No 3 (light) labour, and they should not be required to do work of a heavier type than their labour grade (SO 6A, para 9). Prisoners who are ill may be completely excused from work by the medical officer (r 31(2)).

10.35   The Young Offender Institution Rules 1988 require that prisoners are engaged in education, training courses, work and physical education for up to eight hours per day (r 34). Where young offenders are under the age of 17, they should participate in education or training courses for at least 15 hours per week (r 35). All male YOI inmates and women aged under 21 should receive an average of two hours physical education per week (r 38), and this is included in the working week. Work provided in young offender institutions:

> 'shall so far as is practicable, be such as will foster personal responsibility and prisoners' interests and skills, and help them to prepare for the return to the community.' (r 37)

10.36   The governor should ensure that safe systems of work are in operation, and delegates this responsibility to the members of staff who are in charge of each work area. Health and Safety Executive Inspectors may conduct inspections under the Health and Safety at Work Act 1974 (SO 6A, paras 14–15).

10.37 Standing Order 6 provides for ex-gratia payments to be made for prisoners who are injured at work and are subsequently incapacitated upon their release from prison. Such payments should be made 'at the same rate as disablement benefit under the Industrial Injuries Acts following examination by a Medical Board of the Department of Social Security' (SO 6A, para 16). Members of staff who witness any such injury should complete reports of the accident and detail whether there was any degree of negligence, and upon receipt of this information the governor should make enquiries and arrange for the prisoner to be examined by the medical officer if appropriate.

10.38 Earlier versions of the Prison Rules included a requirement that prisoners not engaged in outdoor work or in an open prison should have one hour's exercise per day if the weather permits. This duty has been diluted and r 30 now states:

'If the weather permits and subject to the need to preserve good order and discipline, a prisoner shall be given the opportunity to spend time in the open air at least once a day, for such period as may be reasonable in the circumstances.'

Detailed guidance on this provision is given in PSO 4275. This distinguishes between prisoners in normal location and those in segregation either as punishment or under r 45. For the latter governors:

'must ensure that ... [they] are provided with the opportunity to spend a minimum of one hour in the open air each day. This requirement will also apply to unconvicted prisoners who exercise their right not to participate in work or other activities.' (para 2)

The PSO states that no special arrangements need to be made for those engaged in outside work, or whose activities involve substantial access to the open air (para 6). It also makes clear that Health Care advice is that all prisoners should ideally have one hour in the open air. Where time in the open air is cancelled because of weather or in the interests of good order and discipline, prisoners (other than those segregated) should be able to spend the time in association with access to recreational or PE facilities where possible, 'subject to the need to maintain good order and discipline' (para 11).

10.39 Rule 31(6) of the Prison Rules makes provision for adult prisoners to be paid for their work, and r 34(5) of the Young Offender Institution Rules provides for young offenders to be paid for their work or other participation in the regime related activities. Convicted prisoners for whom no work is available are paid at a basic rate (currently £2.50 per week), and prisoners who are unable to work are paid at the same rate. In addition, there is a retirement rate of pay (£3.50 per week) which is given to prisoners who choose to retire when they reach retirement age. Such prisoners may elect to continue working if they so choose so long as the medical officer passes them as fit to work. Prisoners who refuse to work will not be paid, and they will also be likely to be charged with an offence against prison discipline (ie if they refuse a lawful order that they should work).

10.40 The Prisoners' Pay Manual was introduced in November 1992, and recognised that the previous levels of prisoners' pay did not even amount to 'pocket money' and provided no incentive for prisoners to work. It aimed to implement Woolf's recommendation of an average weekly pay of £8.00 per week for prisoners who were working. The new pay scheme aimed to provide a framework within which prisoners could be rewarded for taking part in 'purposeful activity' (work, training and daytime education) and be encouraged to put 'sustained effort' into their work (para 2.1).

10.41   Governors set standard rates of pay for each job available in the prison (which cannot be less than the employed rate specified by Prison Service Headquarters), and prisoners who complete their task to an acceptable level of quality are paid at that level. Bonuses for productivity and for attaining qualifications can be paid in certain circumstances. If a prisoner's work is of a sub-standard level deductions from pay of up to £1.00 per week can be made, unless the prisoner is guilty of a 'major failure to match standard performance', in which case it is possible for the pay to be reduced to nothing and the prisoner charged with a disciplinary offence.

10.42   Access to the best jobs and to schemes involving higher rates of pay than the standard rates is now linked to prisoners' behaviour and which level they are on in the prison's Incentives and Earned Privileges Scheme (see chapter 9). Where prisoners are earning higher rates of pay (for example when working outside prison when in a resettlement unit), the current legal position is that no deductions from their earnings can be made for 'board and lodging'. Such deductions were being made until 1998, when the legality of the deductions was challenged in judicial review proceedings. The prisoners argued that although the Prisoners' Earnings Act 1996 allowed for such deductions, it had never been brought into force (and this remains the case). In the absence of such statutory authority, and in light of the fact that Prison Act 1952, ss 51and 53 require that the costs of maintaining prisoners 'be defrayed out of moneys provided by Parliament', there was no power to make the deductions as this amounted to requiring the prisoner to pay for the costs of his own imprisonment. The prisoners were granted permission to bring the proceedings, and in PSI 9/1999 directed governors to stop making the deductions. PSO 4100 was subsequently issued to give guidance on how to process claims from prisoners who had amounts unlawfully deducted. PSI 9/1999 stated that 'work is proceeding with a view to implementation, later this year, of the Prisoners' Earnings Act 1996', but at the time of writing it has still not been brought into force.

FOOD

10.43   Prison Rule 24 provides that:

> 'the food provided shall be wholesome, nutritious, well prepared and served, reasonably varied and sufficient in quality'. (r 24(2))

10.44   Despite this, many prisoners consistently complain about the quality of the food given to them, and will also find it difficult to obtain meals which fit in with their religious or medical dietary requirements.

10.45 The Prison Service Order on Race Relations (PSO 2800 issued in 1997) contains a policy statement that:

> 'An adequate and suitable diet is a basic human need. It is clear that in Prison Service establishments inadequate provision for dietary needs or preferences can become a source of complaint and conflict and that proper attention to dietary matters can reduce problems in this area'. (para 5.7.1)

Thus it is recommended that diet should 'should, as far as is practicable, take account of the religious requirements and cultural preferences of prisoners from different ethnic groups'. The Order anticipates that most religious and cultural 'preferences' will be dealt with by use of a 'menu management' system.

10.46 Vegetarian dishes should be available to any prisoner who expresses a personal preference, whereas vegan diets are only provided to prisoners who 'are able to demonstrate a commitment to the principles of veganism' (PSO 2800, para 5.7.3) which may arise from a personal commitment or from religious belief. Likewise, in order to qualify for a special diet, members of some religions must be able to 'demonstrate an adherence' to the dietary laws of their religion (CI 37/91). Recognised religious leaders and organisations may be allowed to provide food for prisoners during religious festivals (PSO 2800, para 5.7.6).

10.47 There are special arrangements for Orthodox Jewish prisoners who are able to 'demonstrate to the satisfaction of the visiting Rabbi that they normally adhere to Jewish dietary laws' (para 5.7.2) who will have one frozen kosher meal a day brought in from outside the prison at the prison's expense (see IG 17/1995). The Prisons Ombudsman has upheld a complaint from a prisoner that he had been refused a kosher diet (including the frozen meal) because he had not attended synagogue regularly. The Ombudsman stated that the policy, which appears to require a prisoner to demonstrate formal links with a synagogue, was unfair as it did not take into account those who observed their faith but had no such formal links, or those who wished to revert to their faith or change their faith whilst in prison. He recommended that the visiting Rabbi should determine 'whether the prisoner had a sincerely held belief and desire to follow the Jewish religion'. In his 1998/99 Annual report he stated that this recommendation had been accepted (1998/99 Annual Report, Cm 4369 p 37).

10.48 The medical officer of the prison and the Board of Visitors are both under statutory duties to inspect the food before and after it is cooked, and must report upon their findings to the governor (rr 24(3) and 78(2)). Such inspections do not have to take place every day. It is common practice for governors to taste the food prepared at their establishments on a daily basis, although this is not a statutory requirement.

10.49 PSO 5000 on Prison Catering Services gives guidance to establishments on food hygiene and safety and prisons' compliance with the Food Safety (General Food Hygiene) Regulations 1995. It also provides guidance on menu management and permissible variations in diet, according to religion and other preferences. The Food Safety Act 1990 is binding in prison establishments.

10.50 One of the main problems affecting the provision of meals to prisoners is that of transportation from a central kitchen to the wings. In his Annual Report 1992–93, the Chief Inspector of Prisons found that:

'the food, which was acceptable when it left the kitchen in a container, can become a tepid stewed mush by the time a prisoner has collected it on the wing and taken it up the stairs to his cell, where he has to eat often without a chair or table but off his bed, in a cell shared by another inmate, a pot or a toilet'. (para 3.11)

10.51 Another major problem is that prisoners' meal times are planned around staffing hours and thus three meals tend to be crammed into eight or nine hours of the day, for example with breakfast being taken at around 7.45 am, lunch at 11.15 am, and dinner at 4.20 pm (see Chief Inspector's *Report into HMP Wandsworth following an inspection on 13–16 July 1999* Appendix II). The Prison Service Standard on catering creates an auditable standard that 'if the gap between the evening meal and breakfast exceeds fourteen hours and prisoners are locked up in the evening, establishments provide an additional snack and hot drink for consumption later in the evening'.

10.52 Prisoners may complain about the food through the requests/complaints procedure to the governor and area manager. The Prisons' Ombudsman has on occasion upheld prisoners' complaints concerning food, and made recommendations to the Prison Service for improvement.

THE USE OF FORCE, SPECIAL ACCOMMODATION AND MECHANICAL RESTRAINTS

Violent and refractory prisoners

10.53 Rule 49 of the Prison Rules and r 49 of the Young Offender Institutions Rules allow prison governors to direct that prisoners over the age of 17 may be put under restraint 'where this is necessary to prevent the prisoner from injuring himself or others, damaging property or creating a disturbance'. Prisoners may not be kept under restraint for longer than necessary, and this must not exceed 24 hours unless written authorisation is given by a member of the Board of Visitors or an officer of the Secretary of State. Where authorisation is given this must give reasons for the restraint, and the time that it is to continue for (r 49(4)). Guidance on the use of these powers is provided in PSO 1600 (which replaced Standing Order 3E in 1999). This makes it clear that the use of restraint must only be used for the purposes set out in the Rules and 'every effort must be made to avoid the use of mechanical restraint' and that the use of special cells (see below) should be considered first (para 4.4.2). Prisoners must not be restrained as a punishment and any mechanical restraint must be removed as soon as the original justification for its use has ceased (para 4.4.4).

10.54 The only mechanical restraint that the Order authorises for restraint under Rule 49 is 'a body belt (with metal cuffs for both male and female prisoners)' (para 4.3.1). Approval must be given by the governor in charge, or if unavailable an officer who is of the rank of principal officer unless no such officer is available, in which case the most senior officer on duty should make the decision (para 4.6.1). The governor should see the prisoner before the mechanical restraint is applied, or as soon as possible afterwards (para 4.6.2) and the decision should be recorded on form F2323. The medical officer should be informed of the decision, and should examine the prisoner 'as soon as practicable', following which the medical officer will inform the governor of his opinion as to whether there are any 'clinical contra-indications' to the use of a body belt. If so, the prison doctor can order the immediate removal of the body belt, and either way must endorse the F2323 (para 4.8.3).

10.55 The use of mechanical restraints must be closely monitored so that the requirement that it should continue no longer than necessary is met. The duty governor or officer in charge of the prison must visit the prisoner hourly, and the governor in charge must 'personally observe' the prisoner at least twice in every 24-hour period and endorse the F2323. A prison doctor must also visit the prisoner twice each 24 hours and record the visits both on the F2323 and the continuous inmate medical record. The doctor should also examine the prisoner when the restraint is removed (para 4.2). The decision to remove the restraint must be recorded on the F2323 and copies sent to the Boards of Visitors and to the prison doctor.

10.56 The Prison Rules also provide for 'refractory or violent' prisoners to be kept in a 'special cell' temporarily until they have ceased to be violent or refractory (YOI Rules 1998, r 48). Prisoners may not be detained in such accommodation as a punishment. Authority must be given by the governor in charge of the prison, and the procedure for the granting of initial authority of up to 24 hours and subsequent authority for a longer period is the same as that outlined above in the use of mechanical restraints, and uses the same documentation. A prisoner in special accommodation must also be observed at least every 15 minutes by an officer (para 4.12.5).

10.57 Section 14(6) of the Prison Act 1952 provides that:

> 'In every prison special cells shall be provided for the temporary confinement of refractory or violent prisoners.'

The special accommodation used must either be that which has been certified as a 'special cell' under s 14 or an ordinary cell which has had the usual furniture removed and which is either totally unfurnished or does not contain basic items of furniture such as a table and a chair (para 4.4.4). In designated special cells, which are somewhat like a cell within a cell, and are soundproofed with double doors, opaque windows and dim lighting, any furniture would be designed so that no injury could be caused to the prisoner.

10.58 In extreme cases both special accommodation and mechanical restraint are authorised by the Order, but only where 'a prisoner cannot safely be left in special or unfurnished accommodation'. In theory, the use of restraints and special accommodation would be terminable by judicial review proceedings, however, in practice, it is highly unlikely that the prisoner would be able to inform anyone of his plight whilst so confined.

10.59   PSO 1600 also gives guidance on the use of force by officers short of where the extended restraint measures outlined above are needed. Rule 47 of the Prison Rules 1999 and r 47 of the Young Offender Institutions Rules 1998 provide that 'an officer dealing with a prisoner shall not use force unnecessarily and, when the application of force is necessary, no more force than is necessary shall be used'. The PSO states that the use of force 'must always be regarded as a last resort' (para 1.1.3) and that where it is necessary only approved control and restraint (C and R) techniques should be used unless this is impractical. The Prison Service has issued C and R manuals but these documents are classified. Every time C and R techniques are used, a Use of Force report form, F2326, must be completed and held in a central file (para 2.3.1) and a reference inserted in the prisoner's own record. Clearly where unnecessary or excessive force is used, the prisoner may have a claim for assault or misfeasance in a public office.

10.60   The use of ratchet handcuffs should only be used if, following a violent outburst, it is necessary to remove a prisoner from one part of the prison to another and either some distance is involved or the route would make it difficult to maintain approved holds, or the prisoner is 'particularly violent and powerful and failure to restrain the prisoner is likely to result in injury to the prisoner, another prisoner or member of staff, or in the escalation of the incident' (para 2.6). They cannot be used as a 'mechanical restraint' under the Order.

10.61   The Order also gives guidance on the use of staves and batons. Staves must not be used in open or womens' prisons or in juvenile units. Their use in YOIs is at the governor's discretion (para 3.1). Staves may only be used defensively and directed at the prisoner's arms and legs only. They may only be used as an 'exceptional measure' where:

'(i)   necessary for the officer to defend him or herself or a third party from an attack threatening serious injury;

(ii)   and there is no other option open to the member of staff to prevent injury to him or herself or another person but to employ a technique which involves striking a prisoner.' (para 3.1.5)

10.62   Mini-batons may be carried only by female officers. Their use must only be as an exceptional measure where it is judged that approved techniques are unlikely to succeed without their use, and where their use is necessary to prevent injury to the officer or another person, or damage to property (para 3.2.3). Side-arm batons are issued to C and R advanced trained staff. Again their use must be seen as an exceptional measure. They must only be used defensively and aimed at the prisoner's arms and legs. They can only be used:

'(i)   on the instruction of a C & R unit or section commander, where such action is considered necessary to prevent serious injury to staff or others; or

(ii)   on the judgement of an individual member of staff who becomes detached from the body of the response force and needs to exercise personal discretion, where such action is necessary to prevent serious injury; or

(iii)   there is no option open to the member of staff to save him/herself or another person but to employ a technique which entails striking a prisoner.' (para 3.3.3)

Whenever a stave or baton is drawn or used, a Use of Force report form (F2326) must be completed and submitted to the governor. A prison doctor must also examine a prisoner against whom a stave or baton has been used and complete a form (F213) on the prisoner's condition. A doctor's report must be made even if the prisoner does not appear to have sustained any injury (para 3.5.1).

Escorts

10.63   Section 13(2) of the Prison Act 1952 provides that prisoners remain in legal custody whilst being escorted by an officer for the purposes of the Act, and Prison Rules 1999, r 40(1) states that prisoners 'shall be exposed as little as possible to public observation, and proper care shall be taken to protect him from curiosity and insult'. The rule also provides that prisoners are able to wear their own clothes, or civilian clothes provided by the governor, if being taken to court. Prisoners who are under escort to another prison or elsewhere outside the prison may be handcuffed. Escort procedures are dealt with in chapter 37 of PSO 1000, the Security Manual. For the escort of one prisoner from a closed prison, there should normally be at least two officers and use of restraints (para 37.17). The available restraints are standard handcuffs for male prisoners, ratchet handcuffs for male prisoners where standard handcuffs do not provide a close enough fit, ratchet handcuffs for female prisoners and special 'Hyatt' handcuffs for private contractors (para 37.65—the national escort system, which will not deal with prisoners who pose a serious risk of escape or disorder has been contracted out to Group 4—see PSI 31/1997). Escorted absences allow prisoners of any category to attend, for example, funerals if they are ineligible for temporary release for the purpose.

10.64   The Security Manual makes it clear that prisoners under escort outside the prison should normally be handcuffed at all times except:

'(i)   when prisoners are being moved to an open prison;

(ii)   when prisoners from open prisons are being escorted unless being returned to closed conditions;

(iii)   on a mentally disordered prisoner who is subject to an order or direction for compulsory detention under the Mental Health Acts, unless the governor, with the agreement of the Medical Officer, directs that handcuffs must be used because the prisoner poses a security problem;

(iv)   on prisoners attending for medical treatment outside the prison, if the prisoner's medical condition renders restraint inappropriate or a risk assessment demonstrates they are unnecessary in all the circumstances. restraints will not normally be necessary when the prisoner's mobility is severely limited, eg when he or she is on crutches;

(v)   when the Medical Officer recommends this on health grounds;

(vi)   on a category C life sentence prisoner on escorted absence who had been risk assessed under the terms of PSI 73/97.' (para 37.93)

Handcuffs can still be used in the above situations where the prisoner becomes violent or tries to escape, although a written report must be made to the governor on return to prison (para 37.93).

10.65   The use of other restraints for escorts (body belts or a loose canvas restraint jacket) can only be used exceptionally and not by escort contractors. Body belts can only be used on the same grounds as set out above (para 10.53). Use of a canvas restraint jacket must be authorised by the medical officer and confirmed by the governor (para 37.69) and authorisation for either form of restraint only applies until the prisoner reaches the receiving prison. If either of these restraints are used, a member of staff from the healthcare centre must accompany the prisoner to monitor the prisoner's condition and the restraint use must be recorded on appropriate forms, which are also sent to Headquarters.

10.66   Whilst under escort, prisoners who have been handcuffed may have the handcuffs removed in the following circumstances:

(i)   if they are being transported in a cellular vehicle and the doors have been locked (unless there is reason to believe that they have a hidden weapon);

(ii)   if they are produced in court (unless the judge orders that the handcuffs should not be removed);

(iii)   during a marriage ceremony (but only the ceremony itself);

(iv)   during a funeral but only where the funeral is to take place in a hospital and following a risk assessment the governor decides handcuffs are not necessary;

(v)   when in an outside hospital during treatment unless a risk assessment shows the risk of escape is too high;

(vi)   in an emergency when life is being threatened;

(vii) during visits to dying relatives if the governor decides, although Category A prisoners must remain restrained;

(viii) when a woman prisoner is attending an antenatal check, or giving birth. Restraints must not be used for women giving birth from the time of arrival at hospital to the time of leaving;

(ix)   on board an aircraft, unless the operator has given prior consent;

(x)   when the Medical Officer requests their removal on health grounds. Even in these circumstances the treating healthcare professional can request their removal if there is an immediate risk to health, if the prisoner is in pain or discomfort, or because the restraint is impeding essential treatment. In other cases where the healthcare professional requests removal escorting officers can insist restraints will remain in place if they believe a risk escape remains in which case they must contact the governor who will make the decision. (para 37.92).

Escorting staff must not remove handcuffs from a prisoner to allow him or her to use the toilet in an insecure area without first applying an escort chain (para 37.91).

RACE RELATIONS

10.67   The Prison Service published a Race Relations Manual in April 1991. This has been updated and is now the Prison Service Order on Race Relations (PSO 2800). The Order aims to set out the Prison Service's policies and their implications in terms of prison life, to provide a means by which prisons can audit their application of the policies and improve this, and to explain the responsibilities of individual members of staff in implementing the policies.

10.68 The Prison Service's Race Relations Policy Statement is as follows:

> 'The Prison Service is committed to racial equality. Improper discrimination on the basis of colour, race, nationality, ethnic or national origins, or religion is unacceptable, as is any racially abusive or insulting language or behaviour on the part of any member of staff, prisoner or visitor, and neither will be tolerated.' (para 2.13.1 PSO 2280)

10.69 A new overall standard was adopted with the issue of PSI 3/2000. It states:

> 'The Prison Service will have policies and practices which will eliminate improper discrimination. Racially abusive or insulting language or behaviour on the part of any member of staff, prisoner or visitor will not be tolerated'.

The Order itself is based on nine mandatory standards relating to key aspects of race relations policy. These are:

'1. The establishment must adopt policies and practices aimed at eliminating improper discrimination on the basis of race, colour, nationality, ethnic or national origin, or religion. Racially abusive or insulting language or behaviour on the part of any member of staff, prisoner or visitor is not to be tolerated.

2. Maintain a Race Relations Management Team (RRMT) which develops local race relations strategies and monitors performance to ensure implementation of the national race relations policy.

3. Appoint a Race Relations Liaison Officer (RRLO) to provide information to staff and prisoners on national and local policies and to monitor race relations in the establishment.

4. Implement systems designed to assess the overall impact of the race relations policies of the Service and monitor performance.

5. Make comprehensive use of ethnic monitoring data to identify and remedy any discrimination within the establishment.

6. All prisoners will have equality of opportunity to use the facilities and services provided by the establishment.

7. Develop and maintain an effective system for reporting and investigating complaints and racist incidents.

8. Develop contacts and effective working relations with the Race Equality Council and other community groups locally or nationally.

9. Staff, prisoners and visitors to the establishment to be familiar with the Prison Service's Race Relations Policy Statement. Key staff to be familiar with the contents of the Race Relations Order. The RRLO and RRMT members to receive central training. Other race relations training to be delivered locally.'

Each standard in the Order is accompanied by a set of mandatory levels for compliance together with non-mandatory recommendations. However, no mention is made of any sanction being imposed upon prisons and staff who act in breach of any policy.

10.70   The RRMT 'develops local race relations strategies and monitors performance to ensure implementation of the national race relations policy' (para 3.5.1) and must be chaired by the governor or deputy governor of the prison. It should meet at least quarterly and should include the RRLO, other staff and a member of the Board of Visitors to observe, and a representative from a local community body or relevant outside body. Prisoner representation must be considered but is not mandatory (para 3.5.7).

10.71   The RRLO's role is to be a link between the prisoners and the RRMT, and it should 'act as a source of information to both prisoners and staff and be prepared, where necessary, to discuss complaints of a racially sensitive nature with prisoners'. S/he should also report any racist incidents or issues to the governor and/or the RRMT. The definition of racist incident in the Order was amended after the Home Secretary's acceptance that criminal justice agencies should adopt the definition formulated by the McPherson Inquiry into the murder of Stephen Lawrence, that is 'any incident which is perceived to be racist by the victim or any other person' (para 6.2.1). All racist incidents should be reported to the RRLO, and although the Order does not make them mandatory, it is recommended that standard racist incident forms be used. Unfortunately it is not unknown for prisoners complaining of officers' racism to be formally disciplined. The Prisons Ombudsman in his 1998/99 Annual Report gives an example of this where he upheld the prisoner's complaint. The Director General, while accepting the recommendation, stated that it should be 'open to an officer to make a proper judgement as to whether a prisoner is airing a genuine grievance or indulging in insulting behaviour' (p 19). It will clearly undermine race relations policies if the decision to discipline a prisoner complaining of racism is left to the officer who is the subject of that complaint.

10.72   At Prison Service Headquarters the Director General chairs the Advisory Group on Race which aims to ensure 'that race relations remains at the core of Prison Service policy and practice'. Despite these initiatives, prisoners still often complain of institutionalised racism within the prison system, and their complaints range from being at the receiving end of racist and abusive language from officers, to being given the worst labour allocations.

10.73   There is only one reported case of a prisoner taking a successful case under the Race Relations Act 1976, and this also established that prisoners have the right to bring proceedings under the Act, which had previously been disputed by the Home Office. In *Alexander v Home Office* [1985] CLY 1669 a West Indian prisoner was compensated for having been refused jobs in prison on racist grounds. This limited use of the race relations legislation is due partly to the fact that up to now claims for discrimination against the Prison Service have only been possible in relation to the provision of 'goods, facilities and services', and also the problem of collecting evidence. The court accepted in *Alexander* that the allocation of work within a prison could come within the definition of 'facility' for the purpose of the Race Relations Act 1976, s 20. By contrast other decisions, such as those relating to security categorisation or to segregate do not come under s 20, as these are not the provision of 'facilities or services' but an exercise of the duty to control prisoners.

10.74 This position will be radically changed once the Race Relations (Amendment) Bill is brought into force. This piece of legislation was drafted as a response to the McPherson Inquiry to extend the scope of the 1976 Act to make it unlawful for a public body to discriminate 'in carrying out any of its functions' (cl 1). In a written answer on the 27 January 2000, Jack Straw confirmed the draft legislation would be amended so as to include both direct and indirect discrimination. This had initially been resisted because of concerns that this would leave 'public bodies open to routine legal challenge in circumstances where their policies were entirely proper', but was accepted after consultation.

10.75 When the Bill becomes law, probably some time in 2000, prisoners will be able to bring claims for discrimination in all contexts such as prison discipline, categorisation, segregation or transfer. This will be an extremely important development for prisoners, especially in cases that also raise issues under the Human Rights Act 1998. Evidence will remain a problem, but , for example, because indirect discrimination will be covered, statistics showing a disproportionate number of segregations involving ethnic minorities (which prisons are under a duty to monitor—PSO 2800, para 6.1) may provide prima facie evidence of discrimination.

10.76 PSO 2800 states that a prisoner can complain of racist incidents orally to staff, through the request/complaint procedure (see chapter 9), on a locally designed incident form, or directly to the Commission for Racial Equality (para 6.2.2). The Prisons Ombudsman will also consider complaints and make recommendations. The CRE will provide advice, and in some cases support, to those making complaints. Prisoners can also contact their local racial equality council.

HEALTH CARE

10.77 Rules 20–22 of the Prison Rules 1999 make provision for prisoners to receive medical attention whilst they are serving their sentences or on remand. These lay down a system whereby the prison medical officer has responsibility for the physical and mental health of all prisoners detained in that prison, and has discretion to arrange for other practitioners to be consulted. There are two situations where a prisoner may be allowed to be seen by another doctor: an unconvicted prisoner may apply to the governor to be attended upon by another doctor, but if this request is granted, the prisoner will be responsible for paying any charge incurred (r 20(5)); and a prisoner who is taking legal action may be given 'reasonable facilities' to see a doctor in connection with those proceedings. Such a consultation should take place within the sight, but out of the hearing, of prison officers (r 20(6)).

10.78 The Prison Service Standard on Health Services for Prisoners issued in 1999 sets as an auditable standard:

'To provide prisoners with access to the same range and quality of services as the general public receives from the National Health Service.'

The actual experience for prisoners is often that healthcare is of a poor standard, and is often the subject of criticism by the Chief Inspector of Prisons. In November 1996 he published a discussion document, *Patient or Prisoner* which recommended that responsibility for prison health care services be taken over by the NHS. As yet this has not happened.

10.79   More detailed guidance upon health care for prisoners is found in Standing Order 13. This outlines the roles of all health care staff, and gives guidance upon how they should discharge their responsibilities. This will in due course be replaced with a comprehensive PSO on health care.

10.80   Most importantly, each prison should appoint a managing medical officer who should arrange for a doctor to attend the prison every weekday, and for a doctor to be on call at all other times. The following tasks must be routinely completed by prison doctors:

'(a) separately examine as soon as possible and no later than 24 hours after reception all prisoners received
      —for the first time from court
      —from court after conviction or sentence
      —on transfer from another prison or return from an outside hospital after in-patient treatment or observation
      —after any temporary release under police escort
      —after any other temporary absence unless in a category specified by the managing medical officer after consultation with the governor as one in respect of which an examination need not routinely be carried out;
 (b) conduct surgeries for all prisoners who wish to see a medical officer (in this connection the managing medical officer will ensure that adequate facilities exist for prisoners to apply to see a member of the medical staff and for such applications to be recorded);
 (c) visit prisoners undergoing in-patient treatment or observation or who are under special supervision in any location;
 (d) visit at least twice daily any prisoner placed in special accommodation or under body restraint;
 (e) visit as soon as possible after adjudication or removal from association, and thereafter as considered necessary any prisoner undergoing cellular confinement as a consequence of a disciplinary award or removal from association for the maintenance of good order and discipline;
 (f) visit as soon as possible after removal from association and thereafter at least every seven days any prisoner removed from association in his own interests;
 (g) examine prisoners for the purpose of such reports as are required for official purposes;
 (h) if a pharmacist is not in attendance, supervise the preparation of medicinal products; and
 (i) separately examine every prisoner to be discharged or transferred to another prison, and those to be temporarily released or discharged to court other than in prison custody, and make arrangements for continuity of medical care if appropriate.'

10.81   Prisoners who wish to see the doctor for non-urgent problems should report sick in the morning 'sick parade' or put in an application to see the doctor. However, when they are taken to the prison health care centre, it is likely that they will first be seen by a member of the medical staff who may be a prison officer working as a 'hospital officer'. These officers do not have formally recognised medical qualifications, although they undergo a prison service run course in basic health care. Many prisoners complain that if the officer considers that there is nothing wrong that warrants further medical investigation, they are simply returned to the wing after being given aspirins.

10.82 Prisoners who are in urgent need of medical treatment or who are too ill to get to the health care centre should be seen immediately by a member of the medical staff who will decide whether to call the medical officer, if the prisoner can be safely moved to the health care centre, and whether it would be appropriate to send the prisoner to an outside hospital (SO 13, para 28).

10.83 Many prisons contain 'hospitals' where prisoners can be treated as in-patients, and at a few prisons surgical operations may be conducted. Prisoners are able to accept or decline treatment, and must sign their consent for any invasive surgery unless their lives may be endangered, serious harm would be likely or there would be an irreversible deterioration in the prisoner's condition. Subject to the above, the consent of a parent or guardian should be obtained where a prisoner is under 18 years old, and must be obtained if the prisoner is under 16 years of age (SO 13, para 25).

10.84 When prisoners go on hunger strike, this must be reported to the medical officer, and it is standard practice for such prisoners to be admitted to the health care centre in order that their physical condition may be monitored. If the prisoner continues to refuse food and water and their weight drops significantly or it is considered that their health is in danger of being damaged as a result of the hunger strike, an outside consultant may be called in. Such a consultant would be asked to assess whether the prisoner is suffering from a mental or physical illness which impairs their rational judgement. If so, a decision may be made to feed the prisoner artificially, and this should be taken by the medical officer in consultation with the outside consultant. If the prisoner is not found to be irrational, the medical officer should advise him/her that there will be a deterioration in their health if the hunger strike continues, and that this will continue unless the prisoner specifically asks for medical intervention (SO 13, paras 39–41).

10.85 The Prison Services' policy on AIDS and HIV aims to prevent the spread of infection, protect the health of prisoners and staff and provide care and support for infected prisoners (CI 30/91, Annex A). The policy on the issue of condoms is contained in a 'dear doctor' letter (DDL(95)10). These are centrally-issued letters of guidance to prison health care staff. The policy is that medical officers should be 'encouraged to prescribe condoms and lubricants, when in their clinical judgement there is a known risk of HIV infection as a result of HIV risk sexual behaviour'. A challenge to the rationality of this policy on the basis that as a request for condoms inevitably meant that a prisoner was to engage in sexual conduct and so they should be issued on request failed. The court held that it was not unreasonable for control to be exercised over their issue as they could be used for 'other purposes', and as the real issue was one of health the policy was not irrational for making it a decision for the medical officer (*R v Secretary of State for the Home Department, ex p Fielding* (1999) Times, 21 July). Tablets for disinfecting syringes have been issued to prisoners and should be freely available within prisons (IG 96/95). Education is considered to be the 'vital element in the prevention strategy' and to this end the Prison Service has produced an educational package 'AIDS Inside and Out', which explains ways of avoiding infection.

10.86   Prisoners may be tested for HIV/AIDS at their own request whilst they are in prison, and will not be tested unless they consent. Prisoners who are HIV positive or who have AIDS should generally be located on normal location within prison, and should have access to the same regime facilities, including education and employment and recreation, as other prisoners held on the same wing (CI 30/91, Annex A, para 18). However, governors do have discretion to opt out of this policy, and in some prisons, prisoners have been placed under 'viral infectivity restrictions'. This entails removing them from normal location to a different part of the prison, and excluding them from employment which carries the risk of physical injury, for example working with sharp implements (CI 30/91, Annex A, para 19). However, the Prison Service has announced that as from 1 November 1995, prisoners should no longer be subjected to viral infectivity restrictions on the basis that the risk of infection in the course of ordinary day-to-day contact with infected prisoners is 'insignificant' (IG 98/95). The same instruction also makes it clear that only health care staff should be aware of prisoners' HIV positive status.

10.87   The Prison Service has a policy of aiming to 'provide for identified HIV infected inmates no less a quality of care than they could expect to receive outside' (CI 30/91, Annex A, para 23), and to this end a proactive clinical approach is recommended, involving regular physical and psychological monitoring. Although a hospital for prisoners with HIV-related illnesses was purpose built in the late 1980s, this has never been used for its intended purpose. Current policy is to locate such prisoners as near to their homes as possible in a prison health care centre with a full time medical officer, night nursing cover, and links with NHS facilities. Where prisoners become too ill to be managed by prison health care centres, they may be transferred to an NHS hospital or a hospice (CI 30/91, Annex A, para 27).

10.88   Problems relating to health care issues can be extremely difficult to deal with, and letters from solicitors asking that their client be treated often appear to meet with hostile responses from medical officers.

10.89   Prisoners may submit requests/complaints about their treatment to the managing medical officer as well as to the governor and area manager, and can also complain to the Directorate of Prison Health Care at Prison Service Headquarters. The Prisons Ombudsman's remit does not extend to examining the clinical decisions of prison health care staff, despite his calls for the remit to be so amended. However, other decisions relating to health care issues will fall within the scope of the Ombudsman's investigatory powers. For example, if the managing medical officer says that a prisoner has not got a broken arm and is suffering from psychosomatic symptoms, this cannot be investigated by the Ombudsman. Conversely, if the managing medical officer suspects that a prisoner's arm may be fractured, and asks that he is conveyed to an outside hospital for an x-ray, the Ombudsman could investigate the governor's failure to ensure that the prisoner is taken to hospital.

10.90   Where the prison's failure to treat a prisoner causes damage to his health, the normal rules of clinical negligence will apply. One case has suggested that in respect of establishing negligence, the standard of psychiatric care in prisons would not be expected to meet that provided by hospitals outside in terms of suicide prevention (*Knight v Home Office* [1990] 3 All ER 237). The rationale was that the standards of care provided could be different as prisons and outside hospitals were different institutions performing different functions. The courts have not accepted this as a general principle, holding for example that woman prisoners are entitled to the same standard of obstetric care as women in outside hospitals (*Brooks v Home Office* [1999]2 FLR 33).

DISABILITY

10.91   The Disability Discrimination Act 1995 prohibits discrimination in the provision of 'goods, facilities and services' on the basis of disability. The Prison Service is covered by the Act. Extensive guidance to governors is given in PSO 2855. This confirms that governors and directors of private prisons are responsible for compliance with the Act and must ensure that:

(i)   Consideration is given about what reasonable adjustments can be made to meet the needs of disabled prisoners and visitors (para 1.3.1);

(ii)   Arrangements must be made for an assessment of prisoners' needs, at the reception stage (para 2.1.1);

(iii) A record must be kept of all disabled prisoners about their communication and mobility needs (para 2.1.2);

(iv)   Prisoners who have difficulty in understanding the Prisoners' Information Book must have their rights and obligations explained to them. They must in particular be advised of the requirements of the Prison Rules (para 2.1.4);

(v)   All establishments must be prepared, as far as possible, to provide appropriate interpretation services for the purpose of necessary communication with prisoners who have a hearing impairment (paras 2.1.5 and 4.4);

(vi)   The level of an individual's mobility, daily living skills and confidence in navigating his or her environment must be taken into account in the allocation of accommodation (para 2.2.1);

(vii) Establishments must take reasonable steps to ensure that disabled prisoners have access to the full range of employment opportunities available, including access to workshops (para 3.1.1);

(viii) Establishments must take reasonable steps to ensure that disabled prisoners have access to education and physical education facilities (para 3.2.2);

(ix)   The Library must arrange to supply large print or talking books to those prisoners who have a visual disability (para 3.3.1).

The Act imposes a qualified duty to 'take such steps as it is reasonable, in all the circumstances' to make modifications to practices, policies or procedures which make it impossible or unreasonably difficult to make use of a service. As reasonableness will include resources available, this will limit the extent to which prisoners will be able to argue for modifications.

10.92   A person is disabled for the purposes of the Act if they have 'a physical, sensory or mental impairment which has a substantial and long-term effect on their ability to carry out normal day-to-day activities'. A person who suffers discrimination on the basis of their disability may take proceedings in the county court. Complaints can also be made through the requests/complaints procedure, and following that to the Prisons Ombudsman. Once the Human Rights Act is in force if a Convention right is engaged (for example the right to family life under art 8, if visiting facilities are more restricted for the disabled than for the rest of the prison population) then disabled prisoners may be able to also rely on art 14, the prohibition on discrimination.

RELIGION

10.93   Section 10(5) of the Prison Act 1952 requires the governor to 'record the religious denomination to which the prisoner declares himself to belong' and Prison Rule 13 states that a prisoner 'shall be treated as being of the religious denomination stated in the record' made under the Act but may direct that the record be amended 'in a proper case and after due enquiry'. Standing Order 7A confirms that prisoners should:

> 'have the right to practise this religion within its regulations and within the limits of any agreement that may have been reached between the relevant religious body and Headquarters, or, in the absence of such agreement, in a manner that does not discriminate unfairly against adherents of this religion.'

10.94   CI 51/1989 stated that certain religious registrations would not be permitted, namely Scientology, Black Muslim and Rastafarianism (para 4). These restrictions on self-certification may be subject to challenge as breaching art 9 of the ECHR, the right to freedom of religion, on the basis that prisoners should be able to have access to facilities and to engage in conduct which directly expresses their religion or belief. The provision of such facilities is clearly tied to the process of registration.

10.95   The Prison Service has produced a Directory and Guide on Religious Practices in HM Prison Service which details all the major faiths and the permitted observances and facilities in prisons for each of them. It also contains a security summary relating security issues to religious belief, for example that during searches 'the holy books and religious artefacts of any faith . . . whilst subject to search should be treated with the greatest respect.'

EDUCATION, LIBRARY AND ACCESS TO INFORMATION

10.96 Prison Rule 32 states that 'Every prisoner able to profit from the education facilities at a prison shall be encouraged to do so' (r 32(1)). The Rule also states that classes 'shall be arranged at every prison' and that 'special attention shall be paid to the education and training of prisoners with special needs'. Prisoners of compulsory school age must participate in education or training courses for at least 15 hours within 'the normal working week' (r 32(4)). Prisoners who wish to improve their education by distance learning shall be afforded 'reasonable facilities' to do so (r 32(2)). In relation to Open University courses prisons operate a 'sift' procedure and applications must be supported by the education officer and approved by the governor (PSO 4201). The education courses available to prisoners will be related to sentence planning issues (see chapter 6).

10.97 The Rules require prisons to have libraries from which prisoners may borrow books. In relation to legal resources IG 73/1996 includes a long list of books that libraries must have, including texts on criminal and prison law. Prison Rule 10 states that within 24 hours of reception into prison prisoners should be given written information about the Rules including 'earnings and privileges, and the proper means of making requests and complaints' (r 10(1)). The Prison Reform Trust, in conjunction with the Prison Service, has produced a series of Prisoner Information Books which explain the basic provisions of the Rules and which are provided to all prisoners on reception. Prisoners should also be provided with a copy of the Prison Rules on request (r 10(3)).

10.98 With respect to policy guidance, para 1.4.1 of PSO 0300 states: 'As a general principle, prisoners will be allowed access, through libraries in Prison Service establishments, to all Orders and Instructions which affect them.' Some will not be open for security reasons (for example some chapters of PSO 1000, the Security Manual). In practice many prisons maintain a culture based on an assumption that prisoners are not entitled to information about the legal context of their incarceration, and prisoners have extreme difficulty in accessing PSOs and other policy documents.

10.99 With regard to their own records, prisoners are entitled to see their sentence planning documents, and recategorisation forms (see chapter 6). They are entitled to free copies of records of hearing and evidence relating to disciplinary hearings (para 9.5 of the Prison Discipline Manual). Parole is an open process and prisoners see all reports with limited exceptions (see chapter 12). The main anomaly now is the reports prepared for Category A reviews, which are not disclosed but are digested into a 'gist'. Since November 1991 prisoners can have access to their medical records under the Access to Health Records Act 1990 unless the medical officer believes it would be likely to cause serious harm to the mental or physical health of the patient or of any other individual, or where it is likely to identify any person other than the prisoner.

10.100   With regard to other records (such as the prisoner's record on Form F2050) the Prison Service adhere to the Code of Practice on access to information which creates a presumption of disclosure subject to restrictions on, for example, security or third-party confidence grounds. In a letter to *Inside Time* at the end of 1999, the Prison Service confirmed that:

> 'the general policy is that information held about a prisoner should be disclosed on request to him or her unless there are clear and justifiable security grounds for not doing so, including the prevention of crime or the protection of third parties'.

Clearly the most contentious information, such as untested allegations made by staff or other prisoners included on Security Information Reports (SIRs), which could result in a prisoner's segregation or transfer, will not be disclosed to the affected prisoner. When investigating a complaint the Prisons Ombudsman will be able to access these records, but will not include their details in his report. Requests can be made for records held on computer (basic personal details, court appearance information, adjudication record and work/activities timetable) through the Data Protection Act on payment of a fee.

UNCONVICTED PRISONERS

10.101   The main differences between the way that unconvicted and convicted prisoners are treated relate to work, private cash, visits, letters and medical treatment. They are dealt with in the appropriate sections of this text. In addition, unconvicted prisoners generally have the right to wear their own clothing, so long as it is 'suitable, tidy and clean' and their visitors may bring clean clothes for them to change into (r 23(1)). However, if they so wish, unconvicted prisoners may elect to wear prison clothing. In this case, their uniform will be brown, rather than the blue worn by convicted prisoners. Instruction to Governors 78/95 reflected a change in r 23(1), which places important restrictions upon unconvicted prisoners' right to wear their own clothes. Governors may now require unconvicted prisoners who are provisionally category A or on the escape list to wear prison uniform unless they are produced in court.

CIVIL PRISONERS

10.102   Civil prisoners are those who are committed to prison for contempt of court, or 'for failing to do or abstain from anything required to be done or left undone' (SO 12, para 1) (eg defaulting on maintenance payments, civil debts, legal aid contributions etc.).

10.103   Essentially, civil prisoners are treated in the same way as convicted prisoners, except with regard to sentence calculation (see chapter 6), arrangements for them to receive visits and send letters (see chapter 9). In addition civil prisoners may wear their own clothing so long as they are not working outside the prison or associating with convicted prisoners (SO 12, para 4(2)). In these respects, civil prisoners are treated in the same way as unconvicted prisoners.

10.104   If a civil prisoner is employed in his or her cell, the governor has the discretion to leave the door unlocked (Standing Order 12, para 4(3)).

DEATHS IN CUSTODY

Introduction

10.105   Deaths in prison custody have become a matter of increasing public concern over recent years. There has been a steadily rising number of deaths in prison and much warranted attention has been focused on the very serious problem of self-inflicted deaths within prison. Lawyers and families can have a vital role in ensuring that these deaths are subjected to proper public scrutiny *and* that systemic failings are highlighted to try and ensure that similar fatalities do not occur in the future.

10.106   Legal representation can assist the family in understanding the procedures following the death. The inquest is an opportunity for the bereaved to hear evidence from all the witnesses that the coroner considers relevant and to have questions asked about the treatment and care of the deceased in order to gain as full as picture as possible of what happened. In this section, the statutory materials referred to are to the Coroners Act 1988 (CA 1988) and the Coroners Rules 1984 (CR 1984).

The prison response following a death

10.107   Prison Service Order 2710 'Follow up to deaths in custody', lays down the procedures to be followed by the Prison Service and contracted out services where a prisoner dies in custody.

10.108   **Family liaison and investigations following the death**   In the event of a death the prison should inform the nominated next of kin and any other person the prisoner has reasonably requested be informed of the death. A senior member of staff will be appointed as the family's named point of contact in the prison and should provide a factual account of the events leading up to the death. They should also offer the family the opportunity to visit the prison and see where the death occurred. The police will have notified the coroner of the death and the prison governor will have provided basic details of the death, including a copy of any memorandum from the medical officer notifying the governor of the death. After someone has died in prison the police will be called and initial inquiries made. If the police decide there are no grounds to suspect a criminal offence such as to require a formal police investigation there will be a Prison Service internal inquiry.

10.109   In apparent self-inflicted deaths and 'non natural' deaths, an investigation will be carried out by a senior investigating officer from outside the establishment. In deaths that are apparently due to 'natural' causes a clinical review will be conducted and a liaison officer will be appointed whose responsibility it is to draw together the necessary documents for the investigating officer. If the police are carrying out an inquiry, the report and file will be passed to the Crown Prosecution Service which will decide if criminal charges are to be brought. This is very rare save in cases of homicides by other prisoners. If it is decided not to prosecute anyone in relation to the death the inquest will take place, usually some considerable time after the death.

Personal property

10.110   The coroner or the police will take the decision about what property needs to be retained for evidence. The prison will release any cash or property not needed as evidence when the coroner authorises them to do so. Most items can be released at an early stage and the prison will contact family to let them know when they can recover the deceased's belongings. Unfortunately personal items such as letters and other writings are usually amongst those needed as evidence and this sometimes means the intended recipient of a letter written by the deceased may not be able to obtain it until quite some time after the death. The coroner may recognise that this can cause a great deal of additional distress and use his discretion to release a copy of any such letter earlier on.

Funeral arrangements

10.111   The funeral can go ahead as soon as the coroner issues an interim death certificate following the formal opening of the inquest. If there are no executors/personal representatives (or they decline to take responsibility for the funeral arrangements) the prison chaplain has an obligation (the Prison Rules 1999, r 14(1)(b)) to ensure that there are appropriate arrangements for the conduct of the service. If the person or their partner who has taken responsibility for making the funeral arrangements has been awarded certain income-based benefits they are eligible to make a claim for a Social Fund Funeral Payment. This is a grant, not a loan, and is not repayable by the claimant although it is recoverable from the deceased's estate if one exists. The governor has a discretion to meet any funeral expenses not covered by the Social Fund payment or, in the event that the next of kin is not entitled to such a payment, can make a payment direct to the funeral director (normally up to a maximum of £2,000). The area manager can authorise amounts in excess of this.

THE INQUEST PROCEDURE

Introduction

10.112   Coronial law is a specialist area and INQUEST, the advice and campaign group concerned with deaths in custody and their investigation can advise on solicitors and counsel working in this field or work with lawyers new to this area of work. This section is not intended to be a comprehensive review of coronial law and for further consideration one of the standard texts relating to inquests, such as *Jervis on the Office and Duties of Coroners* (11th edn, 1993), should be considered.

Duty to hold an inquest

10.113   The requirement to hold an inquest in the case of deaths in prison dates back to the thirteenth century. The present statutory framework (CA 1988, s 8 (1)(c)) requires that there must be an inquest into all deaths in prisons whatever the circumstances. The inquest must, under CA 1988, s 8(3)(a), be held with a jury. The use of the term prison is not defined but according to *Jervis on the Office and Duties of Coroners*, it does not include youth custody centres (now young offender institutions). The Home Office does recognise that an inquest should be held in all cases where the deceased has been in lawful custody at the time of the death, including where a prisoner has been transferred to a hospital before the death occurred (Home Office circulars 35/1969 and 3/1981).

Persons entitled to ask questions at the inquest

10.114   A properly interested person is entitled to examine any witness at an inquest either in person or by an authorised advocate as defined by the Courts and Legal Services Act 1990, s 119(1) (CR 1984, r 20(1) as amended by the Coroners (Amendment) Rules 1999). A properly interested person is defined under r 20(2) of the Rules as:

(i)   a parent, child, spouse and any person representative of the deceased;
(ii)   any beneficiary under a life insurance policy;
(iii)   the insurer under a life insurance policy;
(iv)   any person whose act or omission or that of his agent or servant may in the opinion of the coroner have caused, or contributed to, the death of the deceased;
(v)   any person appointed by a trade union to which the deceased at the time of his death belonged, if the death of the deceased may have been caused by an injury received in the course of his employment or by an industrial disease;
(vi)   an inspector of an enforcing authority, or a person appointed by a government department eg the health and safety executive;
(vii)   the chief officer of police;
(viii) anyone else who in the opinion of the Coroner is a properly interested person.

10.115   It is for the coroner to decide who is a properly interested person, and a decision can only be challenged if it has been made unreasonable or taking into account irrelevant considerations. The last category of properly interested person can properly be used to extend the class of family beyond the identified degrees of kindred set out above (*R v South London Coroner, ex p Driscoll* (1993) 159 JP 45, DC and also *Practice Note for Coroner approved by the Council of the Coroners' Society of England and Wales on 19 November 1998*). It could also apply to close friends of the deceased if the Coroner is of the view that they have a proper interest.

The post mortem

10.116 Following the death, the body of the deceased will have be taken to a hospital or mortuary. The coroner's office should be contacted as soon as possible as a post mortem will be held and family members may wish to view the body before this takes place. A family member has the right to attend or be represented at the post mortem. If family members have notified the coroner of their desire to do so they should, unless it is impracticable or will cause undue delay, be notified of when it is taking place (CR 1984, r 7).

10.117 A Home Office approved pathologist carries out the initial post mortem on behalf of the Coroner. In some cases, usually involving potential issues about the use of force or neglect, there will also be a pathologist instructed on behalf of the Prison Service and/or the individual prison officers. The decision as to whether the family of the deceased should arrange for their own pathologist to undertake a further post mortem examination in advance of the burial/cremation depends on the circumstances of the individual case. However, in all suspected deaths involving restraint and/or use of force (as opposed to self-inflicted deaths where the medical cause of death is not likely to be in issue) an independent post mortem report is usually invaluable. Funding to instruct a pathologist can be obtained under the Legal Advice and Assistance Scheme or the certificated Legal Aid Scheme if the family of the deceased contemplates a civil action for damages (see chapter 13).

10.118 If the body has already been cremated or buried and there is concern about the medical cause of death there is still an opportunity to, if appropriate, instruct a pathologist to advise on the Home Office post mortem report. Specialist advice can also be sought to advise on the need for any toxicology or other specialist/expert reports.

10.119 A properly interested person or his or her lawyers are entitled to a copy of the post mortem report or any other notes of evidence or any document put in evidence at the inquest (CR 1984, r 57(1)). The post mortem report should also have attached all the toxicology results.

The opening of the inquest

10.120 The inquest proceedings will usually be opened within a few days of the death and then adjourned. There is considerable variation between coroners as to how they conduct the opening of the inquest. In general very brief evidence is heard about details of the deceased and the circumstances of the death. In some cases the pathologist is called to give evidence about the medical cause of death. The family does not need to attend but it can sometimes be helpful to have someone in attendance on their behalf in case more evidence is given. The coroner's officer can be contacted as to the practice of the particular coroner.

Adjournment of inquest pending arrest/criminal proceedings

10.121 Section 16(1) of the Coroners Act 1988 and rr 26 and 27 of the Coroners Rules 1984 provide for the circumstances of when the inquest must or may be adjourned pending arrest or the outcome of criminal charges arising out of the death. After the conclusion of the relevant criminal proceedings the coroner has discretion under the CA 1988, s 16(3) to resume the inquest proceedings. However, the coroner is not obliged to resume the inquest, but his decision may be subject to judicial review in an appropriate case (*R v Inner West London Coroner, ex p Perks* (1993) Independent, July 13, DC). If the inquest is resumed following an adjournment under CA 1988, s 16(1), s 16(7) provides that the findings of the inquest as to cause of death must not be inconsistent with the outcome of the relevant criminal proceedings. A not guilty verdict of a named defendant will not necessarily preclude an inquest jury concluding that the death was the result of an unlawful killing.

The remit of the inquest

10.122 Although the inquest is often the only forum for the family to explore the circumstances of the death, the inquest proceedings have a very narrow remit. It is important that practitioners make their clients aware of the limitations of the proceedings. In order to consider this area the statutory provisions and their interpretation in the case law have to be considered.

The statutory position

10.123 Section 11(5) of the CA 1988 and CR 1984, r 36 of the Rules provide that the proceedings and evidence at an inquest shall be directed solely to ascertaining the following matters, namely:

(i)   who the deceased was;

(ii)   how, when and where the deceased came by his death;

(iii)   the particulars for the time being required by the Registration Act.

10.124 Rule 42 of the CR 1984 provides that:

'No verdict shall be framed in such a way as to appear to determine any question of—

(a)   criminal liability on the part of a named person, or

(b)   civil liability.'

The case law

10.125 The most significant coronial law case in recent years is the Court of Appeal decision in *R v HM Coroner for North Humberside and Scunthorpe, ex p Jamieson* [1995] QB 1. Although dealing specifically with the issue of whether on the particular facts of the case—a self-inflicted death of a prisoner—'neglect' (see further below) should have been left to the jury, the

Court of Appeal extensively reviewed the relevant statutory and judicial authorities. Giving the judgment of the court, Bingham LJ then set out a number of general conclusions, some of which apply to all deaths in prison.

10.126   At conclusion (1) Bingham LJ emphasised that usually, the issue of how the deceased came by his death, is the question that the majority of the evidence at the inquest will be directed towards. At conclusion (2) Bingham LJ held that:

> '"how" is to be understood as meaning "by what means" ... the task is not to ascertain how the deceased died, which might raise general and far reaching issues but "how the deceased came by his death", a more limited question directed to the means by which the deceased came by his death.'

It must be emphasised, however, that this does not mean that the consideration of the means by which a person died should be limited to the last link in the chain of causation (*R v Inner London Coroner, ex p Dalagio and Lockwood Croft* [1994] 4 All ER 139). The Divisional Court in *R v HM Coroner for Western District of East Sussex, ex p Homber* (1994) 158 JP 357 has also emphasised that the:

> 'question of how the deceased came by his death is of course wider than merely finding the medical cause of death and it is therefore right and proper that the coroner should inquire into acts and omissions which are directly responsible for death.'

10.127   This means that despite the prohibition in CR 1984, r 42, the coroner and jury are able to explore facts bearing on criminal and civil liability. At conclusion (2) in *ex p Jamieson* (above) Bingham LJ confirmed that the statutory duty to ascertain how the deceased came by his death prevails over the prohibition in r 42 which applies only to the verdict. At conclusion (14) in *Jamieson*, Bingham LJ emphasised that it is:

> 'the duty of the coroner ... to ensure that the relevant facts are fully, fairly and fearlessly investigated. He is bound to recognise the acute public concern rightly aroused where deaths occurred in custody. He must ensure that the relevant facts are exposed to public scrutiny, in particular if there is evidence of foul play, abuse or inhumanity. He fails in his duty if the investigation is superficial slipshod or perfunctory.'

PRE-INQUEST DISCLOSURE

The law

10.128   There are no parties at an inquest and neither the Rules nor the Act provide the coroner with a mandatory duty of disclosure of documentation before the giving of oral evidence, save for the post mortem report and special examination reports (CR 1984, r 57) and uncontroversial documentary evidence (CR 1984, r 37). The case law (most notably the cases *R v Hammersmith Coroner, ex p Peach* [1980] QB 211 and *R v Southwark Coroner, ex p Hicks* [1987] 2 All ER 140) has held that there is no breach of natural justice in a failure to provide copies of the evidence prior to the inquest hearing. It has also been established that the Coroner has no power to disclose to an interested person documents which have been disclosed to him in confidence. There is, though, no legal prohibition on institutions such as the Prison Service voluntarily disclosing or agreeing to the coroner disclosing evidence.

Prison service policy on pre-inquest disclosure following a death in prison

10.129 As a result of lobbying by organisations such as INQUEST, and increasing disquiet at the secrecy surrounding prison deaths, the Prison Service has recognised that lack of pre-inquest disclosure is counterproductive to the effectiveness of the inquest. INQUEST has been in close dialogue with the Prison Service about disclosure and the recently issued Standing Orders and Instructions on deaths in prison. The prison service policy on pre-inquest disclosure (PID) is contained within Prison Service Order *Follow up to deaths in custody* (see para 10.107) and the protocol, which came into effect on 28 April 1999. This guidance applies to all deaths in prison custody and deaths in the custody of services contracted by the Prison Service, or which occur as a direct result of actions whilst in that care. It applies to all deaths that occur after April 1999. The protocol acknowledges that:

> 'Voluntary disclosure of information held by the Authorities in advance of the inquest should help to ensure all those involved including the bereaved that a full and open investigation has been conducted and that they and their legal representatives will not be disadvantaged at the inquest.'

10.130 The full report of the investigation will be given to the coroner who will be asked for his or her views on whether it is a case where a pre-inquest hearing may be appropriate, and whether he objects to its disclosure to interested parties prior to the hearing or anticipates that such disclosure could damage the conduct of the hearing. The report of the internal investigation into a death in prison custody and statements taken from witnesses in the course of its preparation remains the property of the Prison Service (*ex p Peach*, para 10.129). Disclosure is therefore a voluntary act by the Prison Service.

10.131 The report will then be offered to the family and or their legal representative. It is recommended by the protocol that arrangements for pre-inquest disclosure should take place as soon as the Prison Service is satisfied the material may be disclosed and in any case no later than 28 days before the date of the inquest. The cost of reproduction of documents, and for the family to receive pre-inquest disclosure, should be met by the Prison Service. In cases awaiting CPS consideration on criminal proceedings disclosure should not take place until the CPS has advised against a prosecution or any criminal proceedings have finished.

10.132 The protocol provides for some kinds of material which require particular consideration when pre-inquest disclosure is being arranged, namely:

(i)   Where the disclosure of certain material may have an impact on the fairness of possible subsequent proceedings, whether criminal, civil or disciplinary. It is submitted that these reasons would only justify withholding documents or parts of documents where there was a genuine risk that disclosure would have a prejudicial effect.

(ii) There may be material that contains sensitive or personal material about the deceased or their family or other material, which may cause concern or distress to the family of the deceased. The handling of such material should be discussed with the family or the family's lawyer.

(iii) Personal information about third parties which is not material to the inquest—for example, the addresses of witnesses—should be deleted from documents to be disclosed. If further details of witnesses are considered necessary their consents should be sought.

(iv) Security or other information whose disclosure beyond the coroner could do real or substantial harm to the public interest.

10.133 Any person who is asked to give a statement during the course of an investigation should be made aware that their statement would be used in the context of an inquest and disclosed in accordance with the guidance. As well as the internal investigation report the following documents should be disclosed, subject to the coroner's consent:

(i) governor's and managing medical officer's short letter to the coroner notifying of the death;

(ii) inmate Medical Record and the nursing/treatment records (these are subject to statutory disclosure in any event under the Access to Health Records Act 1990);

(iii) relevant entries from the Inmate Personal Record (F2050);

(iv) relevant entries from the Wing Occurrence Book or Wing Diary;

(v) suicide/self harm referral forms (current or closed F2052SHs);

(vi) any warnings received from other agencies (eg PER form);

(vii) any note left by the deceased (if a copy is available).

It is important that the disclosed documentation is considered carefully prior to the inquest hearing so that any requests for additional disclosure are promptly made.

10.134 Interested persons or their representatives are usually required by the Prison Service to sign an undertaking that the disclosed documents will not be used for any other purpose than the inquest or disclosed to any third party. It is recognised that it is a legitimate concern that the inquest or any other proceedings should not be prejudiced by the inappropriate disclosure of confidential material. It is arguable, however, that given the provisions of the Contempt of Court Act 1981 the wide terms of the confidentiality agreement are unnecessarily restrictive and have caused unnecessary anxiety. For example, a strict interpretation of the agreement may prevent disclosure of information by the family member who is instructing the solicitor to others who have a proper interest in the inquest proceedings.

Witnesses and evidence at the inquest

10.135 As there are no parties to an inquest the coroner has the sole power to call witnesses who are considered to give relevant evidence. The Divisional

Court has suggested that as a matter of good practice that the coroner should circulate a provisional list of witnesses he is proposing to call to interested parties prior to the inquest hearing together with a short statement of their evidence (*R v Lincoln Coroner, ex p Hay* (1999) Times, 30 March, DC). Rule 37(3) of the CR 1984 provides that if the coroner wishes to admit documentary evidence he must make a public announcement at the beginning of the inquest that he wishes to admit it and must allow a properly interested person to see a copy and to object to its admission. Again it is submitted that as a matter of good practice that any documentary evidence that is proposed to be adduced under CR 1984, r 37(3) should be disclosed well in advance of the inquest hearing so that in the event of an objection an adjournment to call the relevant witness is not required.

10.136 The family and their legal representatives have a vital role in assisting the coroner to focus on relevant issues to be dealt with at the inquest (*R v HM Coroner for Coventry, ex p O'Reilly* (1996) 160 JP 749). Although it is solely a matter for the coroner to decide what evidence should be heard and what witnesses should be called, the coroner should be directed towards relevant evidence and witnesses that he or she may not be aware of. In the context of a prison death this may be the evidence of other prisoners. A failure of the coroner to call evidence from relevant witnesses may lead to the Divisional Court quashing the inquisition (see, for example, *ex p Hay* referred to in para 10.135 above).

10.137 The coroner will usually wish to call as a witness at the inquest a family member who had contact with the deceased to give evidence, and it is important that the coroner is made aware of the concerns that the family have about the circumstances of the death and a full statement supplied. A family member attending the inquest as a witness, as opposed to in their capacity as a properly interested person will be entitled following the inquest to be paid their expenses (CA 1988, ss 24 and 26).

Verdicts

10.138 Strictly speaking the 'verdict' means the entirety of the answers to the form of inquisition which is as follows:

(i)   the name of the deceased if known;
(ii) the time, place and circumstances at or in which injury was sustained;
(iii) the conclusion of the jury as to the death;
(iv) the registration particulars.

Colloquially the 'verdict' is understood as meaning the conclusion as to death.

10.139 If there is sufficient evidence on which a jury properly directed could return a specific verdict it is the duty of the coroner to leave such a verdict (*R v HM Coroner for Inner London, ex p Diesa Koto* (1993) 157 JP 857). Before reaching a particular verdict, the jury must be satisfied on the requisite standard of proof. For a verdict of suicide or unlawful killing the standard is the criminal standard—beyond reasonable doubt—and for all other verdicts it is the lesser civil standard—on the balance of probabilities.

In the context of a death in custody the likely possible verdicts are:

(i)   suicide;
(ii)   accident/misadventure;
(iii)   open verdict;
(iv)   unlawful killing;
(v)   natural causes;
(vi)   neglect.

10.140   **Suicide** should never be presumed. The test of sufficiency of evidence has been stated to be 'have all other possible explanations been totally ruled out' (*R v Essex Coroner, ex p Hopper* (13 May 1988, unreported), DC).

10.141   Accident/misadventure involves the conclusion that the deceased died as an unexpected result of a deliberate act. In a self-inflicted death it would cover the situation where the deceased did not intend the consequences of his/her actions.

10.142   Open verdict   If the jury agree on the balance of probabilities that there is insufficient evidence to prove the other available verdicts then they should record an open verdict. This includes the situation where they are not satisfied of a verdict to the requisite standard of proof.

10.143   Unlawful killing covers all cases of homicide.

10.144   Natural causes   Ie where the death was due to the normal consequences of a natural illness.

10.145   Neglect   Neglect is not the same as civil negligence, and a verdict of neglect as an adjunct to another verdict such as misadventure or suicide will only be left to a jury in very limited circumstances. The leading case on neglect is the Court of Appeal decision in *ex p Jamieson* (para **10.125**). At conclusion (9) Bingham LJ defines neglect as:

> 'a gross failure to provide adequate nourishment or liquid, or provide or procure basic medical attention or shelter or warmth for someone in a dependent position (because of youth, age, illness or incarceration) who cannot provide it for himself. Failure to provide medical attention for a dependent person whose physical condition is such as to show that he obviously needs it may amount to neglect.'

10.146   It is possible, therefore, that the dependent person's mental condition is relevant to such a finding. For example, if a mental nurse observed that a patient had a propensity to swallow razor blades and failed to report this propensity to a doctor and the patient had no intention to cause himself injury, but did thereafter swallow razor blades with fatal results. In both cases the crucial consideration will be what the dependent person's condition, whether physical or mental, appeared to be.

10.147   At conclusion (11) dealing with a situation where the deceased took his own life Bingham LJ held that:

> 'On certain facts it could possibly be correct to hold that neglect contributed to that cause of death, but this finding would not be justified simply on the ground

that the deceased was afforded an opportunity to take his own life even if it was careless (as that expression is used in common speech or in the law of negligence) to afford the deceased that opportunity. Such a finding would only be appropriate in a case where gross neglect was directly connected with the deceased's suicide (for example, if a prison warder observed a prisoner in his cell preparing to hang a noose around his neck, but passed on without any attempt to intervene).'

10.148 If 'neglect' is to form part of the verdict Bingham LJ held at conclusion (12) that there must 'be a clear and direct causal connection ... established between the conduct so described and the cause of death'. Cases following the decision in *Jamieson* have emphasised that errors in clinical or lay judgment are matters for the law of negligence and not neglect (*R v Birmingham Coroner, ex p Cotton* (1995) 160 JP 123 and *R v HM Coroner for South Yorkshire, ex p Tremble* (1995)159 JP 761). However, a failure to make a properly informed judgment based on relevant and reasonable obtainable information may give rise to the primary cause of death being aggravated by neglect (there is authority for this proposition is the unreported decision of the Divisional Court in *R v HM Coroner Swansea and Gower, ex p Tristram* (7 October 1999, unreported).

10.149 The coroner has power under the CR 1984, r 43 following the inquest to report in writing to the Prison Service or other appropriate authority the circumstances of the case so that remedial action can be taken to try to prevent any future fatality. It is submitted that consideration should be given to requesting that the coroner use his powers in appropriate cases where the circumstances of the death have highlighted systemic failures.

Applications under the CA 1988, s 13 and judicial review

10.150 Section 13 of the CA 1988 provides that the High Court can quash the inquisition and order a fresh inquest or order that an inquest is held in the following circumstances:

(i)   that the coroner refuses or neglects to hold an inquest;
(ii) where an inquest has been held that (whether by reason of fraud, rejection of evidence, irregularity of proceedings, insufficiency of inquiry, the discovery of new facts or evidence or otherwise) it is necessary or desirable in the interests of justice that another inquest should be held.

An application must be made for the Attorney General's authority or fiat, which must be obtained in order to pursue the review under the CA 1988, s 13. If an inquest has been held it will be necessary to show that there is a possibility of a different verdict. There is no time limit on the application, however delay could be a factor leading to the court finding that, irrespective of the possibility of a different verdict, that it was not necessary or desirable in the interests of justice to hold a fresh inquest (*R v HM Coroner for Wiltshire, ex p Clegg* (1996) 161 JP 521).

10.151 Judicial review (see generally chapter 16) is also available to review both interlocutory decisions of the coroner and also the inquisition. Applications for review of the inquisition can be made in conjunction with an application under the CA 1988, s 13.

Remedies following death in custody

10.152   Fatal Accidents Act 1976 and the Law Reform (Miscellaneous Provisions) Act 1934   A person who suffers injury, physical or psychiatric, in consequence of negligence or an assault and battery may bring an action for damages for that injury. Any personal injury action maintainable by a living person survives for the benefit of the estate and may be pursued after death. Claims arising from the death of an individual caused by tortious conduct are brought under the Fatal Accidents Act 1976 or the Law Reform (Miscellaneous Provisions) Act 1934. The 1976 Act enables those who were financially dependent upon the deceased to recover damages for the loss of dependency, and there is also a bereavement allowance payable to the spouse of a deceased or a parent of a deceased child under 18 at the time of death (Fatal Accidents Act 1976, ss 1 and 1A). The 1934 Act enables damages to be recovered on behalf of the deceased's estate and may include any right of action vested in the deceased at the time of the death together with funeral expenses.

10.153   European Convention on Human Rights and Human Rights Act 1998   The families of many who die in custody do not have viable claims under the 1934 and 1976 Acts as the deceased was over 18 with no dependants. The European Commission in *Keenan v United Kingdom* [1998] EHRLR 648 held that although the inquest provides an effective investigation mechanism, by its inquisitorial nature it did not provide a forum for establishing the responsibility of the prison authorities for failure to protect the deceased or obtaining damages. The restrictions provided by the 1934 and 1976 Act violated art 13 requiring the state to provide an effective domestic remedy.

10.154   The circumstances of the death may also give rise to a violation of art 2 of the European Convention on Human Rights. The European Court held in the case of *Osman v United Kingdom* [1999] 1 FLR 193 that there would be a violation of the state's positive obligation to protect life if it was established that the state knew or ought to have known at the time of the death of the existence of a real and immediate risk to life and that the state failed to take measures which, if judged objectively, might have been expected to avoid that risk.

Other remedies

10.155   A death in custody cannot form the subject matter of a complaint to the Prison Ombudsman as his remit (see chapter 4) only allows a complaint by a prisoner, rather than a prisoner's family, to be investigated. The Parliamentary Ombudsman has, however, been prepared to investigate complaints of administrative failings on the part of the Prison Service referred through a Member of Parliament (for example, the death of Kenneth Severin in HMP Belmarsh in 1995). Complaint to the Parliamentary Ombudsman is an avenue to consider in cases that raise questions of maladministration and misfeasance in public office.

10.156   Clinical failings of doctors and concerns about prison medical care can be referred for investigation to the General Medical Council. Lawyers representing the families of two prisoners who died in Brixton prison from overdoses of methadone prescribed by the prison medical officer complained that he had been reckless in his prescribing and had breached good medical practice. As a result of the evidence heard at the hearing the former medical officer was found guilty of serious professional misconduct and struck off by the GMC.

Funding

10.157 A 'properly interested person' can be advised on the inquest procedure and preparation for the inquest can be undertaken under the Legal Aid Advice and Assistance Scheme. Despite the fact that the Prison Service is invariably represented at the inquest by counsel paid out of public funds, legal aid is not available for representation for interested parties. However, grants may be made by the Lord Chancellor in exceptional cases to enable representation at inquest proceeding (Legal Aid Act 1988, s 4(2)(B)). INQUEST Lawyers Group co-ordinates a national pool of lawyers who are members of INQUEST and are willing to provide preparation and legal representation for the families of the bereaved. INQUEST can assist members through its extensive work on deaths in prison and inquest law generally. It can also provide information about its lobbying and campaigning work.

SUICIDE PREVENTION POLICY

10.158 The number of prisoners taking their own lives in prison has been steadily rising through the 1990s to an all time high of 91 in 1999. In May 1999 the Chief Inspector of Prisons published *Suicide is Everyone's Concern: A Thematic Review of Prisons for England and Wales*. Its terms of reference were to offer informed advice to the Prison service to enable it to maintain best practice in every establishment to assist and support:

(i)   prisoners at risk of suicide and self harm;
(ii)   the next of kin of prisoners who appear to have committed suicide;
(iii) staff and prisoners affected by the above.

10.159   Prison Service Order 2700 (*Caring for the Suicidal in Custody* (2000)) is the PSO which describes current prison service policy on suicide prevention. It draws upon recommendations of the thematic review and brings all previous instructions on suicide prevention into a new standard format.

10.160   In terms of their duty to care for prisoners, the Prison Service states that they aim to identify, and provide special care for prisoners in distress and despair and so reduce the risk of suicide and self harm. The Prison Service's overall strategy in reducing incidents of suicide and self-harm stresses the multi-disciplinary and multi-agency approach to suicide prevention.

10.161   The policy emphasises the importance of the screening procedure on reception into prison, specifically form F2169 which is a health screening form completed on reception when an initial assessment of suicide risk will be made by a member of the health care staff. In the case of first receptions and reception following conviction, sentence or transfer, a doctor will see the prisoner within 24 hours of reception.

10.162   A Self Harm at Risk form F2052SH should be raised where a prisoner has been identified as being at risk of suicide or self harm, and all relevant information should be recorded within in it, including assessments, instructions, observations about the prisoner, support by staff or others and information received from outside the establishment. The needs of at risk prisoners will be kept under regular review by staff, in consultation with the prisoner and a daily Supervision and Support Record will be maintained. The F2052SH will be closed by the unit manager when the prisoner appears to be coping satisfactorily. The strategy recognises the importance of communication between staff about at risk prisoners, particularly when they move within or between establishments.

10.163   Prisoners who are identified as suicidal or likely to self-mutilate should be seen by a doctor 'as soon as possible and in any event within 24 hours' and it is then up to the doctor to decide whether they should be treated as an in-patient or allowed to remain on normal location within the prison. In general, 'at risk' prisoners should be located in a cell with another prisoner, although exceptions will be made if their behaviour is considered 'too disturbing to other prisoners'. Prisoners who continue to be held in single cells are generally subject to a '15 minute watch'.

10.164   Staff responsible for the care of an 'at risk' prisoner should always be informed at shift handovers and when prisoners are being transferred between establishments or to court. 'At risk' prisoners should have their situations regularly reviewed, and should be monitored on a daily basis until it appears that they are able to 'cope satisfactorily'.

10.165   The Prison Service's strategy for aiming to reduce the number of suicides and incidents of self-harm in prison addresses the wider effects upon the whole of the prison community. Aftercare should be provided for 'close family and friends' as well as prisoners and prison staff who are affected.

10.166   The Prison Service has stated that the whole of the prison system shares 'a responsibility to be aware of and support those in distress'. Such responsibility is discharged by providing staff training and support, encouraging other prisoners to share responsibility for each other, working with prisoners' families and community organisations, and ensuring co-operation between all of those individuals and agencies working with prisoners. The Samaritans and Listener Schemes are widely used in prisons.

10.167   Where someone commits suicide in custody, the prisoner's spouse or next of kin should be informed 'at once', as should any one else who 'the prisoner may reasonably have asked' to be told (r 22(1)). The governor should also tell the coroner, the Board of Visitors and the Secretary of State (r 22(2)). The detailed provisions for reporting deaths in custody are contained in the Prison Service Order, *Follow up to deaths in custody* (see paras 10.105–10.111). In essence, this states that governors must inform the Home Office Press Office and the Incident Management Support Unit of the death in discharging their duty under r 22(2).

CHAPTER 11
LIFERS

MANDATORY LIFERS

11.1 When a person is convicted of murder, the court has no discretion as to the sentence that must be imposed—all persons convicted of a murder committed after the prisoner reached the age of 21 years will be sentenced to life imprisonment (Murder (Abolition of Death Penalty) Act 1965). Thus a life sentence for murder imposed on a person over the age of 21 years is known as a mandatory life sentence. There are a range of other life sentences that can be imposed, including the discretionary life sentence, the automatic life sentence, detention at her Majesty's Pleasure and custody for life. These sentences are dealt with later in this chapter.

PRISONERS CHARGED WITH MURDER

11.2 Prisoners charged with murder and remanded in custody are held in local category B prisons until the time of their trial, and will be treated in line with the criteria for unconvicted prisoners. However, Circular Instruction 30/90 contains detailed instructions about the medical assessment of prisoners who are charged with murder. This states that the medical officer should keep a written record of the physical and mental condition of the prisoner, and this may be done on a daily basis. In order that the medical officer may form an adequate assessment of the prisoner's mental condition, a copy of the depositions taken before the magistrates and coroner will be requested from the Crown Prosecution Service. The guidance states that these depositions 'are furnished only so that he may be in possession of important and true particulars of the prisoner's recent history insofar as it has a bearing upon his mental state' (para 10).

11.3 When a prisoner charged with murder is committed for trial, the governor is instructed to forward a report from the medical officer to Prison Service Headquarters. This report should give the medical officer's opinion of the case and whether it is considered that any further psychiatric examination should be carried out. If such an examination is suggested on the grounds that 'there is reason to believe that the prisoner is not mentally normal' (para 11), the services of a psychiatrist independent of the Directorate of Prison Health Care should be carried out.

11.4 The medical records of prisoners charged with murder should be kept in locked cabinets and access to them should be restricted to the medical officer and hospital officers of principal officer rank and above.

ADULT PRISONERS CONVICTED OF MURDER

11.5   Mandatory life sentences have three distinct elements. The first element is the part of the sentence which is set by the Home Secretary to reflect the minimum period of time that the lifer should serve in the interests of deterrence and retribution, and is commonly known as the 'tariff' or the 'penal' element. After completion of this period, lifers may still be held on the basis that they represent a risk to the public. Finally, and most controversially, according to recent policy changes lifers who have served their tariffs and are considered to be no risk may be held in custody in order to maintain the public's confidence in the criminal justice system.

The tariff

11.6   The tariff is the punitive part of the life sentence. All lifers have to serve up to their tariff date, and there is no prospect of release before this period has expired (unless the very stringent criteria for compassionate release are met, see chapter 12).

11.7   The tariff is set by the Home Secretary, who seeks recommendations from the trial judge and the Lord Chief Justice as to the appropriate term to be served in the circumstances of the offence. These recommendations are not binding on the Home Secretary, who has reserved the power to take into account other factors, including public policy considerations. There is no obligation to set the tariff in line with the judicial views and it is apparent that the tariff is often set at a considerably higher number of years than that sentencing judge has recommended.

11.8   Until 1994, past mandatory lifers did not have the right to know the basis upon which their tariffs were set, or whether the Home Secretary had set them at a higher level than that recommended by the judiciary. The tariff setting procedure was examined in the case of *R v Secretary of State for the Home Department, ex p Doody* [1994] 1 AC 531, HL. The judgment in this case gave mandatory lifers the right to know the minimum period the judge thought that they should serve and the gist of the reasons why that recommendation was made; the right to make representations in respect of the tariff before it is set; and the right to be informed of the reasons for any departure from the judge's recommendation when the tariff is set. The tariff unit at Prison Service Headquarters is responsible for administering the tariff review process. Their role is to disclose the relevant material to prisoners, to obtain their written representations and to submit the case to ministers for a decision to be made.

11.9   Lifers whose tariffs were set before the new arrangements came into effect have also benefited from the judgment. Following the *Doody* judgment all mandatory lifers received a letter outlining the gist of the judicial recommendation as to tariff, the level at which the tariff was set, and any reasons given by the Home Secretary of the day for that decision. They have the opportunity to make representations to the Home Secretary so that their tariff periods can be reviewed.

11.10   However, the disclosure which took place under the new arrangements initially proved far from adequate and consisted of a brief letter setting out the judicial recommendations and ministerial decision in a few lines. In some cases tariffs had been increased by up to 10 years above the trial judge's recommendation with no substantive reason given by the Home Secretary.

11.11   The cases of *R v Secretary of State for the Home Department, ex p Raja and Riaz* (16 December 1994, unreported), DC questioned whether this level of disclosure complied with the principles established in *Doody*. In these cases, tariffs had been set at 20 and 25 years respectively, increases of 10 years above the trial judges' recommendations. The court criticised the disclosure of the judge's comments as 'woefully inadequate' and considered that 'the reasons of the Secretary of State for differing from the judges were inadequately disclosed'.

11.12   Since 1994 the level of disclosure has improved, and prisoners who have indicated that they wish to make representations are sent copies of information which will be placed before the Home Secretary when the tariff representations are considered. These should include letters and reports from the trial judge which relate to tariff setting considerations, and the verbatim comments of the Lord Chief Justice.

11.13   It would appear that in the past poor records have been kept of the actual information which was placed before the Home Secretary when the tariff was originally set, and the tariff unit are sometimes able to do little more than speculate as to this. Furthermore, in some cases the Home Secretary of the day appeared not to have recorded reasons for deviation from the judicial recommendation. The tariff unit may seek to withhold information on the basis that although it was probably before the Home Secretary of the day when the tariff was originally set, it will not be placed before him when the matter is reviewed. In response to this, lifers and their representatives may argue that the principles of administrative fairness outlined in *Doody* entitle them to see all information placed before the Home Secretary when the original tariff decision was made.

11.14   It became apparent after the new open procedures were introduced that there were a few mandatory lifers for whom a tariff had not been set, despite having served many years in prison custody. These tended to be prisoners who were convicted of two or more homicide offences, and at the time that their tariffs were considered the Home Secretary merely stated that they should have their first Parole Board review at 17 years. This was in line with the policy in operation up to 1994, when a review at the 17 year stage indicated that the tariff was set at 20 years or more, and there was no obligation on the Prison Service to inform lifers of the actual length at which the tariff had been set. Prisoners falling into that category should by now have received full tariff disclosure and had the opportunity to have their tariffs reviewed. However, such cases must be approached very carefully as, if no tariff was actually fixed, the Secretary of State still has free rein to set the tariff at the level he feels is appropriate. This was one of the problematic issues in the *Hindley* case (see below).

11.15   The process of tariff disclosure has lead to important litigation on the tariff setting process, which has resulted in numerous further policy statements made by the Home Secretary as well as three further applications to the House of Lords. In order to make sense of the current law and system of review, it is helpful to review the key litigation and policy statements in this field, commencing with the 1983 Brittan policy and the decision in *Re Findlay* [1985] AC 318. Leon Brittan, the Home Secretary of the day, put in place a restricted parole policy whereby certain classes of lifers could expect to serve minimum sentences of 20 years. This affected some prisoners who had understood that they would be considered for parole at an earlier date (despite never having had a formal tariff communicated to them). A challenge to this restrictive policy was dismissed by the House of Lords on the basis that all a prisoner could expect is for his/her parole application to be considered under the criteria in application at the time their individual case is reviewed. The policy was held to be lawful because the Home Secretary had reserved his power to consider exceptional cases outside of this normal policy, thereby ensuring that his discretion was not fettered (at 336A–F). This decision thus created a precedent whereby the Home Secretary has an enormously wide discretion in the administration of the life sentence.

11.16   Lord Mustill's decision in *Doody* had particular importance in understanding the theory and practice of the mandatory life sentence and the concept of tariff. He explained that although the sentence is indeterminate, it does not operate in this fashion in practice. The very concept of a 'tariff' indicates that the sentence does contain within it a 'fixed term of years apt to reflect not only the requirements of deterrence but also the moral quality of the individual act (retribution)' (at 556B–D). To that extent, the manner in which the tariff is set does bear similarities to a sentencing exercise. In response to this judgment, Michael Howard, the then Home Secretary issued two policy statements. The first, on 27 July 1993, indicated the arrangements put in place to implement the judgment (as outlined above) but went on to explain that he reserved the right to increase tariffs previously fixed in cases where the requirements of retribution and deterrence had not been met (Official Report, columns 861–864). On 7 December 1994, Mr Howard explained for the first time that there was a category of prisoners for whom whole life tariffs may be fixed. He put in place two ministerial reviews of tariffs, one after 10 years and the second after 25 years, to establish whether any grounds existed for reducing tariff (Official Report, columns 234–235).

11.17   The impact of these policy announcements did not come to be fully understood until two successive House of Lords judgments in June and July 1997 (*R v Secretary of State for the Home Department, ex p Thompson and Venables* [1998] AC 407 and *R v Secretary of State for the Home Department, ex p Pierson* [1998] AC 539). *Ex p Thompson and Venables* concerned the setting of HMP tariffs. These are now a distinct class of prisoner from adult mandatory lifers, and the full implications of the judgment are discussed below. The key importance of that decision was to characterise the tariff-setting exercise as being essentially a sentencing exercise (see the speeches of Lords Goff, Steyn and Hope). The decision conflicted with the Home Office approach, which is to see tariff setting as an executive function with elements that are entirely distinct from judicial sentencing.

11.18 In the *Pierson* case, the House of Lords quashed a decision by the Home Secretary to maintain a tariff at 20 years despite having accepted that the facts were less serious than when the 20 year tariff was originally fixed. It was successfully argued that against this factual background the Home Secretary had effectively increased the tariff. Unfortunately, the Lords were in disagreement over the more fundamental issues in the case, as to whether it was lawful to increase a previously fixed sentence and whether tariff setting is a sentencing exercise or not. Although Lord Steyn felt that the binding authority from the *Thompson and Venables* case was that tariff-setting is a sentencing exercise, even for adult mandatory lifers, Lords Browne-Wilkinson and Lloyd disagreed, leaving the issue still be determined.

11.19 In response to the *Pierson* decision, the current Home Secretary Jack Straw issued a new and the current policy statement in relation to tariff setting (7 November 1997). He reasserted the right for the Home Secretary to increase a tariff fixed at an earlier date but introduced a new policy whereby the progress of life sentenced prisoners would be monitored and, in cases where there had been exceptional progress in prison custody, the tariff could be reduced. This power is of particular importance in relation to the issue of whole life tariffs. In July 1998, Mr Straw announced that the 10 year ministerial review had been abolished.

11.20 This 1997 statement was made with particular thought to the challenge being brought by Myra Hindley seeking to impeach the legality of 'whole life tariff'. Her challenge was founded upon the arguments that her tariff had been increased from the period of 30 years originally envisaged and that it was unlawful to impose a whole life tariff once it has been recognised that the mandatory life sentence is in fact composed of a fixed punitive period as well as a protective post tariff period. The challenge was unsuccessful in the Court of Appeal (*R v Secretary of State for the Home Department, ex p Hindley* [2000] 1 QB 152), with the court deciding that the flexibility in the policy whereby tariffs would be reviewed in exceptional circumstances was adequate protection against the arbitrariness of a whole life tariff. The challenge on the grounds that the tariff was increased was rejected on the facts, with the court finding that the tariff had only ever been provisionally set and never communicated to the appellant. The House of Lords upheld this decision, expressly approving the reasoning of the Court of Appeal, in February 2000: [2000] 2 WLR 730.

11.21 This plethora of litigation and policy announcements has left the current situation very confused. In brief, the official stance pursued by the Home Office can be summarised as follows: tariff setting is not a judicial exercise but an administrative exercise carried out by the executive; the Home Secretary can choose to increase tariffs (both over judicial recommendations and to increase tariffs previously set); whole life tariffs can be set, subject to the requirement for future reviews; all tariffs can be reviewed at any time; tariffs may be reduced in exceptional circumstances (see the Prison Service's Lifer Manual, chapter 3). Legally, the situation is slightly more complex. There is conflicting authority from the House of Lords as to the extent to which tariff setting is a sentencing exercise or not and the extent to which a tariff, once set, can be increased. Although it is not possible to give a definitive answer to these questions, it is advisable to proceed on the basis that tariff setting is akin to sentencing and, absent substantial changes in the factual situation, it is not possible to increase a tariff already set or communicated.

11.22 The possibility of a reduction in tariff on the grounds of 'exceptional progress' has excited much interest amongst life sentenced prisoners. Unfortunately, no further guidance has been issued on this topic and each case will have to be approached on its own merits. Indications are that exceptional progress will have to go beyond the good conduct in prison that the authorities hope lifers will exhibit. In practice, it is likely that applications based on conduct in prison will need to be supported by recommendations to this effect from prison staff.

The Human Rights Act and tariffs

11.23 The Human Rights Act 1998 may have implications for the manner in which the domestic courts approach tariff setting for mandatory life sentenced prisoners. In *Wynne v United Kingdom* (1994) 19 EHRR 333 the European Court of Human Rights held that art 5(4) does not apply to mandatory lifers. Article 5(4) relates to the need for detention to be reviewed by an independent tribunal with the power to order release, and the court was of the opinion that as a mandatory life sentence authorises life long detention, providing the trial process was fair no further Convention issues arose in relation to the release procedures for such prisoners. The rationale behind that decision appears to be increasingly weak given the successive decisions of the House of Lords which have recognised that a mandatory life sentence does in fact contain a fixed punitive term. It is therefore arguable that art 6(1) of the Convention, which applies to the application of sentences following criminal convictions, should safeguard the tariff setting process. The judgment of the court in *V v United Kingdom* [2000] Crim LR 187 applied this logic to HMP tariff setting, providing some support for such an argument for mandatory lifers. Although it seems unlikely that the European Court itself will intervene in this area as it is likely to consider itself bound by the *Wynne* decision, the inconsistency of domestic and European law could well lead to a resolution in the domestic courts.

Progression through the life sentence system

11.24 Following conviction, the local prison where the lifer has been held will send an Initial Life Sentence Report to the Lifer Management Unit (LMU) at Prison Service Headquarters. This report contains details of the offence, whether the lifer is considering an appeal and any previous convictions. Personal information and details of custodial behaviour whilst on remand are also asked for (Lifer Manual, chapter 4). This form is used to assist the LMU in deciding the appropriate prison to allocate the lifer to.

11.25 Lifers are centrally managed at Prison Service Headquarters, and governors of prisons are only responsible for their day-to-day management. Permanent transfers are always arranged by the LMU, as are changes in security categorisation. Prison governors may transfer lifers in the interests of good order and discipline under IG 28/93 (see chapter 7), but they would then have to ask the LMU to arrange a permanent move.

11.26   The majority of male life sentence prisoners will initially be allocated to one of the main lifer centres. These are at Brixton, Gartree, Long Lartin, Wakefield and Wormwood Scrubs prisons. Women lifers will be allocated to closed conditions. Category A status overrides all other considerations and so male category A prisoners will go to one of the dispersal prisons, and women category A lifers will go to HMP Durham. Category B male lifers should be allocated to the main lifer centre which affords the easiest access to their visitors, so long as there is space available. If a male lifer has been convicted of a sexual offence in the past, or if it is considered that the murder that he committed was sexually motivated, then he would be most likely to be transferred to Brixton or Wakefield as they are sex offender treatment assessment centres.

11.27   Most lifers remain at their initial allocation for at least three years, as this is considered to give them a chance to settle down and come to terms with the offence and their sentence. During this period staff should carry out initial assessments of the needs of each lifer, the areas of concern in their behaviour and identify factors which may have lead them to commit the offence for which they have been convicted.

11.28   Comprehensive reports are made about lifers throughout their sentences. Every lifer should have an internal review board each year, which assesses the progress that has been made and the outstanding areas of concern that need to be addressed. The Board must invite the home probation officer to attend and include the personal officer for the lifer. Lifers should be allowed to sit in on the review and to comment on the views that have been gained about them at the prison (Lifer Manual, chapter 5, p 1). A summary of the review board's decision is sent to the LMU, which will consider its contents in making a decision to reallocate lifers. Brief summaries of these reports are also considered by the Parole Board when they eventually consider lifers' prospects for progression to open conditions or release.

11.29   In addition to the long term review board, F75 reports are completed on lifers every three years, and thus the first set will be completed as most lifers are nearing the end of their period in a main lifer centre. These are more detailed reports and make recommendations as to where lifers should be allocated to serve the next part of their sentence. The F75 reports are forwarded to the LMU, which will consider them and decide whether to act on the recommendations of the prison staff. Although there is not any specific legal obligation on the prison to disclose the reports to the prisoner, this is recommended as good practice by the Prison Service and if the governor wishes to withhold the reports, advice must be sought from LMU (Lifer Manual, para 5.4.1). Lifers are able to make representations to the LMU if they so wish.

11.30   The progress of lifers will vary dramatically after the completion of their first F75 reports. Some may be transferred to category C conditions, others will be transferred from dispersal conditions to category B training prisons.

These decisions will be made depending on behaviour in prison, the degree of risk thought to be posed by each lifer, whether they have come to terms with their offence and begun to address their offending behaviour and how long of their tariff there is left to serve. Category A lifers will remain in dispersal conditions until the Category A Review Committee has downgraded their security categorisation.

11.31 Life sentence prisoners continue to have their progress monitored by prison staff at long-term review boards and by completion of F75 reports. This ensures that the question of allocation is kept under review and progressive transfers to lower security conditions may be made. Likewise, if a lifer's behaviour gives cause for concern, the LMU may arrange a transfer to higher security conditions.

11.32 Lifers cannot progress to open conditions without the Home Secretary's approval, and this will only be considered after a favourable recommendation has been made by the Parole Board. In general lifers are required to progress through all of the different types of prison before the Parole Board is likely to recommend that they are ready to move to open conditions.

Parole board reviews and release from prison

11.33 Mandatory lifers may only be released from prison under a tripartite procedure which involves a recommendation for release by the Parole Board, the views of the Lord Chief Justice and the trial judge (if still available) being obtained and finally, if approved by the Secretary of State (Crime (Sentences) Act 1997, s 29). Parole Board reviews of detention are therefore the first stage in this lengthy process. There is no statutory procedure for this review process, but Prison Service policy in force since the early 1980s has dictated that lifers should have their cases reviewed by the Parole Board for the first time when they are three years away from reaching the expiry of their tariffs. However, in cases where the lifer has been in a category C prison for 12 months or more when the tariff still has three and a half years to run, the review will be brought forward by six months (ministerial announcement of 9 July 1998 *and R v Secretary of State for the Home Department, ex p Roberts* (8 July 1998, unreported), DC). The purpose of advancing the review date for this group of lifers was to ensure that in cases where release on tariff might be possible, the review would take place in sufficient time to allow this to happen.

11.34 Prison staff prepare detailed reports about each life sentence prisoner and submit these to the Lifer Review Unit at Prison Service Headquarters. These form the bulk of the lifer's parole dossier. Other documents included in the dossier are a Home Office Summary of the offence, psychiatric reports produced at trial (if in existence), a list of the prisons where the lifer has been held during the period of imprisonment and a summary of the reports that have been submitted about them during their sentence.

11.35 On 16 December 1992 the then Home Secretary, Kenneth Clarke, announced that mandatory lifers would be given access to their Parole Board dossiers and would be given reasons for decisions reached about their subsequent management following Parole Board reviews. This was aimed to bring mandatory lifers in line with determinate sentenced prisoners following the commencement of the Criminal Justice Act 1991, and also to give them some of the benefits which had been extended to discretionary life sentence prisoners following the case of *Thynne, Wilson and Gunnell v United Kingdom* (1990) 13 EHRR 666, Series A, No 190. The arrangements for disclosure came into effect for all mandatory lifer reviews starting after 1 April 1993.

11.36 Lifer dossiers are disclosed to lifers by staff at the prison, and prisoners may arrange to have them photocopied at their own expense. Otherwise, lifers are entitled to have access to the dossier in order to be able to prepare their representations. Legal representatives can obtain a copy of the dossier direct from Lifer Review Unit (LRU) at Prison Service Headquarters free of charge providing they have signed authority from the lifer for disclosure. Representations should normally be submitted within 14 days of the dossier being received at the prison, although extensions of time are allowed on request. Many lifers ask solicitors to prepare representations for them, and this can be done under the public funding advice and assistance scheme.

11.37 Representations are submitted to the LRU, which attaches these to the parole dossier and arranges for a Parole Board member to travel to the prison and interview the lifer. The interview follows the same format as for determinate sentenced prisoners. Following the interview the Parole Board member's report is disclosed to the lifer, who may wish to submit further representations. The report and any further representations are added to the dossier which is then submitted to the Parole Board secretariat and sent to the Parole Board panel who will be considering the case.

11.38 The Home Secretary has given guidance to the Parole Board on how they should consider the cases of mandatory life sentence prisoners (Lifer Manual, appendix 7). The Directions to the Parole Board on the Release of Mandatory Life Sentence Prisoners state that in considering whether a prisoner may be released they should have regard to the 'degree of risk involved of the lifer committing further imprisonable offences after release' and in view of this 'whether it remains necessary for the protection of the public for the lifer to be confined' (para 2). The directions state:

'In making this decision, the Parole Board should consider whether:

(a) the lifer has shown by his performance in prison that he has made positive efforts to address his attitudes and behaviourial problems and the extent to which progress has been made in doing so such that the risk that he will commit a further imprisonable offence after release is minimal;

(b) the lifer is likely to comply with the conditions of the life licence and the requirements of supervision.' (para 4)

11.39 In addressing their minds to the above, the Parole Board should have regard to the Home Secretary's Training Guidance on the Release of Mandatory Life Sentence Prisoners. This advises:

'The following factors should generally be taken into account when recommending release on life licence. The weight and relevance attached to each factor may vary according to the circumstances of the case:

(a) the offender's background, including any previous convictions and their pattern;

(b) the nature and circumstances of the original offence and the reasons for it;

(c) where available, the sentencing judge's comments and probation and medical reports prepared for the court;

(d) attitude and behaviour in custody, including offences against prison discipline;

(e) behaviour during any home leave or other outside activities undertaken while in open conditions;

(f) attitude to other inmates and staff and positive contributions to prison life;

(g) insight into attitudes and behavioural problems, attitude to the offence and degree of remorse and steps taken to achieve the treatment and training objectives set out in the life sentence plan;

(h) (i) realism of the release plan and resettlement prospects, including home circumstances and the likelihood of co-operation with supervision, relationship with the home probation officer, attitude of the local community,

    (ii) extent to which the release plan continues rehabilitative work started in prison and the extent to which it lessens or removes the occurrence of circumstances which led to the original offence;

(i) any risk to other persons, including the victim's family and friends or possibility of retaliation by the victim's family or local community;

(j) possible need for special licence conditions to cover concerns which might otherwise militate against release;

(k) any medical, psychiatric or psychological considerations (particularly where there is a history of mental instability).'

11.40   Following consideration of the above factors, the Parole Board may decide to recommend the release of the lifer under review. For many years, the Board were asked to recommend a 'provisional release date' with the lifer first spending a period of time in an open prison or on a pre-release employment scheme hostel. However, current policy is for all lifers to go to open prison conditions before release will be authorised. The Directions issued to the Parole Board on this issue state:

'A period in open conditions is essential for most life sentenced prisoners ("lifers"). It allows the testing of areas of concern in conditions which are nearer to those in the community than can be found in closed prisons. Lifers have the opportunity to take home leave from open prisons and, more generally, open conditions require them to take more responsibility for their actions.' (Lifer Manual, appendix 7, p 4)

11.41   The policy whereby all lifers must first go to an open prison is relatively inflexible and the first parole review will therefore always be concerned with assessing suitability for a transfer to an open prison. This policy was upheld by the House of Lords in *R v Secretary of State for the Home Department, ex p Stafford* [1998] 1 WLR 503. However, it must be remembered that the first duty of the Board is to look at suitability for release and it is only once that determination has been made that other options should be considered.

11.42   The Parole Board are instructed to 'balance the risks against the benefits to be gained by such a move' and to take into account the following factors:

'(a)   whether the lifer has made *sufficient* progress towards tackling offending behaviour to minimise the risk and gravity of re-offending and whether the benefits suggest that a transfer to open conditions is worthwhile at that stage; and

(b)   whether the lifer is trustworthy enough not to abscond or to commit further offences (either inside or outside the prison).' (para 3)

11.43   The Directions go on to say that in making a recommendation to transfer a lifer to open conditions the Parole Board should consider whether:

'(a)   the extent to which the risk that the lifer will abscond or commit further offences while in an open prison is minimal;

(b)   the lifer has shown by his performance in closed conditions that he has made positive efforts to address his attitudes and behavioural problems and extent to which significant progress has been made in doing so;

(c)   the lifer is likely to derive benefit from being able to continue to address areas of concern in an open prison and to be tested in a more realistic environment.'

11.44   The Directions are supported by Training Guidance on the Transfer of Life Sentence Prisoners to Open Conditions, and these are almost identical to those outlined above in the Training Guidance on the Release of Mandatory Life Sentence Prisoners, except they ask the Parole Board to consider any outstanding areas of concern in the lifer's offending behaviour and the benefits to the lifer of a transfer to open conditions. Furthermore, the Parole Board is told that the emphasis should be on the 'risk' aspect of a move to open conditions, and the 'need to have made significant progress in changing attitudes and tackling offending behaviour' (para 3).

11.45   If the Parole Board does not find the lifer suitable for release or for transfer to open conditions, they may nevertheless recommend a progressive move, for example to a category C prison, and they should also outline any areas of concern or points that should be clarified before the next Parole Board review. The Home Office are generally quite hostile to recommendations outside of those concerning release or open conditions, but the Board's comments on moves within the closed prison estate should be sought, particularly if there are concerns about the lifer's management by LMU.

11.46   Whatever the Parole Board's recommendation, they are required to give reasons which will be disclosed to the lifer. If the Parole Board do not recommend release, then they will recommend when the next review should take place. Normally this will be in a minimum of two years' time (Directions to the Parole Board on the Release of Mandatory Life Sentence Prisoners), except in cases where a transfer to an open prison has been made. The review period after a transfer to an open prison is now set at 18 months following the announcement made by the Home Secretary on 9 July 1999 (see para 10.33 above). Lesser or greater periods between reviews can be recommended and if this is done, the Parole Board should give reasons for their recommendation.

11.47 Recommendations made by the Parole Board are merely advisory and are considered by the Home Secretary. In practice, this means that recommendations for progression to category C conditions will be considered by senior staff in the LMU, who will either accept the recommendation and make arrangements for the prisoner to be transferred to category C conditions, or reject the recommendation and decide whether the lifer should be transferred to another prison of the same security categorisation as that where the review started. If the Parole Board has recommended release or transfer to open conditions then this will be considered by the Prisons Minister and possibly by the Home Secretary in person. If the Parole Board has not recommended release, then the Home Secretary has no power to release a lifer.

11.48 A decision to release a lifer at his or her first Parole Board review would be very unusual, because at that time the lifer would still have approximately three years to serve before expiry of the tariff and release dates are not normally set so far in advance. Thus lifers who have progressed through their sentence will generally hope that the Parole Board recommend transfer to open conditions with a further review in two years, by which time they will be close to completion of the tariff. If the two years in open conditions go smoothly and there are no outstanding areas of concern, the second Parole Board review may recommend release, which would be via a Pre-Release Employment Scheme Hostel if the lifer is of working age. In this way, it is possible that lifers may be released upon completion of tariff.

Detention on the basis of risk and the need to maintain public confidence in the criminal justice system

11.49 Lifers who have completed their tariffs may be held on the basis that they may pose a 'risk' to the community, or that their release may undermine the public's confidence in the criminal justice system. In theory this period may last indefinitely. Lifers held on either basis will continue to have long-term review boards each year and Parole Board reviews at intervals set by the Home Secretary taking into account the recommendations that the Parole Board has made as to when the lifer should next be reviewed. However, no lifer will be released unless the Parole Board recommend that s/he should be, and the Home Secretary accepts that recommendation.

11.50 The proper test to apply in determining whether a mandatory lifer should be released is whether that individual poses a risk of committing further imprisonable offences. For many years, there was no distinction in Home Office policy between the test for the release of discretionary lifers ('unacceptable risk to life and limb') and mandatory lifers. Indeed, in many applications for judicial review, the case for the Home Secretary was put on this basis. However, the Straw statement of 10 November 1997 made it clear that release would only be sanctioned in cases where the tariff had expired and on the Home Secretary being satisfied that 'the level of risk of his committing further imprisonable offences presented by his release is acceptably low'. It was this test that was upheld by the House of Lords in *R v Secretary of State for the Home Department, ex p Stafford* (para 10.39).

11.51   The House of Lords approved the decision of the Court of Appeal in the same case ([1998] 1 WLR 503) in which Buxton LJ had expressed concern that the test was cast so wide that it raised some concern as to whether moral considerations could influence the decision (at 530). Shortly after that decision, Turner, J quashed a decision made by the Secretary of State to refuse to release a recalled lifer due to concerns, inter alia, that he might return to making pornographic films (*R v Secretary of State for the Home Department, ex p Freeman* (5 June 1998, unreported)). The judgment highlights the practical problems that can arise with such a widely-cast test.

11.52   Various attempts have been made through the domestic and European courts to introduce an independent system of review which is binding upon the Home Secretary, the most important being the case of *Wynne v United Kingdom* (1994) 19 EHRR 333, Series A, Vol 294–A 1994. In that case, the European Commission of Human Rights upheld the distinction that has been drawn between mandatory and discretionary life sentences and confirmed that mandatory lifers have no right to review of their detention before a 'court-like body' pursuant to art 5(4) of the Convention. The rationale for the decision was that, despite the fact that the mandatory sentence contains a punitive and protective period, it is essentially fixed by law with no element of discretion. The court commented that:

> 'the fact remains that the mandatory life sentence belongs to a different category from the discretionary sentence in the sense that it is automatically imposed as the punishment for the offence of murder irrespective of considerations pertaining to the offender. That mandatory life prisoners do not actually spend the rest of their lives in prison and that a notional tariff period is also established in such cases ... does not alter this essential distinction between the two types of sentence.'

11.53   It is the Home Secretary's discretion in such cases that is at the root of the concern over the mandatory life sentence. The decision as to whether to authorise release is primarily based upon whether the lifer continues to pose a risk to the public. However, Home Secretary Michael Howard specifically reserved the power to take into account the distinctly political considerations of 'public acceptability'. In a Parliamentary answer of 27 July 1993, he stated that:

> 'I wish to state that a mandatory life sentence prisoner should not assume that once the minimum period fixed for retribution and deterrence has been satisfied he will necessarily be released if it is considered that he is no longer a risk ... Accordingly, before any such prisoner is released I will consider not only (a) whether the period served by the prisoner is adequate to satisfy the requirements of retribution and deterrence and (b) whether it is safe to release the prisoner, but also (c) the public acceptability of early release. This means that I will exercise my discretion to release only if I am satisfied that to do so will not threaten the maintenance of public confidence in the system of criminal justice.'

This approach was confirmed by Jack Straw in his policy announcement of 7 November 1997.

11.54   The right that mandatory lifers now have to the disclosure of their Parole Board dossiers has brought to light the degree of subjectivity in the process of release and the extent to which both the Parole Board and the Home Secretary can choose not to accept the recommendations of report writers. In the case of *R v Secretary of State for the Home Department and Parole Board, ex p Evans* (2 November 1994, unreported), DC a lifer sought to challenge the refusal of the Parole Board and the Home Secretary to authorise release from a closed prison, despite the fact that the reports prepared took the view that he was suitable for release and no longer presented a risk to the public. Indeed, the report writers were so incensed by the decision that they took it upon themselves to write letters of complaint to the Home Office about the decision reached. Leave had been granted to challenge the refusal on the basis that the reasons given for the decision were inadequate, and a detailed affidavit was filed to expand upon the reasoning applied. Simon Brown LJ refused to quash the decisions made but was very critical of the failure to give adequate reasons prior to the commencement of proceedings. He commented that:

> 'The Board's duty to give reasons is not in dispute ... where the Board find themselves unable to follow what I have already described as the clear, emphatic and unanimous view of the LRC [Local Review Committee] and those reporting to them, they should explain why in language sufficiently clear and terms sufficiently full to ensure that the LRC properly understand the basis of the difference between them'. (pp 16–7 of transcript)

11.55 It is clear that this duty applies equally to the Home Secretary as it does to the Board and in his final comments, Lord Justice Simon Brown made the point that the case contained important lessons for both the Board and the Secretary of State.

11.56 In the case of *R v Secretary of State for the Home Department, ex p Pegg* (1994) Times, 11 August, DC) a decision of the Secretary of State not to release a lifer was also under scrutiny. Steyn, LJ, in accepting the fact that the mandatory life sentence system is one which has evolved by executive decree, expressed his disquiet at the fact that the present system, from a constitutional point of view, 'makes no sense'. However, as the power to correct this lies with Parliament and not the courts, he went on to say that:

> 'Given the essential unfairness of the system in relation to prisoners serving mandatory life sentences the courts have to bear in mind that fundamental rights are at stake. But courts can do no more that be extra vigilant in the exercise of their powers of judicial review.' (p 15 of transcript)

11.57 These comments are quite extraordinary in the context of the mandatory life sentence and the operation of executive power. The fact that the Home Secretary is exercising powers which are judicial in their nature has prompted the courts to subject these decisions to a very high level of scrutiny. However, the courts are still reluctant to interfere with substantive decisions, and although it seemed at one stage as if the courts were moving towards a very tight judicial control of the life sentence, there has been a perceptible trend in recent years for the courts to shy away from imposing further procedural safeguards. For example, a challenge to the time scale for the review process (*R v Secretary of State for the Home Department, ex p Roberts* (8 July 1998, unreported), DC) was unsuccessful, as was an attempt to impose a requirement on the Home Secretary to issue 'minded to refuse' notifications in cases where he was not prepared to acept the recommendations of the Parole Board (*R v Secretary of State for the Home Department, ex p Draper* (21 January 2000, unreported). There has been a great deal of speculation that oral parole hearings will be introduced for mandatory lifers as a result of the implementation of the Human Rights Act 1998. The current interpretation of the courts is that the Parole Board has an inherent jurisdiction to convene an oral hearing if it is necessary to properly determine a lifer's parole application (*R v Parole Board, ex p Davies* (25 November 1996, unreported)). While the logic of the current judicial thinking on the mandatory life sentence would seem to indicate that in the long term, release procedures should be determined through an independent tribunal having directive powers of release, this is likely to be the last aspect of the life sentence to be changed, either legislatively or through the common law.

Recall

11.58   Once a mandatory lifer has been released from prison, s/he will remain subject to the terms and conditions of a life licence. This is the method by which the sentence is made truly indeterminate—the licence provides for a mandatory lifer to be supervised for the remainder of his/her life. This means that such a person may be recalled to prison at any time for the remainder of his or her life.

11.59   The procedure for the recall of lifers is contained in the Crime (Sentences) Act 1997, s 32. The procedure for initial recall envisages that this may be done by the Secretary of State either acting on the recommendation of the Parole Board (s 32(1)) or, where it is expedient in the public interest, by the Secretary of State acting alone (s 32(2)). In practice, the Minister will normally make the initial recall decision and this will then be put to the Parole Board for approval. The most common reasons for a decision to recall a lifer are that new criminal charges have been made or on the advice of the supervising probation officer.

11.60   Once a lifer has been recalled, under either set of procedures, s/he is entitled to have fresh consideration of the decision by the Parole Board. In accordance with the policy of open reporting before the Parole Board and in order to accord with the rules of natural justice, recalled lifers are entitled to receive the reasons for their recall together with any reports or other material that will be placed before the Board when the recall is reconsidered. There is statutory provision for written representations to be made to the Board in such cases (C(S)A 1997, s 33(3)(a)). It is always advisable for a lifer to have legal advice concerning these representations, as they will be crucial in determining the length of time that will be spent in custody.

11.61   The Board must be concerned with the level of dangerousness that a lifer poses when considering such cases, rather than factors such as disobedience unless the disobedience goes to risk (*R v Secretary of State for the Home Department, ex p Cox* (1992) 5 Admin LR 17). In practice, it is not always a simple matter to persuade the Board to make such a distinction and it is important to bear in mind the circumstances of the original offence when addressing the Board on dangerousness in such cases. For example, if the original conviction was for a crime committed on the spur of the moment, a rational and thought-out decision or course of action, even if criminal, may not necessarily be linked to the 'dangerousness' apparent in the original offence. Alternatively, if the new behaviour is thought to be impulsive and irrational, then links could reasonable be drawn.

11.62 The Parole Board holds a unique power when considering the recall of mandatory lifers in that if they recommend immediate release, this is the only occasion on which the Secretary of State is bound by the decision (C(S)A 1997, s 32(5)). If any other recommendation is made, this is purely advisory as with other life sentence reviews and the Secretary of State has the discretion not to accept the recommendation (*R v Secretary of State for the Home Department, ex p Gunnell* [1998] Crim LR 170). The prisoner will then fall to be detained under the terms of the original sentence with reviews and release at the discretion of the Secretary of State.

11.63 The meaning of immediate release is of some importance to prisoners in this position as it has been held to be precisely that, namely that the prisoner can be released that day (per *Gunnell*). This has been the cause of some difficulty, particularly where the prisoner is subject to further criminal charges which may not have been heard or has received a short custodial sentence. In such cases, if the Board recommends release at the end of the sentence this is not a binding recommendation for immediate release (*R v Secretary of State for the Home Department, ex p De Lara* (22 March 1995, unreported)). Similarly, if the Board decide that they wish to defer their decision pending the outcome of further charges, the Secretary of State can treat this as a decision and the prisoner then falls to be reviewed under the terms of the original sentence and the Board loses its powers to make binding recommendations. In such cases, representations should be submitted to the Board with the addendum that if immediate release is the recommendation that they wish to make, they should formally adjourn the case without reaching a decision and then reconvene when the obstacle to immediate release has been removed. This is particularly important in cases where further charges are pending, as the Board's decision may be completely dependent on whether a conviction is obtained.

11.64 Once a lifer has been recalled, progress towards release will be governed in precisely the same manner as for lifers who have never been released. Re-release will be dependent upon a positive recommendation from the Parole Board being accepted by the Secretary of State under the procedures put in place pursuant to the Crime (Sentences) Act 1997, s 29. There is one difference. If a lifer has spent some time in the community and does not spend a great deal of time back in custody on recall, the need to be sent to an open prison is less compelling. In the *Stafford* case, the House of Lords approved the judgment of Bingham, LCJ given in the Court of Appeal which explained:

> 'While a powerful case can be made for testing in open conditions a mandatory life sentenced prisoner who has been institutionalised by long years of incarceration in closed conditions, such a case loses much of its force in the case of a man who has, since serving the punitive term of his life sentence, demonstrated a capacity for living an independent and apparently lawful life by doing so for a number of years.' (*R v Secretary of State for the Home Department, ex p Stafford* [1998] 1 WLR at 518)

Human Rights Act and release procedures

11.65 There have been many criticisms of the recall procedure and the lack of any real judicial element to the procedures. These are compounded by the fact that in most cases, the Parole Board will be fulfilling a dual function of recommending the initial recall and then reviewing their own decision. Attempts to bring this procedure within the ambit of art 5(4) of the European Convention on Human Rights, which ensures that all persons have the right to have their detention reviewed speedily by a court-like body have so far been unsuccessful (see eg *Wynne v United Kingdom* (1994) 19 EHRR 333, Series A, volume 294–A). It is possible, however, that with the introduction of the Human Rights Act 1998 the domestic courts will be prepared to engage in a further examination of this area. Recall decisions are especially difficult as they often involve disputed facts which can be difficult to determine on a paper review. The High Court has already held that an oral hearing might be necessary in some cases to allow for a fair determination of the case (*R v Parole Board, ex p Davies* (25 November 1995, unreported)). Given the nature of the rights at stake and the policy that detention in such cases is determined solely by risk, it is arguable that the chain of causation with the original life sentence has been broken and that the recall decision should accord with art 5(4) standards.

CUSTODY FOR LIFE

11.66 The mandatory sentence of custody for life is imposed upon persons convicted of murder committed whilst over 18 and under 21 (Criminal Justice Act 1982, s 8). This category of prisoners will be dealt with in precisely the same manner as adult mandatory lifers save that their first allocation will normally be to a Young Offender's Institution. The YOIs that normally take such prisoners on first allocation after conviction are Aylesbury, Castington, Moorland or Swinfen Hall.

PERSONS DETAINED AT HER MAJESTY'S PLEASURE

11.67 The sentence of detention at 'Her Majesty's Pleasure' (HMP) was originally conceived in an attempt to ensure that children did not face the death penalty for murder. The Children and Young Persons Act 1933, s 53(1) authorises the detention of people under the age of 18 who are convicted of murder to be detained at HMP. Section 8 of the Criminal Justice Act 1982 authorises the detention of persons between the ages of 18–21 who are convicted of murder to be detained for life. Prisoners who receive such sentences are treated as if they have received a mandatory life sentence.

11.68 At the present time, the law is in a state of flux following the successive decisions of the European Court of Human Rights in *Hussain and Prem Singh v United Kingdom* (1996) 22 EHRR 1, *V and T v United Kingdom* [2000] Crim LR 187 and the House of Lords decision in *R v Secretary of State for the Home Department, ex p Thompson and Venables* [1998] AC 407. Until the *Hussain* decision, the sentence of detention at HMP was administered in precisely the same manner as the adult mandatory life sentence. However, the effect of these judgments has been to transform the sentence into one that mirrors the discretionary life sentence in its entirety.

11.69   In *Hussain v United Kingdom*, the European Court held that the sentence did not authorise lifelong punitive detention and that the sentence actually contained a fixed punitive element followed by detention on the basis of risk alone. The decision was highly influenced by the arguments that the sentence was partly imposed in the interests of the welfare of the child. As a result of that decision, the release procedures for HMP prisoners were brought in line with those for discretionary lifers with the release decision now being taken by the Parole Board alone (Crime (Sentences) Act 1997, s 28). The release procedures for these prisoners are set out in the following section. There is, however, one important distinction which is not reflected in the statutory release test. Discretionary lifers will have received their sentence because a finding has been made in the trial process that they pose a risk to the public of committing further offences in the future. No such finding will ever have been made for HMP detainees and so it is wrong for the Parole Board to make any assumptions as to the 'pathology' of this class of prisoner. This was accepted in a judicial review application made by one such recalled HMP prisoner (although the application failed on other grounds) by Dyson, J:

> 'It is quite wrong to make any assumptions about the dangerousness of an HMP detainee. When considering whether the prisoner poses a risk to life and limb that is more than minimal, the Board must apply the most careful scrutiny since a fundamental human right, the right to liberty, is at stake. I am prepared to accept the submission [of the Applicant] that the Board require cogent evidence before being satisfied that a prisoner poses more than a minimal risk of danger to life and limb.' (*R v Parole Board, ex p Curley* unreported, 22 October 1999, HC)

Tariff setting

11.70   Until January 2000, HMP tariffs were set in precisely the same manner as for adult lifers. Some changes were introduced to the system following the House of Lords decision in *R v Secretary of State for the Home Department, ex p Thompson and Venables* [1998] AC 407. The Lords held that tariff setting in such cases is essentially a sentencing exercise and placed upon the Secretary of State a duty to keep such prisoners under close and constant review. As a result, the Prison Service put in place a system for Tariff Assessment Reviews which allowed for a yearly review of the prisoner to assess whether there any considerations which would warrant a reduction in tariff based on the individual's personal development in custody, general welfare and the public interest (Lifer Manual, appendix 3). In addition, a more detailed review is held at the halfway point of the tariff to determine whether the original tariff remains appropriate and the prisoner is entitled to submit representations at this stage. The criteria for assessment are:

> '(i)   Has there been any significant change in maturity and outlook since the offence was committed?

(ii) Are there any risks to the detainee's continued development that cannot be sufficiently mitigated or removed in the custodial enviroment (ie will continued detention harm the detainee's development)?
(iii) Is there anything that casts doubt on the appropriateness of the original tariff?' (Lifer Manual, appendix 3, pp 3–4)

11.71 Although this system of review was introduced in 1999, some doubt has been cast on the future of such reviews by the decision of the European Court of Human Rights in *V and T v United Kingdom* [2000] Crim LR 187. The European Court found that tariff setting for HMP detainees is in fact a sentencing exercise which should be carried out by the judiciary as occurs for discretionary lifers. In light of this judgment, new legislation will have to be enacted to enable tariffs to be set in the same manner as for discretionary lifers. The Home Secretary confirmed his intention to introduce such legislation in a statement to the House of Commons on 13 March 2000. The interim arrangements announced were:

(i)   For new convictions, tariffs will be set at the level recommended by the Lord Chief Justice.
(ii)   All existing HMP prisoners will be invited to submit fresh representations.
(iii) If no representations are made, the tariff will be fixed at the level originally recommended by the LCJ.
(iv)   No tariff previously set will be increased.
(v)   If representations are made, these will be forwarded to the LCJ and his recommendation on tariff will be accepted.

11.72 The proposals for the changes to tariff setting are likely to generate a further round of legal challenges on two grounds. First, the argument that the European Court decision conflicts with the House of Lords judgment is problematic. The rationale for the House of Lords judgment does not seem to be based on the 'unfairness' of the executive setting the tariff, but more on the need for this particular group of prisoners to be kept under close and constant review. Even if the tariff is judicially set, it is difficult to see why this approach should be abandoned.

11.73 Second, the certification process whereby all tariffs will now be fixed at the level of the judicial recommendations arguably does not satisfy the art 6(1) requirement for sentence to be fixed by a court in public (see eg *Eckle v Germany* (1982) 5 EHRR 1). A similar certification process was adopted for discretionary lifers following the implementation of the Criminal Justice Act 1991 and an attempt to challenge the lack of an oral hearing was unsuccessful, permission to move for judicial review being refused by the Court of Appeal (*R v Secretary of State for the Home Department, ex p Easterbrook* (22 March 1999, unreported). In dismissing the application Lord Woolf did not rule out the possibility of an oral hearing if the individual facts of a case demanded it, but rejected the argument that it was required in all cases as a matter of law. However, the issue is the subject of an application to the European Court and may result in further changes to the tariff setting process for HMP prisoners.

DISCRETIONARY LIFE SENTENCED PRISONERS

11.74   The discretionary life sentence may be imposed for a number of offences, commonly manslaughter, buggery, arson or rape. The rationale for the sentence is that offences have been committed which are grave enough to require a long sentence, that the person is of unstable character and is likely to commit such offences in the future and that the nature of these offences is such that the consequences will be particularly injurious to others (such as offences of a sexual nature).

11.75   There is a not inconsiderable overlap between the imposition of such a sentence and an order made under the Mental Health Act 1983. The court must be satisfied when passing such a sentence that there is some element of unpredictability and dangerousness that, whilst it may diminish with the passing of time, means that the person presents a serious danger to life and limb and that the person cannot be dealt with under the Mental Health Act 1983. At the same time, the purpose of the sentence is only to detain the person so long as they may cause a danger to others (see eg *R v Wilkinson* (1983) 5 Cr App Rep (S) 105). Although the classic interpretation of the sentence required some form of medical evidence to support the imposition of the sentence, more recent authorities, particularly in the field of sexual offending, tend to the view that the sentence can be imposed in the absence of medical evidence if the offence has particular aggravating features (see eg *R v Billam* (1986) 82 Cr App Rep 347; *A-G's Reference (No 76 of 1995) (R v Baker)* [1997] 1 Cr App R (S) 81). The Court of Appeal did affirm, however, that in all cases the offence must pass a certain threshold of gravity for the sentence to be imposed in the first place (*R v Chapman* [2000] 1 Cr App Rep (S) 377).

11.76   Historically, discretionary lifers were treated in precisely the same manner as mandatory lifers with the same tariff setting and release procedures. In recent years, although the fundamental nature of the sentences has diverged considerably in terms of tariff setting and release procedures, treatment within the prison system itself is still fairly similar. In terms of what a discretionary life-sentenced prisoner can expect from the prison system, there is virtually no difference to that for mandatory lifers and so the same reception and allocation decisions will be made. The differences in the procedures for tariff setting and release that need to be explored have resulted from both domestic court decisions and from statutory changes imposed following a decision of the European Court of Human Rights.

Tariffs

11.77   In 1987, the Divisional Court considered the procedure for the setting of tariffs for discretionary lifers (*R v Secretary of State for the Home Department, ex p Handscomb* (1987) 86 Cr App Rep 59). It was held that the procedure whereby no tariff was set for the first three or four years of a sentence had the effect of delaying the potential release of a prisoner until some six or seven years had been served, due to the lengthy reviews whereby release comes to be authorised. Consequently, this amounted to a minimum sentence for all discretionary lifers which was at variance with the concept that the prisoner was only to be detained until safe for release. This procedure made no allowance for the widely different sentence lengths that may be appropriate for such prisoners.

11.78 The result of this case was that the sentencing judge was to obtain the view of the trial judge on the length of tariff immediately after the trial and that the first Parole Board review would be set in accordance with the judicial view. This effectively removed the Secretary of State's discretion and imposed a judicial tariff for discretionary lifers.

11.79 The Criminal Justice Act 1991 formalised the tariff-setting procedures for discretionary lifers. The Act made substantial changes to the entire discretionary life sentence system as a result of the European Court's decision in *Thynne, Wilson and Gunnell* (1990) 13 EHRR 666. In respect of tariff, the CJA 1991, s 34 authorised the sentencing judge to specify the relevant part of the sentence that must be served, taking into account the seriousness of the offence. The Lord Chief Justice has directed that it is only in very exceptional cases that the trial judge can decline to make such an order (*Practice Direction (Life Sentences)* [1993] 1 WLR 223). The provisions of s 34 were repealed by Crime (Sentences) Act 1997, s 28 which makes provision for the length of tariff to be set by the sentencing judge.

11.80 Tariffs for discretionary lifers are now, therefore, almost identical to determinate sentences in the manner in which they are set. The Court of Appeal has decided that it has the authority to exercise control over the 'relevant period' to be served on the basis that it is an order within the meaning of Criminal Appeal Act 1968, ss 9 and 50(1) and have reduced tariffs in many cases (see eg *R v Dalton* [1995] QB 243).

11.81 The manner in which the tariff or relevant period is to be fixed is based upon a comparison with the equivalent determinate sentence that would have been imposed had a life sentence not been considered necessary (see eg *R v O'Conner* (1993) 15 Cr App R (S) 473; *R v Secretary of State for the Home Department, ex p McCartney* (1994) Times, 25 May, CA; and *R v Secretary of State for the Home Department, ex p Chapman* [1994] 42 LS Gaz R 38, DC). The precise method of calculation was later made clearer when it was established that the sentencing court should first decide upon the appropriate determinate sentence and then look at the point where a prisoner could be eligible for parole. As determinate prisoners can apply for parole at one half of their sentence and are automatically released after two thirds, the tariff should be set at somewhere between one half and two thirds of the equivalent determinate sentence. In subsequent decisions, the courts have tended towards the view that tariff should be as close to one half the determinate sentence as possible to reflect the fact that life sentences have very severe consequences in terms of potential release. Indeed, in *R v Secretary of State for the Home Department, ex p Furber* [1998] 1 All ER 23, Simon Brown LJ expressed the view that the reality of the life sentence, including the delays built in to the release procedures for lifers, should bear upon the court when setting the tariff. In *R v Marklew* [1999] 1 Cr App Rep (S) 6,

Bingham LCJ stated that in cases where the tariff was to be more than one half of the determinate sentence, the court should explain why it had been deemed appropriate to set the longer period.

11.82   When setting the tariff, the court should specify how it has taken account of any time spent on remand (*R v Marklew* [1999] 1 Cr App Rep (S) 6) and any time spent abroad awaiting extradition (*R v Howard* [1996] Crim LR 756). For discretionary lifers sentenced prior to the implementation of the C(S)A 1997, for the purposes of sentence calculation remand time is to be calculated on the same grounds as for determinate sentenced prisoners, so remand time counts towards sentence (Criminal Justice and Public Order Act 1994, s 46 and Sch 9).

Discretionary lifer panels/oral parole hearings

11.83   The gradual acceptance of the domestic courts that discretionary and mandatory life sentences could be distinguished was formalised by the Criminal Justice Act 1991, introduced to comply with the requirements of the European Court (see *Thynne, Wilson and Gunnell v United Kingdom* (1990) 13 EHRR 666). The court accepted that as there was a distinct, fixed element to the sentence, prisoners were entitled to a proper review of their detention at the expiry of the tariff period by a court-like body in accordance with art 5(4). Paper reviews by the Parole Board, even with full disclosure of documents, do not meet this criteria and as such a mechanism for a proper oral hearing had to be established.

11.84   The result was the present system of discretionary lifer panels (DLPs) which replaced the reviews that still exist for mandatory lifers. Although these are referred to as DLPs for ease of reference, they now encompass oral parole hearings for HMP detainees (HMPs) and automatic lifers (ALPs). The same procedures apply in all three cases. Discretionary lifers are still subject to internal lifer reviews held within the prison to assess their progress and they are subject to a formal Parole Board review three (or three and a half) years before the expiry of tariff to determine whether they are suitable for a transfer to open prison conditions. However, release is now decided by a panel of the Parole Board following an oral hearing.

11.85   The Crime (Sentences) Act 1997, s 28 (replacing the Criminal Justice Act 1991, s 34(5)) contains the right for discretionary lifers to require the Secretary of State to refer their case to the Parole Board at any time after the relevant part of the sentence has been served, or if it is more than two years since the Board last considered a reference. In practice, such a reference should be automatically made by the Lifer Review Unit and there is no necessity for the prisoner to make such an application.

11.86   The actual timing of the reference has been the subject of litigation as to precisely when this reference should take effect. The wording of the statute is for the reference to take place once the relevant period has expired. The actual administrative procedures for a review means that DLP hearings are fixed on six months' notice (see below). This means that if a reference takes place on the date that the tariff expires, the detention will not actually be reviewed until at least six months after the tariff has expired. In 1995, it was held that the system whereby prisoners may be required to wait for up to a year over tariff before the DLP was constituted was unfair and unreasonable (*R v Secretary of State for the Home Department, ex p Norney* (1995) Independent, 28 September). The court commented that the present system may also be considered to be in breach of the European Convention. The effect of this judgment is that references for DLP hearings now take place six months before tariff expiry in order to potentially allow release on the expiry of tariff. A subsequent decision of the European Commission of Human Rights, ratified by the Committee of Ministers, held that delays of 12 months in fixing the first review were in breach of art 5(4) (*AT v United Kingdom* (1995) 20 EHRR CD 59). That case also raised the possiblity that the fixed two-year period between reviews may not be adequate to satisfy the requirements of a regular review of detention, and this is an area which could well fall to be examined further following the introduction of the Human Rights Act (see eg *Hirst v United Kingdom*, admissibility decision 40787/98, 21 March 2000).

Procedure at DLPs/oral parole hearings

11.87   The procedural rules for DLP hearings are set by the Secretary of State (CJA 1991, s 35(2)) and the Parole Board Rules 1997 (previously issued in 1992) were issued under this authority. Discretionary Lifer panels are appointed by the Chair of the Parole Board and must be chaired by a judge, in the more serious cases a High Court judge and in others, a circuit judge. The second member will normally be a psychiatrist but can be a psychologist or probation officer if there is no serious area of psychiatric concern. The third member is a lay member of the Board.

11.88   Prisoners will be notified of the date of the hearing 26 weeks before it is due to take place. They are given five weeks to inform the Board as to whether they wish an oral hearing to take place and whether they wish to attend in person. In that time, the Board must also be notified as to whether a representative will appear on behalf of the prisoner. Representatives may not include serving prisoners, people who have been released from prison but are on licence, people with unspent criminal convictions or people who are liable to be detained under the Mental Health Act 1983 (PBR 1997, r 6). Legal aid is available (ABWOR, ie assistance by way of representation) and in most cases, solicitors will be appointed as the representative.

11.89   Within eight weeks of the reference, the prisoner is entitled to receive the information that is prepared on behalf of the Secretary of State for the purposes of the hearing (PBR 1997, r 5(1)). This will comprise of a dossier, not dissimilar to a mandatory lifer's dossier, containing details of the offence, behaviour in custody, previous DLP decisions and a series of current reports prepared by prison and probation staff together with psychiatric and psychologists' reports. This will also contain the Secretary of State's view as to the prisoner's future. It is often the case that these reports are not prepared by the deadline, and all subsequent actions should only be undertaken once the dossier has been disclosed.

11.90   On receipt of the dossier, the prisoner has four weeks to notify the Board as to what witnesses will be called and a further three weeks to submit any written representations deemed to be necessary. The Chair of the Board will then decide what witnesses will be called to give oral evidence. It may be the case that expert witnesses will be required, particularly if psychiatric evidence in is dispute. Payment for the cost of the preparation of expert reports and attendance at the hearing can be applied for under the ABWOR certificate.

11.91   There is a discretion to withhold information from the prisoner if the Secretary of State considers that it would adversely affect the health and welfare of that prisoner or others (PBR 1997, rr 5(2) and 9(1)(d)). In such cases it will be served on the Chair of the Board who will decide whether to uphold that decision. If the information is to be withheld, it will still be disclosed to the prisoner's representative. Any part of the hearing dealing with that information will be conducted in the absence of the prisoner. A recent protocol agreed by the Parole Board Users' Group (a group convened to exchange ideas for good practice and procedure between the Board, the Home Office and legal practitoners) established that representatives should be warned in advance of disclosure that the Board have material which they intend not to disclose to the prisoner and that it will only be sent to the representative on receipt of an undertaking not to disclose it. The Group has also prepared a number of leaflets for participants at these hearings.

11.92   The hearing itself is normally held in the prison where the prisoner is detained, although hearings can be constituted elsewhere, normally at another prison (PBR 1997, r 12). The time and location of the hearing are given out three weeks in advance (PBR 1997, r 11(2)). Details of the proceedings may not be made public. Part III of the Rules allow the hearing to be conducted in a manner which the panel considers appropriate for the just handling of the case and that formality should be avoided (PBR 1997, r 13(2)). When reviewing the procedure at panel hearings, the Divisional Court criticised situations whereby a report writer who may be required to give evidence at a hearing can appear as a representative for the Secretary of State, and emphasised the incompatibility of the two roles. It further decided that the chair is under a duty to record in writing the reasons for any decisions reached, with reference to the substantial points that have been raised and the established points of law on which they rely (*R v Parole Board, ex p Gittens* ((1994) Times, 3 February, DC)). For a while, this lead to tape recording of DLPs with the transcripts being prepared in the event of a judicial review being commenced. This practice has now ceased and the onus is once again on the chair and the panel secretary to keep notes of evidence and decisions.

11.93   The decision of the DLP must be communicated to the prisoner in writing within seven days of the hearing (PBR 1997, r 15(2)) and, if the panel cannot agree, a majority decision is acceptable (r 15(1)). A decision to direct release is binding upon the Secretary of State but all other decisions are advisory only (C(S)A 1997, s 28(3)). If a decision other than release is made, the DLP can recommend that a hearing be held in less than the two-year period that applies by statute. Again, this recommendation is not binding.

11.94 The panel must be satisfied that the prisoner no longer needs to be confined for the protection of the public before release can be ordered. This is a test often referred to as the 'life and limb' test as the danger posed by the lifer must be of violent re-offending rather than the much narrower test of 'any imprisonable offence' applied to mandatory lifers (see eg *R v Parole Board, ex p Bradley* [1991] 1 WLR 134). The courts have consistently held that the Parole Board are making a subjective decision based on the material before them. The courts will therefore be very reluctant to quash decisions for being unreasonable, providing proper reasons have been given for the conclusions reached. For example, a decision that a prisoner who had made great progress and had very positive reports should be transferred for further testing in open conditions was commended as being a responsible and well-thought out conclusion (*R v Parole Board, ex p Telling* (1993) Times, 10 May). The burden of proof rests with the prisoner to establish that s/he does not represent a risk to the public, and not with the Secretary of State. Leggatt LJ took the view that:

'the Board must be satisfied that it is not necessary that he should be kept in prison and not that there would be a substantial risk if he were released. In other words it must be shown that the risk is low enough to release him, not high enough to keep him in prison.' (*R v Parole Board, ex p Lodomez* (unreported, 4 May 1994), DC, p 18 of transcript)

11.95 In 1997/98, the Parole Board convened 278 oral parole hearings. Release was directed in 39 cases, with a transfer to open conditions being recommended in another 36 cases (Annual Report of the Parole Board 1997/98, Cm 1089, p 46). The last year where full figures are available for the acceptance of recommendations other than for release is 1993, in which 76% were accepted (Annual Report of the Parole Board 1994, p 13). In contrast, in the same year, of 52 recommendations for the release of mandatory lifers, six were rejected by the Secretary of State. A rejection rate of 10% in respect of release recommendations for mandatory lifers shows the importance to the prisoner of the binding powers that exist following an oral hearing, as opposed to the purely advisory powers following a paper consideration.

11.96 In cases where the Secretary of State rejects a recommendation made by the Parole Board after an oral hearing, the prisoner will inevitably feel concerned at the outcome. However, the courts have refused to impose any higher duty on the Secretary of State in such cases than that which exists for mandatory lifers. An attempt to have a 'minded to refuse' procedure introduced was rejected on the grounds that the Board's recommendation carries all the weight the prisoner needs to support his/her case (*R v Secretary of State for the Home Department, ex p Bushell* (14 December 1994, unreported), DC). However, the High Court has stated that in cases where the panel has heard oral evidence which is significant and which is relevant to their decision, a note of this should be forwarded to the Secretary of State with the panel's formal decision—otherwise, the Secretary of State may be unaware of its relevance and importance (*R v Secretary of State for the Home Department, ex p Blackstock* (3 November 1999, unreported).

Recall

11.97   A discretionary lifer, HMP detainee or automatic lifer may be recalled to prison on an emergency basis in the same manner as a mandatory lifer (C(S)A 1997, s 32). However, in such cases, if the prisoner makes representations against the recall, an oral hearing similar to a DLP must be constituted speedily to decide whether the prisoner's licence should be revoked. At these hearings, the prisoner will normally receive a copy of the last parole dossier prepared before release was initially authorised, together with the decision made to revoke the licence and any material relied upon when reaching that decision or prepared subsequently.

11.98   Recall hearings can be the most difficult parole hearings that take place. They will often involve substantial disputed evidence and will require preparation similar to that for a criminal trial. In cases where criminal charges have been laid, it is always advisable to ensure that these are concluded. Otherwise, it is not uncommon for the CPS to withdraw the charges in the knowledge that the Parole Board will have the power to keep the prisoner in custody under the terms of the original sentence. The Board have a lower standard of proof than the criminal courts and need only be satisfied on the balance of probabilites that an offence or course of action occurred. Thus, even in cases where a prisoner has been acquitted in criminal proceedings, the Board can still lawfully effect a recall if they consider that the behaviour alleged has been proven on the balance of probabilities and that it demonstrates that the prisoner poses an unacceptable risk to the safety of the public.

11.99   The issue of the burden of proof is contentious in these circumstances. A lifer will understandably feel aggrieved that an acquittal in the criminal courts can be followed by a recall to custody in any event. It is a problem that is likely to be tested further with the direct implementation of art 5(4) into English law through the Human Rights Act.

AUTOMATIC LIFE SENTENCES

11.100   The Crime (Sentences) Act 1997, s 2 introduced a new class of life sentenced prisoner. This group of lifers automatically receive a life sentence if convicted for the second time of one of the following offences:

(i) attempted murder, incitement or conspiracy or soliciting to commit murder;
(ii) manslaughter;
(iii) wounding or committing GBH with intent;
(iv) rape or attempted rape;
(v) sexual intercourse with a girl under 13;
(vi) possession of a firearm with intent to injure;
(vii) use of a firearm with intent to resist arrest;
(viii) carrying as firearm with criminal intent;
(ix) armed robbery.

11.101   Although the first conviction can have occurred at any time, the second conviction must have taken place after 1 October 1998 (the date when the C(S)A 1997 was implemented), and the person convicted must have been over the age of 18 when the second qualifying offence was committed. The first offence will not count as a qualifying offence if a non-custodial sentence was imposed at the time. The sentencing court has a little discretion over the imposition of the sentence, hence the reference to this group as automatic lifers. However, there is an overriding discretion not to impose the sentence where exceptional circumstances arise. The Court of Appeal has held that 'exceptional' must be given its everyday meaning and will not apply simply because the first offence was committed many years ago or the offences are not especially serious (*R v Kelly, R v Sandford* [2000] 1 QB 198). However, a sentence was quashed for a second offence of armed robbery where the robber had written his demand on a note containing his name and address and then sat down patiently to wait. The Court of Appeal stated that although the offence was serious, the firearm was imitation and could not have caused injury, it was never produced and no gain was made, rendering the circumstances exceptional (*R v Buckland* [2000] 1 All ER 907). It should be noted that many people who would have previously received discretionary life sentences will now instead be 'automatic lifers' with the discretionary sentence being reserved for very serious first offences.

11.102   Automatic lifers are, for all intents and purposes, the same as discretionary lifers. The only difference is that they will often have very short tariffs, the shortest so far being nine months. In consequence, it is not possible for them to progress through the normal life sentence plans and reviews. The Prison Service have set up two special centres, at Brixton for tariffs of less than five years and at Swaleside for tariffs of five to seven years, to try to process this group effectively towards release. At the time of writing, it is too soon to comment on whether these interim measures will prove successful, although early evidence indicates that proper sentence planning is proving impossible for those with very short tariffs and first reviews are not taking place on tariff expiry.

11.103   The test for release is the same as at normal DLP hearings. However, for those with short tariffs, the need to go to open conditions will be less important as they will not have been institutionalised by many years in custody. The prospect of treatment in the community should also be greater as there cannot be an automatic assumption that the lifer is 'dangerous' in the same sense that a discretionary lifer has been classified as dangerous (a pre-requisite of the discretionary life sentence). As the first cases come to be reviewed and the sentence develops, there is likely to be increasing guidance from the courts as to how the Parole Board should address such cases.

Human Rights Act 1998 and automatic life sentences

11.104   There have been arguments advanced that the automatic life sentence can potentially breach the European Convention and there may be challenges to such sentences once the Human Rights Act 1998 comes into force in October 2000. The Convention arguments that have been considered relate to the

221

possibility that the sentence amounts to a retrospective penalty under art 7, as it relies upon a conviction pre-dating the introduction of the legislation. It has also been suggested that the imposition of an automatic life sentence in the absence of any finding of dangerousness could potentially be considered arbitrary and may even amount to inhuman and degrading treatment. The extent to which any such challenges are likely to be successful will depend partly on the facts of individual cases, but is also likely to be assessed in light of the developing case law on the extent to which the sentencing court can chose not to impose the sentence in 'exceptional circumstances' (see further *Archbold News* Issue 4, 9 May 2000, pp7–8).

CHAPTER 12

PAROLE AND RELEASE

THE PAROLE SYSTEM

12.1   The system for the early release of prisoners was radically overhauled by the Criminal Justice Act 1991 ('the Act'). The Act appears to have been designed to implement two main policy objectives, these being the need to ensure a more rapid throughput of prisoners in order to ease overcrowding, whilst at the same time ensuring that those convicted of more serious crimes would be obliged to spend a greater part of their sentence in custody.

12.2   The Act divides prisoners into three categories and operates differing release schemes for each. The categories are:

(i)   Sentences of less than 12 months;
(ii)   Sentences of less than four years but 12 months or more;
(iii)   Sentences of four years or more.

Prisoners in groups (i) and (ii) are described by the Act as 'short-term' prisoners and those in group (iii) as 'long-term prisoners' (s 33(5)).

12.3   The Act came into force on 1 October 1992. Prisoners who were serving sentences imposed before that date, but who remain in custody, are defined as 'existing prisoners.' Any existing prisoner who receives a further sentence after 1 October 1992, will have their total sentence calculated into a single term and will continue to be treated as an existing prisoner (see chapter 6). Existing prisoners have their cases considered under the new parole system but retain their right to a PED at one-third of their sentence and licence conditions can only be imposed up until the two-thirds point of their sentence (see below).

The automatic unconditional release scheme

12.4   Prisoners serving sentences of less than 12 months will be released after serving one-half of that sentence (s 33(1)(a)). Release is automatic and the release date can only be deferred where additional days of imprisonment have been awarded at adjudication. Release is unconditional and is not subject to any licence conditions or probation supervision.

12.5 Approximately one week before release under the AUR scheme, prisoners are issued with an 'At Risk Notice,' advising them that they may be returned to custody if they should commit a further imprisonable offence before their sentence expiry date (see further below).

Automatic conditional release scheme

12.6 Prisoners serving less than four years but more than 12 months must be released on licence after serving one-half of their sentence (s 33(1)(b)). Again, there is no discretion in the matter and the Secretary of State is under a duty to authorise release. All prisoners falling within this scheme will be supervised by a probation officer upon their release from prison at the half-way point, until their licence expiry date (LED). For the majority of prisoners the LED falls at the three-quarters point of their sentence (some sex offenders must be supervised until the expiry of their sentence (s 44)).

12.7 As the scheme is automatic, responsibility for its administration lies with the governor of the individual prison rather than with the Home Office, and detailed guidance is given in PSO 6000. All references below relate to PSO 6000 unless otherwise stated.

12.8 It is the duty of the prison receiving short-term prisoners from the sentencing court to notify them of their conditional release date (ie the half-way point of their sentence) and to remind them that they will be under supervision on release (para 3.3.1). Prisoners should also be told of the standard conditions of the automatic release licence and how long the licence will last. This procedure should also be followed whenever a prisoner is transferred to another prison.

12.9 Each prisoner will be allocated to a probation officer on reception to prison. This officer has responsibility for drawing up a supervision plan and to participate in sentence planning procedures at the prison (para 3.4.1). The Probation Service National Standards require probation officers to submit a pre-discharge report to the relevant establishment at least one month before release. This should contain relevant information on prisoners' home circumstances and may contain recommendations as to any additional licence conditions that are felt to be necessary. Shortly before release, prisoners' personal officers must send a discharge report to the supervising probation officer, and at the end of the supervision period the probation officer should send a feedback report to the prison (para 3.8.1).

12.10 The licence is produced by the governor of the holding prison and is a pro forma (a sample copy is reproduced in PSO 6000 at appendix A, p 6). If the probation officer asks that additional conditions are included on the licence, the governor is able to authorise these if they are standard conditions contained in annex B to PSO 6000, chapter 3. Any other agency (police, social services) asking for additional licence conditions to be imposed should be referred to the supervising probation officer. In exceptional cases non-standard conditions can be included in a licence but the governor must clear these with the Parole Unit at Prison Service Headquarters (para 3.9.2).

12.11 The licence must be signed and issued by the governor or an officer duly authorised by the governor. When it is given to the prisoner the reporting instructions, other requirements of supervision, the length of supervision and the penalties for breach must be explained. The prisoner should then be invited to sign the licence but if s/he refuses, the governor must certify that the requirements have been explained and that the prisoner refused to sign (para 3.9.1).

12.12 Where a prisoner refuses to sign, release must still proceed as the Secretary of State has no discretion to defer release (except in cases where additional days have been awarded, see chapter 8). The governor must ensure that suitable reporting instructions are given to the prisoner and if s/he does not have a release address then the reporting arrangements must be made within the prisoner's usual home area, or the petty sessional area in which s/he was tried (para 3.11.1).

The discretionary release scheme

12.13 The parole system is now entitled the Discretionary Release Scheme (DCR) and applies only to long-term prisoners serving sentences of four years or more. The Act provides that the Secretary of State may release long-term prisoners after they have served one-half of their sentence, if so recommended by the Parole Board (s 35(1)). Until 1992, parole eligibility commenced at one-third of the sentence and the DCR scheme can therefore be seen to have significantly lengthened the possible time to be served in prison as well as reducing the number of reviews to which a prisoner will be entitled.

12.14 Prisoners who were convicted before 1 October 1992 will continue to be considered for parole after they have served one-third of their sentences and will have an annual parole review thereafter.

12.15 The decision as to release in the case of all long-term prisoners rests with the Secretary of State providing the Parole Board has made such a recommendation. However, the Secretary of State has delegated this power to the Board in the case of prisoners serving sentences of less than fifteen years (Parole Board (Transfer of Functions) Order 1998).

12.16 The most important aspect of the system is the policy decision to have an 'open reporting' process. This provides for prisoners to be given access to a copy of the dossier once it has been prepared. This policy decision was made following considerable debate in the House of Lords, reports from government committees and pressure from the courts (see eg the interlocutory applications in *R v Secretary of State for the Home Department, ex p Benson* [1989] COD 329). Home Office resistance to the concept of open reporting does, however, provide limits to the extent of disclosure. PSO 6000 provides that whilst the general principle is for the entire dossier to be disclosed, documents can be withheld for the following reasons:

'(a) in the interests of national security;
(b) for the prevention of crime or disorder, including information relevant to prison security;
(c) for the protection of information received in confidence from a third party, or other information which may put a third party at risk;
(d) if, on medical and/or psychiatric grounds, it is felt necessary to withhold information where the mental and/or physical health of the prisoner could be impaired.' (para 4.15.1)

12.17   The governor may seek guidance from the Parole Unit as to whether or not to withhold any report from the prisoner, particularly where there are considerations of national security or the prevention of crime or disorder. In coming to a decision about disclosure the governor should consider whether the report might be re-written for disclosure, or whether a summary or edited version might be disclosed.

12.18   If the report is not disclosed to the prisoner then s/he must be advised of the decision in writing on a 'disclosure form' which is attached to the parole dossier. Such decisions are susceptible to judicial review. In one case a prisoner's parole decision alluded to undisclosed police intelligence information. Permission to apply for judicial review was refused but the proceedings were withdrawn when the applicant was released on licence a matter of days before the renewed application of his case.

12.19   The review process for release on parole licence commences some 26 weeks before the prisoners' PED. At this time the prisoner receives notification that the review process will commence and is invited to sign a form consenting to be reviewed (para 4.12.1). Once the prisoner has indicated his/her consent, requests for the preparation of reports will be sent out.

The parole dossier must be structured chronologically and should consist of the following reports:

(a) Summary sheet/index;
(b) Crown court order for imprisonment and record of conviction including the sentencing judge's comments;
(c) Court of Appeal papers (if applicable);
(d) Post-trial police reports;
(e) Previous convictions;
(f) Pre-sentence/social enquiry reports;
(g) Pre-sentence psychiatric/medical reports;
(h) Sentence plan and parole initial profile;
(i) Sentence plan review forms;
(j) Adjudications and additional days awarded;
(k) Reports on offence related work;
(l) Prison parole assessment;
(m) Prison medical officer's report;
(n) Prison chaplain's report;
(o) Parole assessment report (home circumstances report);
(p) Additional information (including job offers, letters of support);
(q) Previous review papers;
(r) Copy of decisions in previous reviews.

12.20 On receipt of the dossier, the prisoner will be invited to sign a form indicating the documents that have been disclosed and to make written representations in support of the application. If difficult issues of law or fact arise, it is advisable for the prisoner to seek legal advice at this stage and if appropriate, for a legal adviser to draft these representations.

12.21 A prisoner should be interviewed by a member of the Parole Board approximately 16 weeks before his/her PED. The interview is designed to be structured around the criteria which are used by the Board when assessing the application (see below). The member's record of interview is subsequently passed to the prisoner for further comment before the papers are finally placed before a panel of the Board.

12.22 The Secretary of State is empowered to give directions to the Board as to the matters it must take into account when considering applications. The two main criteria are described as the need to protect the public from serious harm and the desirability of preventing the commission of further offences and of securing rehabilitation (CJA 1991, s 6). Under this power, the Secretary of State wrote to the chairman of the Board in 1992 to set out the main criteria. These are available from the Parole Unit at Prison Service Headquarters but they may be summarised as follows:

> 'The decision should be focused on the risk of further offences being committed when the offender would otherwise be in prison. A balance must be reached between this and whether early release under supervision would aid rehabilitation and lessen the chance of re-offending. The Parole Board must be satisfied that the release plan will help secure rehabilitation and that the offender has demonstrated, through behaviour and attitude in custody that positive efforts have been made to address offending behaviour.'

12.23 There are a number of factors to be considered in each case:

(i) The prisoner's background, previous criminal record and response to previous supervision;

(ii) The nature and circumstances of the offence;

(iii) The risk that may be posed to the victim or other persons, including those outside the jurisdiction (a consideration upheld in the case of *R v Parole Board, ex p White* (1994) Times, 30 December 1994, where the court upheld a refusal to release a discretionary life sentence prisoner on completion of his tariff even though the prisoner was subject to a deportation order);

(iv) The likely response of the local community and the victim or the victim's family;

(v) Statistical indicators as to the likelihood of re-offending;

(vi) Behaviour in custody including offences against discipline, attitude to other inmates and the contribution made to prison life;

(vii) Remorse and insight into offending behaviour including steps taken within available resources to achieve treatment and training objectives (an application for leave to move for judicial review was granted in the case of *R v Parole Board, ex p Watson* (24 November 1994, unreported), HC in respect of a decision not to authorise release for failure to address offending behaviour when the dossier indicated that the applicant had completed all offending behaviour courses available within the prison. The applicant was released before a full hearing could take place);

(viii) The realism of release plans including home circumstances reports.

12.24 The interpretation of these criteria will naturally involve the Board making a subjective assessment on the available information. The Board is required to give reasons for any refusal to authorise parole and the normal principles of administrative law will apply when scrutinising such decisions.

12.25 The Divisional Court has set out the duty to give reasons for determinate parole cases in some detail (*R v Secretary of State for the Home Department, ex p Lillycrop* (1996) Times, 13 December, DC). It was held that the decision letter, 'should contain a succinct and accurate summary of the reasons leading to a decision reached.' This did not require an elaborate or detailed analysis of the facts but:

> 'The reasons must be such that the prisoner will know why a decision unfavourable to him has been reached. The whole of the reasoning process of the Board need, however, not be set out. In particular, while it is clear that the Board must have regard in coming to its decision to matters favourable to the prisoner which are included in the dossier, the Board need not set out in its decision letter the matters pointing towards release which it has taken into account.' (Butterfield J, transcript, p 9)

These comments indicate that the duty is similar to that imposed on the reviews for life sentenced prisoners, albeit slightly less onerous. In the case of *R v Secretary of State for the Home Department and Parole Board, ex p Evans* (2 November 1994, unreported), DC, Simon Brown LJ commented that:

> 'The Board's duty to give reasons is not in dispute...[where] the Board find themselves unable to follow what I have already described as the clear, emphatic and unanimous view of the LRC and those reporting to them, they should explain why, in language sufficiently clear and terms sufficiently full to ensure that the LRC properly understand the basis of the difference of the opinion between them.' (transcript, pp 16–17)

12.26 There is no right of appeal against a refusal to grant parole. Prisoners may submit a requests/complaints form querying the decision to the Parole Board Secretariat. In practice, however, this is unlikely to elicit any further reasons. The present policy applied by the Board is only to reconsider cases where there has been a substantial procedural irregularity or if significant new information is made available. These decisions fall outside of the remit of the Prisons' Ombudsman who has no powers to investigate complaints concerning decisions made by agencies outside of the Prison Service such as the Parole Board.

12.27 When advising on the possibility of judicial review, it is important to closely cross-reference the reports prepared with the criteria for release and the reasons given. Whilst the Board will necessarily be making subjective decisions, the proper balance between the various criteria must be achieved. Applications to the High Court for leave have been approved in various cases and these have subsequently lead to a voluntary reconsideration of the application and release. An application for leave in the case of *R v Parole Board, ex p Riley* (7 July 1994, unreported), was made where the applicant had been refused release by the Board for failing to address her offending behaviour. She in fact maintained her innocence of complex and technical financial offences but was described as a 'model prisoner' who was allowed regular temporary releases. The leave application was granted on the basis that the Board's decision was irrational, but the case settled before a full hearing.

12.28 The principle that maintaining innocence is not an automatic barrier to release on licence was upheld in the case of *R v Parole Board, ex p Zulfikar* (1995) Times, 26 July, DC (see also *R v Secretary of State for the Home Department, ex p Lillycrop* (1996) Times, 13 December, DC) and has received recent publicity in *R v Parole Board, ex p Oyston* (14 October 1999, unreported), HC. In the *Oyston* case parole was refused on the basis that the prisoner, imprisoned following convictions for sex offences, had failed to address his offending behaviour and that the Board could not be satisfied that the risk that he posed was sufficiently low to authorise release on licence. Although the prisoner had maintained his innocence, parole had been recommended on the basis that his high public profile and his wealth meant that re-offending was unlikely. In quashing the decision, Hooper J held that parole had in reality been refused on the sole basis that the prisoner had not admitted his guilt. The High Court's decision was affirmed by the Court of Appeal in March 2000.

12.29 The relationship between innocence and parole refusal still remains complex and there is an absence of any real judicial guidance beyond the simple principle that refusal to admit guilt is not grounds in itself to refuse release on licence. In *Zulfikar*, Stuart-Smith LJ suggested that each case will depend on its own particular facts and that the court should, 'avoid trying to lay down principles that may not be universally applicable' (transcript, p 24). He distinguished the case of a first time offender with, for example, a persistent sex offender, pointing out that the risk of future re-offending might be easy to assess in some cases, irrespective of whether guilt is admitted, whereas it will be more complex in others. This approach was followed in the *Lillycrop* case in which Butterfield J confirmed that the Board must assume each prisoner is properly convicted and that the nature of the offence and the offender's history are relevant. The difficulties that arise are perfectly illustrated by the subsequent decision in *Zulfikar (No 2)*. When the Parole Board reconsidered the case following the decision of the court, parole was refused again. That decision was upheld by Buxton J who considered that the reasoning applied by the Board did not rely solely upon the refusal to admit guilt and was within its discretion (*R v Secretary of State for the Home Department, ex p Zulfikar (No 2)* (1 May 1996, unreported), HC). When the *Oyston* judgment is read in light of these cases, it is possible to discern particular facts which rendered the case unusual, the applicant being a first time offender from a wealthy background who was in the public eye. It is difficult to discern any statements of principle which go beyond the earlier decisions.

Subsequent reviews

12.30   If parole is not granted at the first review, a prisoner may be entitled to further reviews depending on the length of sentence being served. The minimum parole licence period is one month and, therefore, a prisoner may be entitled to a further review if the anniversary of his/her PED is at least one month before his/her non-parole release date (ie two-thirds of the sentence).

12.31   The Parole Board describes the period of eligibility for parole as a 'parole window.' In order to qualify for a second review, a prisoner will have to be serving a minimum of 66 months' imprisonment. The first review will be completed by 33 months and the second review by 45 months. The next parole review date will then fall after 46 months.

12.32   The Board does retain the right to order early or special reviews in exceptional circumstances. This will commonly include ordering a review when there is no longer one scheduled or advancing the date of the next review by six months. The Home Office guidance for when this would be appropriate is contained in Circular Instruction 26/92, paras 59–60. Examples include allowing monitoring of progress on a drugs rehabilitation course or other offence-based work and where there are new factors which substantially change the prisoner's circumstances. In addition an early review may be ordered where there were procedural irregularities in consideration of the case. It is arguable that in such cases the prisoner is entitled to immediate reconsideration with supplementary reports if necessary. This will necessarily depend on the nature of the irregularities discovered.

Licence conditions

12.33   When a prisoner is released on licence, in most cases this will remain in force until the three-quarters point of the sentence (CJA 1991, s 37(1)). However, the sentencing court does have the power to order that the licence should remain in force until the entire sentence has expired (s 44). This power is reserved for prisoners convicted of sexual offences or in cases where the court feels it is necessary to prevent the commission of further offences or to protect the public from serious harm (see the definitions at s 32(6)).

12.34   The prisoner is obliged to comply with the conditions of the licence (s 37(4)) and these may be varied after consultation with the Board. Any prisoner who refuses to sign a DCR parole licence will not be released on parole.

NON-PAROLE RELEASE

12.35   Long-term prisoners who are not granted parole will nevertheless be released on licence at the two-thirds stage of their sentence (subject to additional days awarded at adjudication). All prisoners will be on licence until the three-quarter stage (or until the sentence expiry date in the case of some sex offenders where this was directed at their sentence hearing under the CJA 1991, s 44). 'Existing' prisoners, who were serving their sentences before commencement of the Act will be released unconditionally at the two-thirds point.

12.36   Approximately 10 weeks before release on non-parole licence, the parole clerk at the prison should make contact with the supervising probation officer and discuss any need for additional conditions on the non-parole licence. In some cases such conditions will have been recommended by the Parole Board at the last (unsuccessful) review. If additional conditions are thought necessary then the supervising probation officer will be required to make an application to the prison six weeks in advance of the release date. A dossier (including an application to the Parole Board, a report from the supervising officer setting out the reasons for the request, previous convictions, and reports relating to the offence) will be prepared and disclosed to the prisoner, who will be given the opportunity to make representations. The dossier and representations are then forwarded to the Parole Board for consideration (para 5.3.2).

12.37   The non-parole licence is issued at the prison, and signed by the governor or an officer authorised by him. Conditions on the licence must be explained to the prisoner, as should the consequences of breach. Where the prisoner refuses to sign the licence, s/he must still be released. In cases where the prisoner does not have a home address the governor will make arrangements for him/her to report to a probation officer in his/her usual home area, or the petty sessional area in which s/he was convicted.

YOUNG OFFENDERS

12.38   The release and supervision arrangements for young offenders, whilst operating under the same general principles, do vary from those for adult prisoners (CJA 1991, ss 43 and 65).

12.39   Young offenders who are serving sentences of 12 months or less are to be released after serving one-half of their sentence on a notice of supervision. This is issued by the governor of the releasing prison on behalf of the Home Secretary. The period of supervision is to be three months or until the prisoners' 22nd birthday, whichever is the shorter period. Supervision for this period is obligatory, even when it will extend beyond the length of the sentence.

12.40   Young offenders who are serving sentences of over 12 months are released on the standard automatic conditional release licence, discretionary conditional release licence or non-parole licence, as above. However, supervision must continue for a minimum of three months regardless of the length of the sentences.

12.41   The Criminal Justice Act 1991, s 43(2) makes an important change for young offenders sentenced to periods of imprisonment under the Children and Young Persons Act 1933, s 53(2) in that they are now eligible for parole. Previously such sentences did not attract early release on licence.

DEPORTEES

12.42   Prisoners who are liable to deportation or removal from the UK will still fall under the release schemes as outlined above. Thus, those serving less than four years will be released from their sentence automatically at the half-way point. Prisoners will be issued with the appropriate 'at risk' notice or licence despite the fact that they will not be remaining in the jurisdiction. An automatic conditional release licence will contain a standard condition requiring a deportee to comply with removal directions and to submit to supervision if released from custody in the UK or if allowed to return to the UK during the licence period.

12.43   The parole clerk at the prison will liaise with the Immigration and Nationality Department to arrange removal from the country. If the Immigration and Nationality Department are not able to make travel arrangements on the date of release, then further detention must be authorised under Immigration Act powers.

12.44   Prisoners serving more than four years will be considered under the discretionary conditional release scheme. However, there are significant differences from the scheme for domestic prisoners.

12.45   Deportees cannot opt out of the parole process. They are automatically considered when they reach the half-way point of their sentences (unless they are 'existing' prisoners, in which case they will be eligible after serving one-third).

12.46   A parole dossier is collated and prepared as for domestic prisoners, but includes a Prison Assessment for Deportation. There will not be a report from a Parole Board member, although prisoners must still be interviewed in order that they can put forward their case for release on licence. In practice, this role falls to the Board of Visitors.

12.47   Once completed, the dossier is sent to the Parole Unit, who will make a decision as to whether or not to grant the application on behalf of the Secretary of State. If release is not authorised then reasons will be given for refusal.

12.48   Where release on licence is granted, a licence will be issued. If removal directions are not made, and the prisoner is detained under Immigration Act powers, the licence must be supervised by the probation service (para 8.9.2).

RECALL OF DETERMINATE SENTENCE PRISONERS

Short-term prisoners sentenced before 1 January 1999

12.49   The recall of short-term prisoners serving less than four years' imprisonment has been altered by the Crime and Disorder Act 1998, s 103. This transferred the power to recall short-term prisoners from the courts to the Parole Board following breach of licence conditions. The new recall powers apply to all short-term prisoners who were released from prison on licence and whose original offence was committed on or after 1 January 1999.

12.50 Where the original offence was committed before 1 January 1999 the prisoner may be convicted of breaching their licence by a magistrates court (CJA 1991, s 38). This criminal offence is punishable by a fine. In addition, the court can order that the parole licence is suspended for six months, or the remainder of the licence period, if this is shorter.

12.51 There is no emergency recall provision for short-term prisoners whose original offence was committed before 1 January 1999.

Short-term prisoners sentenced after 1 January 1999 and long-term prisoners

12.52 Under the Criminal Justice Act 1991, s 39, prisoners serving sentences of four years or more may be recalled to prison following breach of their licence conditions (including non-parole licences), or if it is considered that they may pose a risk.

12.53 In order to recall a prisoner, reference must be made to the Parole Board. Section 39(1) provides that the Parole Board may recommend to the Secretary of State that a prisoner's licence is revoked. However, if it is considered that there is an immediate risk to the public of re-offending, a prisoner can be recalled before his case has been considered by the Board (s 39(2)). Such decisions are taken on behalf of the Secretary of State by senior officials in the Parole Unit, usually outside of working hours. In these circumstances the case must be referred to the Board as soon as practicable after revocation, and if it does not uphold the decision to recall the prisoner, the prison will be instructed to release him/her immediately.

12.54 Where the Parole Unit receives notification from the Probation Service that an offender is not complying with the conditions on his licence, the Parole Unit should prepare a dossier for submission to the Parole Board.

12.55 In considering whether to revoke the licence (or uphold the Secretary of State's decision to revoke it), the Parole Board should consider the Secretary of State's *Directions to the Parole Board—Recall of Determinate Sentence Prisoners*:

'1. In deciding whether or not to recommend the recall of a prisoner who has been released on licence, or to recommend the immediate release of such a prisoner who has been recalled, the Parole Board shall consider whether the prisoner's continued liberty or, as the case may be, immediate release, would present an unacceptable risk to the public of further offences being committed.
2. In considering this issue, the Board shall, in particular, take into account:
(a) whether the prisoner is likely to commit further offences; and
(b) whether the prisoner has failed to comply with one or more of his licence conditions or might be likely to do so in the future.'

12.56 The Parole Board must also take account of the views of the supervising probation officer, and any representations made by the prisoner. Training guidance has been issued to the Board by the Home Secretary, and so it should also have regard to the following factors:

(i) the offender's background, including any previous convictions and their pattern, and in particular, performance during any previous periods of supervision;

(ii) the nature and circumstances of the original offence and the offender's present attitude to it;

(iii) how far the causes of offending behaviour have been addressed on release, together with any new areas of concern that have arisen on licence;

(iv) general behaviour on licence, including response to supervision, compliance with licence requirements, co-operation with the supervising officer and general attitude to authority;

(v) the proportion of the licence already served and the seriousness of the breach in relation to the amount of licence period successfully completed;

(vi) the extent and seriousness of any further offences committed while on licence and/or charges which have been laid in connection with such offences;

(vii) the suitability of the offender's current accommodation;

(viii) the offender's relationships with his or her family and people outside the family circle;

(ix) any contact by the offender with, or concerns expressed by, the victim or victim's family, any adverse local reaction to the offender's release on licence;

(x) work record—the extent to which jobs have been held down, relationships with colleagues and employer;

(xi) current medical and psychiatric views, if any;

(xii) any other information, including representations from other people or bodies (eg police, social services) which may have a bearing on whether the offender should be permitted to remain on licence.

12.57 When a prisoner is recalled, the governor will be advised as to the reasons why, and be asked to convey that information to the prisoner. Prisoners will be given the dossier considered by the Parole Board and the reasons for confirming the recall decision. They have the right to make written representations (s 39(3)(a)). These will be referred back to the Parole Board for its consideration.

12.58 If the Parole Board accepts the representations, the Parole Unit will order the prison to release the prisoner immediately, and the prisoner will then be supervised in the community on the original licence. However, in some cases, the Parole Board may decide to impose additional licence conditions. If so, a fresh licence will be prepared and issued.

12.59 Where the decision to revoke the licence is upheld, the prisoner will be advised of their post recall release date (PRRD) which is the same as their original licence expiry date with any time spent unlawfully at large added. The Parole Board has the power to authorise further reviews of a case at any time. If an earlier review is not requested then it will review prisoners whose licences have been revoked on an annual basis. A prisoner with less than 13 months to serve following confirmation of revocation will not have an automatic right to a review, but if there is fresh information which could be considered by the Parole Board, it would be worth making representations.

12.60   If there is any delay between a revocation of a parole licence and arrest, then an offender will be unlawfully at large. The Prison Act 1952 provides that in calculating a prison sentence, no account is taken of any time during which a person sentenced to imprisonment is unlawfully at large (s 49) and thus the licence expiry date will be pushed back by the number of days that the prisoner was UAL.

The 'at risk' period

12.61   Prisoners sentenced after commencement of the CJA 1991 are subject to an 'at risk' period which runs until that sentence expires. This means that if they commit a further offence punishable by imprisonment during that period, they may be returned to prison for the whole or any part of the period between the commission of the offence and the expiry of the original sentence (s 40).

12.62   A section 40 order is imposed by the court which convicts the prisoner of the new offence, and as such is appealed through the usual criminal procedures.

12.63   The relationship between s 40 and s 39 of the CJA 1991 has been examined by the courts on many occasions. In *R v Sharkey* [2000] 1 WLR 160, CA, it was held that it was appropriate to impose an order returning an offender to prison under s 40 even where s/he had already been recalled to prison under s 39. This decision contradicts the judgment in *R v Governor of HMP Elmley, ex p Moorton* [1999] 2 Cr App Rep (S) 165, DC, in which Simon Brown LJ and Astill J both commented that a prisoner who had already been recalled to prison under s 39 should not be returned under a s 40 order as well. In *Sharkey*, Bingham LCJ felt that the administrative provisions allowing for recall under s 39 could not oust the power to impose a further criminal sentence under s 40.

12.64   In *R v Giacopazzi* (9 July 1999, unreported), CA, a s 40 order returning the appellant to prison for one year was quashed in the Court of Appeal. The appellant's original trial had taken place before commencement of the CJA 1991, but the conviction had been quashed and a re-trial ordered. He was convicted a second time after commencement of the Act. Whilst serving that sentence he was treated by the prison as an existing prisoner and was released at the two-thirds point of his sentence without any licence being issued. However, before the sentence expiry date he was convicted of further imprisonable offences, and a s 40 order imposed. The Criminal Cases Review Commission referred the case back to the Court of Appeal on the basis that the Criminal Appeal Act 1968, Sch 2, para 2(3) refers any sentence imposed on retrial back to the time when a sentence imposed at the original trial would have commenced.

HOME DETENTION CURFEW

12.65   The Home Detention Curfew scheme (HDC) came into effect on 28 January 1999 and was introduced under the CJA 1991, s 34A (as amended by the CDA 1998, s 99). This provides for most prisoners serving over three months and under four years to be released on a licence containing a curfew condition. The scheme is to be viewed as a 'normal part of ... progression through the sentence' (PSO 6700, para 1.4). However, evidence filed on behalf of the Respondent in *R v Secretary of State for the Home Department, ex p Allen* (21 November 1999, unreported), QBD, showed that only 31% of prisoners eligible for release on HDC had been so released.

Eligibility

12.66   Statutory exceptions to eligibility are contained in s 34A. Prisoners not eligible to be released on home detention curfew are:

(a)   violent and sexual offenders currently serving an extended sentence under CDA 1998, s 58;

(b)   prisoners serving a sentence under the Prisoners (Return to Custody) Act 1995, s 1;

(c)   prisoners currently subject to a hospital order, hospital direction or transfer direction under the Mental Health Act 1983, ss 37, 45A, or 47;

(d)   prisoners currently serving a sentence imposed under the CJA 1991, Sch 2, para 3(1)(d) or 4 (1)(d) in a case where the prisoner had failed to comply with a requirement of a curfew order;

(e)   prisoners who have at any time been recalled to prison from a home detention curfew order under the CJA 1991, s 38A(1)(a), unless the prisoner successfully appealed against the recall;

(f)   prisoners currently liable to removal from the UK under the CJA 1991, s 46;

(g)   prisoners who have, during the current sentence, been released on home detention curfew or given early compassionate release under the CJA 1991, s 36 and have been recalled to prison under the CJA 1991, s 38(1) or (2);

(h)   prisoners who have at any time been returned to prison under the CJA 1991, s 40;

(i)   prisoners who have not served the requisite period of their sentence until there are fewer than 14 days remaining until the half-way point of the sentence;

(j)   prisoners who have not yet reached the age of 18 years.

12.67   In addition to the above, fine defaulters and those held in contempt of court are not eligible as they are not serving a sentence of imprisonment. Prisoners who have been recalled to prison at any time under the CJA 1991, s 39 whilst on home detention curfew should only be assessed for release under the scheme if there are exceptional circumstances (PSO 6700, para 2.3.1).

12.68   There are special provisions in relation to the eligibility of sex offenders. Thus, those prisoners who will be required to register with the police under the Sex Offenders Act 1997, Pt 1, must be checked by an authorised governor. If it is decided that a full assessment for HDC is warranted then Prisoner Administration Group at Prison Service Headquarters must be informed immediately, and the police consulted to ascertain the prisoner's antecedents and relevant criminal intelligence. Where the full assessment shows that a prisoner appears to meet the criteria for release, the case must be referred to the area manager. Authorisation by the Director General of the Prison Service is required before such a prisoner can be released on HDC (PSO 6700, para 2.4.1).

12.69   Prisoners eligible for release on HDC will be informed of their curfew eligibility date upon their reception to prison. Those serving more than three months but less than four months will have to serve a minimum of thirty days in custody before becoming eligible; those serving more than four months but less than eight months will have to serve one-quarter of their sentence; and those serving between eight months and four years will serve 60 days less than half of their sentence before they may be released on HDC.

Risk assessment

12.70   Risk assessment for HDC commences ten weeks before a prisoner's eligibility date. If the prisoner is a sex offender required to register under the Sex Offenders Act 1997, an assessment will only be commenced if the governor believes that there are exceptional circumstances. A judicial review application in which a prisoner contended that as those required to register under the 1997 Act were not statutorily excluded from the scheme, unlike those with extended sentences, it was irrational to have a policy where they would only be released on HDC in exceptional circumstances, failed (*R v Secretary of State for the Home Department, ex p Willis* [2000] 10 LS Gaz R 35). The court also rejected the suggestion that the prisoner was entitled to disclosure of the material on which the decision as to whether there were any exceptional circumstances was based, prior to the decision being made. Category A prisoners serving less than four years will only be assessed if they make an application for release on HDC and the governor decides that there are exceptional circumstances (PSO 6700, para 5.1.2).

12.71   There are two risk assessment procedures. A standard 'suitability assessment' must be used in relation to all prisoners; an 'enhanced assessment' is also applied in cases where the prisoner is serving more than one year and does not have a successful record of temporary release during their sentence, are scored as high risk on the predictor scores for violent or sex offences, or risk of re-imprisonment, or are considered to require more in-depth consideration by the suitability assessment (para 5.3.3).

12.72   Both risk assessments are carried out on standard forms (HDC 1 for the suitability assessment, and HDC 4 for the enhanced assessment). These are appended to PSO 6700.

12.73   The suitability assessment is usually carried out by a prison probation officer or a prison officer with experience of completing risk assessments. Information is obtained from the prisoner, a member of staff in daily contact with him/her, and the probation service in the area in which it is anticipated that the prisoner will be released. When the relevant information has been gathered the probation officer will be required to complete form HDC 1, summarising the prisoner's suitability for release on HDC. The summary should include a review of the information outlined above, the prisoner's risk prediction scores, and a recommendation as to suitability for release, or a referral for the enhanced assessment.

12.74   Where release is recommended, the governor will be required to confirm the recommendation and authorise release.

12.75   If an enhanced assessment is required then the matter will be referred to an assessment board containing a governor, a seconded probation officer or member of the throughcare team (who supervises those on HDC until the end of their licence period), and a member of staff who is in regular contact with the prisoner. The board will consider the HDC 1 and core documentation and will note the prisoner's previous criminal history and evidence as to the causes of offending behaviour; participation in and response to offending behaviour work in prison; response to periods of release on temporary licence; relevant behaviour in prison; external factors affecting the likelihood of re-offending; home circumstances and stability of close relationships (PSO 6700, para 5.10.4). The chairperson of the board will complete form HDC 4 recording the decision and the reasoning behind it. An authorised governor will then be required to confirm any decision to release or to refuse the application.

12.76   PSO 6700 gives detailed guidance as to risk assessment (chapter 5). In general, prisoners should normally be released on HDC unless there are 'substantive' reasons for retaining him/her in custody. The reasons must fall under one of the following headings:

'(a)   an unacceptable risk to the victim or members of the public;
 (b)   a pattern of offending which indicates a likelihood of re-offending during the HDC period;
 (c)   a likelihood of failure to comply with the conditions of the curfew;
 (d)   lack of suitable accommodation for HDC [the home must be in England or Wales, and have a fixed or metered supply of electricity];
 (e)   shortness of the potential curfew period [this must usually be at least 14 days].' (para 5.13.3)

Licence conditions

12.77   There are two types of HDC licence, one for prisoners serving less than 12 months and one for prisoners serving over 12 months and for young offenders. The latter contains requirements for probation supervision throughout the licence period. Prisoners serving less than twelve months will remain on licence until the half-way stage of their sentences and those serving more than twelve months will be on licence until they have reached the two-thirds point. They will remain at risk of being returned to prison if they commit further offences (CJA 1991, s 40), as outlined above.

12.78   The authorising governor must set licence conditions and these will include the place and times of curfew. In exceptional cases it is possible to curfew a prisoner to more than one address (eg home and workplace) if this is essential to the supervision plan.

12.79   Curfew periods must be for at least nine hours per day, and usually twelve hours. However, they may vary from day to day, for example, in order to enable the prisoner to work, care for children or have routine medical appointments.

12.80   Prisoners must agree to sign their HDC licences. If they refuse to do so then they cannot be released until their conditional or automatic release date (PSO 6700, para 6.3.1).

12.81   All HDC licences contain a condition that the prisoner will agree to bear the cost of the electricity used by the monitoring unit installed at his/her address. Where the prisoner has a telephone line in his or her own name, s/he will be required to agree that the contractor may use it. If there is no telephone line at the HDC address this can be installed by the contractor.

Refusal to grant release

12.82   If release on HDC is refused, reasons will be given to the prisoner on form HDC 6. The reports upon which that refusal is based should also be disclosed, including the risk assessments on HDC 1 and HDC 4 (PSO 6700, para 7.2). In some circumstances information may be withheld (see paras 12.16–12.18 above).

12.83   It is open to prisoners to appeal against refusal to release on HDC via the requests/complaints system and/or to instruct solicitors to challenge the decision on their behalves. Governors are advised that they should deal with such appeals as a 'priority' (para 7.10). If the refusal is upheld then it is appropriate to appeal to the area manager and the Ombudsman, if there is time.

12.84   Judicial review proceedings may also be appropriate. In *R v Secretary of State for the Home Department, ex p Allen* (12 November 1999, unreported), QBD, a prisoner successfully challenged the procedural fairness in the eligibility assessments for HDC as the scheme did not envisage disclosure of the reports in order that representations could be submitted in advance of the HDC decision. The Respondents were granted permission to appeal against the decision on the grounds this was an issue of public importance. Following the judgment, the revised PSO 6700, issued in January 2000, contained a provision in para 7.3 that disclosable reports, including either the standard or enhanced assessment forms (HDC 1 or 4):

> 'must be made available to the prisoner if requested ... Where a request for disclosure is made in advance of the consideration of the case, the prisoner must be given the opportunity to make oral or written represenations prior to the board's decision on Home Detention Curfew.'

Notwithstanding this, it was the Prison Service's contention in the appeal of the *Allen* decision (unreported, CA), that procedural fairness did not require prior disclosure. When a prisoner appealed against a decision using the requests/complaints procedure there was disclosure of the reports and an opportunity to make oral representations to a governor who would make a new decision. Given the contents of the revised PSO it is unclear why the Prison Service sought to challenge the court's finding at first instance, as now a refusal to allow disclosure before the decision is made will breach a prisoner's legitimate expectation based on para 7.3 even if the courts have decided that it is not strictly required for procedural fairness.

Post release

12.85   A prisoner who has been released on HDC may apply to the governor of the establishment from which s/he was released for licence conditions to be varied (although the contractor responsible for installing the equipment and monitoring compliance may authorise some one-off absences).

12.86   In coming to a decision as to whether to grant an application for variation, the governor may consult a seconded probation officer or a member of the prison's throughcare team. If the prisoner is also under supervision by the probation service, it is likely that their views will also be sought.

12.87   Where the application is refused, the curfewee should be given written reasons for that decision and would be able to appeal against it to the governing governor (see also para 12.84 above), and to Prison Service Headquarters.

Recall

12.88   Curfewees may be recalled to prison under the CJA 1991, s 38A(1) if:

(a)   they fail to comply with the curfew conditions on their licence;
(b)   it is no longer possible to monitor the curfew at the specified address; or
(c)   the offender is considered to represent a threat to public safety.

These recall powers are in addition to those powers outlined above in relation to the breach of conditions on automatic unconditional release and automatic unconditional release licences.

12.89   The Parole Unit is responsible for decisions as to whether to revoke an HDC licence and recall the prisoner. Once the licence is revoked the prisoner will then be unlawfully at large until such a time as s/he is arrested by the police and returned to the nearest local prison.

12.90   Within 24 hours of being notified of the prisoner's return to custody, the Parole Unit should fax the prison with a revocation dossier, including a letter to the prisoner explaining the reasons for the decision to revoke the licence and giving details of the procedure by which that decision can be challenged. These should be given to the prisoner within one working day of receipt at the prison.

12.91 If the prisoner wishes to appeal against the recall decision a statement of his/her intention to do so should be forwarded to the Parole Unit by the following day. Any representations should then be sent to the Parole Unit the next working day (ie within three days of the Parole Unit being advised of the prisoner's return to custody) (PSO 6700, para 9.7).

Re-release

12.92 If an appeal against recall is unsuccessful, the prisoner will be released at their conditional or automatic release date at the half-way point of their sentence.

12.93 In cases where the recall was based upon the unsuitability of the HDC address, prisoners may be re-released on curfew once an appropriate alternative address has been found and assessed by the probation service. The governor will consider whether the prisoner's previous behaviour on HDC gave any cause for concern, and will consult the Parole Unit to ascertain if they have any additional information which may be relevant to the decision (PSO 6700, para 9.81).

COMPASSIONATE RELEASE

12.94 The Criminal Justice Act 1991, s 36, contains a wholly discretionary power for the Secretary of State to authorise release from a prison sentence on compassionate grounds. The Crime (Sentences) Act 1997, s 30, introduced an identical power in respect of life sentenced prisoners. Prior to the commencement of the Act, release before the prisoner was granted parole could only be achieved by the exercise of the Royal Prerogative of Mercy. This was generally considered to be unsatisfactory in that the sentence was remitted and once released the prisoner would receive no supervision in the community and could not be recalled to prison if his/her conduct gave cause for concern.

12.95 The Criminal Justice Act 1991, s 36, makes provision for the Secretary of State to release a prisoner on compassionate grounds at any point in the sentence if he is satisfied that 'exceptional circumstances' exist (s 36(1)). Before taking the decision the Secretary of State is under a duty to consult the Parole Board unless circumstances render such consultation impracticable (s 36(2)). A prisoner released on compassionate grounds is subject to licence conditions and may be recalled to prison at any time until the licence expires.

12.96 Early release on compassionate grounds may be applied for by any prisoner serving any length of sentence, provided that they have not yet reached their parole eligibility date/automatic release date. PSO 6000 states that prisoners who have reached their parole eligibility date can have their compassionate circumstances considered by the Parole Board as part of their statutory parole review or as part of a 'special parole review' (para 10.2.1). A special parole review would be applied for in exactly the same way as early release on compassionate grounds for prisoners who were not yet eligible for release on licence.

12.97   There are two main types of case where early release on compassionate grounds may be granted—where this is warranted by the medical condition of a prisoner or if there are tragic family circumstances. In both cases, before lending support to an application, the governor must be satisfied that the prisoner's needs cannot be met by release on temporary licence (para 10.1).

12.98   Medical condition.   The types of medical condition which may render a prisoner suitable for early release on compassionate grounds are set out in PSO 6000, para 10.4:

(i)   Where a prisoner is suffering from a terminal illness and death is likely to occur 'soon' (within three months is suggested as a guideline). For the application to be successful it must be considered that there is no prospect of the prisoner committing further offences and that medical care will be available to the prisoner in the community;

(ii)   Where a prisoner will be 'bedridden or severely incapacitated' until the end of the sentence and there is no risk of further offences being committed before then. Examples given of the kinds of illness that would attract such compassionate release are wheelchair-bound prisoners, stroke victims, or prisoners who are paralysed;

(iii) Where the prisoner's continued imprisonment would endanger his/her life or seriously shorten their life expectancy.

12.99   If a prisoner's medical condition is self-induced then they would not usually be considered for compassionate release. This provision will apply most commonly to hunger strikers.

12.100   In deciding whether a prisoner's medical condition is one for which they might be released on compassionate grounds, criteria set out in PSO 6000, chapter 10, appendix A are applied. These are:

'(i)   the prisoner is suffering from a terminal illness and death is likely to occur soon; or the prisoner is bedridden or similarly incapacitated; *and*

(ii)   the risk of further crime is past; *and*

(iii) there are adequate facilities for the prisoner's care and treatment outside prison; *and*

(iv)   early release will bring some significant benefit to the prisoner or his/her family;

(v)   the diagnosis and prognosis, in particular whether there is a specific estimate of life expectancy; and the degree of incapacitation.'

12.101   In addition, for both types of compassionate release case, the following considerations should also be taken into account:

(i)   whether temporary release under the Prison Rules could significantly reduce the prisoner's and/or family's suffering;

(ii)   the length of the sentence still outstanding; the effect on the overall sentence passed by the court if compassionate release is granted; and any remarks which the trial judge made on sentencing which have a bearing on the question of release;

(iii) the wishes of the prisoner and his/her family and the level of benefit which would derive to the prisoner and/or the family from permanent release.

12.102   An application for early release on the basis of medical condition is made to the prison itself in the first instance. The managing medical officer at the prison is required to complete forms giving details of the medical condition and including medical reports from consultants or others involved in the care and treatment of the prisoner. The prison probation officer will also be required to report upon the prisoner's home circumstances, and the governor will report as to whether the prisoner's medical condition was known to the court at the time that s/he was sentenced.

12.103   Tragic family circumstances. PSO 6000 sets out the types of .circumstances which may be considered to constitute tragic family circumstances for the purposes of compassionate release (para 10.5 and appendix A to chapter 10):

(i)   Where a prisoner's spouse is seriously ill, or has died, and there is no one to care for their young children. The support available to such a family would be taken into account—in particular how much other family members, friends, or social services are able to assist. The prisoner must be able and willing to care for the children;

(ii)   Where a prisoner's spouse is seriously ill but there are no children compassionate release may still be granted. This will be dependent on the particular illness, life expectancy, and whether anyone else is able to care for the spouse;

(iii)   Where a prisoner's parents are ill, compassionate release may be considered if the circumstances are 'exceptionally tragic.' This may apply in cases where there is only one parent who is suffering from an incurable illness and there is no one else who is able to care for him/her;

(iv)   Compassionate release as a result of the serious illness or death of a child is not normally considered to constitute grounds for compassionate release from prison. However, if it is considered that 'the effect on the other parent combines with other factors to create exceptionally difficult domestic circumstances,' the possibility of compassionate release will arise.

12.104   The criteria for compassionate release due to tragic family circumstances is also set out at PSO 6000, chapter 10, annex A. These provide that for an application to be successful it must be shown that:

'(i)   the circumstances of the prisoner or the family have changed to the extent that if s/he served the sentence imposed, the hardship suffered would be of exceptional severity greater than the [sentencing] court could have foreseen; *and*

(ii)   the risk of further crime is past; *and*

(iii)   it can be demonstrated beyond doubt there is a real and urgent need for the prisoner's permanent presence with his/her family; *and*

(iv)   early release will bring some significant benefit to the prisoner or his/her family.'

It is important to be aware that all of the criteria must be proven.

12.105   The additional grounds listed in para 12.101 above will also apply in tragic family circumstances cases. Applications for compassionate release on this basis should be made to the governor of the prison establishment who will report to Prison Service Headquarters on whether the prisoner's domestic circumstances were known to the court when the prisoner was sentenced, the circumstances of the case, the prisoner's custodial behaviour, and an assessment of the risk of re-offending before the sentence is ended. The prison probation officer will also be asked to contribute to the report, and may contact the external probation service to gain further details of the circumstances and supporting evidence, for example medical reports.

12.106   In order for an application for compassionate release to be considered, reports from the prison will be forwarded to the Parole Unit at Prison Service Headquarters. If the Parole Unit considers that there are sufficient grounds for the application to be considered further, it will normally be forwarded to the Parole Board for further advice in accordance with the Criminal (Sentences) Act 1997, s 30(2). Release may only be authorised by ministers, although senior officers in the Parole Unit have delegated authority to refuse applications.

12.107   There are no set time limits for the consideration of cases, but guidance is given to the effect that decisions should be reached within two weeks of submission to Headquarters. Where an application is refused, the prison may keep the case under review and reactivate it if the situation should deteriorate, by submitting further reports to the Parole Board.

12.108   If it is decided that a prisoner is eligible to be released on the basis of his/her compassionate circumstances, the Parole Unit will send a licence to the prison to be issued. Conditions may be attached to the licence, and may be varied throughout the period that it is in force. The licence will expire at the two-thirds point of the sentence if the prisoner was sentenced before 1 October 1992, at the one-half point if s/he is serving 12 months or less, or at the three-quarters point for all other prisoners, except some sex offenders whose licences will not expire until the full term has passed.

12.109   Prisoners released on compassionate grounds may be recalled to prison at any time. However, changes in the circumstances which lead to their release will not constitute grounds for recall. The position is similar to the recall of determinate prisoners who have been released on licence in that the following factors will be grounds for recall to prison:

(i)   where the prisoner's behaviour is posing, or likely to pose, a threat to the safety of the public; *or*

(ii)   there has been a breach of conditions on the licence; *or*

(iii) further offences have been committed.

12.110   In practice, the Home Secretary appears reluctant to exercise the power to release prisoners under the Criminal (Sentences) Act 1997, s 30. Between October 1992 and December 1998 only 54 determinate sentenced prisoners were released on compassionate grounds. There have been very few legal challenges to refusals to release prisoners on compassionate grounds. The difficulty that arises in such cases is the absolute discretion afforded to the Secretary of State by statute which means that challenges to the 'reasonableness' of refusals will always be extremely difficult.

12.111   One interesting area relates to applications where prisoners are seeking to argue that the conditions of their detention are such that they are likely to cause or accelerate death. An application was granted in the case of a prisoner with a serious heart condition whose consultant was of the opinion that prison conditions would greatly exacerbate the possibility of a fatal heart attack occurring. The application was approved only after the prisoner had suffered a number of heart attacks in prison, each one increasing in seriousness. In the case of *R v Secretary of State for the Home Department, ex p Grice* (application for leave, 10 December 1993, HC), a prisoner was serving a four year sentence and had developed AIDS before being sent to prison. He was held in an old Victorian prison and his consultant felt that this was unsuitable for someone in his condition. The insanitary conditions were thought to greatly increase the risk that he may develop a potentially fatal infection. Nevertheless, the Home Secretary refused his application for compassionate release on medical grounds, and he was only released following a special early parole review after the High Court granted him leave to apply for judicial review.

DISCHARGE GRANTS

12.112   On release many prisoners are entitled to apply for discharge grants. The purpose of the grant is to provide sufficient money to meet their immediate needs. The rates are closely linked to social security benefit levels and change each year.

12.113   In order to qualify, the prisoner must be eligible for income support and be travelling to an address within the UK. Those not eligible include prisoners to be deported, civil prisoners, young offenders under the age of 18 (unless exceptional circumstances apply, see below) and unconvicted prisoners released on acquittal or in other circumstances. The grants are payable at standard and higher rates, the higher rate being paid to prisoners who have a need to seek, obtain and pay for accommodation (Standing Order 1I). The payment of discharge grants is based on equivalent payments of income support and covers living expenses for one week only. This does create substantial difficulties for those people who need to make a claim for state benefits on release as the application cannot be made until two weeks after release. The organisation UNLOCK has been campaigning for a change in the payment rules to prevent released prisoners from falling into this benefits gap.

12.114   Young offenders aged 16 or 17 may be paid discharge grants where there is a genuine need to seek, obtain and pay for accommodation. This means that where a young offender qualifies for such a grant, it will always be paid at the higher rate. Young offenders aged 14 and 15 do not receive any grant as they are ineligible for statutory social security benefits.

12.115   Travel warrants are given to all prisoners on discharge, save for those who are to be deported. The warrant (or payment of fares) is to their home or a destination in the UK. Prisoners not receiving a discharge grant will be paid a subsistence allowance for the period of their journey or, if necessary, for the full period until a local office of the Department of Social Security can be reached. This will include any intervening night or weekend (Standing Order 1I, para 27).

246

SECTION III

CHAPTER 13
LEGAL AID

INTRODUCTION

13.1 One of the major problems that prisoners have tended to face when seeking legal representation is that lawyers have found it difficult to obtain payment for work undertaken, or have been unaware of what the proper source of legal aid income is for prisoners' cases. The confusion that surrounds this issue has been compounded by the introduction of franchising and contracting and the uncertainty that this has produced. Unfortunately, at the time of writing the precise situation with franchises and contracts has not fully been resolved and whilst this chapter is based upon the situation as set out by the Legal Aid Board in March 2000, it is possible that it could be changed.

13.2 As from April 2000, the Legal Aid Board in its current format ceased to exist (Access to Justice Act 1999). Legal aid is administered through the Legal Services Commission ('LSC') which has responsibility for two bodies: the Community Legal Service ('CLS') which administers the system for civil legal aid; and the Criminal Defence Service ('CDS') which administers criminal legal aid through an exclusive contracting system for advice and assistance from October 2000.

13.3 Work relating to prisoners' rights initially fell between these two services. Although prisoners' rights work is primarily civil in scope, it is very often dealt with by criminal practitioners. At one stage, it was envisaged that a prisoners' rights category would be developed within the civil contracting arrangements, but in October 1999 the Legal Aid Board decided to transfer this category of work to the CDS. This could have caused a problem for those undertaking prisoners' rights work, but without a general criminal practice. However the Legal Aid Board made it clear in March 2000 that those lawyers specialising in prison law who did not undertake general crime work and could not therefore obtain a general crime franchise could apply for a niche prison law franchise, which in turn would lead to a prison law contract from October. Although, initially, those with general criminal contracts will be able to take on prison law cases, eventually, it is envisaged that all firms wishing to undertake prisoners' rights work will be required to demonstrate some form of specialism in this as a specific area of work (see Legal Aid Board Focus, 28th and 29th edns, 1999). It has also been decided that judicial review work in respect of prisoners will fall to be dealt with through the CDS, despite it being ostensibly 'civil' work. Legal aid certificates will still be issued on a case by case basis rather than as part of a general contract in the first instance.

13.4   There will still be some cross over with the CLS and civil work. Actions for damages for prisoners, arising from personal injury or death, will still fall within the civil contracting scheme (although all legally aided advice and assistance in relation to property claims will cease). Practitioners will only be able to provide advice and assistance in respect of these matters when the claim is based on alleged negligence through the personal injury franchise, and claims will be dealt with on a case by case basis rather than being assessed for a specific number of case starts in the contract (Legal Aid Focus 28, p 23). This does leave uncertainty as to how claims resulting from intentional torts (eg assault, misfeasance in public office) or neglect of duty will be administered and funded. At the time of writing, no answer to this problem had been proposed by the Legal Aid Board.

13.5   The final complicating factor arises from the creation of a franchise category for public law. This is a category that will bridge both the CDS and the CLS, administered initially by the CLS for firms who have been able to demonstrate a specialism in public law and civil rights work. The franchise does encompass judicial review and will enable practitioners who have expertise in public law to deal with judicial review cases for prisoners. Any applications for judicial review or habeas corpus will fall to be defined by the franchise category from which the matter originates. Applications concerning prisoners' rights will therefore be within the crime franchise, funded by the CDS and outside the scope of the general civil contracts (LAB Focus 28, p 17). Those with public law contracts with the CLS will be able to contract with the CDS in respect of the cases that fall within its scope.

PUBLIC FUNDING

13.6   The legal aid scheme makes provision for lawyers to receive payment when acting for prisoners in three ways; for general advice and assistance (previously known as the Green Form or the Claim 10 scheme), for advocacy assistance at oral parole hearings and for prison disciplinary proceedings (previously known as ABWOR) and for full public funding certificates to be issued for representation in litigation. These three levels of possible legal help will be rationalised, but preserved under the CDS. This chapter assumes that practitioners are familiar with the generality of the legal aid scheme and will focus on particular problems that may arise when acting for prisoners.

ADVICE AND ASSISTANCE

13.7   The vast majority of work that is undertaken on behalf of prisoners will be carried out under the advice and assistance scheme (previously known as Claim 10 or Green Form scheme). In general, physical representation for prisoners is either not permitted (eg when the Parole Board consider determinate prisoners' and mandatory lifers' cases), or is completely discretionary and very rarely permitted (eg adjudications or internal decision-making 'boards' in the prison itself). The only exception to this general rule is in the case of oral parole hearings where legal representation is generally permitted as of right (subject to financial eligibility).

13.8 By far the majority of cases in which prisoners will seek legal advice will first involve representations being made on their behalf. These representations may be made with the intent of changing an adverse decision, such as re-categorisation or temporary release, or may be made with a view to securing a favourable outcome to a decision yet to be made, such as release on parole licence. In either situation, litigation cannot normally be contemplated until initial representations have been made and it is not possible to assess in advance whether there will be grounds to apply for a full legal aid certificate to commence litigation. As a consequence, by far the majority of work undertaken for prisoners will only be covered by the advice and assistance scheme and this may never progress further. Lawyers engaged in this area of work are therefore far more likely to be dependent on this scheme than lawyers involved in any other type of work with the possible exception of immigration law.

13.9 The particular problem with prisoners seeking to receive advice has been the manner in which they come to instruct solicitors. As the normal route of booking an appointment and attending the solicitor's office is not possible, prisoners will generally seek to obtain advice either by telephoning a solicitor or writing to him/her. The problem the solicitor and prisoner will then face is how the solicitor will come to be paid for this work. This will be equally as true for existing clients who raise new issues relating to their imprisonment as it is for new, possibly unsolicited enquiries.

13.10 It is possible for firms holding criminal franchises or prisoners' rights franchises to accept an application for advice and assistance from a prisoner either over the telephone (Legal Aid Board *General Civil Contract Regulations* (October 1999), rr 2.9 and 3.12) or to send out an application form to be signed through the post. Where telephone advice is given, the form can then be posted to the client to be signed. The cost of travelling to see a prisoner can be problematic. In most areas of work, travelling time of more than one hour each way will not be authorised. However, for prisoners the situation is more complex as they can be moved around the country with no control over their location and many prisons are located a long way from the nearest solicitor's office. In such cases, it is likely that the solicitor will have to demonstrate on each individual case why lengthy travelling time is justified, either by prior involvement in the case or through particular expertise that cannot be met by a solicitor closer to the prison (see eg the finding codes for immigration law published by the LAB in October 1999).

13.11 As at March 2000, the LAB had not published the supervisor standards or transaction criteria that will be applied to the prisoners' rights franchise. These are likely to be akin to those applied in the areas of mental health and immigration. Eventually, it is likely that the specialist prisoners' rights franchise will supersede the crime franchise in this area, although there will remain tolerance for solicitors specialising in crime to deal with limited areas of prisoners' rights work such as sentence calculation and parole. This will mean that to obtain a specialist prisoners' rights franchise under the CDS contracts, solicitors are likely to need to show that they have spent a minimum of 350 hours a year working on prisoners' rights in the preceding three years and will have to demonstrate a variety of work ranging from pure advice through to representation at oral parole hearings and advice on potential judicial review applications.

ADVOCACY ASSISTANCE

13.12   Advocacy assistance (currently operated through the ABWOR scheme) allows for representation in those proceedings where physical representation is permitted. This is presently restricted to oral parole hearings (ie for discretionary lifers, automatic lifers and HMP detainees) and at prison disciplinary proceedings where representation has been authorised by the adjudicator. Representation in such cases is normally granted as of right as the matters relate directly to the liberty of the subject. Although payment for oral parole hearings is made at a rate slightly higher than for other areas of advocacy representation, there is no provision for enhancement of rates. Applications can be made to authorise counsel to be instructed but counsel's payment will also be limited to the prescribed rates.

LEGAL AID CERTIFICATES

Financial assessment

13.13   When prisoners' make an application for a legal aid certificate for the purposes of litigation, the appropriate form for assessment of their finances relates to people not in receipt of state benefits (currently CLSMEANS 1). Whilst this may seem unusual for people with little or no income (as income support is not available to those serving custodial sentences), a full financial assessment is required. Prisoners should be advised to include details of their prison wages in the section headed 'Other Relevant Information' and not in the section that deals with employment. This is because prison employment is not contractual but is part of the disciplinary code and so these 'wages' are not paid in the course of employment. If prison wages are entered in the 'employment' section of the form, it will delay the application as the LSC will ask for a form confirming the amount of wages received (currently L17) to be submitted even though prison wages can never bring an individual above the financial eligibility. The one exception will be for those prisoners located in resettlement units and prisons who are employed outside of the prison and receive a wage.

13.14   The major problem that will arise with the financial side of the application is the question of whether the finances of a prisoner's partner should also be assessed. The regulations provide that the income and capital of spouses shall be treated as the resources of the applicant, unless they are living apart or the spouse has a contrary interest in the subject matter of the application. Opposite sex couples who live in the same household as if married are also covered by this provision (Civil Legal Aid (Assessment of Resources) Regulations 1989, reg 7).

13.15   In the past, the Legal Aid Board have widely interpreted this to include couples who *normally* live together as if they are married and this wording appears on the top of the assessment form. Area offices have sent forms to the spouses and partners of prisoners to declare details of their finances. This can potentially create problems, either if the partner does not comply with the completion of the forms or if they are above the financial limit. It is arguable that in the majority of cases, prisoners' partners should not be included in the financial assessment. Many relationships will not survive the stress of imprisonment and it is not really practical for a long-term prisoner to be classed as 'normally' living with a person outside of prison. Financially, prisoners can only receive a set amount of income each year and their partner will not usually have any direct interest in the outcome of an application. Whilst this argument may be less valid for very short-term prisoners who have a firm intention to return to a matrimonial home at the end of the sentence, refusals to grant legal aid based on the financial situation of a partner may be vulnerable to challenge.

The 'merits test'

13.16   The merits test for civil legal aid is something which practitioners will be generally familiar with and does not require any lengthy explanation. In applications involving compensation claims, this will require an individual assessment of the facts of each case. For public law challenges, the merits test is usually satisfied if permission to move for judicial review would be granted (*R v Legal Aid Board, ex p Hughes* (1992) 24 HLR 698, CA). As from October 2000, the merits test will be replaced by the relevant funding code for criminal judicial review applications. The full details of the funding code insofar as it relates to prisoners' cases have not been published by the CDS as at March 2000.

Satisfying the 'benefit' test

13.17   Legal aid certificates can be refused, even where a good case on the merits has been established, if the benefit to the client is not deemed sufficient to justify the costs of the proceedings. In compensation claims this is a relatively straightforward assessment to make based on the damages that might be awarded. In cases concerning public law matters, the assessment is more complex and the decision will depend upon the nature of the right at stake. This means that cases concerning the liberty of the subject will be more likely to satisfy the test than those concerned with, for example, living conditions in prison. The importance of the matter to the prisoner, particularly if the case raises an allegation of discrimination or a breach of human rights is a relevant consideration (see eg Legal Aid Handbook, 1998–99, paras 7-03.10-11).

13.18   In applications for judicial review of administrative decisions, it will normally be necessary to demonstrate that there is some benefit to the applicant that is of sufficient importance to override the question of costs. The Legal Aid Board has often used this ground as a reason for refusing initial applications unless it has been specifically addressed in the statement of case. In some applications, the benefit will be obvious. This would commonly include applications to challenge a refusal to release a prisoner on parole licence, or a life sentenced prisoner challenging the decision of the Secretary of State following a parole review. Nevertheless, it is advisable to spell out that the application relates to the release of a person from prison in such cases to ensure that this test is satisfied.

13.19   In other applications, the benefit may not be immediately obvious to those who are not familiar with prison law and procedure and so it is necessary to explain this in more detail. By and large, the majority of decisions made in respect of prisoners which lead to complaints and applications for judicial review will have a direct impact on either the conditions in which they are held and/or their long-term prospects of progression and release. An award of additional days at an adjudication extends the time that must be served in custody, and a decision to re-categorise a prisoner to a higher security category will result in poorer conditions of detention and decrease the prospects of parole.

13.20   The judicial view of administrative decision-making in respect of prisoners has largely accorded with this view since the judgment in *ex p Doody*. In 1993, Rose LJ commented on the process whereby prisoners are made category A, and compared it to the length of lifers' tariffs. He accepted counsel's arguments that:

> 'In each case reports are made and considered, the decision is based on information about the offence and the prisoners' character, and there is a significant effect on when the prisoner may be released.'
> (*ex p Duggan* [1994] 3 All ER 277)

It is difficult to envisage any adverse decisions made in respect of prisoners that will not have similar consequences on conditions of detention and the prospects of release from prison and this point must be made to the LSC when submitting applications.

Personal injury claims

13.21   As was explained at the start of this chapter, the precise mechanics for state funding of cases concerning prisoners' rights remained unclear as at March 2000. Although it is clear that 'legal aid' will only be administered through the franchising and contracting scheme, it remains unclear as to what work falls into what franchise. The decision to remove state funding for personal injury claims has been tempered by the commitment to ensure that legal aid will remain for cases involving actions against the state where it is alleged that there has been abuse of power. This does create some difficulties in assessing when it is appropriate for legal aid to be granted to prisoners for compensation claims and under which franchise.

13.22   There are usually two types of 'personal injury' claims that prisoners wish to pursue. There are those involving negligence on the part of prison staff and those involving deliberate abuses of power (eg assaults by staff). It appears that negligence cases will be restricted to those firms holding personal injury (or medical negligence) franchises as from April 2000 and may possibly end up being removed from the legal aid scheme in their entirety. However, cases concerning assaults and misfeasance in public office will remain part of the legal aid scheme, probably through the prisoners' rights franchise, but possibly dealt with by personal injury franchise holders as well. It is unfortunate that the LSC have failed to provide any firm answers to these problems when the franchising and contracting schemes are at such an advanced stage. All solicitors involved in this area of work are strongly advised to discuss their particular needs with their franchise liaison officers to ensure that they do not find themselves barred from conducting their normal caseload.

Property claims

13.23   As stated at the start of this chapter, prisoners' property claims cannot be conducted under any of the legal aid schemes as from April 2000 (Legal Aid Board Focus (28th edn, 1999), p 17).

CHAPTER 14

PRISONERS' PROPERTY CLAIMS

INTRODUCTION

14.1 Prisoners are entitled to receive compensation when their property is lost in prison so long as they are able to show that the Prison Service is liable for their loss. Applications may be taken by prisoners themselves through the requests/complaints procedure or through their legal advisers.

14.2 Compensation claims for lost property are initially submitted to the governor of the prison where the property was lost. PSO 0150, Reform of the Civil Justice System, advises governors that upon receipt of a request/complaint or a letter of claim they should collect all relevant documentation, decide whether it is 'worth contesting the claim considering the value involved,' and decide who should deal with any contested case. All claims under £5,000 should be dealt with 'informally' (paras 30–32). Higher value claims will be referred to the Treasury Solicitor.

14.3 It is possible to appeal against decisions made by the governor by submitting an appeal to the area manager, either through the requests/complaints procedure or through a legal representative. If the area manager refuses to authorise compensation or offers a derisory sum, a complaint can be made to the Prisons Ombudsman.

14.4 Applications for compensation should give full details of the lost items, where and when they were purchased, receipts (if possible), and the circumstances of the loss. If no receipts are available, the letters or statements from the persons who purchased the property on behalf of the prisoner should be obtained.

14.5 Prisons keep extensive documentation on prisoners' property and these include records of stored property (property held in boxes in the reception of the prison), in possession property (property which prisoners keep in their cells), and details of boxes of prisoners' property which is in transit between different prisons. In addition, where prisoners are removed from their cells on normal location, officers complete cell clearance sheets (itemised statements of everything removed from the cell). In putting together a property claim it is often helpful to obtain copies of prisoners' property records in order to prove that the items being claimed for were the responsibility of the prison at the time of the loss.

14.6 If claims are successful the money will normally be paid into the prisoner's private cash account at the prison.

ESTABLISHING LIABILITY

14.7 If *stored property* is either lost in reception or in transit then so long as it is clear from the property cards that the prisoner actually owned that property and it was held in the prison then the Prison Service will be liable.

14.8 The Prison Service does not normally accept liability for 'in possession' property (ie property held in the prisoner's cell) on the basis that the inmate may have given it to other prisoners or exchanged it for other items. There are exceptions to this and these are based upon the law of negligence:

(i) Where the prisoner has been removed from normal location (eg to the segregation block) without prior warning and has therefore been unable to secure his/her property;

(ii) Where the prisoner has been removed from normal location because of illness;

(iii) Where the prisoner has been temporarily released;

(iv) Where the prisoner has absconded or escaped.

14.9 In situations (i) and (ii) above, in possession property is deemed to be no longer under the inmate's control and thus responsibility reverts back to the Prison Service. Therefore it is important to take instructions from prisoners on whether they have any knowledge of whether the cell was sealed immediately after their removal from normal location (eg via other inmates or if the cell was unsealed on their return to normal location). If the cell was not sealed immediately, was unsealed at any point before the cell was cleared, or if property shown on the cell clearance sheet was never returned to the prisoner, then the Prison Service would be liable for the loss (*Winson v Home Office* (18 March 1994, unreported), Central London County Court; *Ross v Home Office* (unreported)).

14.10 In situation (iii) above the Prison Service will argue that the prisoner should have taken reasonable steps to secure his property before temporary release. It is therefore important to obtain instructions as to whether the prisoner was advised by staff to store property in reception during their absence, or if they asked to do so and were refused. If prisoners are temporarily released on a daily basis they should be warned of the increased risk to their property by staff.

14.11 In situation (iv) above the Prison Service will not accept liability for property lost between the time of the abscond/escape and the disappearance being confirmed. When disappearance is confirmed prison staff should take immediate action to secure the in possession property—the cell should be sealed and then cleared without delay. Circular Instruction 48/92 states that the property should be stored until six months after the date of the abscond/escape. At that time the next of kin should be contacted to ask if they wish to claim the property. If after three years the property still has not been claimed,

Circular Instruction 48/92 states that it may be disposed of either by competitive tender, or if the items have no value they may be destroyed.

14.12 In all cases a failure to handle a prisoner's property in accordance with the instructions in the Inmate Personal Records System Manual will create a strong presumption in favour of paying compensation (Prisoners' Requests/Complaints Procedure Staff Manual, annex I, para 2), and so it is important to check that the relevant signatures are on property cards, and that there is no evidence that the property has been misrecorded at some stage.

LEGAL ACTION

14.13 The level of compensation that will be offered, whether by the Prison Service or through a court award, is based on the value of the property at the time it was lost and not on the replacement costs of new items. It is possible to argue that the value of a relatively small claim is substantially greater to a prisoner due to the low level of prison wages (eg a claim of £500 is equal to at least six months of prison earnings). However, in most cases legal aid will be refused.

14.14 Due to the fact that public funding is no longer available in most cases, complaints to the Prisons Ombudsman are very often the best course of action to pursue before commencing legal proceedings. The Ombudsman's annual report for 1998–99 shows that property claims 'form a significant proportion of the complaints I investigate.' Although the Ombudsman reported a reduction in the number of property claims upheld following investigation, he voiced concern at Prison Service procedures:

> 'it is disappointing that, year after year, I have to deal with numerous complaints where the losses could easily have been avoided if accurate records had been kept and the agreed procedures followed.' (Prisons Ombudsman Annual Report 1998/9, p 27)

14.15 When a complaint is made to the Ombudsman in cases where legal aid is not available, the primary aim is to secure a favourable recommendation which will be accepted by the Prison Service. In cases where a favourable recommendation is not accepted, the report can form the basis of an application to the county court as it will often contain a clear and impartial account of the loss and where liability should rest. This is, however, a double-edged sword and if the complaint is not upheld it can undermine any potential litigation.

14.16 Where public funding is not available, prisoners should be advised to commence their own proceedings in the county court local to the prison in which they are located. A summons and explanatory leaflet will be sent to the prisoner on a request to the Chief Clerk. Prisoners should be advised of the following points:

(i)   The proper defendant is the Home Office (not the governor of the prison concerned);

(ii) The address for service is that of the Treasury Solicitor (Queen Anne's Chambers, 28 Broadway, London SW1H 9JS);

(iii) A waiver of court fees may be obtained by making an application to the Lord Chancellor's Office or by completing the county court form 'Application For a Fee Remission' and sending it to the Clerk to the County Court together with the summons;

(iv) The claim is for negligence, and/or conversion, and/or trespass to goods;

(v) If attendance at court is necessary, either for the final hearing or interlocutory applications, the normal rules on production at court will apply.

CHAPTER 15

PERSONAL INJURY AND ASSAULT CLAIMS

INTRODUCTION

15.1 The substantive law relevant to prisoners' claims for personal injury and assault is discussed in section I, chapter 3. Personal injury claims by prisoners will usually be concerned with three scenarios: assaults by other inmates, assaults by prison officers or claims arising from negligent medical treatment. Lawyers who are familiar with conducting claims for damages will often be unfamiliar with the bureaucracy of the Prison Service and may face difficulties in obtaining records relevant to the claim. Other aspects of normally routine advice, such as reporting alleged criminal offences to the police and making claims to the Criminal Injuries Compensation Authority (CICA) also need to be considered. This chapter is not designed to provide a detailed examination of how to conduct a personal injury/medical negligence action, but to deal with the particular areas that need to be addressed when advising prisoners in respect of these matters.

REPORTING INCIDENTS TO THE POLICE

15.2 Prisoners may report any incident in which they allege a criminal offence has been committed to the police. There is no restriction on this right simply by virtue of the fact that one is in custody. The practical problem that is faced is how to physically make the report. The police are reluctant to commence an investigation on the basis of information received from a telephone call and will not generally visit prisoners to take a statement without some form of written statement being provided in advance. In cases where a prisoner wishes to make a report, the quickest method of doing this is to make a signed, handwritten statement and for this to be sent to the police station closest to the prison. Most forces have a prison liaison officer who will then arrange to attend the prison to take a more formal statement, although in some cases, an investigation can commence simply on the basis of the information in the original statement prepared by the prisoner. Complaints and handwritten statements can also be forwarded by friends or legal representatives.

15.3 In certain circumstances, the governor of a prison may be under a duty to report a matter which could subsequently form the basis of a personal injury claim to the police, such as incidents where an assault is alleged to have been committed by another prisoner. The following guidelines have been issued to governors when deciding whether to report an incident to the police (CI 3/92, appendix A):

(i)   serious assaults including allegations of non-consensual buggery or rape, attempted murder and manslaughter and threats to kill where there is a genuine intent;

(ii)   assaults that result in serious injury, hostage-taking, the use of a weapon that is capable of causing serious injury or persistent sexual violations other than rape and buggery;

(iii) criminal damage or arson unless the damage is negligible and no injury or substantial financial loss has been incurred;

(iv)   robbery.

The governor should also report any incidents where the victim of an alleged crime asks for the police to be notified or where there is evidence of racial motivation.

CLAIMS TO THE CRIMINAL INJURIES COMPENSATION AUTHORITY

15.4 Prisoners are able to make claims for compensation to the Criminal Injuries Compensation Authority (CICA) in precisely the same circumstances as any other citizen. It is for this reason that many prisoners are keen to have assaults reported to the police. In practice, claims on behalf of prisoners will rarely be successful. The CICA operates within a discretionary framework whereby it is empowered to make ex gratia awards. Paragraph 6(c) of the scheme allows awards to be refused if it is considered inappropriate having taken account of the applicant's character as shown by his/her criminal convictions. As all prisoners, save for remand and civil prisoners, will necessarily have criminal convictions, this is a major barrier to making a claim.

15.5 The decision to refuse an award on these grounds is not confined to convictions which have a causal connection with the assault on the inmate. Similarly, convictions of all types, not just those of violence can be considered by the CICA when reaching a decision on these grounds. The Court of Appeal has upheld the power of the Board to refuse awards on these grounds even where the applicant's conduct, character and past way of life had no bearing on the incident that lead to the injury (*R v Criminal Injuries Compensation Board, ex p Thompstone* [1984] 1 WLR 1234).

15.6 Prisoners with convictions for violence will face great difficulty in mounting a challenge to a refusal on these grounds. The Court of Appeal did state that this power also exists in cases where there are convictions for dishonesty, but the power must be exercised reasonably and each application must be considered on its own merits. Blanket refusals to any persons serving custodial sentences regardless of the nature and extent of their convictions would be susceptible to challenge by way of judicial review.

ACCESS TO MEDICAL RECORDS

15.7 Prison doctors are required to maintain a 'continuous inmate medical record.' This is akin to the notes kept by a GP and will record all entries relevant to a prisoner's medical history whilst in custody. The Access To Health Records Act 1990 allows access to all such records made since 1 November 1991. Prisoners may make an application in writing to see their records and they should be made available within 40 days. Copies can also be obtained, although a copying charge is normally made.

15.8 There will also be reference to medical issues in other parts of a prisoner's files, although it is arguable that a prison doctor should also make a note of these on the continuous records. These will include any reception medical examination and views expressed on health and fitness to work, records kept by the prison hospital, if a prisoner has been admitted and any reports of injury to a prisoner. This last document, known as form F213, is required to be completed by the medical officer whenever a prisoner has been injured. This can be of crucial importance to prisoners who wish to commence personal injury actions as contemporaneous proof of the injuries that they allege were suffered and, in cases where limitation dates are close to expiring or where there are difficulties in obtaining an independent report prior to the issue of proceedings, this can be appended to the summons in place of a more detailed medical report to be prepared at a later date. All of these documents form part of the prisoner's health records and disclosure may be sought under the Access to Health Records Act 1990.

15.9 The situation with medical records is generally no different for people who are imprisoned. Therefore, a refusal to release records, particularly those made before November 1991 would be subject to the same rules of disclosure as in any other personal injury case (ie applications for pre-action discovery etc). It is when making such applications, or initial requests for the release of the records that prisoners and their lawyers should be aware of precisely what documents they are seeking.

15.10 The one area of disclosure where problems have arisen has been with psychiatric and psychologists' reports. The general policy applied by the Prison Service is that these documents will only be released where the report writer has given permission for disclosure. It is not always possible to characterise such documents as medical records as they have a more wide ranging ambit, dealing with issues such as classification, allocation, sentence planning and attendance on offending behaviour programmes. This does mean that it can be possible for such reports to be treated as being separate from medical records and so access to these documents will be governed by the general rules of disclosure.

DISCLOSURE OF OTHER RECORDS

15.11 Apart from medical records, there is little information that will be freely disclosed prior to the issue of proceedings. There are, however, certain reports and records that a prisoner has a right to see throughout his/her sentence and it can be advisable to obtain these at an early stage to scrutinise them for relevant information. These will include parole dossiers, if the prisoner has been considered for parole. Parole dossiers will contain general reports on behaviour as well as any relevant medical assessments and records of major disciplinary offences, some or all of which may be relevant. All records of adjudications must also be provided to a prisoner or his/her legal representative on request (Discipline Manual, para 9.5). The medical officer is obliged to examine a prisoner before every adjudication to ensure that the person is well enough to attend the hearing and fit enough for any awards that may be awarded. The adjudication records will note that this examination has taken place. Category A prisoners will have had the gist of reports that are prepared each year disclosed to them and lifers will increasingly be given the reports prepared for internal lifer reviews. All of these reports may contain valuable information as to how a prisoner's behaviour has been perceived by staff and whether any specific problems were identified.

15.12 Aside from the documents that are routinely disclosed, a large number of files and forms will be maintained. These documents will normally only be subject to discovery in the normal course of an action in negligence. The most important of these is the prisoner's personal record, a loose-leaf file which accompanies prisoners through their sentence. This contains the following records:

(i)   details of conviction, sentence and release dates;
(ii)   a record of each transfer together with applications and the governor's observations;
(iii) the medical officer's views on health and work classification;
(iv)   the disciplinary record;
(v)   any time spent in segregation and details of transfers in the interests of good order and discipline;
(vi)   any special security information, which may include details of escapes and escape attempts, intelligence on visits and correspondence and details of suicide attempts and special medical problems.

15.13 In addition to this general record, the prison is obliged to maintain: records of all occasions on which force is used against a prisoner; reports of injuries suffered by prisoners, completed by the medical officer; a register of any non-medical restraints applied to prisoners; and, the authority for segregation and the reasons why the decision was taken. Decisions to continue periods in segregation, whether taken by the Secretary of State or the Board of Visitors must also be recorded. In addition to the formal records that are required to be kept, each wing will maintain its own set of records, including segregation and hospital wings. Significant events should be noted in these on a daily basis.

INDEPENDENT MEDICAL EXAMINATIONS

15.14 There is no general right for convicted prisoners to be examined by a doctor of their own choice. In situations where there is no litigation in progress, prisoners can request to be seen by a doctor/psychiatrist from outside the prison and this is then at the discretion of the governor. The costs of any such examination must be met by the prisoner, although if a legal aid certificate has been granted, authority can be obtained to cover these costs. There is usually little difficulty in obtaining the consent of the governor in such circumstances—a refusal would be suspicious and would merit being brought to the attention of the court.

15.15 The Prison Rules 1999, r 20(6) allows prisoners who are party to any legal proceedings to be afforded reasonable facilities to be examined by a registered medical practitioner selected on his/her behalf. The examination will take place out of the hearing but within the sight of a prison officer. The Secretary of State has also reserved the power to impose directions on this right in particular cases although, at present, no directions have been issued under this power.

OBTAINING AND PRESERVING EVIDENCE

15.16 Prisoners are at a major disadvantage in preparing negligence claims against the Prison Service in that their ability to prepare and secure evidence is severely impaired. This contrasts sharply with the facilities and resources of the Prison Service who maintain detailed records of all incidents. It is therefore important that prisoners are made aware of what steps they can take to maximise their chances of success.

15.17 In cases where prisoners fear assault by another inmate, they must ensure that these fears are brought to the attention of prison staff and comply with any attempts made by staff to ensure their safety (eg through segregation or transfer). Guidance issued to prison staff lists specific steps that should be taken when one prisoner is thought, or known, to pose a threat to the safety of others. These include reporting the matter to the governor, making appropriate searches where it is though that a weapon may be used, and to keep a special watch at recognised 'danger points.' These danger points are commonly perceived to be when prisoners are moving to or from work and exercise, in television rooms, at the servery and in any situation involving queuing.

15.18 The importance of ensuring that prisoners make sure their fears in this regard are known and recorded cannot be emphasised enough. If a prisoner feels that they have not been taken seriously or that no formal record has been made of the problem, it is advisable to issue a requests/complaints form on the matter to ensure that a formal record is kept. The case law on this area suggests that staff have a duty to balance the need for protection against the need to provide as balanced and open a regime as possible. As a result, in one case where a prisoner was seriously assaulted by another inmate with whom he had previously fought, the claim was unsuccessful as the judge noted that the victim was proficient at defending himself and did not wish to give the appearance of running away from trouble (*Porterfield v Home Office* (1988) Independent, 9 March).

15.19 In all cases, prisoners should keep their own written record wherever possible. When an incident has occurred, it may be some time before a prisoner has access to a solicitor and so by making an immediate record, the events are recorded as contemporaneously as possible. Letters to legal advisers detailing the nature of the complaint can be utilised as such a record. If there are witnesses to an incident, the prisoner should seek to identify them as quickly as possible and ask if they are prepared to make a statement. If they are, then this should be written down immediately rather than waiting for a solicitor to take it at a later date. A solicitor can always expand on this statement subsequently. If the complaint relates to a lengthy series of conduct, the prisoner would be advised to keep a diary of all events so that specific times and dates can be given to alleged actions.

15.20 If injuries have been suffered, prisoners should request a copy of the record of those injuries prepared by the medical officer. If s/he feels that the record is not accurate, then a formal request for amendment should be made. It is important that this request is made formally (eg through the requests/complaints procedure) to ensure that the extent of the disagreement is recorded.

15.21 When solicitors receive instructions from prisoners in this situation, then this advice can be given immediately as there is likely to be some delay between the receipt of the complaint and the time when a legal visit can be arranged. Solicitors can themselves shoulder the burden of these duties by raising matters in writing with the governor of the prison in advance of any legal visit.

CHAPTER 16

APPLICATIONS FOR JUDICIAL REVIEW

WHAT DECISIONS ARE REVIEWABLE?

16.1 Judicial review is of crucial importance to prisoners as, aside from investigations by the Prisons Ombudsman, it is the only formal method by which an independent body can exercise control over decisions made in respect of prisoners. The fact of prison life is that each day, many administrative decisions will be made in respect of each prisoner, some of these will be of crucial importance to the individual and others will be more mundane. These decisions can be made by a wide variety of people, from prison officers, to governors, to civil servants acting on behalf of the Secretary of State and the Secretary of State in person.

16.2 The gradual process whereby the courts have extended their jurisdiction to deal with prisoners' applications has left virtually all decisions made in respect of prisoners amenable to this remedy. Thus, the courts will entertain applications concerning the categorisation of prisoners, the calculation of their sentences, disciplinary proceedings, the use of quasi-disciplinary powers such as transfers and segregation, medical treatment (eg *R v Secretary of State for the Home Department, ex p Drew* [1987] 1 WLR 881 where a prisoner sought an order for mandamus to require specific medical treatment to be given. The treatment had been provided by the time the case came to be heard and the application was struck out with the prisoner being informed that the proper course of action was then to commence a negligence claim), length of tariff and decisions concerning release. In all cases where a prisoner makes a complaint about the treatment that has been accorded to him/her, if there is no personal injury or financial loss resulting from that treatment, the practitioner should immediately be alerted that judicial review is likely to be the only legal remedy available.

16.3 The use of this remedy is of such importance that all advice given to prisoners, and all action taken on their behalf, should be done with this remedy in mind. It is therefore essential for practitioners to bear in mind the basic principles that apply to applications for judicial review and the relief that is available. The technical nature of the remedy is such that many prisoners mistakenly see it as a form of appeal of decisions rather than a process of review. Lord Hailsham emphasised this point clearly when he commented:

'It is important to remember in every case that the purpose of ... [judicial review] is to ensure that the individual is given fair treatment by the authority to which he has been subjected and that it is no part of that purpose to substitute the opinion of the judiciary or of individual judges for that of the authority constituted by law to decide the matters in question.'
(*Chief Constable of North Wales Police v Evans* [1982] 1 WLR 1155)

16.4   These comments define the area to which the court may direct its powers to cases where an authority has acted without jurisdiction or in excess of its jurisdiction, where there is a failure to follow the rules of natural justice, where there is an error of law on the face of the record or where the decision is unreasonable in the *Wednesbury* sense. The remedies that are available are for the court to quash decisions (certiorari), to prohibit actions or further actions which are unlawful (prohibition), to require the performance of a duty (mandamus) or to make a declaration that an action or decision is unlawful. The court also has powers to grant an injunction and in limited cases to award damages (RSC Ord 53, r 1). These remedies do not allow the court to substitute its own decision for that which is being challenged but merely to proscribe unlawful decisions and, if appropriate, to require the body to make a fresh decision in accordance with the law.

16.5   The immediate problem that faces prisoners in such cases is that the majority of administrative decisions made in respect of them have, to a greater or lesser extent, an element of discretion on the part of the decision maker. Given the court's inability to substitute its own opinion for that of the decision maker, it is essential to establish either an error in procedure or law or to obtain evidence to show that the decision was *Wednesbury* unreasonable.

16.6   A further fundamental principle that must be considered is that the court will not normally consider an application for judicial review where there is another avenue of appeal. Although there are circumstances when it may be impractical to pursue all avenues of appeal (*R v Epping and Harlow General Comrs, ex p Goldstraw* [1983] 3 All ER 257), the general principle is that judicial review is a remedy of last resort. Practitioners must therefore be satisfied that they have sought to utilise the formal methods that are in place to appeal or review adverse decisions before making an application to the court.

16.7   The final principle to bear in mind is that judicial review is a discretionary remedy. Even if a case falls into a category from which an application for judicial review lies, the court is not bound to grant it. It is important to consider the purpose of the application and whether, even if there is no practical remedy available, there is a point of law that is important enough to warrant the intervention of the court. For example, if a prisoner is segregated for a period of three days and then is allowed back on to normal location, the court would be unable to provide any tangible relief to that prisoner but may decide to hear an application on the grounds that an important point of law or principle was at issue in terms of how the decision was reached. Conversely, there will be cases where the court will decide that although an unlawful action has taken place, it may not be desirable to grant any relief. An example occurred with an application by a prisoner in connection with compulsory deductions from prisoners' wages for the 'common purpose fund' (a fund designed to provide extra amenities for prisoners). By the time the case came to court, the Prison Service had halted the deductions and the court refused to grant any relief on the basis that the actions had now stopped and that the sums of money were sufficiently small to make it impractical and undesirable for all of the contributions to be traced and restored.

AGAINST WHOM DOES THE APPLICATION LIE?

16.8 Administrative decisions will be made by a sometimes bewildering variety of individuals and departments. However, this vast administration actually derives its authority from a limited number of sources and consequently, applications for judicial review lie against only a small number of people. In effect, these will be the governor of a prison, the Secretary of State for the Home Department and the Parole Board.

The governor

16.9 The majority of decisions made inside a prison are done so on the authority of the governor of that prison. The governor obviously does not personally make each decision, but retains the power to delegate them to a number of other people in the prison. These can range from other governor grades (eg at adjudications or when authorising segregation) to less senior members of staff (eg senior and principal officers will commonly make decisions concerning categorisation or transfers). Whoever formally makes the decision in an individual case, this is ultimately done on the governor's authority.

16.10 It is possible to list the powers that a governor will exercise in which the responsibility for the decision rests with the individual and not higher up the chain of command. These are commonly concerned with the maintenance of security and good order and discipline within the prison and include the following:

(i)   Adjudications which must be heard by a governor;
(ii)   Decisions to segregate prisoners for the first three days (thereafter, the consent of the Board of Visitors is required and the decision is effectively made by the two bodies in tandem);
(iii)   Decisions to transfer prisoners, other than category A prisoners and lifers;
(iv)   The security categorisation of prisoners, other than those in category A;
(v)   Whether to grant temporary release, except for lifers or in cases where the authority of the area manager is required;
(vi)   The allowance of visits and correspondence and restrictions placed thereon, such as closed visits;
(vii)   Decisions relating to the administration of the Incentives and Earned Privileges Scheme;
(viii) In addition, the governor will have responsibility for ensuring that national rules and guidelines for the provision of facilities and the observance of legal rights are followed. An example of when the action lies against the governor rather than the Secretary of State would be if the governor was not allowing prisoners to receive sealed, privileged legal correspondence contrary to the instructions issued.

16.11 It is possible for all decisions made by prison governors to be 'appealed' to the area manager for that prison, for a complaint to be lodged with the Board of Visitors or for a petition to be presented to the Secretary of State. The question in such cases is whether these options represent established appeal procedures which must be followed before lodging an application to the court. It is safe to say that complaints to the Board of Visitors and petitions cannot properly be considered an established appeals process with the power to overturn the decision of the governor. In *Ex p Leech* [1988] AC 533, Lord Bridge specifically dismissed the concept that a petition could be an adequate remedy and was highly critical of the concept of a 'faceless authority in Whitehall' looking at governors' decisions as representing a proper appeals process.

16.12 That decision was made before the present requests/complaints procedure was introduced. It is arguable that the fact that there is now a formal, established mechanism for reviewing governors' decisions where the decision is vulnerable to modification or to be quashed, means that an effective internal remedy has been established that must now be followed. There will be an element of discretion depending on the individual facts of each case when deciding whether to pursue this appeal. In some cases, when an application for permission is lodged, particularly when dealing with adjudications, the court will adjourn the application to enable the area manager to conduct a review of the decision. In general, it is always advisable to use this process for adjudications, particularly in light of the powers contained in the Prison Rules for the Secretary of State to review findings of guilt (Prison Rules 1999, r 61). An example where it may not be appropriate may include where legal correspondence is constantly being interfered with and the governor, whilst accepting the ambit of the relevant rules, is unable to establish a system of ensuring they are complied with. An appeal to the area manager would be of little assistance in such cases. However, as a general rule it would be imprudent not to fully consider whether an internal appeal should be used, as the client does face the prospect of further delay if the application is adjourned for further consideration or, in the worst scenario, the risk of having the application dismissed.

Decisions of the Secretary of State

16.13 The Prison Service was constituted to have agency status but remains a department of the Home Office. As such, all decisions made by staff at Prison Service Headquarters are done on behalf of the Home Office and under the authority of the Secretary of State. Consequently, the proper defendant in all such cases is the Secretary of State for the Home Department. The range of decisions that this will encompass will include the majority of decisions concerning category A prisoners and lifers, policy decisions on areas such as temporary release or the provision of facilities and decisions made concerning prisoners in the special units and close supervision centres.

16.14 There is no method to appeal against decisions made at this level. It is possible for representations and requests/complaints forms to be submitted if a prisoner is unhappy about a decision, but the review will be undertaken by the same department, and usually the same person who made the initial decision. On a practical level, it is often worthwhile making written representations to the decision maker partly to seek modification, but more importantly, to define the issues which will form the subject of any application to the High Court. There is not, however, any obligation to undertake this course of action and an application for judicial review may be made immediately.

The Parole Board

16.15   The Parole Board was created by statute (Criminal Justice Act 1967), and as such, it is an independent public body whose decisions are amenable to judicial review. Historically, the number of applications made against the Board were fairly few but this can be attributed to the fact that the decision-making process was secretive with neither the material before the Board nor the reasons for the decision being disclosed to the prisoner. This secrecy meant that the material necessary to determine whether a decision was reviewable was simply not available. Since the policy has been changed and all prisoners now have the right of disclosure of all material before the Board and to know of the reasons for decisions, the number of applications for judicial review has increased greatly.

16.16   As with decisions made by the Secretary of State, there is no formal right of appeal against Parole Board decisions. Whilst the Board will consider requests/complaints forms and written representations made in respect of its decisions, the general policy is only to reconsider cases where new and previously unconsidered information is disclosed. The same matters as are relevant in decisions made on the authority of the Secretary of State should be considered when advising clients as to whether to lodge an appeal. It is important to remember that in the case of determinate prisoners serving sentences of 15 years or more, all recommendations for release by the Board will be reviewed on behalf of the Secretary of State. If such a decision is to be challenged, it is important to establish whether the Board recommended release and this was not approved by the minister or whether it was the Parole Board who rejected the application. This should be apparent from the wording of the letter of refusal of parole.

Time limits

16.17   Applications for judicial review must be lodged 'promptly' and in any event within three months from the date when the grounds for the application first arose (RSC Ord 53, r 4). The requirement is for the application to be made promptly and the three month time limit is the final deadline. The court can and will dismiss an application made within the three month limit if it feels that it was not made promptly enough (*R v Independent Television Commission, ex p TV NI Ltd* (1991) Times, 30 December, CA). Given the delays that can often occur before prisoners seek legal advice, it is often essential for immediate action to be taken to ensure that the application is admissible.

16.18 The Rules of the Supreme Court 1965, Ord 53 refers to the date when the grounds of the action first arose when calculating the appropriate time limits. Problems can arise in cases where representations are made in an attempt to appeal a decision or to have it modified before proceedings are issued, not least because the Prison Service sets itself a six week deadline to reply to such matters. There are three matters to bear in mind if it is thought that the deadline for issuing the application may be exceeded:

(i)   If a formal appeal has been lodged, time will start to run from the date that a reply is received to the appeal. Therefore, if a prisoner wishes to challenge an adjudication that took place several weeks ago, an appeal can be lodged with the area manager and if this is unsuccessful, the application should be made as promptly as possible thereafter;

(ii) It is possible to lodge representations to try and secure the modification or substitution of a decision for which there is no right of appeal. It is arguable that the time for judicial review commences from the date of the reply to those representations on the basis that it is the later decision, taken with the benefit of full argument and representations on behalf of the prisoner, that is the subject of court scrutiny;

(iii) Where time limits are an issue, set a definite deadline for a reply and reserve the right to issue proceedings without further notice after that date. This can be particularly important with annual decisions such as parole reviews where a lengthy delay in issuing proceedings in the first place can mean that any judgment of the court would be made redundant by virtue of a new decision being made.

THE OMBUDSMAN AND JUDICIAL REVIEW

16.19 The Ombudsman is unable to accept complaints that are subject to legal proceedings and so it is not possible to pursue both courses of action at the same time. Prisoners are not required to make a complaint to the Ombudsman before making an application for judicial review as the Ombudsman has only an advisory capacity. If a prisoner's complaint is upheld, the Ombudsman can make a recommendation to the Director General of the Prison Service but has no power to make binding directions. Consequently, it is not possible to argue that this provides an effective remedy that must be pursued before making an application to the court.

16.20 Although prisoners cannot be required to complain to the Ombudsman before applying for judicial review, it can be advisable to take this course of action in cases where further information is necessary to strengthen the application or if the matter is relatively trivial and might not pass the threshold for the grant of legal aid (see chapter 13). If the Ombudsman finds in favour of the prisoner, a recommendation is issued to the Prison Service. This recommendation will result in a new decision being made in respect of that prisoner. The new decision, if unfavourable and, more particularly, if it is contrary to the Ombudsman's report, is more likely to be vulnerable to judicial review. The Ombudsman's report will also often contain a wealth of information that may not otherwise be available. Practice has shown that the courts tend to be very open to receiving applications from prisoners where they are seeking to have an Ombudsman's recommendation accepted and there are no reported cases where applications have been dismissed for being out of time. It is important when considering this course of action, however, to advise the client that if the report does not uphold the prisoner's complaint, it can effectively remove any possibility of subsequently applying to the court.

HOW THE COURTS VIEW PRISONERS' APPLICATIONS

16.21   The history of applications for judicial review brought by prisoners is detailed in section I, chapter 3. Over the past two decades, the courts have steadily exerted their authority to consider all aspects of public decision-making and nowhere is this more apparent that in the field of prison law. However, for the mere fact that the judiciary has successfully established the concept of the judge looking over the shoulder of all decision makers, there is still something of a dichotomy between the willingness of the courts to look at these areas and their willingness to overturn decisions.

16.22   It is almost possible to divide applications for judicial review brought by prisoners into two categories, those which the courts consider are concerned with fundamental rights and freedoms and those which are more concerned with the day-to-day management of prisoners. The judiciary has shown that it is prepared to be relatively interventionist in matters concerning release from prison and the administration of the mandatory life sentence which has frequently been the subject of judicial criticism.

16.23   In contrast, applications seeking to impeach decisions concerning the day-to-day management of the prison are far more difficult. For example, the Court of Appeal in *Ex p Ross* (1994) Times, 9 June, CA, a case concerning a governor's decision to transfer an allegedly disruptive prisoner, made it clear that judges found it difficult to review prison governors' decisions. In rejecting a renewed application for leave, Waite LJ held that the need for fairness was discharged by giving general reasons for the transfer of a disruptive prisoner and that the governor was best placed to make that assessment. He accepted that administrative procedures had to be properly followed and that the right to be given reasons for adverse decisions was a valid one, but the approach to the actual substantive issue of the management and control of prisoners was scarcely different from that of Lord Denning in *Becker v Home Office* [1972] 2 QB 407 some 20 years earlier.

16.24   The difficulty for prisoners remains that the vast majority of decisions made about them will arise from the use of discretionary powers. As the discretion afforded to the decision maker is usually very wide, the courts have very limited powers to intervene. Whilst there will always be cases where *Wednesbury* arguments are appropriate, by and large, the strongest cases will remain those where there has been some form of procedural error in the decision-making process or where the Prison Service has failed to introduce systems which accord with the requirements of fairness set down in *Doody* [1994] 1 AC 531. It is also apparent that the courts will pay very close attention to the nature of the right at stake before assessing the extent to which the requirements of fairness will allow judicial imposition of procedural safeguards onto statutory provisions which remain silent in this regard (eg *R v Secretary of State for the Home Department, ex p Hepworth* [1998] COD 146 and *R v Secretary of State for the Home Department, ex p Mehmet and O'Conner* (1999) 11 Admin LR 529, HC).

CHAPTER 17

CRIMINAL OFFENCES COMMITTED IN PRISON

INTRODUCTION

17.1 In recent years, there has been a significant shift towards police involvement in offending within the confines of a prison. Historically prison governors adjudicated upon disciplinary offences and Boards of Visitors heard proceedings which related to 'grave' or 'especially grave' offences. Thus, offences such as escape, violence upon prison officers and riot were delegated to the Boards of Visitors who had power to order that a prisoner should lose up to 180 days' remission for any one grave offence and unlimited remission for an especially grave offence. By contrast the maximum number of days' loss of remission that a governor could award was limited to 28. In 1983, Boards of Visitors' disciplinary powers were limited in terms of the punishments that they could award, and the distinction between grave and especially grave offences was removed in 1989. Awards of loss of remission were then limited to 120 days per disciplinary offence.

17.2 The prison disciplinary system was revisited in the aftermath of the Strangeways disturbance of 1990 and, in his report, Lord Justice Woolf recommended that a clear distinction should be drawn between prison disciplinary offences and criminal offences committed in prison. His view that the latter should be dealt with in the criminal courts was adopted by the Prison Service. Internal prison disciplinary matters are dealt with in chapter 8 of this book.

17.3 This section is not intended to provide a detailed guide to criminal law. Rather, its purpose is to deal with particular matters which criminal practitioners should be aware of when advising prisoners in relation to criminal proceedings, arising from allegations of offending during their imprisonment.

REFERRING SERIOUS OFFENCES TO THE POLICE

17.4 Where a serious criminal offence has been committed, this should be reported to the governor immediately regardless of whether or not the offender has been identified. The governor should decide whether the police need be informed and should give details of the incident to the Intelligence and Incident Support Unit at Prison Service Headquarters (Prison Discipline Manual, para 11.1).

17.5   Any suspects should be charged with an offence against prison discipline within 48 hours of discovery of the offence, but if the matter is being investigated by the police an adjudication should be opened and then adjourned pending the outcome of their enquiries. If the police or Criminal Prosecution Service decide not to prosecute, the governor should decide whether to pursue the internal charge at that stage.

17.6   Circular Instruction 3/92 gives guidance to governors on when offences should be referred to the police for investigation. Broadly, offences falling within the following categories should be referred:

(a)   Assault—alleged murder, manslaughter, non-consensual buggery and rape, attempts at the above, threats to kill if there appears to be intent, assaults with a weapon likely to cause serious injury, where serious violence has been used or serious injury caused, sexual assaults involving violence or where the victim was especially vulnerable, and hostage-taking;

(b)   Escape—from closed establishments or secure escorts and alleged escape attempts provided that the attempt is more than preparation;

(c)   Possession of unauthorised articles—allegations that a prisoner was in possession of firearms or explosives, other offensive weapons if there is evidence that the weapon was to be used to commit a serious criminal offence, class A drugs, class B drugs if there appears to have been intention to supply;

(d)   Criminal damage, arson—where the cost of the damage exceeds £2,000, or there was a risk of the fire taking hold;

(e)   Robbery—with serious violence or the threat or use of a weapon;

(f)   Major disturbances—involving a number of prisoners where the governor appears to be in danger of losing control or has lost control over any part of the establishment, and mass disobedience involving the use or threat of violence or the commission of serious criminal offences.

17.7   If there is clear evidence of racial motivation in any of the offences described above, the case for referral will be strengthened (Discipline Manual, appendix 3, para 7). Otherwise, the governor should make a referral if any victim asks for a police investigation (appendix 3A, para 6).

17.8   Prison governors are advised that the chances of successful prosecution of an offender will be enhanced if the police are called immediately when an offence is discovered. Any notes taken by staff in relation to an incident should be 'carefully preserved' and placed in prisoners' records (appendix 3A, paras 8–9).

17.9   Following the discovery of a serious offence in a prison establishment, prison staff are expected to follow a series of practical procedures in order to preserve physical evidence at the crime scene. However, staff are told that they must not take on the role of an investigating officer. Rather they should take action which will assist the police's task in the gathering of evidence.

'(1)   The prison officer first on the scene must take charge of the incident until assistance arrives.

(2)   If identified, the alleged offender must be detained and removed from the scene as early as practicable.

(3)   The identity of any witnesses, whether staff or prisoners must be noted.

(4)   Questioning of victims, alleged offenders and witnesses must be limited to establishing what has happened. Prison officers must not conduct lengthy interviews or take written statements from prisoners. This should be left to the police where criminal proceedings are a possibility. A court may exclude evidence if correct procedures have not been followed in taking statements.

(5)   As soon as possible after dealing with the incident, the prison officer first on the scene and other staff witnesses must make written notes. These will form the basis of both the witness statement to the police and form F254 in relation to internal proceedings. Each note should be recorded on form F2147, which should be available on every wing. The note must record details of:

- how the officer became aware of the incident (was he or she present throughout? Was it reported to him or her? Who reported it etc);
- what the officer observed, for example injuries or damage;
- potential exhibits left at the scene of the incident;
- what those involved said initially;
- the date and time the note is made.

(6)   The police should be contacted immediately on discovery of an alleged offence which may lead to a prosecution. Subject to their advice, after the prisoners concerned in the incident have been removed, the scene must be sealed and nothing disturbed unless it is unavoidable. While awaiting the arrival of the police investigating officer, if exceptionally someone has to enter the sealed area, it is essential to inform the police investigating officer, if possible in advance.

(7)   Items at the scene must not be handled unless this is essential. In this event there must be minimum contact to reduce damage to marks or other evidence. Covering the hands before touching does not preserve such evidence.

(8)   The police may seize items of a prisoners clothing which could be evidence if this is necessary to prevent concealment, loss or damage.

(9)   Guidance on giving evidence in court is contained in the card Prosecution Witnesses in the Crown Court and Magistrates Courts and in CI 7/1991.

(10) Charges should be laid in the normal way within 48 hours of the discovery of the alleged offence in case the referral does not result in a prosecution.' (Prison Discipline Manual, appendix 3B, paras 1–10)

OFFENCES COMMITTED IN PRISON

17.10   Very few offences are particular to prisons. The crime of prison mutiny was introduced following the disturbances at HMP Strangeways. The law is framed in such a way as to make it easier to achieve a successful prosecution for prison mutiny than riot, which requires 12 participants (Public Order Act 1986, s 1), although the maximum period of imprisonment for the two offences is the same.

17.11   The offence of prison mutiny is contained in the Prison Security Act 1992, s 1:

'(1) Any prisoner who takes part in a prison mutiny shall be guilty of an offence and liable, on conviction on indictment, to imprisonment for a term not exceeding ten years or to a fine or both.

(2) For the purposes of this section there is a prison mutiny where two or more prisoners, while on the premises of any prison, engage in conduct which is intended to further a common purpose of overthrowing lawful authority in that prison.

(3) For the purposes of this section the intentions and common purpose of prisoners may be inferred from the form and circumstances of their conduct and it shall be immaterial that conduct falling within subsection (2) above takes a different form in the case of different prisoners.

(4) Where there is a prison mutiny, a prisoner who has or is given a reasonable opportunity of submitting to lawful authority and fails, without reasonable excuse, to do so shall be regarded for the purposes of this section as taking part in the mutiny.'

17.12   Prison mutiny is a more serious offence than violent disorder (Public Order Act, s 2), which is also often used against prisoners following smaller disturbances within prisons. In recent years there have been mutiny trials at Hull Crown Court (*R v Edmonds* August 1998) and Newcastle Crown Court (*R v Francis* February–March 1999), both of which stemmed from disturbances at HMP Full Sutton on 20–21 January 1997 when prisoners took over B and C wings of the prison. Three prisoners out of four were convicted in the Hull trial, and seven out of nine were acquitted at Newcastle. Five prisoners were acquitted of violent disorder arising from an incident at HMP Parkhurst on 8 November 1998 (*R v Nash* March–May 1999 at Portsmouth Crown Court), and seven prisoners are to due to be tried in 2000 in relation to an alleged violent disorder at HMP Full Sutton on 26 April 1998.

17.13   Other offences peculiar to prisons and prisoners include the common law offence of breaking prison which requires the use of force in escaping, for example by cutting through fences or bars. Breaking prison is a more serious offence than escape.

17.14   There are many offences relating to escape—prisoners may be tried for escapes, conspiracies to escape and attempts; prison officers for permitting an escape, police officers for negligently permitting an escape, and others for aiding or assisting escapes (Prison Act 1953, s 39) or, at common law, for rescuing a prisoner in custody. Further offences relating to escape include harbouring escaped prisoners (Criminal Justice Act 1961, s 22(2)).

17.15   The vast majority of offences committed in prison and referred to the police for prosecution are assaults on prisoners by prisoners. These will range from a very few cases of murder and hostage-taking, and many reported offences of grievous bodily harm (Offences Against the Person Act 1861, ss 18 and 20) and actual bodily harm (Offences Against the Person Act 1861, s 47).

THE POLICE INTERVIEW

17.16   Different police forces take different approaches with regard to interview arrangements. In practice the majority of police interviews will take place in legal visiting rooms in prison, although in some cases prisoners may be taken to a police station.

17.17   The 'spirit of' the Police and Criminal Evidence Act 1984 and Codes of Practice apply to all police interviews which take place in prison (see CI 10/89). However, police officers can be particularly unaccommodating when it comes to the time constraints imposed by the prison regime, as the usual period for legal visits tends to be two or two-and-a-half hours long. Thus, if a solicitor meets police officers to obtain disclosure at the beginning of the visiting period, the police will often interrupt private consultation if they are of a view that the solicitor has been with the client so long that there will not be enough time left for the interview afterwards. In view of this it is worth considering whether to meet the police to obtain disclosure before being taken to the legal visiting room in the prison, or booking two legal visits in succession.

17.18   Prisoners can be subjected to a 'compulsory' interview by the police (CI 10/88). Any prisoner who is to be interviewed by the police should be given an information notice (F2042) advising them that if the police consider that there are reasonable grounds for suspecting that they have committed an arrestable offence they must remain in an interview room whilst questions are put to them. The notice also advises prisoners that they have a right to have a solicitor of their choice present at interview and that legal aid should be available for this purpose. In view of this prisoners cannot avoid the possibility of adverse inferences being drawn against them (under the Criminal Justice and Public Order Act 1994, s 34) by refusing to see the police at interview.

17.19   In the trial of *R v Francis* at Newcastle Crown Court between 1 February 1999 and 25 March 1999, the trial judge's summing up invited the jury to draw an adverse inference against one of the defendants who had left the interview room before the police had cautioned him or asked any questions. The police failed to exercise their power to compel him to stay in the room whilst questions were put. It is submitted that the trial judge was wrong in this approach. However, as the defendant in question was acquitted of mutiny, there was no appeal on the point.

Charging

17.20   Different police forces have different practices. In some geographical areas prisoners are almost always informed that they will be reported for summons, and they will then experience a time of uncertainty before a decision as to whether to summons them is made. Summonses are often used for serious offences such as prison mutiny, s 18 GBH and attempted murder.

17.21 In other geographical areas the police will attend the prison and charge a prisoner in the normal way. Prisoners are entitled to have a solicitor with them when they are charged, and procedures are the same as outlined above for interviews.

PREPARING THE DEFENCE CASE

Disclosure

17.22 In addition to the usual documents created in the course of a criminal enquiry, the Prison Service will also have a large amount of documentation in its possession. Whether or not the police have seized this will depend upon their diligence and/or their familiarity with prosecuting offences that have occurred within the confines of a prison.

17.23 In the course of preparing the defence case, it may be helpful to request the following items from the prosecution:

(a) Forms relating to the charging of a prisoner for an internal disciplinary offence arising from the same incident and the transcript of any adjudication proceedings (F256 and F1127). These can be requested for the defendant(s) and suspects who have been eliminated;

(b) Records of segregation of the defendant(s), or prisoner witnesses/victims (F1299B/C/D);

(c) Medical records of the victim or the defendant if he was injured in the incident (it is common for prison staff to be attended by a prison doctor in the first instance, and so it is worth asking for the records of prison officer victims as well as prisoners);

(d) Prison history sheets (F2052A);

(e) Report of Injury to Inmate/Prison Staff;

(f) Serious Incident Reports completed by prison officers who are prosecution witnesses;

(g) Security Intelligence Reports completed by prison officers who are prosecution witnesses;

(h) Disciplinary findings against prison officer witnesses;

(i) Records of sick leave taken by prison officer victims;

(j) CICA (Criminal Injuries Compensation Authority) claims completed by victims;

(k) Reports of any internal enquiries conducted by the Prison Service in the aftermath of the incident (the presence of these will depend upon the seriousness of the incident);

(l) Requests/complaints forms relating to the incident (eg where a defendant has complained to the governor that s/he was assaulted by staff);

(m) Control and Restraint (use of force) records;

(n) Use of Special Cell forms (if it is not clear whether a prisoner was held in a special cell, the Cell Certificate, indicating type of cell, can be requested);

(o) Fifteen minute watch forms;

(p) Audio tapes of relevant telephone calls made by prisoners;

(q)   Video tapes from any CCTV cameras in the vicinity of the incident;

(r)   A list of all prisoners who were in the prison/on the wing at the time of the incident, and an up-to-date list of their locations. This information is held on computer at each prison and can be invaluable in tracking down witnesses;

(s)   Prison disciplinary findings against prisoner victims/prisoner prosecution witnesses;

(t)   Criminal convictions of prisoner and prison officer witnesses;

(u)   Emergency Control Room logs. These are created in the course of more serious incidents or where incidents last for a protracted period of time, and should provide a contemporaneous record of the actions of prison staff involved in managing the incident, and information coming into the control room from other sources;

(v)   Photographs/plans of the area of the prison in which the incident took place.

17.24   Where the police have not already seized those items, in some circumstances the CPS will instruct them to approach the prison in order to ask for disclosure. At other times, the CPS will refer requests for disclosure to the Treasury Solicitor. In such cases the Treasury Solicitor will consider the rules on third party disclosure and may ask lawyers to address them on materiality and relevance before making any decision. If the Treasury Solicitor refuses to disclose the documentation, then an application for a third party witness summons should be considered.

Double jeopardy

17.25   Any internal disciplinary proceedings against a prisoner should be opened and then adjourned whilst a police investigation is ongoing (Prison Discipline Manual, para 4.15).

17.26   Where an offence is reported to the police, but this does not result in a prosecution, the governor must decide whether or not to proceed with the adjudication. Governors are advised that, where the CPS have decided not to pursue a prosecution on the basis that there is insufficient evidence against the prisoner, they must dismiss the disciplinary charge. However, in other cases the governor may decide to proceed with the charge (Prison Discipline Manual, para 11.6). Likewise, governors may re-open adjudications where criminal proceedings are discontinued, or it is directed that the charge should lie on file (para 11.7).

17.27   In cases where prisoners are cautioned by the police, governors are advised that they may still go ahead and hear an adjudication, on the basis that 'no formal proceedings will have taken place and no evidence will formally have been presented' (Prison Discipline Manual, para 11.8).

17.28   In any case where the CPS proceed with a prosecution and present evidence in court, the adjudication must not be continued (Prison Discipline Manual, para 11.10).

17.29   There appear to be a small number of cases where these rules were not followed, and prisoners were found guilty at adjudication and found guilty again at court. In such circumstances, the Prison Service has quashed the finding of guilt at adjudication, remitted any additional days awarded and, exceptionally, taken a punishment of cellular confinement into account when considering applications for the restoration of additional days awarded at adjudications in connection with other matters.

17.30   Anecdotal evidence also suggests that prisoners who have been found guilty at adjudication before the criminal proceedings have commenced have successfully run the special plea in bar, *autrefois convict*.

Visits to the crime scene

17.31   The Prison Service is usually amenable to allowing defence lawyers to attend a prison to view the scene of the incident and to take photographs of it. Whilst it is usually appropriate to liaise with the police in relation to this, security governors at establishments can also be approached in order to arrange access. Views of prisons tend to take place over the lunch time 'bang up' period.

17.32   If it is important to see any area of the prison other than the one in which the incident took place (eg the segregation block, any sterile areas, sight lines from cells or from the grounds of the prison into the prison) it is advisable to make a written request to the governor beforehand in order that any security arrangements can be made.

17.33   Juries are sometimes taken to view the prison during the course of the trial. In such cases it can be invaluable to have advance knowledge of the lay out of the jail as this will enable informed discussion with the prosecution as to which areas of the prison it would be useful for the jury to see.

ISSUES ARISING AT COURT

Handcuffing

17.34   The Prison Service Security Manual (chapter 38) deals with all issues relating to security at court. Court escorts are often contracted out, and so the policy applies equally to private contractors and prison staff on escort duty. In practice, prison staff are generally used to escort category A prisoners to court; the lower security categories are normally escorted by private security companies.

17.35   Prisoners should not normally be handcuffed in the courtroom, but they will usually be so restrained when moving from their cells in the court to the dock if the route between the two is insecure (Prison Service Security Manual, para 38.28).

17.36   Where high risk or exceptional risk category A prisoners are to be produced in court, the manager of the escort team is instructed to make an application to the CPS for the prisoner to be handcuffed in the dock (Prison Service Security Manual, para 38.29). A similar application should be made for lower security category prisoners where the courtroom is considered insecure, and the defendant is on the escape list (or has previously escaped or recently attempted to escape), if there is intelligence that the prisoner is likely to escape, or if the prisoner is considered violent, likely to take a hostage or to pose a danger to the public.

17.37   The decision as to whether any prisoner should be handcuffed in the dock is for the judge or the magistrate to make (Prison Service Security Manual, para 38.30). In practice it is highly unusual for a prisoner to remain handcuffed throughout a trial even if he is high or exceptional risk category A. However, it is much more common for such prisoners to be handcuffed in the less secure courtrooms provided in the magistrates' courts.

17.38   Some private contractors do not strictly adhere to the provisions of the Security Manual and will often ask the CPS to apply for handcuffs to be kept on for lower security category prisoners, particularly in cases where there is more than one defendant in the dock.

Training to give evidence

17.39   The Prison Service is often very anxious to secure convictions against prisoners for offences committed in custody, particularly if such offences have been widely reported in the media.

17.40   Criminal practitioners should be aware that the desire for a successful prosecution has led to training sessions where prison officers who are due to be witnesses in criminal proceedings have been given briefings as to how to give their evidence. At the Whitemoor escape trial (*R v McGhee* January 1997, Woolwich Crown Court), it emerged that prison officer witnesses had attended full day training sessions in HMP Whitemoor's education department.

17.41   In response to a parliamentary question, Richard Tilt (then Director General of the Prison Service) stated that:

'Three training sessions aimed at preparing staff to give evidence in court have been run at Whitemoor Prison since September 1996. This training was chosen by the Governor at Whitemoor particularly because a number of staff at the prison were expected to be asked to give evidence in the coming months... Governors have been encouraged, at least since 1991, to provide training to staff on what is involved in being a witness to reduce the possibility of trials being prejudiced as a result of inappropriate action by staff.' (Letter from Richard Tilt to Mr Kevin McNamara MP dated 7 February 1997)

Prisoner witnesses

17.42   Applications to witness summons serving prisoners should be made in the usual way. However, the summons should be directed to the governor of the relevant prison, and should ask him to produce a named prisoner at court. Prison governors will usually accept service of a summons by fax.

17.43   In large trials involving several prisoners it is likely that the prison will appoint a court/prison liaison officer. S/he will be responsible for ensuring that all prisoner witnesses are brought to court in good time to give their evidence.

CHAPTER 18

THE HUMAN RIGHTS ACT 1998 AND THE EUROPEAN CONVENTION ON HUMAN RIGHTS

INTRODUCTION

18.1 The Human Rights Act 1998 (HRA) comes into force in October 2000 and will make the majority of the European Convention on Human Rights directly enforceable in English law. The practical implications of the HRA on specific subjects are discussed in context in section II and this chapter will look at the wider implications in terms of the possible changes in philosophy and approach that the HRA may have on this area of law as a whole. In order to assess the likely impact of the HRA on the law relating to prisoners, it is most helpful to look at the Convention itself in the first place. There are now a large number of practitioners guides to the Convention and the HRA and it is strongly suggested that this chapter should be used as a starting point of reference for use with a more detailed guide.

18.2 The Convention has a somewhat paradoxical place in prisoners' litigation. On the one hand, applications brought by individual prisoners have lead to some of the more progressive changes to prison law whereas on the other hand, the length of time that it takes for a case to be decided and for the effects of any subsequent changes in the law to be implemented is such that only long-term prisoners will individually benefit from their applications. Nevertheless, in light of the extent to which the UK government does in fact comply with European Court judgments, it is a remedy that has been often utilised by and on behalf of prisoners to the extent that British prisoners have been one of the largest class of applicants to the European Court in the whole of Europe.

THE RELEVANT ARTICLES

18.3 The Convention came into force on 3 September 1953 and the UK was the first state to ratify it. Although it does not formally become part of domestic law until October 2000, the UK has recognised the right of individuals to petition since 1965.

18.4 The aim of the Convention is to protect those rights that are perceived as fundamental in free societies, the context having been set by the Universal Declaration of Human Rights issued by the United Nations in the immediate aftermath of the second world war. The Convention was drafted with the recent experiences of Nazi Germany very much in mind. The full text of the articles of most relevance to prisoners are reproduced in the appendices and these can be summarised as follows:

(i)   Article 2—protects the right to life;
(ii)   Article 3—this prohibits the use of torture or inhuman or degrading treatment or punishment;
(iii)   Articles 5(1) and (4)—no detention without due process and the right of everyone deprived of their liberty to have the lawfulness of that detention decided speedily by a court and release ordered if the detention is not lawful: compensation may be claimed for breaches of this article;
(iv)   Article 6—fair trial procedures;
(v)   Article 7—a prohibition against any criminal penalties being imposed retrospectively;
(vi)   Article 8—the right to a private and family life and to one's home and correspondence;
(vii)   Article 9—freedom of thought, conscience and religion;
(viii) Article 10—freedom of expression and to impart ideas and information;
(ix)   Article 12—the right to marry and found a family;
(x)   Article 13—the requirement for there to be an effective remedy in domestic law;
(xi)   First Protocol, Article 1—the right to the peaceful enjoyment of possessions;
(xii)   Article 14—freedom from discrimination in the enjoyment of any of these rights, although this article can only be invoked in connection with a complaint under one of the other articles.

18.5 Each of these articles must be approached with a degree of caution and the full text examined. This is because save for arts 2 and 3, the rights protected are not generally absolute, but are expressed subject to an acceptance that there may be restrictions legitimately placed upon those rights in domestic law. For example, the right to a private and family life (art 8) is subject to such controls as may be necessary in a democratic society in the interests of public safety. Similarly, art 4 which prohibits enforced labour does not prevent people who are lawfully detained from being required to undertake ordinary unpaid work as part of the prison disciplinary regime.

PROCEDURE AT THE EUROPEAN COURT

18.6 The process by which an individual may make a complaint that his/her rights under the Convention have been breached is remarkably straightforward compared to domestic court procedures. There is a two-tier mechanism whereby applications are initially made to the first tier of the Court, comprising of a representative appointed from each member state. This was previously administered through the European Commission of Human Rights and when looking at historical decisions, reference is often made to the findings of the Commission. The administration was rationalised in 1999 when the Court took on direct responsiblity for all aspects of applications. The processes have scarcely changed as a result.

18.7 The first task of the Court is to decide whether an application is admissible. Admissibility falls into three areas: whether the application has been made within the relevant time limits; whether all domestic remedies have been exhausted; and whether the application is 'manifestly ill founded' (ie has no merits).

18.8 In order to lodge the application, the Court provides a fairly straightforward form to be completed. It is not necessary to actually use this form but the application must contain a minimum amount of detail that includes the name, date and place of birth of the applicant, the nationality of the applicant, the state against whom the complaint is made, the articles that are alleged to have been breached and a brief statement of the facts of the application. In cases where the application needs to be lodged urgently, these details can be very brief and must simply contain the bare minimum to enable the application to be registered. The Court administrators will then send requests for further information which they need to process the case. A fuller application, even one which expands the alleged breaches to other articles, can be lodged at a later date. It is not unheard of for the Court to identify breaches themselves that were not particularised in the initial application.

18.9 The Court conducts its own investigation into the application and will set a procedural timetable in each individual case. The Court retains the power to extend the time limits if it is considered necessary for the proper preparation of a case. If the application is not struck out at this preliminary stage, then in most cases it will formally communicate the application to the state against which it is lodged and invite written representations. These observations will in turn be communicated to the applicant who has the opportunity to reply. At this point, the Court will decide whether it requires a hearing to help determine the issues, although hearings at this stage are likely to be far less common than they were when the Commission administered this part of the process.

18.10 The procedure at this stage is still primarily concerned with the issue of admissibility, however it is normal practice for a preliminary view to be taken on the merits of the application. If an oral hearing is held, it is entirely different from those in domestic courts. Each party is allotted 30 minutes to address the Court and this is done in turn. The Court can decide that witnesses should be asked to give evidence but there is no power to compel their attendance and this rarely happens. Following the delivery of speeches, the members of the Court will set questions to the parties and after a short adjournment will ask for replies to be given.

18.11 At this stage, the Court will reach a decision as to whether the application is admissible. If it is declared inadmissible, that is the end of the matter and there is no right of appeal. If an application is considered to be admissible, a preliminary report on the merits will be drawn up. The Court has a duty to try and secure a friendly settlement where possible (art 38) and proposals will be sought from both parties. If no friendly settlement can be reached, then the Court will formally publish its decision on the merits of the application. At this stage, either the Court or a member state can refer the matter to the full Court or the Committee of Ministers. As a general rule, cases which raise new points will be referred to the full Court whereas cases concerning established breaches will be sent to the Committee of Ministers. There is no right for the individual to require reference of the case to the Court or Committee of Ministers.

18.12 The procedure before the full Court is not dissimilar to that before the first tier of the Court and can be decided on the basis of either written representations or an oral hearing. There is no formal method of enforcing decisions made by the Court or Committee of Ministers. The Committee of Ministers will usually seek reports from member states as to how they have complied with a decision, but ultimately, the only sanction is to expel the member state from the Council of Europe.

18.13 There is no right of appeal against decisions made by the Court at any stage of the process. If, for example, the Court dismisses the case on first receipt for being outside of the relevant time limits, then this is the end of the matter. If a case is considered to be potentially admissible on first receipt, the Court administrators draw up a summary of the facts and a list of questions for the government to address. This is a crucial stage as it is this summary and the list of questions that will determine how the case proceeds in the future. The minimum aim of any application should be to reach this stage.

IS THE APPLICANT A VICTIM?

18.14 Article 34 defines who may be considered to be victims. In effect it states that the applicant must have been particularly affected in some way by the breach of the Convention. This is not limited simply to the direct victim, but can include near relatives or third parties who are so prejudiced by the violations that they have a valid personal interest. It is also possible to commence actions to try and prevent a future breach if it can be shown that the applicant belongs to a particular class and that a potential violation already affects their lives (see eg *Norris v Ireland* (1988) 13 EHRR 186, Series A, no 12).

EXHAUSTING DOMESTIC REMEDIES

18.15 It is a general principle that all domestic remedies must be exhausted before the Court can consider an application (art 35). This applies only to remedies which can be described as 'effective and sufficient' and so lawyers must pay particular attention to this requirement when advising a client to lodge an application. Remedies that are wholly discretionary are not deemed to be sufficient and as such do not have to be exhausted before an application is lodged. In the prison context, this raises important considerations as to whether internal prison complaints procedures can be considered effective remedies and more fundamentally, whether judicial review needs to be pursued.

18.16 The internal Prison Service complaints procedures do not appear to be sufficiently effective to be considered as remedies within the meaning of the Convention. These do not provide for any proper independent system of investigation and in many cases will not have the ability to offer proper redress for the wrong that has occurred (*Raphie v United Kingdom* 2 December 1993, No 20035/92). Similarly, complaints to the Prisons Ombudsman cannot be seen as an effective remedy as the powers of the Ombudsman are solely to make recommendations and are not mandatory.

18.17 The most difficult remedy to assess is that of judicial review. It was long argued that as judicial review is a discretionary remedy, it was not sufficient to satisfy the requirements of art 13 and did not have to be exhausted prior to lodging an application. This point of view is no longer fully sustainable. The European Court has defined effective remedies in the following terms:

> 'The only remedies which Article 26 requires to be exhausted are those that relate to the breaches alleged and which are at the same time available and sufficient. The existence of such remedies must be sufficiently certain not only in theory but also in practice, failing which they will lack the requisite accessibility and effectiveness: it falls to the Respondent state to establish the various conditions are satisfied.' (*Navarra v Spain* Series A/273–B, para 24)

18.18 The reality of the present situation is that each application will have to be judged on its own facts in light of what may be obtained by way of judicial review. For example, there have been cases where the inability of the domestic courts to examine the merits of a case on judicial review have resulted in the European Court deciding that it is not an effective remedy within the meaning of art 13 (*Chahal v United Kingdom* (1996) 23 EHRR 413, para 150). On the other hand, the increasingly pro-active attitude of the domestic courts whereby the requirements of the Convention come under more 'anxious scrutiny' have lead to the Court taking the view that judicial review can promote an effective remedy (see *Vilvarajah v United Kingdom* (1991) 14 EHRR 248, Series A, No 215). Clearly, when the HRA comes into force and is formally part of domestic law, it will be increasingly difficult to argue that judicial review should not be utilised before making an application directly to the European Court itself.

TIME LIMITS

18.19 Article 35(1) requires that applications must be lodged within six months of the violation or of the exhaustion of domestic remedies. This time limit is strictly observed. Problems can arise for applicants in complying with this time limit when considering whether domestic remedies have been exhausted. The danger is that a domestic remedy will be pursued unsuccessfully, only for the Court to decide that the remedy was not effective and the time limit has been exceeded. Alternatively, an application submitted at an early stage can be declared inadmissible on the grounds that domestic remedies have not been exhausted.

18.20 In cases where there is some doubt and the six month time period from the original violation is approaching, it is prudent to lodge an initial application whilst the question of domestic remedies is explored. The Court are, in many cases, prepared to register an application and then not to proceed with the investigation into admissibility for a set period of time whilst the possibility of a domestic remedy is pursued. In any event, if an application is declared inadmissible on the grounds that domestic remedies have not been exhausted, it can always be resubmitted once this has been done.

LEGAL AID

18.21 The Court operates a legal aid scheme, but this bears little resemblance to that in operation in this country. The Rules of the Court allow legal aid to be made available where it is deemed necessary for the proper discharge of their duties and where the applicant is financially eligible. Legal aid is not, therefore, available from the outset and applications can only be submitted from the time that the applicant is asked to make written submissions in reply to the government's observations. There is no method of obtaining payment for the initial application.

18.22 When the legal aid application is submitted, the Court requires proof of the applicant's financial situation. This is done by submitting both the Court's own legal aid application form and the appropriate English form to the Legal Aid Assessment Department at the Department of Social Security in Preston. They will complete an assessment stating whether the applicant qualifies under the English scheme and this must be forwarded to the Court with their own form. Legal aid payments are based upon fixed rates for preparing observations and attending any hearing before the Court and are not assessed according to the time that has been spent on the case. The fixed rates are really no more than nominal, although travelling expenses and costs for attending any hearing are paid in full.

APPLICATIONS FROM ENGLISH PRISONERS

18.23 There is no doubt that applications made to the Court have had a considerable impact on the prison system and the rights of prisoners. These range from the right to marry (*Hamer v United Kingdom* (1979) 4 EHRR 139), disciplinary procedures (*Campbell and Fell v United Kingdom* (1984) 7 EHRR 165, Series A, No 80) and access to the courts (*Silver v United Kingdom* (1983) 5 EHRR 347, Series A, No 61). Major legislative changes have also been adopted in relation to the release of discretionary life sentenced prisoners in the form of the Criminal Justice Act 1991 (*Thynne, Wilson and Gunnell* (1990) 13 EHRR 666, Series A, No 190).

18.24 There is always a tension between the role of the Court in protecting the most fundamental of human rights and the lack of any formal constitution or bill of rights in this country. Consequently, whilst prisoners can be subject to conditions and decisions that many would consider to be prima facie breaches of the Convention, the fact that the Convention allows a deal of discretion to domestic governments in deciding what constraints are necessary in the wider public interest can prevent these breaches from being successfully pursued. The cases where the Court has been most willing to find in favour of prisoners have included the right to proper access to lawyers (see eg *Campbell and Fell v United Kingdom* (1984) 7 EHRR 165, Series A, No 80; *Silver v United Kingdom* (1983) 5 EHRR 347, Series A, No 61; *Campbell v United Kingdom* (1992) 15 EHRR 137, Series A, No 233–A), basic rights to maintain family contact, and the mechanisms by which people's detention is subject to review (*Thynne, Wilson and Gunnell* (1990) 13 EHRR 666, Series A, No 190; *Hussain and Singh v United Kingdom* (1996) 22 EHRR 1). In contrast, applications concerning the day-to-day treatment of prisoners and the general conditions in prisons have been markedly less successful.

18.25 It is a very common complaint from prisoners that general conditions inside of prisons are so poor as to be in breach of art 3. In recent years, three applications have been considered on this subject, all of which have been unsuccessful. One failed in a complaint about a decision to segregate him in conditions that attracted severe criticism by the Chief Inspector of Prisons and the International Committee for the Prevention of Torture. The Commission decided that segregation does not constitute the severe ill treatment necessary to establish a violation and that conditions would have to be particularly severe to succeed (*Delazarus v United Kingdom* 16 February 1993, No 17525/ 90). An application by a Scottish prisoner concerning 14 months in a lockdown regime where association had been suspended and exercise was not always available, did not breach art 3 as there was not complete sensory and social isolation (*Windsor v United Kingdom* 6 April 1993, No 18942/91). The third case was declared inadmissible for being brought outside of the time limits (*Raphie v United Kingdom* 2 December 1993, No 20035/92).

18.26 These cases illustrate the sensitivity of such applications and the fact that the Commission will require extremely severe facts to find that particular conditions are in breach of art 3. Whilst there is still plenty of scope for such applications to be brought, the prospect that the Convention will provide a long-term panacea to prison conditions in this country is highly unlikely, particularly as more and more countries from the old Eastern Bloc with far worse prison conditions become signatories to the Convention.

THE CONVENTION AND DOMESTIC LAW

18.27 Two concepts are crucial in assessing the impact that the Convention has had on domestic law and the likely ramifications of the HRA, these being 'proportionality' and the 'margin of appreciation.' The role of the Court is subsidiary to the role of domestic law in protecting human rights. It is for the government to secure the rights protected by the Convention and the Court's role is to enforce that compliance. Many of the rights protected by the Convention are subject to restrictions that can be imposed by the domestic authorities and it is this room for manoeuvre that is termed the 'margin of appreciation.'

18.28 In the case of *Handyside v United Kingdom*, the Court gave an explanation of the extent to which it allows this margin of appreciation to domestic authorities. They explained that English courts are better placed to assess the necessity of a restriction placed upon a Convention right, 'by reason of their direct and continuous contact with the vital forces of their countries' ((1976) 1 EHRR 737 at para 48). So, for example, attempts made by British prisoners to have the right to conjugal visits, a right that has been rejected by the UK government on the grounds of security, have proven unsuccessful when taken to the European Court (see eg *ELH and PLH v United Kingdom* [1998] EHRLR 231). The extent of the margin of appreciation depends largely on the importance of the right itself and the degree to which there is room for departure from the wider consensus as to how such a right should be protected (for a fuller discussion, see Starmer *European Human Rights Law* (1999) Legal Action Group).

18.29 The need for a balance to be struck between the rights of the individual and wider interests of society has been termed as 'proportionality.' Although the concept is a complex one in application, in purely theoretical terms it simply requires that any interference with a Convention right must be proportionate to the aim of the interference. The European Court has set down a number of guiding principles that can be applied to this balancing act:

(i)   whether relevant and sufficient reasons have been given for the interference;
(ii) whether there is a less restrictive alternative;
(iii) whether the decision-making process has been procedurally fair;
(iv) whether there are adequate safeguards against abuse; and
(v)   whether the restriction actually extinguishes the essence of the right itself (see Starmer (1999) at p 170ff and for a discussion on these tests in the context of particular rights).

18.30 The extent to which domestic courts have been required to take account of Convention rights and European Court decisions has been the subject of considerable judicial consideration over the years. The situation has veered from disregarding the Convention entirely (*Uppal v Home Office* (1978) Times, 11 November), to a strained and technical approach of its impact (*R v Secretary of State for the Home Department, ex p Brind* [1991] 1 AC 696; *Bugdaycay v Secretary of State for the Home Department* [1987] AC 514), through to the current view that it must be assumed, unless there is evidence to the contrary that the intention of the legislature and executive is to comply with the Convention (*R v Secretary of State for the Home Department, ex p Ahmed and Patel* [1998] INLR 570). With the effective incorporation of the Convention into domestic law through the HRA 1998, it is no longer necessary to contemplate how to raise Convention arguments in domestic proceedings. To the contrary, it is now potentially negligent for them to be ignored.

THE HUMAN RIGHTS ACT 1998

18.31 The Human Rights Act 1998 makes virtually the whole Convention directly part of domestic law, protecting arts 2–12, 14, arts 1–3 of the first protocol and art 1 of the sixth protocol (s 1(1)). It provides that:

(i)   All legislation, primary and subordinate shall be interpreted to be compatible with the Convention so far as is possible (s 3(1));
(ii)   It is unlawful for a public authority to act in a way which is incompatible with the Convention (s 6);
(iii) If subordinate legislation cannot be so construed, it can be struck down;
(iv)   If primary legislation cannot be so construed, any court from the High Court up can issue a declaration of incompatibility which then requires Parliament to either amend the legislation or affirm that it should continue despite the finding (s 4(1));
(v)   Individuals whose Convention rights have been infringed by a public authority can bring legal proceedings against it (including a claim for damages)(ss 7–8).

18.32 Although the Human Rights Act does not make decisions of the European Court of Human Rights binding in English law, it does require domestic courts and tribunals to take account of such decisions (HRA 1998, s 2(1)). In effect, this means that a whole new body of jurisprudence will become part of our common law and will have to be considered when commencing proceedings. This is especially relevant in the field of judicial review which is concerned almost exclusively with the acts and omissions of public bodies.

18.33 The lengthy history of applications to the European Court by British and other European prisoners makes the situation particularly complex in the field of prison law. On the one hand, the very nature of prison law whereby the state is required to place limitations on the rights which people at liberty enjoy means that there is enormous scope for argument on the lawfulness and necessity of such restrictions. On the other hand, there is in existence a large body of case law from the European Court which has defined and limited those rights. So, for example the Court has already upheld matters such as the ban on conjugal visits (*ELH and PBH v United Kingdom* [1998] EHRLR 231) or the right to require prisoners to undertake mandatory drugs tests in custody (*Peters v Netherlands* 6 April 1994, Application No 21132/93).

18.34 In seeking to assess the possible implications of the HRA 1998, the key areas on which to concentrate are: the impact of the concept of proportionality; the requirement on the state to take positive obligations to secure Convention rights; and the implications of the absence of the margin of appreciation in domestic law.

Proportionality under the HRA

18.35 The concept of proportionality is explained at para 18.29 above. It is a concept that has often conflicted with domestic law, particularly in the field of prison law. The tension arises as the prison authorities will very often seek to justify an interference with family visits (art 8) or legal correspondence (arts 6 and 8) on the grounds that this is necessary in the interests of prison security.

18.36 In *R v Secretary of State for the Home Department, ex p Leech* [1994] QB 198, Steyn LJ was of the view that the appropriate test in domestic law was essentially the same as under the Convention, being whether an interference was the 'minimum necessary' to achieve the stated aim. This is often referred to as the 'minimum interference test.' The judgment was concerned with the vires of secondary legislation, the legislation in question being a prison rule which only allowed for confidential correspondence between prisoners and their legal advisers in limited circumstances. However, the Court of Appeal later expressed doubt that this was the appropriate test, preferring instead the proposition that prisoners forfeited certain rights through the fact of their imprisonment and the onus was then upon the prisoner to demonstrate that the restriction was unjustified (*R v Secretary of State for the Home Department, ex p O'Dhuibhir* [1997] COD 315, CA). In that case, the Court of Appeal stated that even if the minimum interference test was appropriate when assessing legislative provisions, it could not be applied to policies put in place by the prison authorities under legislation which was itself lawful. Kennedy LJ fell back on the old concept that the prison authorities should be left to make their own assessments as to what the needs of security demanded.

18.37 The proper construction of the test was eventually clarified by the House of Lords in 1999 and provides a strong indication of how the courts will approach the concept of proportionality under the HRA 1998 (*R v Secretary of State for the Home Department, ex p Simms and O'Brien* [1999] 3 All ER 400. The Lords were called upon to assess whether restrictions imposed upon journalists wishing to visit prisoners who maintained their innocence were valid. The lead judgment was given by Lord Steyn, allowing him to revisit his own comments in *Leech* (above). It was held that the legislative provisions and the policy document setting out the restrictions were valid, but that the prison authorities were implementing those policies in an invalid manner. The appropriate test for assessing the extent of a restriction on fundamental or Convention rights, whether arising from statute or policy, was affirmed as the minimum interference test. The judgment was strongly influenced by the acceptance that art 6 was an issue as well as art 8 to the extent that access to a journalist was often the only method for a wrongly convicted prisoner to have his/her case returned to the Court of Appeal. However, even with that proviso, the judgment provides helpful guidance as to the acceptance in advance of the HRA 1998 that Convention approaches to such issues will predominate.

Positive obligations

18.38 Another area which is, at first blush, unfamiliar to domestic law is the concept that the authorities owe a positive obligation to uphold Convention rights rather than to simply refrain from infringing them. The Convention requires states to 'secure' (art 1) the rights protected and to provide effective domestic remedies (art 13) and this can impose a requirement to take positive action, such as the provision of a system of legal aid in criminal cases under art 6(3)(c)(I) (see eg *Benham v United Kingdom* (1996) 22 EHRR 293).

18.39 The European Court has not been directive in its approach to this area, recognising that the state has to strike a fair balance between the individual and the community (*Powell and Rayner v United Kingdom* (1990) 12 EHRR 355). The scope of the duty has therefore come to be expressed in general terms, encompassing matters such as the duty to prevent breaches (*Osman v United Kingdom* [1999] EHRLR 228), to respond to breaches (*Aydin v Turkey* (1997) 25 EHRR 251), to provide resources to individuals to prevent breaches (*Airey v Ireland* (1979) 2 EHRR 305) and to put in place a legal framework to respond to breaches (*X and Y v Netherlands* (1985) 8 EHRR 235).

18.40 The positive obligations that have been set out by the European Court will form part of the consideration that must be given by the domestic courts. The 'incorporation' of the substantive articles themselves has taken place to fulfil the art 1 obligation to 'secure' rights and the inclusion of courts and tribunals within the ambit of public authorities (HRA 1998, s 6(3)(a)) imposes this duty directly upon them. The extent to which positive obligations do arise does depend on the nature of the right at stake, the general principle being that the more fundamental a right is, the more onerous the burden becomes.

The absence of the margin of appreciation

18.41 The margin of appreciation that is afforded to member states under the Convention has a considerable impact upon the manner in which the European Court has assessed applications made against the UK government. The Court has recognised the need for member states to maintain their own distinct legal systems and traditions and does not seek to impose uniformity.

18.42 When Convention rights are considered in the domestic courts, the margin of appreciation is an irrelevant concept. The domestic courts will form part of the mechanism for protecting Convention rights and will have a distinct function from the supervisory role of the European Court itself. This does not mean that domestic courts will be prohibited from allowing a degree of discretion to the bodies whose decisions are under review, but the extent of that discretion will have to be considered in light of the importance of the right at stake and the interference that has taken place.

18.43 The absence of the margin of appreciation does mean that domestic courts may actually be able to re-examine areas of law which the European Court has not found to breach the Convention. The domestic courts will be required to look at the Convention rights in a more practical form rather than in a purer supervisory role and to match the reality of domestic law with the issues falling to be determined. For example, although the European Court has held that the current procedures for administering the mandatory life sentence after conviction do not breach the Convention, that approach does not match the reality of the developments that have occurred domestically. The European Court has accepted the government's arguments that the sentence is entirely distinct from the discretionary life sentence as it authorises life-long punitive detention. The reality is somewhat different and successive House of Lords decisions have confirmed that the mandatory life sentence is in fact comprised of a fixed punitive term followed by detention on the basis of risk alone (see chapter 11). In consequence, it may well be open to the domestic courts to re-examine matters such as tariff setting, release procedures and recall on the basis of the domestic authorities.

Conclusions

18.44 At the start of this chapter it was explained that the impact of the HRA 1998 on specific aspects of prisoners' rights has been discussed in the context in which they arise in section II. The following is a very general guide to the subjects where Convention rights are likely to be invoked in future applications:

Article 2   suicides and deaths in custody; provision of medical treatment;

Article 3   overcrowding; strip searching and intimate searches; conditions in CSCs;

Article 5   awards of additional days at adjudications; recall procedures for mandatory lifers;

Article 6   adjudications, particularly for young offenders; tariff setting procedures for mandatory lifers;

Article 8   visits, telephone calls, allocation and family ties in general, particularly for young offenders and women prisoners with children;

Article 9   non-recognised religious practices (eg Rastafarianism);

Article 10   access to the media, censorship;

Article 12   conjugal visits; artificial insemination;

Article 14   discriminatory practices, especially for foreign prisoners, immigration detainees and prisoners with disabilities;

First protocol, Article 1   education provisions for young offenders;

First protocol, Article 3   the right to vote.

PRISON ACT 1952

1952 Chapter 52

An Act to consolidate certain enactments relating to prisons and other institutions for offenders and related matters with corrections and improvements made under the Consolidation of Enactments (Procedure) Act 1949

1st August 1952

Central administration

1 General control over prisons

All powers and jurisdiction in relation to prisons and prisoners which before the commencement of the Prison Act 1877 were exercisable by any other authority shall, subject to the provisions of this Act, be exercisable by the Secretary of State.

Annotations

This section does not extend to Scotland.

3 Officers and servants of [the Secretary of State]

(1)   The Secretary of State [may, for the purposes of this Act, appoint such officers and [employ such other persons] as he] may, with the sanction of the Treasury as to number, determine.

(2)   There shall be paid out of moneys provided by Parliament to [the officers and servants appointed under this section] such salaries as the Secretary of State may with the consent of the Treasury determine.

Annotations

Section heading: words in square brackets substituted by virtue of SI 1963/597, art 3(2), Sch 1.

Sub-s (1): first words in square brackets substituted by SI 1963/597, art 3(2), Sch 1, words in square brackets therein substituted by the Criminal Justice and Public Order Act 1994, s 168(2), Sch 10, para 7.

Sub-s (2): words in square brackets substituted by SI 1963/597, art 3(2), Sch 1.

This section does not extend to Scotland.

4 General duties of [the Secretary of State]

(1) [The Secretary of State] shall have the general superintendence of prisons and shall make the contracts and do the other acts necessary for the maintenance of prisons and the maintenance of prisoners.

(2) [Officers of the Secretary of State duly authorised in that behalf] shall visit all prisons and examine the state of buildings, the conduct of officers, the treatment and conduct of prisoners and all other matters concerning the management of prisons and shall ensure that the provisions of this Act and of any rules made under this Act are duly complied with.

(3) [The Secretary of State and his officers] may exercise all powers and jurisdiction exercisable at common law, by Act of Parliament, or by charter by visiting justices of a prison.

Annotations

Section heading: words in square brackets substituted by virtue of SI 1963/597, art 3(2), Sch 1.

Sub-ss (1)–(3): words in square brackets substituted by SI 1963/597, art 3(2), Sch 1.

This section does not extend to Scotland.

5 Annual report of [the Secretary of State]

[(1) The Secretary of State shall issue an annual report on every prison and shall lay every such report before Parliament.]

(2) The report shall contain—

(a) a statement of the accommodation of each prison and the daily average and highest number of prisoners confined therein;

(b) such particulars of the work done by prisoners in each prison, including the kind and quantities of articles produced and the number of prisoners employed, as may in the opinion of the Secretary of State give the best information to Parliament;

(c) a statement of the punishments inflicted in each prison and of the offences for which they were inflicted . . .

Annotations

Section heading: words in square brackets substituted by virtue of SI 1963/597, art 3(2), Sch 1.

Sub-s (1): substituted by SI 1963/597, art 3(2), Sch 1.

Sub-s (2): words omitted repealed by the Criminal Justice Act 1967, s 103(2), Sch 7, Part I.

This section does not extend to Scotland.

[5A Appointment and functions of Her Majesty's Chief Inspector of Prisons]

[(1) Her Majesty may appoint a person to be Chief Inspector of Prisons.

(2) It shall be the duty of the Chief Inspector to inspect or arrange for the inspection of prisons in England and Wales and to report to the Secretary of State on them.

(3)   The Chief Inspector shall in particular report to the Secretary of State on the treatment of prisoners and conditions in prisons.

(4)   The Secretary of State may refer specific matters connected with prisons in England and Wales and prisoners in them to the Chief Inspector and direct him to report on them.

(5)   The Chief Inspector shall in each year submit to the Secretary of State a report in such form as the Secretary of State may direct, and the Secretary of State shall lay a copy of that report before Parliament.

[(5A) *Subsections (2) to (5) apply to detention centres (as defined by section 147 of the Immigration and Asylum Act 1999 and including any in Scotland) and persons detained in such detention centres as they apply to prisons and prisoners.*]

(6)   The Chief Inspector shall be paid such salary and allowances as the Secretary of State may with the consent of the Treasury determine.]

Annotations

Inserted by the Criminal Justice Act 1982, s 57.

Sub-s (5A): inserted by the Immigration and Asylum Act 1999, s 152(5). Date in force: to be appointed: see the Immigration and Asylum Act 1999, s 170(4).

This section does not extend to Scotland.

. . . boards of visitors

6 . . . boards of visitors

(1)   . . .

(2)   The Secretary of State shall appoint for every prison . . . a board of visitors of whom not less than two shall be justices of the peace.

(3)   Rules made as aforesaid shall prescribe the functions of . . . boards of visitors and shall among other things require members to pay frequent visits to the prison and hear any complaints which may be made by the prisoners and report to the Secretary of State any matter which they consider it expedient to report; and any member of a . . . board of visitors may at any time enter the prison and shall have free access to every part of it and to every prisoner.

(4)   . . .

Annotations

Section heading: words omitted repealed by virtue of the Courts Act 1971, ss 53 (3), 56(4), Sch 7, Part II, para 4, Sch 11, Part IV.

Paras (1)–(4): words omitted repealed by the Courts Act 1971, ss 53 (3), 56(4), Sch 7, Part II, para 4, Sch 11, Part IV.

This section does not extend to Scotland.

Prison officers

7 Prison officers

(1)   Every prison shall have a governor, a chaplain and a medical officer and such other officers as may be necessary.

(2) Every prison in which women are received shall have a sufficient number of women officers; . . .

(3) A prison which in the opinion of the Secretary of State is large enough to require it may have a deputy governor or an assistant chaplain or both.

(4) The chaplain and any assistant chaplain shall be a clergyman of the Church of England and the medical officer shall be duly registered under the Medical Acts.

(5) . . .

Annotations

Sub-s (2): words omitted repealed by the Sex Discrimination Act 1975, s 18(2).

Sub-s (5): repealed by SI 1963/597, art 3(2), Sch 1.

Modified, in relation to contracted out prisons, by the Criminal Justice Act 1991, s 87.

This section does not apply to Scotland.

8 Powers of prison officers

Every prison officer while acting as such shall have all the powers, authority, protection and privileges of a constable.

Annotations

Modified, in relation to contracted out prisons, by the Criminal Justice Act 1991, s 87.

This section does not extend to Scotland.

[8A Powers of search by authorised employees

(1) An authorised employee at a prison shall have the power to search any prisoner for the purpose of ascertaining whether he has any unauthorised property on his person.

(2) An authorised employee searching a prisoner by virtue of this section—

  (a) shall not be entitled to require a prisoner to remove any of his clothing other than an outer coat, jacket, headgear, gloves and footwear;

  (b) may use reasonable force where necessary; and

  (c) may seize and detain any unauthorised property found on the prisoner in the course of the search.

(3) In this section 'authorised employee' means an employee of a description for the time being authorised by the governor to exercise the powers conferred by this section.

(4) The governor of a prison shall take such steps as he considers appropriate to notify to prisoners the descriptions of persons who are for the time being authorised to exercise the powers conferred by this section.

(5) In this section 'unauthorised property', in relation to a prisoner, means property which the prisoner is not authorised by prison rules or by the governor to have in his possession or, as the case may be, in his possession in a particular part of the prison.]

Annotations

Inserted by the Criminal Justice and Public Order Act 1994, s 152(1).

Modified, in relation to contracted out prisons, by the Criminal Justice Act 1991, s 87.

This section does not extend to Scotland.

9 Exercise of office of chaplain

(1)   A person shall not officiate as chaplain of two prisons unless the prisons are within convenient distance of each other and are together designed to receive not more than one hundred prisoners.

(2)   Notice of the nomination of a chaplain or assistant chaplain to a prison shall, within one month after it is made, be given to the bishop of the diocese in which the prison is situate; and the chaplain or assistant chaplain shall not officiate in the prison except under the authority of a licence from the bishop.

Annotations

This section does not extend to Scotland.

10 Appointment of prison ministers

(1)   Where in any prison the number of prisoners who belong to a religious denomination other than the Church of England is such as in the opinion of the Secretary of State to require the appointment of a minister of that denomination, the Secretary of State may appoint such a minister to that prison.

(2)   The Secretary of State may pay a minister appointed under the preceding subsection such remuneration as he thinks reasonable.

(3)   [The Secretary of State] may allow a minister of any denomination other than the Church of England to visit prisoners of his denomination in a prison to which no minister of that denomination has been appointed under this section.

(4)   No prisoner shall be visited against his will by such a minister as is mentioned in the last preceding subsection; but every prisoner not belonging to the Church of England shall be allowed, in accordance with the arrangements in force in the prison in which he is confined, to attend chapel or to be visited by the chaplain.

(5)   The governor of a prison shall on the reception of each prisoner record the religious denomination to which the prisoner declares himself to belong, and shall give to any minister who under this section is appointed to the prison or permitted to visit prisoners therein a list of the prisoners who have declared themselves to belong to his denomination; and the minister shall not be permitted to visit any other prisoners.

Annotations

Sub-s (3): words in square brackets substituted by SI 1963/597, art 3(2), Sch 1.

Modified, in relation to contracted out prisons, by the Criminal Justice Act 1991, s 87.

This section does not extend to Scotland.

11 Ejectment of prison officers and their families refusing to quit

(1) Where any living accommodation is provided for a prison officer or his family by virtue of his office, then, if he ceases to be a prison officer or is suspended from office or dies, he, or, as the case may be, his family, shall quit the accommodation when required to do so by notice of [the Secretary of State].

(2) Where a prison officer or the family of a prison officer refuses or neglects to quit the accommodation forty-eight hours after the giving of such a notice as aforesaid, any two justices of the peace, on proof made to them of the facts authorising the giving of the notice and of the service of the notice and of the neglect or refusal to comply therewith, may, by warrant under their hands and seals, direct any constable, within a period specified in the warrant, to enter by force, if necessary, into the accommodation and deliver possession of it to [a person acting on behalf of the Secretary of State].

Annotations

Sub-ss (1), (2): words in square brackets substituted by SI 1963/597, art 3(2), Sch 1.

Modified, in relation to contracted out prisons, by the Criminal Justice Act 1991, s 87.

This section does not extend to Scotland.

Confinement and treatment of prisoners

12 Place of confinement of prisoners

(1) A prisoner, whether sentenced to imprisonment or committed to prison on remand or pending trial or otherwise, may be lawfully confined in any prison.

(2) Prisoners shall be committed to such prisons as the Secretary of State may from time to time direct; and may by direction of the Secretary of State be removed during the term of their imprisonment from the prison in which they are confined to any other prison.

(3) A writ, warrant or other legal instrument addressed to the governor of a prison and identifying that prison by its situation or by any other sufficient description shall not be invalidated by reason only that the prison is usually known by a different description.

Annotations

Modified, in relation to contracted out prisons, by the Criminal Justice Act 1991, s 87.

This section does not extend to Scotland.

13 Legal custody of prisoner

(1) Every prisoner shall be deemed to be in the legal custody of the governor of the prison.

(2) A prisoner shall be deemed to be in legal custody while he is confined in, or is being taken to or from, any prison and while he is working, or is for any other reason, outside the prison in the custody or under the control of an officer of the prison [and while he is being taken to any place to which

he is required or authorised by or under this Act [or the Criminal Justice Act 1982] to be taken, or is kept in custody in pursuance of any such requirement or authorisation].

Annotations

Sub-s (2): first words in square brackets inserted by the Criminal Justice Act 1961, s 41(1), Sch 4, words in square brackets therein inserted by the Criminal Justice Act 1982, s 77, Sch 14, para 4.

Modified, in relation to contracted out prisons, by the Criminal Justice Act 1991, s 87.

Modified, in relation to contracted out functions at directly managed prisons, by the Criminal Justice Act 1991, s 88A.

Modified, in relation to contracted out functions at directly managed secure training centres, by the Criminal Justice and Public Order Act 1994, s 11(3).

This section does not extend to Scotland.

14 Cells

(1) The Secretary of State shall satisfy himself from time to time that in every prison sufficient accommodation is provided for all prisoners.

(2) No cell shall be used for the confinement of a prisoner unless it is certified by an inspector that its size, lighting, heating, ventilation and fittings are adequate for health and that it allows the prisoner to communicate at any time with a prison officer.

(3) A certificate given under this section in respect of any cell may limit the period for which a prisoner may be separately confined in the cell and the number of hours a day during which a prisoner may be employed therein.

(4) The certificate shall identify the cell to which it relates by a number or mark and the cell shall be marked by that number or mark placed in a conspicuous position; and if the number or mark is changed without the consent of an inspector the certificate shall cease to have effect.

(5) An inspector may withdraw a certificate given under this section in respect of any cell if in his opinion the conditions of the cell are no longer as stated in the certificate.

(6) In every prison special cells shall be provided for the temporary confinement of refractory or violent prisoners.

Annotations

Modified, in relation to contracted out prisons, by the Criminal Justice Act 1991, s 87.

Modified, in relation to contracted out functions at directly managed prisons, by the Criminal Justice Act 1991, s 88A.

Modification: references to an inspector to be construed as references to an officer (not being an officer of the prison) acting on behalf of the Secretary of State, by virtue of the Prison Commissioners Dissolution Order 1963, SI 1963/597, art 3(2), Sch 1.

This section does not extend to Scotland.

16 Photographing and measuring of prisoners

The Secretary of State may make regulations as to the measuring and photographing of prisoners and such regulations may prescribe the time or times at which and the manner and dress in which prisoners shall be measured and photographed and the number of copies of the measurements and photographs of each prisoner which shall be made and the persons to whom they shall be sent.

Annotations

This section does not extend to Scotland.

[16A Testing prisoners for drugs

(1)   If an authorisation is in force for the prison, any prison officer may, at the prison, in accordance with prison rules, require any prisoner who is confined in the prison to provide a sample of urine for the purpose of ascertaining whether he has any drug in his body.

(2)   If the authorisation so provides, the power conferred by subsection (1) above shall include power to require a prisoner to provide a sample of any other description specified in the authorisation, not being an intimate sample, whether instead of or in addition to a sample of urine.

(3)   In this section—

'authorisation' means an authorisation by the governor;

'drug' means any drug which is a controlled drug for the purposes of the Misuse of Drugs Act 1971;

'intimate sample' has the same meaning as in Part V of the Police and Criminal Evidence Act 1984;

'prison officer' includes a prisoner custody officer within the meaning of Part IV of the Criminal Justice Act 1991; and

'prison rules' means rules under section 47 of this Act.]

Annotations

Inserted by the Criminal Justice and Public Order Act 1994, s 151(1).

Modified, in relation to contracted out prisons, by the Criminal Justice Act 1991, s 87.

This section does not extend to Scotland.

[16B Power to test prisoners for alcohol

(1)   If an authorisation is in force for the prison, any prison officer may, at the prison, in accordance with prison rules, require any prisoner who is confined in the prison to provide a sample of breath for the purpose of ascertaining whether he has alcohol in his body.

(2)   If the authorisation so provides, the power conferred by subsection (1) above shall include power—

(a)   to require a prisoner to provide a sample of urine, whether instead of or in addition to a sample of breath, and

(b)   to require a prisoner to provide a sample of any other description specified in the authorisation, not being an intimate sample, whether instead of or in addition to a sample of breath, a sample of urine or both.

(3)   In this section—

'authorisation' means an authorisation by the governor;

'intimate sample' has the same meaning as in Part V of the Police and Criminal Evidence Act 1984;

'prison officer' includes a prisoner custody officer within the meaning of Part IV of the Criminal Justice Act 1991;

'prison rules' means rules under section 47 of this Act.]

Annotations

Inserted by the Prisons (Alcohol Testing) Act 1997, s 1.

This section does not extend to Scotland.

17 Painful tests

The medical officer of a prison shall not apply any painful tests to a prisoner for the purpose of detecting malingering or for any other purpose except with the permission of [the Secretary of State] or the visiting committee or, as the case may be, board of visitors.

Annotations

Words in square brackets substituted by SI 1963/597, art 3(2), Sch 1.

This section does not extend to Scotland.

19 Right of justice to visit prison

(1)   A justice of the peace for any [commission area] . . . may at any time visit any prison in that [area] . . . and any prison in which a prisoner is confined in respect of an offence committed in that [area] . . . , and may examine the condition of the prison and of the prisoners and enter in the visitors' book, to be kept by the governor of the prison, any observations on the condition of the prison or any abuses.

(2)   Nothing in the preceding subsection shall authorise a justice of the peace to communicate with any prisoner except on the subject of his treatment in the prison, or to visit any prisoner under sentence of death.

(3)   The governor of every prison shall bring any entry in the visitors' book to the attention of the visiting committee or the board of visitors at their next visit.

Annotations

Sub-s (1): words 'commission area' in square brackets substituted by the Access to Justice Act 1999, s 76(2), Sch 10, para 21(a); words omitted repealed by the Local Government Act 1972, s 272(1), Sch 30; word 'area' in square brackets in both places it occurs substituted by the Access to Justice Act 1999, s 76(2), Sch 10, para 21(b).

Modified, in relation to contracted out prisons, by the Criminal Justice Act 1991, s 87.

This section does not extend to Scotland.

21 Expenses of conveyance to prison

A prisoner shall not in any case be liable to pay the cost of his conveyance to prison.

Annotations

This section does not extend to Scotland.

22 Removal of prisoners for judicial and other purposes

(1)   Rules made under section forty-seven of this Act may provide in what manner an appellant within the meaning of [Part I of the Criminal Appeal Act 1968], when in custody, is to be taken to, kept in custody at, and brought back from, any place at which he is entitled to be present for the purposes of that Act, or any place to which the Court of Criminal Appeal or any judge thereof may order him to be taken for the purpose of any proceedings of that court.

(2)   The Secretary of State may—

(a)   . . .

(b)   if he is satisfied that a person so detained requires [medical investigation or observation or] medical or surgical treatment of any description, direct him to be taken to a hospital or other suitable place for the purpose of the [investigation, observation or] treatment;

and where any person is directed under this subsection to be taken to any place he shall, unless the Secretary of State otherwise directs, be kept in custody while being so taken, while at that place, and while being taken back to the prison in which he is required in accordance with law to be detained.

Annotations

Sub-s (1): words in square brackets substituted by the Criminal Appeal Act 1968, s 52, Sch 5, Part I.

Sub-s (2): para (a) repealed by the Criminal Justice Act 1961, s 41(2), Sch 5; in para (b) words in square brackets inserted by the Criminal Justice Act 1982, s 77, Sch 14, para 5.

Modification: references to the Court of Criminal Appeal to be construed as a reference to the criminal division of the Court of Appeal, by virtue of the Supreme Court Act 1981, s 151(4), Sch 4, para 3.

This section does not extend to Scotland.

23 Power of constable etc to act outside his jurisdiction

For the purpose of taking a person to or from any prison under the order of any authority competent to give the order a constable or other officer may act outside the area of his jurisdiction and shall notwithstanding that he is so acting have all the powers, authority, protection and privileges of his office.

Annotations

This section does not extend to Scotland.

Length of sentence, release on licence and temporary discharge

24 Calculation of term of sentence

(1)   In any sentence of imprisonment the word 'month' shall, unless the contrary is expressed, be construed as meaning calendar month.

(2) . . .

Annotations

Sub-s (2): repealed by the Criminal Justice Act 1961, s 41(2), Sch 5.

This section does not extend to Scotland.

28 Power of Secretary of State to discharge prisoners temporarily on account of ill health

(1)   If the Secretary of State is satisfied that by reason of the condition of a prisoner's health it is undesirable to detain him in prison, but that, such condition of health being due in whole or in part to the prisoner's own conduct in prison, it is desirable that his release should be temporary and conditional only, the Secretary of State may, if he thinks fit, having regard to all the circumstances of the case, by order authorise the temporary discharge of the prisoner for such period and subject to such conditions as may be stated in the order.

(2)   Where an order of temporary discharge is made in the case of a prisoner not under sentence, the order shall contain conditions requiring the attendance of the prisoner at any further proceedings on his case at which his presence may be required.

(3)   Any prisoner discharged under this section shall comply with any conditions stated in the order of temporary discharge, and shall return to prison at the expiration of the period stated in the order, or of such extended period as may be fixed by any subsequent order of the Secretary of State, and if the prisoner fails so to comply or return, he may be arrested without warrant and taken back to prison.

(4)   Where a prisoner under sentence is discharged in pursuance of an order of temporary discharge, the currency of the sentence shall be suspended from the day on which he is discharged from prison under the order to the day on which he is received back into prison, so that the former day shall be reckoned and the latter shall not be reckoned as part of the sentence.

(5)   Nothing in this section shall affect the duties of the medical officer of a prison in respect of a prisoner whom the Secretary of State does not think fit to discharge under this section.

Annotations

This section does not extend to Scotland.

Discharged prisoners

[30 Payments for discharged prisoners

The Secretary of State may make such payments to or in respect of persons released or about to be released from prison as he may with the consent of the Treasury determine.]

Annotations

Substituted for existing ss 30–32 by the Criminal Justice Act 1967, s 66(3).

This section does not extend to Scotland.

Provision, maintenance and closing of prisons

33 Power to provide prisons, etc

(1)   The Secretary of State may with the approval of the Treasury alter, enlarge or rebuild any prison and build new prisons.

[(2)   The Secretary of State may provide new prisons by declaring to be a prison—

    (a)   any building or part of a building built for the purpose or vested in him or under his control; or

    (b)   any floating structure or part of such a structure constructed for the purpose or vested in him or under his control.]

(3)   A declaration under this section may with respect to the building or part of a building declared to be a prison make the same provisions as an order under the next following section may make with respect to an existing prison.

(4)   A declaration under this section may at any time be revoked by the Secretary of State.

(5)   A declaration under this section shall not be sufficient to vest the legal estate of any building in the [Secretary of State].

Annotations

Sub-s (2): substituted by the Criminal Justice and Public Order Act 1994, s 100(1).

Sub-s (5): words in square brackets substituted by SI 1963/597, art 3(2), Sch 1.

Modification: sub-s (2) modified, in relation to contracted out prisons, by the Criminal Justice and Public Order Act 1994, s 100(2), (3).

This section does not extend to Scotland.

34 Jurisdiction of sheriff, etc

(1)   The transfer under the Prison Act 1877 of prisons and of the powers and jurisdiction of prison authorities and of justices in sessions assembled and visiting justices shall not be deemed to have affected the jurisdiction of any sheriff or coroner or, except to the extent of that transfer, of any justice of the peace or other officer.

(2)   The Secretary of State may by order direct that, for the purpose of any enactment, rule of law or custom dependent on a prison being the prison of any county or place, any prison situated in that county or in the county in which that place is situated, or any prison provided by him in pursuance of this Act, shall be deemed to be the prison of that county or place.

Annotations

This section does not extend to Scotland.

[35 Prison property

(1)   Every prison and all real and personal property belonging to a prison shall be vested in the Secretary of State and may be disposed of in such manner as the Secretary of State, with the consent of the Treasury, may determine.

(2)   For the purposes of this section the Secretary of State shall be deemed to be a corporation sole.

(3)   Any instrument in connection with the acquisition, management or disposal of any property to which this section applies may be executed on behalf of the Secretary of State by an Under-Secretary of State or any other person authorised by the Secretary of State in that behalf; and any instrument purporting to have been so executed on behalf of the Secretary of State shall be deemed, until the contrary is proved, to have been so executed on his behalf.

(4)   The last foregoing subsection shall be without prejudice to the execution of any such instrument as aforesaid, or of any other instrument, on behalf of the Secretary of State in any other manner authorised by law.]

Annotations

Substituted by SI 1963/597, art 3(2), Sch 1.

See further, in relation to contracted out prisons: the Criminal Justice Act 1991, s 87 and the Criminal Justice and Public Order Act 1994, s 100(2), (4).

This section does not extend to Scotland.

36 Acquisition of land for prisons

(1)   [The Secretary of State may purchase by agreement or] compulsorily, any land required for the alteration, enlargement or rebuilding of a prison or for establishing a new prison or for any other purpose connected with the management of a prison (including the provision of accommodation for officers or servants employed in a prison).

[(2)   The [Acquisition of Land Act 1981] shall apply to the compulsory purchase of land by the Secretary of State under this section . . .]

(3)   In relation to the purchase of land by agreement under this section, [the provisions of Part I of the Compulsory Purchase Act 1965 (so far as applicable) other than sections 4 to 8, section 10, and section 31, shall apply].

Annotations

Sub-s (1): words in square brackets substituted by SI 1963/597, art 3(2), Sch 1.

Sub-s (2): substituted by SI 1963/597, art 3(2), Sch 1; words in square brackets substituted, and words omitted repealed, by the Acquisition of Land Act 1981, s 34, Sch 4, para 1, Sch 6, Part I.

Sub-s (3): words in square brackets substituted by the Compulsory Purchase Act 1965, s 38, Sch 6.

See further: the Criminal Justice Act 1988, s 167.

This section does not extend to Scotland.

37 Closing of prisons

(1)   Subject to the next following subsection, the Secretary of State may by order close any prison.

(2)   Where a prison is the only prison in the county, the Secretary of State shall not make an order under this section in respect of it except for special reasons, which shall be stated in the order.

(3)   In this section the expression 'county' means a county at large.

(4)   For the purposes of this and the next following section a prison shall not be deemed to be closed by reason only of its appropriation for use as a remand centre, [or young offender institution] [or secure training centre].

Annotations

Sub-s (4): first words in square brackets substituted by virtue of the Criminal Justice Act 1988, s 123, Sch 8, para 1; final words in square brackets inserted by the Criminal Justice and Public Order Act 1994, s 168(2), Sch 10, para 8.

This section does not extend to Scotland.

Offences

39 Assisting prisoner to escape

Any person who aids any prisoner in escaping or attempting to escape from a prison or who, with intent to facilitate the escape of any prisoner, conveys any thing into a prison or to a prisoner [sends any thing (by post or otherwise) into a prison or to a prisoner] or places any thing anywhere outside a prison with a view to its coming into the possession of a prisoner, shall be guilty of felony and liable to imprisonment for a term not exceeding [ten years].

Annotations

First words in square brackets inserted and second words in square brackets substituted, by the Prison Security Act 1992, s 2(1), (4).

Felony: this is now to be read as 'shall be guilty of an offence' by virtue of the Criminal Law Act 1967, s 12(5)(a).

This section does not extend to Scotland.

40 Unlawful conveyance of spirits or tobacco into prison, etc

Any person who contrary to the regulations of a prison brings or attempts to bring into the prison or to a prisoner any spirituous or fermented liquor or tobacco, or places any such liquor or any tobacco anywhere outside the prison with intent that it shall come into the possession of a prisoner, and any officer who contrary to those regulations allows any such liquor or any tobacco to be sold or used in the prison, shall be liable on summary conviction to imprisonment for a term not exceeding six months or a fine not exceeding [level 3 on the standard scale] or both.

Annotations

Maximum fine increased and converted to a level on the standard scale by the Criminal Justice Act 1982, ss 37, 38, 46.

This section does not extend to Scotland.

41 Unlawful introduction of other articles

Any person who contrary to the regulations of a prison conveys or attempts to convey any letter or any other thing into or out of the prison or to a prisoner or places it anywhere outside the prison with intent that it shall come into the possession of a prisoner shall, where he is not thereby guilty of an offence under either of the two last preceding sections, be liable on summary conviction to a fine not exceeding [level 3 on the standard scale].

Annotations

Maximum fine increased and converted to a level on the standard scale by the Criminal Justice Act 1982, ss 37, 38, 46.

This section does not extend to Scotland.

42 Display of notice of penalties

The Prison Commissioners shall cause to be affixed in a conspicuous place outside every prison a notice of the penalties to which persons committing offences under the three last preceding sections are liable.

Annotations

Functions of the Prison Commissioners transferred to the Secretary of State for the Home Department, by the Prison Commissioners Dissolution Order 1963, SI 1963/597.

This section does not extend to Scotland.

Remand centres [and young offender institutions]

[[43 Remand centres [and young offender institutions]

(1)   The Secretary of State may provide—

    (a)   remand centres, that is to say places for the detention of persons not less than fourteen but under 21 years of age who are remanded or committed in custody for trial or sentence;

    [(aa) young offender institutions, that is to say places for the detention of offenders sentenced to detention in a young offender institution [or to custody for life];]

    (b), (c) . . . ; [and]

    [(d)   secure training centres, that is to say places in which offenders in respect of whom detention and training orders have been made under section 73 of the Crime and Disorder Act 1998 may be detained and given training and education and prepared for their release.]

(2)   The Secretary of State may from time to time direct—

    (a)   that a woman aged 21 years or over who is serving a sentence of imprisonment or who has been committed to prison for default shall be detained in a remand centre or a [young offender institution] instead of a prison;

    (b)   that a woman aged 21 years or over who is remanded in custody or committed in custody for trial or sentence shall be detained in a remand centre instead of a prison;

    (c)   that a person under 21 but not less than 17 years of age who is remanded in custody or committed in custody for trial or sentence shall be detained in a prison instead of a remand centre or a remand centre instead of a prison, notwithstanding anything in section 27 of the Criminal Justice Act 1948 or section 23(3) of the Children and Young Persons Act 1969.

(3)   Notwithstanding subsection (1) above, any person required to be detained in an institution to which this Act applies may be detained in a remand

centre for any temporary purpose [and a person [aged 18 years] or over may be detained in such a centre] for the purpose of providing maintenance and domestic services for that centre.

(4)   Sections 5A, 6(2) and (3), 16, 22, 25 and 36 of this Act shall apply to remand centres [and young offender institutions] and to persons detained in them as they apply to prisons and prisoners.

[(4A) Sections 16, 22 and 36 of this Act shall apply to secure training centres and to persons detained in them as they apply to prisons and prisoners.]

(5)   The other provisions of this Act preceding this section, except sections 28 and 37(2) above, shall apply to [centres of the descriptions specified in subsection (4) above] and to persons detained in them as they apply to prisons and prisoners, but subject to such adaptations and modifications as may be specified in rules made by the Secretary of State.

[(5A) The other provisions of this Act preceding this section, except sections 5, 5A, 6(2) and (3), 12, 14, 19, 25, 28 and 37(2) and (3) above, shall apply to secure training centres and to persons detained in them as they apply to prisons and prisoners, but subject to such adaptations and modifications as may be specified in rules made by the Secretary of State.]

(6)   References in the preceding provisions of this Act to imprisonment shall, so far as those provisions apply to institutions provided under this section, be construed as including references to detention in those institutions.

(7)   Nothing in this section shall be taken to prejudice the operation of section 12 of the Criminal Justice Act 1982.]

Annotations

Section heading: reference to 'young offender institutions' substituted by virtue of the Criminal Justice Act 1988, s 123(6), Sch 8, para 1.

Substituted by the Criminal Justice Act 1982, s 11.

Sub-s (1): para (aa) inserted by the Criminal Justice Act 1988, s 170, Sch 15, para 11; in para (aa) words 'or to custody for life' in square brackets inserted by the Criminal Justice and Public Order Act 1994, s 18(3); para (b) repealed by the Criminal Justice Act 1988, s 170, Sch 16; word 'and' after para (b) repealed by the Criminal Justice and Public Order Act 1994, s 168(3), Sch 11; para (c) repealed by the Criminal Justice Act 1988, s 170, Sch 16; para (d) and word 'and' preceding it inserted by the Criminal Justice and Public Order Act 1994, s 5(2); para (d) substituted by the Crime and Disorder Act 1998, s 119, Sch 8, para 6.

Sub-s (2): in para (a) words in square brackets substituted by virtue of the Criminal Justice Act 1988, s 123(6), Sch 8, para 1.

Sub-s (3): first words in square brackets substituted by the Criminal Justice Act 1988, s 170(1), Sch 15, para 12, words in square brackets therein substituted by the Criminal Justice Act 1991, s 68, Sch 8, para 2.

Sub-s (4): words in square brackets substituted by virtue of the Criminal Justice Act 1988, s 123(6), Sch 8, para 1.

Sub-ss (4A), (5A): inserted by the Criminal Justice and Public Order Act 1994, s 5(3), (5).

Sub-s (5): words in square brackets substituted by the Criminal Justice and Public Order Act 1994, s 5(4).

This section does not extend to Scotland.

Rules for the management of prisons and other institutions

47 Rules for the management of prisons, remand centres [and young offender institutions]

(1)   The Secretary of State may make rules for the regulation and management of prisons, remand centres[, young offender institutions or secure training centres] respectively, and for the classification, treatment, employment, discipline and control of persons required to be detained therein.

(2)   Rules made under this section shall make provision for ensuring that a person who is charged with any offence under the rules shall be given a proper opportunity of presenting his case.

(3)   Rules made under this section may provide for the training of particular classes of persons and their allocation for that purpose to any prison or other institution in which they may lawfully be detained.

(4)   Rules made under this section shall provide for the special treatment of the following persons whilst required to be detained in a prison, that is to say—

    (a)–(c) . . .

    (d)   any . . . person detained in a prison, not being a person serving a sentence or a person imprisoned in default of payment of a sum adjudged to be paid by him on his conviction [or a person committed to custody on his conviction].

[(4A) Rules made under this section shall provide for the inspection of secure training centres and the appointment of independent persons to visit secure training centres and to whom representations may be made by offenders detained in secure training centres.]

(5)   Rules made under this section may provide for the temporary release of persons [detained in a prison, [remand centre][, young offender institution or secure training centre] not being persons committed in custody for trial [before the Crown Court] or committed to be sentenced or otherwise dealt with by [the Crown Court] or remanded in custody by any court].

Annotations

Section heading: reference to 'young offender institutions' substituted by virtue of the Criminal Justice Act 1988, s 123(6), Sch 8, paras 1, 3(2).

Sub-s (1): words in square brackets substituted by the Criminal Justice and Public Order Act 1994, s 6(2).

Sub-s (4): words omitted repealed and words in square brackets inserted, by the Criminal Justice Act 1967, ss 66(5), 103(2), Sch 7, Part I.

Sub-s (4A): inserted by the Criminal Justice and Public Order Act 1994, s 6(3).

Sub-s (5): first words in square brackets substituted by the Criminal Justice Act 1961, s 41(1), (3), Sch 4, first words in square brackets therein substituted by the Criminal Justice Act 1982, s 77, Sch 14, para 7, second words in square brackets therein substituted by the Criminal Justice and Public Order Act 1994, s 6(4), third and final words in square brackets therein substituted by the Courts Act 1971, s 56(1), Sch 8, Part II, para 33.

Subordinate Legislation

Prison Rules 1999, SI 1999/728.
Young Offender Institution (Amendment) (No 2) Rules 1999, SI 1999/962.
Young Offender Institution (Amendment) Rules 2000, SI 2000/700.
This section does not extend to Scotland.

Miscellaneous

49 Persons unlawfully at large

(1)   Any person who, having been sentenced to [imprisonment or custody for life or ordered to be detained in secure accommodation or in a young offenders institution], or having been committed to a prison or remand centre, is unlawfully at large, may be arrested by a constable without warrant and taken to the place in which he is required in accordance with law to be detained.

(2)   Where any person sentenced to [imprisonment, or ordered to be detained in secure accommodation or in a young offenders institution], is unlawfully at large at any time during the period for which he is liable to be detained in pursuance of the sentence or order, then, unless the Secretary of State otherwise directs, no account shall be taken, in calculating the period for which he is liable to be so detained, of any time during which he is absent from the [place in which he is required in accordance with law to be detained]:

Provided that—

(a)   this subsection shall not apply to any period during which any such person as aforesaid is detained in pursuance of the sentence or order or in pursuance of any other sentence of any court [in the United Kingdom] [in a prison or remand centre, in secure accommodation or in a young offenders institution];

(b), (c) . . .

(3)   The provisions of the last preceding subsection shall apply to a person who is detained in custody in default of payment of any sum of money as if he were sentenced to imprisonment.

(4)   For the purposes of this section a person who, after being temporarily released in pursuance of rules made under subsection (5) of section forty-seven of this Act, is at large at any time during the period for which he is liable to be detained in pursuance of his sentence shall be deemed to be unlawfully at large if the period for which he was temporarily released has expired or if an order recalling him has been made by the [Secretary of State] in pursuance of the rules.

[(5)   In this section 'secure accommodation' means—

(a)   a young offender institution;

(b)   a secure training centre; or

(c)   any other accommodation that is secure accommodation within the meaning given by section 75(7) of the Crime and Disorder Act 1998 (detention and training orders).]

Annotations

Sub-s (1): words from 'imprisonment or custody for life' to 'a young offenders institution' in square brackets substituted by the Crime and Disorder Act 1998, s 119, Sch 8, para 7(1).

Sub-s (2): words 'imprisonment, or ordered to be detained in secure accommodation or in a young offenders institution' in square brackets substituted by the Crime and Disorder Act 1998, s 119, Sch 8, para 7(2)(a); words 'place in which he is required in accordance with law to be detained' in square brackets substituted by the Criminal Justice Act 1982, s 77, Sch 14, para 8(b)(ii); in para (a) words 'in the United Kingdom' in square brackets inserted by the Criminal Justice Act 1961, s 30(4), Sch 4; in para (a) words 'in a prison or remand centre, in secure accommodation or in a young offenders institution' in square brackets substituted by the Crime and Disorder Act 1998, s 119, Sch 8, para 7(2)(b); para (b) repealed by the Criminal Justice Act 1982, s 78, Sch 16; para (c) repealed by the Criminal Justice Act 1961, s 41, Sch 5.

Sub-s (4): words 'Secretary of State' in square brackets substituted by SI 1963/597, art 3(2), Sch 1.

Sub-s (5): inserted by the Crime and Disorder Act 1998, s 119, Sch 8, para 7(3).

Date in force of the Crime and Disorder Act 1998 amendments: 1 April 2000 (except in relation to offenders who are subject to detention or supervision under a secure training order made before that date): see SI 1999/3426, arts 3(b), 4(4)(b).

This section does not extend to Scotland.

Supplemental

51 Payment of expenses out of moneys provided by Parliament

All expenses incurred in the maintenance of prisons and in the maintenance of prisoners and all other expenses of the Secretary of State . . . incurred under this Act shall be defrayed out of moneys provided by Parliament.

Annotations

Words omitted repealed by SI 1963/597, art 3(2), Sch 1.

This section does not extend to Scotland.

52 Exercise of power to make orders, rules and regulations

(1)   Any power of the Secretary of State to make rules or regulations under this Act and the power of the Secretary of State to make an order under section thirty-four or section thirty-seven of this Act shall be exercisable by statutory instrument.

(2)   Any statutory instrument containing regulations made under section sixteen or an order made under section thirty-seven of this Act, . . . shall be laid before Parliament.

(3)   The power of the Secretary of State to make an order under section six or section thirty-four of this Act shall include power to revoke or vary such an order.

Annotations

Sub-s (2): words omitted repealed by the Criminal Justice Act 1967, ss 66(4), 103(2), Sch 7, Part I.

This section does not extend to Scotland.

53 Interpretation

(1)   In this Act the following expressions have the following meanings:—

'Attendance centre' means a centre provided by the Secretary of State under [section 16 of the Criminal Justice Act 1982];

'Prison' does not include a naval, military or air force prison;

. . .

(2)   For the purposes of this Act the maintenance of a prisoner shall include all necessary expenses incurred in respect of the prisoner for food, clothing, custody and removal from one place to another, from the period of his committal to prison until his death or discharge from prison.

(3)   References in this Act to the Church of England shall be construed as including references to the Church in Wales.

(4)   References in this Act to any enactment shall be construed as references to that enactment as amended by any other enactment.

Annotations

Sub-s (1): words in square brackets substituted by the Criminal Justice Act 1982, s 77, Sch 14, para 9; words omitted repealed by the Children and Young Persons Act 1969, s 72(4), Sch 6.

This section does not extend to Scotland.

54 Consequential amendments, repeals and savings

(1), (2)   . . .

(3)   Nothing in this repeal shall affect any rule, order, regulation or declaration made, direction or certificate given or thing done under any enactment repealed by this Act and every such rule, order, regulation, direction, certificate or thing shall, if in force at the commencement of this Act, continue in force and be deemed to have been made, given or done under the corresponding provision of this Act.

(4)   Any document referring to any Act or enactment repealed by this Act shall be construed as referring to this Act or to the corresponding enactment in this Act.

(5)   The mention of particular matters in this section shall not be taken to affect the general application to this Act of section thirty-eight of the Interpretation Act 1889 (which relates to the effect of repeals).

Annotations

Sub-s (1): repealed by the Statute Law (Repeals) Act 1993.
Sub-s (2): repealed by the Statute Laws (Repeals) Act 1974.

This section does not extend to Scotland.

55 Short title, commencement and extent

(1)   This Act may be cited as the Prison Act 1952.

(2)   This Act shall come into operation on the first day of October, nineteen hundred and fifty-two.

(3)   . . .

(4)   Except as provided in . . . [the Criminal Justice Act 1961], this Act shall not extend to Scotland.

[(4A) *Subsections (2) to (5) of section 5A, as applied by subsection (5A) of that section, extend to Scotland.*]

(5)   This Act shall not extend to Northern Ireland.

Annotations

Sub-s (3): repealed by the Statute Law (Repeals) Act 1993.

Sub-s (4): words omitted repealed by the Statute Law (Repeals) Act 1993; words in square brackets substituted by the Criminal Justice Act 1961, s 41, Sch 4.

Sub-s (4A): inserted by the Immigration and Asylum Act 1999, s 169(1), Sch 14, para 33. Date in force: to be appointed: see the Immigration and Asylum Act 1999, s 170(4).

PRISON RULES 1999

SI 1999/728

10th March 1999

PART I
INTERPRETATION

General

1 Citation and commencement

These Rules may be cited as the Prison Rules 1999 and shall come into force on 1st April 1999.

2 Interpretation

(1)   In these Rules, where the context so admits, the expression—

'controlled drug' means any drug which is a controlled drug for the purposes of the Misuse of Drugs Act 1971;

'convicted prisoner' means, subject to the provisions of rule 7(3), a prisoner who has been convicted or found guilty of an offence or committed or attached for contempt of court or for failing to do or abstain from doing anything required to be done or left undone, and the expression 'unconvicted prisoner' shall be construed accordingly;

'governor' includes an officer for the time being in charge of a prison;

'legal adviser' means, in relation to a prisoner, his counsel or solicitor, and includes a clerk acting on behalf of his solicitor;

'officer' means an officer of a prison and, for the purposes of rule 40(2), includes a prisoner custody officer who is authorised to perform escort functions in accordance with section 89 of the Criminal Justice Act 1991;

'prison minister' means, in relation to a prison, a minister appointed to that prison under section 10 of the Prison Act 1952;

'short-term prisoner' and 'long-term prisoner' have the meanings assigned to them by section 33(5) of the Criminal Justice Act 1991, as extended by sections 43(1) and 45(1) of that Act.

(2)   In these Rules—

(a)   a reference to an award of additional days means additional days awarded under these Rules by virtue of section 42 of the Criminal Justice Act 1991;

(b)   a reference to the Church of England includes a reference to the Church in Wales; and

(c)   a reference to a numbered rule is, unless otherwise stated, a reference to the rule of that number in these Rules and a reference in a rule to a numbered paragraph is, unless otherwise stated, a reference to the paragraph of that number in that rule.

PART II
PRISONERS

General

3 Purpose of prison training and treatment

The purpose of the training and treatment of convicted prisoners shall be to encourage and assist them to lead a good and useful life.

4 Outside contacts

(1)   Special attention shall be paid to the maintenance of such relationships between a prisoner and his family as are desirable in the best interests of both.

(2)   A prisoner shall be encouraged and assisted to establish and maintain such relations with persons and agencies outside prison as may, in the opinion of the governor, best promote the interests of his family and his own social rehabilitation.

5 After care

From the beginning of a prisoner's sentence, consideration shall be given, in consultation with the appropriate after-care organisation, to the prisoner's future and the assistance to be given him on and after his release.

6 Maintenance of order and discipline

(1)   Order and discipline shall be maintained with firmness, but with no more restriction than is required for safe custody and well ordered community life.

(2)   In the control of prisoners, officers shall seek to influence them through their own example and leadership, and to enlist their willing co-operation.

(3)   At all times the treatment of prisoners shall be such as to encourage their

self-respect and a sense of personal responsibility, but a prisoner shall not be employed in any disciplinary capacity..

7 Classification of prisoners

(1)   Prisoners shall be classified, in accordance with any directions of the Secretary of State, having regard to their age, temperament and record and with a view to maintaining good order and facilitating training and, in the case of convicted prisoners, of furthering the purpose of their training and treatment as provided by rule 3.

(2)   Unconvicted prisoners:

(a)   shall be kept out of contact with convicted prisoners as far as the governor considers it can reasonably be done, unless and to the extent that they have consented to share residential accommodation or participate in any activity with convicted prisoners; and

(b)   shall under no circumstances be required to share a cell with a convicted prisoner.

(3)   Prisoners committed or attached for contempt of court, or for failing to do or abstain from doing anything required to be done or left undone:

(a)   shall be treated as a separate class for the purposes of this rule;

(b)   notwithstanding anything in this rule, may be permitted to associate with any other class of prisoners if they are willing to do so; and

(c)   shall have the same privileges as an unconvicted prisoner under rules 20(5), 23(1) and 35(1).

(4)   Nothing in this rule shall require a prisoner to be deprived unduly of the society of other persons.

8 Privileges

(1)   There shall be established at every prison systems of privileges approved by the Secretary of State and appropriate to the classes of prisoners there, which shall include arrangements under which money earned by prisoners in prison may be spent by them within the prison.

(2)   Systems of privileges approved under paragraph (1) may include arrangements under which prisoners may be allowed time outside their cells and in association with one another, in excess of the minimum time which, subject to the other provisions of these Rules apart from this rule, is otherwise allowed to prisoners at the prison for this purpose.

(3)   Systems of privileges approved under paragraph (1) may include arrangements under which privileges may be granted to prisoners only in so far as they have met, and for so long as they continue to meet, specified standards in their behaviour and their performance in work or other activities.

(4)   Systems of privileges which include arrangements of the kind referred to in paragraph (3) shall include procedures to be followed in determining whether or not any of the privileges concerned shall be granted, or shall

continue to be granted, to a prisoner; such procedures shall include a requirement that the prisoner be given reasons for any decision adverse to him together with a statement of the means by which he may appeal against it.

(5) Nothing in this rule shall be taken to confer on a prisoner any entitlement to any privilege or to affect any provision in these Rules other than this rule as a result of which any privilege may be forfeited or otherwise lost or a prisoner deprived of association with other prisoners.

9 Temporary release

(1) The Secretary of State may, in accordance with the other provisions of this rule, release temporarily a prisoner to whom this rule applies.

(2) A prisoner may be released under this rule for any period or periods and subject to any conditions.

(3) A prisoner may only be released under this rule:

    (a) on compassionate grounds or for the purpose of receiving medical treatment;

    (b) to engage in employment or voluntary work;

    (c) to receive instruction or training which cannot reasonably be provided in the prison;

    (d) to enable him to participate in any proceedings before any court, tribunal or inquiry;

    (e) to enable him to consult with his legal adviser in circumstances where it is not reasonably practicable for the consultation to take place in the prison;

    (f) to assist any police officer in any enquiries;

    (g) to facilitate the prisoner's transfer between prisons;

    (h) to assist him in maintaining family ties or in his transition from prison life to freedom; or

    (i) to enable him to make a visit in the locality of the prison, as a privilege under rule 8.

(4) A prisoner shall not be released under this rule unless the Secretary of State is satisfied that there would not be an unacceptable risk of his committing offences whilst released or otherwise failing to comply with any condition upon which he is released.

(5) The Secretary of State shall not release under this rule a prisoner serving a sentence of imprisonment if, having regard to:

    (a) the period or proportion of his sentence which the prisoner has served or, in a case where paragraph (10) does not apply to require all the sentences he is serving to be treated as a single term, the period or proportion of any such sentence he has served; and

    (b) the frequency with which the prisoner has been granted temporary release under this rule, the Secretary of State is of the opinion that the release of the prisoner would be likely to undermine public confidence in the administration of justice.

(6)   If a prisoner has been temporarily released under this rule during the relevant period and has been sentenced to imprisonment for a criminal offence committed whilst at large following that release, he shall not be released under this rule unless his release, having regard to the circumstances of this conviction, would not, in the opinion of the Secretary of State, be likely to undermine public confidence in the administration of justice.

(7)   For the purposes of paragraph (6), 'the relevant period':

(a)   in the case of a prisoner serving a determinate sentence of imprisonment, is the period he has served in respect of that sentence, unless, notwithstanding paragraph (10), the sentences he is serving do not fall to be treated as a single term, in which case it is the period since he was last released in relation to one of those sentences under Part II of the Criminal Justice Act 1991 ('the 1991 Act');

(b)   in the case of a prisoner serving an indeterminate sentence of imprisonment, is, if the prisoner has previously been released on licence under Part II of the Crime (Sentences) Act 1997 or Part II of the 1991 Act, the period since the date of his last recall to prison in respect of that sentence or, where the prisoner has not been so released, the period he has served in respect of that sentence; or

(c)   in the case of a prisoner detained in prison for any other reason, is the period for which the prisoner has been detained for that reason;

save that where a prisoner falls within two or more of sub-paragraphs (a) to (c), the 'relevant period', in the case of that prisoner, shall be determined by whichever of the applicable sub-paragraphs produces the longer period.

(8)   A prisoner released under this rule may be recalled to prison at any time whether the conditions of his release have been broken or not.

(9)   This rule applies to prisoners other than persons committed in custody for trial or to be sentenced or otherwise dealt with before or by any Crown Court or remanded in custody by any court.

(10)   For the purposes of any reference in this rule to a prisoner's sentence, consecutive terms and terms which are wholly or partly concurrent shall be treated as a single term if they would fall to be treated as a single term for the purposes of any reference to the term of imprisonment to which a person has been sentenced in Part II of the 1991 Act.

(11)   In this rule:

(a)   any reference to a sentence of imprisonment shall be construed as including any sentence to detention or custody; and

(b)   any reference to release on licence or otherwise under Part II of the 1991 Act includes any release on licence under any legislation providing for early release on licence.

10 Information to prisoners

(1) Every prisoner shall be provided, as soon as possible after his reception into prison, and in any case within 24 hours, with information in writing about those provisions of these Rules and other matters which it is necessary that he should know, including earnings and privileges, and the proper means of making requests and complaints.

(2) In the case of a prisoner aged less than 18, or a prisoner aged 18 or over who cannot read or appears to have difficulty in understanding the information so provided, the governor, or an officer deputed by him, shall so explain it to him that he can understand his rights and obligations.

(3) A copy of these Rules shall be made available to any prisoner who requests it.

11 Requests and complaints

(1) A request or complaint to the governor or board of visitors relating to a prisoner's imprisonment shall be made orally or in writing by the prisoner.

(2) On every day the governor shall hear any requests and complaints that are made to him under paragraph (1).

(3) A written request or complaint under paragraph (1) may be made in confidence.

Women prisoners

12 Women prisoners

(1) Women prisoners shall normally be kept separate from male prisoners.

(2) The Secretary of State may, subject to any conditions he thinks fit, permit a woman prisoner to have her baby with her in prison, and everything necessary for the baby's maintenance and care may be provided there.

Religion

13 Religious denomination

A prisoner shall be treated as being of the religious denomination stated in the record made in pursuance of section 10(5) of the Prison Act 1952 but the governor may, in a proper case and after due enquiry, direct that record to be amended.

14 Special duties of chaplains and prison ministers

(1) The chaplain or a prison minister of a prison shall—

   (a) interview every prisoner of his denomination individually soon after the prisoner's reception into that prison and shortly before his release; and

   (b) if no other arrangements are made, read the burial service at the funeral of any prisoner of his denomination who dies in that prison.

(2) The chaplain shall visit daily all prisoners belonging to the Church of England who are sick, under restraint or undergoing cellular confinement;

and a prison minister shall do the same, as far as he reasonably can, for prisoners of his denomination.

(3) The chaplain shall visit any prisoner not of the Church of England who is sick, under restraint or undergoing cellular confinement, and is not regularly visited by a minister of his denomination, if the prisoner is willing.

15 Regular visits by ministers of religion

(1) The chaplain shall visit the prisoners belonging to the Church of England.

(2) A prison minister shall visit the prisoners of his denomination as regularly as he reasonably can.

(3) Where a prisoner belongs to a denomination for which no prison minister has been appointed, the governor shall do what he reasonably can, if so requested by the prisoner, to arrange for him to be visited regularly by a minister of that denomination.

16 Religious services

(1) The chaplain shall conduct Divine Service for prisoners belonging to the Church of England at least once every Sunday, Christmas Day and Good Friday, and such celebrations of Holy Communion and weekday services as may be arranged.

(2) Prison ministers shall conduct Divine Service for prisoners of their denominations at such times as may be arranged.

17 Substitute for chaplain or prison minister

(1) A person approved by the Secretary of State may act for the chaplain in his absence.

(2) A prison minister may, with the leave of the Secretary of State, appoint a substitute to act for him in his absence.

18 Sunday work

Arrangements shall be made so as not to require prisoners of the Christian religion to do any unnecessary work on Sunday, Christmas Day or Good Friday, or prisoners of other religions to do any such work on their recognised days of religious observance.

19 Religious books

There shall, so far as reasonably practicable, be available for the personal use of every prisoner such religious books recognised by his denomination as are approved by the Secretary of State for use in prisons.

Medical attention

20 Medical attendance

(1) The medical officer of a prison shall have the care of the health, mental and physical, of the prisoners in that prison.

(2) Every request by a prisoner to see the medical officer shall be recorded by the officer to whom it is made and promptly passed on to the medical officer.

(3) The medical officer may consult a medical practitioner who is a fully registered person within the meaning of the Medical Act 1983. Such a practitioner may work within the prison under the general supervision of the medical officer.

(4) The medical officer shall consult another medical practitioner, if time permits, before performing any serious operation.

(5) If an unconvicted prisoner desires the attendance of a registered medical practitioner or dentist, and will pay any expense incurred, the governor shall, if he is satisfied that there are reasonable grounds for the request and unless the Secretary of State otherwise directs, allow him to be visited and treated by that practitioner or dentist in consultation with the medical officer.

(6) Subject to any directions given in the particular case by the Secretary of State, a registered medical practitioner selected by or on behalf of a prisoner who is a party to any legal proceedings shall be afforded reasonable facilities for examining him in connection with the proceedings, and may do so out of hearing but in the sight of an officer.

21 Special illnesses and conditions

(1) The medical officer or a medical practitioner such as is mentioned in rule 20(3) shall report to the governor on the case of any prisoner whose health is likely to be injuriously affected by continued imprisonment or any conditions of imprisonment. The governor shall send the report to the Secretary of State without delay, together with his own recommendations.

(2) The medical officer or a medical practitioner such as is mentioned in rule 20(3) shall pay special attention to any prisoner whose mental condition appears to require it, and make any special arrangements which appear necessary for his supervision or care.

22 Notification of illness or death

(1) If a prisoner dies, becomes seriously ill, sustains any severe injury or is removed to hospital on account of mental disorder, the governor shall, if he knows his or her address, at once inform the prisoner's spouse or next of kin, and also any person who the prisoner may reasonably have asked should be informed.

(2) If a prisoner dies, the governor shall give notice immediately to the coroner having jurisdiction, to the board of visitors and to the Secretary of State.

Physical welfare and work

23 Clothing

(1) An unconvicted prisoner may wear clothing of his own if and in so far as it is suitable, tidy and clean, and shall be permitted to arrange for the supply to him from outside prison of sufficient clean clothing:

Provided that, subject to rule 40(3):

    (a) he may be required, if and for so long as there are reasonable grounds to believe that there is a serious risk of his attempting to escape, to wear items of clothing which are distinctive by virtue of being specially marked or coloured or both; and

    (b) he may be required, if and for so long as the Secretary of State is of the opinion that he would, if he escaped, be highly dangerous to the public or the police or the security of the State, to wear clothing provided under this rule.

(2)   Subject to paragraph (1) above, the provisions of this rule shall apply to an unconvicted prisoner as to a convicted prisoner.

(3)   A convicted prisoner shall be provided with clothing adequate for warmth and health in accordance with a scale approved by the Secretary of State.

(4)   The clothing provided under this rule shall include suitable protective clothing for use at work, where this is needed.

(5)   Subject to rule 40(3), a convicted prisoner shall wear clothing provided under this rule and no other, except on the directions of the Secretary of State or as a privilege under rule 8.

(6)   A prisoner may be provided, where necessary, with suitable and adequate clothing on his release.

24 Food

(1)   Subject to any directions of the Secretary of State, no prisoner shall be allowed, except as authorised by the medical officer or a medical practitioner such as is mentioned in rule 20(3), to have any food other than that ordinarily provided.

(2)   The food provided shall be wholesome, nutritious, well prepared and served, reasonably varied and sufficient in quantity.

(3)   The medical officer, a medical practitioner such as is mentioned in rule 20(3) or any person deemed by the governor to be competent, shall from time to time inspect the food both before and after it is cooked and shall report any deficiency or defect to the governor.

(4)   In this rule 'food' includes drink.

25 Alcohol and tobacco

(1)   No prisoner shall be allowed to have any intoxicating liquor except under a written order of the medical officer or a medical practitioner such as is mentioned in rule 20(3) specifying the quantity and the name of the prisoner.

(2)   No prisoner shall be allowed to smoke or to have any tobacco except as a privilege under rule 8 and in accordance with any orders of the governor.

26 Sleeping accommodation

(1)   No room or cell shall be used as sleeping accommodation for a prisoner

unless it has been certified in the manner required by section 14 of the Prison Act 1952 in the case of a cell used for the confinement of a prisoner.

(2)   A certificate given under that section or this rule shall specify the maximum number of prisoners who may sleep or be confined at one time in the room or cell to which it relates, and the number so specified shall not be exceeded without the leave of the Secretary of State.

27 Beds and bedding

Each prisoner shall be provided with a separate bed and with separate bedding adequate for warmth and health.

28 Hygiene

(1)   Every prisoner shall be provided with toilet articles necessary for his health and cleanliness, which shall be replaced as necessary.

(2)   Every prisoner shall be required to wash at proper times, have a hot bath or shower on reception and thereafter at least once a week.

(3)   A prisoner's hair shall not be cut without his consent.

29 Physical education

(1)   If circumstances reasonably permit, a prisoner aged 21 years or over shall be given the opportunity to participate in physical education for at least one hour a week.

(2)   The following provisions shall apply to the extent circumstances reasonably permit to a prisoner who is under 21 years of age—

(a)   provision shall be made for the physical education of such a prisoner within the normal working week, as well as evening and weekend physical recreation; the physical education activities will be such as foster personal responsibility and the prisoner's interests and skills and encourage him to make good use of his leisure on release; and

(b)   arrangements shall be made for each such prisoner who is a convicted prisoner to participate in physical education for two hours a week on average.

(3)   In the case of a prisoner with a need for remedial physical activity, appropriate facilities will be provided.

(4)   The medical officer or a medical practitioner such as is mentioned in rule 20(3) shall decide upon the fitness of every prisoner for physical education and remedial physical activity and may excuse a prisoner from, or modify, any such education or activity on medical grounds.

30 Time in the open air

If the weather permits and subject to the need to maintain good order and discipline, a prisoner shall be given the opportunity to spend time in the open air at least once every day, for such period as may be reasonable in the circumstances.

31 Work

(1)   A convicted prisoner shall be required to do useful work for not more than 10 hours a day, and arrangements shall be made to allow prisoners to work, where possible, outside the cells and in association with one another.

(2)   The medical officer or a medical practitioner such as is mentioned in rule 20(3) may excuse a prisoner from work on medical grounds, and no prisoner shall be set to do work which is not of a class for which he has been passed by the medical officer or by a medical practitioner such as is mentioned in rule 20(3) as being fit.

(3)   No prisoner shall be set to do work of a kind not authorised by the Secretary of State.

(4)   No prisoner shall work in the service of another prisoner or an officer, or for the private benefit of any person, without the authority of the Secretary of State.

(5)   An unconvicted prisoner shall be permitted, if he wishes, to work as if he were a convicted prisoner.

(6)   Prisoners may be paid for their work at rates approved by the Secretary of State, either generally or in relation to particular cases.

Education and library

32 Education

(1)   Every prisoner able to profit from the education facilities provided at a prison shall be encouraged to do so.

(2)   Educational classes shall be arranged at every prison and, subject to any directions of the Secretary of State, reasonable facilities shall be afforded to prisoners who wish to do so to improve their education by training by distance learning, private study and recreational classes, in their spare time.

(3)   Special attention shall be paid to the education and training of prisoners with special educational needs, and if necessary they shall be taught within the hours normally allotted to work.

(4)   In the case of a prisoner of compulsory school age as defined in section 8 of the Education Act 1996, arrangements shall be made for his participation in education or training courses for at least 15 hours a week within the normal working week.

33 Library

A library shall be provided in every prison and, subject to any directions of the Secretary of State, every prisoner shall be allowed to have library books and to exchange them.

Communications

34 Communications generally

(1)   The Secretary of State may, with a view to securing discipline and good

order or the prevention of crime or in the interests of any persons, impose restrictions, either generally or in a particular case, upon the letters or other communications to be permitted between a prisoner and other persons.

(2)   Without prejudice to the generality of paragraph (1), the Secretary of State may require that any visit, or class of visits, shall be held in facilities which include special features restricting or preventing physical contact between a prisoner and a visitor.

(3)   Without prejudice to sections 6 and 9 of the Prison Act 1952, and except as provided by these Rules, a prisoner shall not be permitted to communicate with any outside person, or that person with him, without the leave of the Secretary of State or as a privilege under rule 8.

(4)   Except as provided by these Rules, every letter or other communication to or from a prisoner may be read, listened to, logged, recorded or examined by the governor or an officer deputed by him, and the governor may, at his discretion, stop any letter or other communication on the ground that its contents are objectionable or that it is of inordinate length.

(5)   Every visit to a prisoner shall take place within the sight of an officer, unless the Secretary of State otherwise directs.

(6)   Except as provided by these Rules, every visit to a prisoner shall take place within the hearing of an officer, unless the Secretary of State otherwise directs.

(7)   The Secretary of State may give directions, generally or in relation to any visit or class of visits, concerning the day and times when prisoners may be visited.

(8)   In this rule:

'communications' includes communications during or by means of visits or by means of a telecommunications system or telecommunications apparatus, and 'telecommunications apparatus' has the meaning assigned by paragraph 1 of Schedule 2 to the Telecommunications Act 1984.

35 Personal letters and visits

(1)   Subject to paragraph (8), an unconvicted prisoner may send and receive as many letters and may receive as many visits as he wishes within such limits and subject to such conditions as the Secretary of State may direct, either generally or in a particular case.

(2)   Subject to paragraph (8), a convicted prisoner shall be entitled—

(a)   to send and to receive a letter on his reception into a prison and thereafter once a week; and

(b)   to receive a visit twice in every period of four weeks, but only once in every such period if the Secretary of State so directs.

(3)   The governor may allow a prisoner an additional letter or visit as a privilege under rule 8 or where necessary for his welfare or that of his family.

(4)   The governor may allow a prisoner entitled to a visit to send and to receive a letter instead.

(5)   The governor may defer the right of a prisoner to a visit until the expiration of any period of cellular confinement.

(6)   The board of visitors may allow a prisoner an additional letter or visit in special circumstances, and may direct that a visit may extend beyond the normal duration.

(7)   The Secretary of State may allow additional letters and visits in relation to any prisoner or class of prisoners.

(8)   A prisoner shall not be entitled under this rule to receive a visit from:

(a)   any person, whether or not a relative or friend, during any period of time that person is the subject of a prohibition imposed under rule 73; or

(b)   any other person, other than a relative or friend, except with the leave of the Secretary of State.

(9)   Any letter or visit under the succeeding provisions of these Rules shall not be counted as a letter or visit for the purposes of this rule.

36 Police interviews

A police officer may, on production of an order issued by or on behalf of a chief officer of police, interview any prisoner willing to see him.

37 Securing release

A person detained in prison in default of finding a surety, or of payment of a sum of money, may communicate with and be visited at any reasonable time on a weekday by any relative or friend to arrange for a surety or payment in order to secure his release from prison.

38 Legal advisers

(1)   The legal adviser of a prisoner in any legal proceedings, civil or criminal, to which the prisoner is a party shall be afforded reasonable facilities for interviewing him in connection with those proceedings, and may do so out of hearing but in the sight of an officer.

(2)   A prisoner's legal adviser may, subject to any directions given by the Secretary of State, interview the prisoner in connection with any other legal business out of hearing but in the sight of an officer.

39 Correspondence with legal advisers and courts

(1)   A prisoner may correspond with his legal adviser and any court and such correspondence may only be opened, read or stopped by the governor in accordance with the provisions of this rule.

(2)   Correspondence to which this rule applies may be opened if the governor has reasonable cause to believe that it contains an illicit enclosure and any

such enclosures shall be dealt with in accordance with the other provision of these Rules.

(3) Correspondence to which this rule applies may be opened, read and stopped if the governor has reasonable cause to believe its contents endanger prison security or the safety of others or are otherwise of a criminal nature.

(4) A prisoner shall be given the opportunity to be present when any correspondence to which this rule applies is opened and shall be informed if it or any enclosure is to be read or stopped.

(5) A prisoner shall on request be provided with any writing materials necessary for the purposes of paragraph (1).

(6) In this rule, 'court' includes the European Commission of Human Rights, the European Court of Human Rights and the European Court of Justice; and 'illicit enclosure' includes any article possession of which has not been authorised in accordance with the other provisions of these Rules and any correspondence to or from a person other than the prisoner concerned, his legal adviser or a court.

Removal, search, record and property

40 Custody outside prison

(1) A person being taken to or from a prison in custody shall be exposed as little as possible to public observation, and proper care shall be taken to protect him from curiosity and insult.

(2) A prisoner required to be taken in custody anywhere outside a prison shall be kept in the custody of an officer appointed or a police officer.

(3) A prisoner required to be taken in custody to any court shall, when he appears before the court, wear his own clothing or ordinary civilian clothing provided by the governor.

41 Search

(1) Every prisoner shall be searched when taken into custody by an officer, on his reception into a prison and subsequently as the governor thinks necessary or as the Secretary of State may direct.

(2) A prisoner shall be searched in as seemly a manner as is consistent with discovering anything concealed.

(3) No prisoner shall be stripped and searched in the sight of another prisoner, or in the sight of a person of the opposite sex.

42 Record and photograph

(1) A personal record of each prisoner shall be prepared and maintained in such manner as the Secretary of State may direct.

(2) Every prisoner may be photographed on reception and subsequently, but no copy of the photograph shall be given to any person not authorised to receive it.

43 Prisoners' property

(1) Subject to any directions of the Secretary of State, an unconvicted prisoner may have supplied to him at his expense and retain for his own use books, newspapers, writing materials and other means of occupation, except any that appears objectionable to the board of visitors or, pending consideration by them, to the governor.

(2) Anything, other than cash, which a prisoner has at a prison and which he is not allowed to retain for his own use shall be taken into the governor's custody. An inventory of a prisoner's property shall be kept, and he shall be required to sign it, after having a proper opportunity to see that it is correct.

(3) Any cash which a prisoner has at a prison shall be paid into an account under the control of the governor and the prisoner shall be credited with the amount in the books of the prison.

(4) Any article belonging to a prisoner which remains unclaimed for a period of more than 3 years after he leaves prison, or dies, may be sold or otherwise disposed of; and the net proceeds of any sale shall be paid to the National Association for the Care and Resettlement of Offenders, for its general purposes.

(5) The governor may confiscate any unauthorised article found in the possession of a prisoner after his reception into prison, or concealed or deposited anywhere within a prison.

44 Money and articles received by post

(1) Any money or other article (other than a letter or other communication) sent to a convicted prisoner through the post office shall be dealt with in accordance with the provisions of this rule, and the prisoner shall be informed of the manner in which it is dealt with.

(2) Any cash shall, at the discretion of the governor, be—

   (a) dealt with in accordance with rule 43(3);

   (b) returned to the sender; or

   (c) in a case where the sender's name and address are not known, paid to the National Association for the Care and Resettlement of Offenders, for its general purposes:

   Provided that in relation to a prisoner committed to prison in default of payment of any sum of money, the prisoner shall be informed of the receipt of the cash and, unless he objects to its being so applied, it shall be applied in or towards the satisfaction of the amount due from him.

(3) Any security for money shall, at the discretion of the governor, be—

   (a) delivered to the prisoner or placed with his property at the prison;

   (b) returned to the sender; or

   (c) encashed and the cash dealt with in accordance with paragraph (2).

(4)   Any other article to which this rule applies shall, at the discretion of the governor, be—

   (a)   delivered to the prisoner or placed with his property at the prison;

   (b)   returned to the sender; or

   (c)   in a case where the sender's name and address are not known or the article is of such a nature that it would be unreasonable to return it, sold or otherwise disposed of, and the net proceeds of any sale applied in accordance with paragraph (2).

Special control, supervision and restraint and drug testing

45 Removal from association

(1)   Where it appears desirable, for the maintenance of good order or discipline or in his own interests, that a prisoner should not associate with other prisoners, either generally or for particular purposes, the governor may arrange for the prisoner's removal from association accordingly.

(2)   A prisoner shall not be removed under this rule for a period of more than 3 days without the authority of a member of the board of visitors or of the Secretary of State. An authority given under this paragraph shall be for a period not exceeding one month, but may be renewed from month to month except that, in the case of a person aged less than 21 years who is detained in prison such an authority shall be for a period not exceeding 14 days, but may be renewed from time to time for a like period.

(3)   The governor may arrange at his discretion for such a prisoner as aforesaid to resume association with other prisoners, and shall do so if in any case the medical officer or a medical practitioner such as is mentioned in rule 20(3) so advises on medical grounds.

(4)   This rule shall not apply to a prisoner the subject of a direction given under rule 46(1).

46 Close supervision centres

(1)   Where it appears desirable, for the maintenance of good order or discipline or to ensure the safety of officers, prisoners or any other person, that a prisoner should not associate with other prisoners, either generally or for particular purposes, the Secretary of State may direct the prisoner's removal from association accordingly and his placement in a close supervision centre of a prison.

(2)   A direction given under paragraph (1) shall be for a period not exceeding one month, but may be renewed from time to time for a like period.

(3)   The Secretary of State may direct that such a prisoner as aforesaid shall resume association with other prisoners, either within a close supervision centre or elsewhere.

(4)   In exercising any discretion under this rule, the Secretary of State shall take account of any relevant medical considerations which are known to him.

47 Use of force

(1)   An officer in dealing with a prisoner shall not use force unnecessarily and, when the application of force to a prisoner is necessary, no more force than is necessary shall be used.

(2)   No officer shall act deliberately in a manner calculated to provoke a prisoner.

48 Temporary confinement

(1)   The governor may order a refractory or violent prisoner to be confined temporarily in a special cell, but a prisoner shall not be so confined as a punishment, or after he has ceased to be refractory or violent.

(2)   A prisoner shall not be confined in a special cell for longer than 24 hours without a direction in writing given by a member of a board of visitors or by an officer of the Secretary of State (not being an officer of a prison). Such a direction shall state the grounds for the confinement and the time during which it may continue.

49 Restraints

(1)   The governor may order a prisoner to be put under restraint where this is necessary to prevent the prisoner from injuring himself or others, damaging property or creating a disturbance.

(2)   Notice of such an order shall be given without delay to a member of the board of visitors, and to the medical officer or to a medical practitioner such as is mentioned in rule 20(3).

(3)   On receipt of the notice, the medical officer, or the medical practitioner referred to in paragraph (2), shall inform the governor whether there are any medical reasons why the prisoner should not be put under restraint. The governor shall give effect to any recommendation which may be made under this paragraph.

(4)   A prisoner shall not be kept under restraint longer than necessary, nor shall he be so kept for longer than 24 hours without a direction in writing given by a member of the board of visitors or by an officer of the Secretary of State (not being an officer of a prison). Such a direction shall state the grounds for the restraint and the time during which it may continue.

(5)   Particulars of every case of restraint under the foregoing provisions of this rule shall be forthwith recorded.

(6)   Except as provided by this rule no prisoner shall be put under restraint otherwise than for safe custody during removal, or on medical grounds by direction of the medical officer or of a medical practitioner such as is mentioned in rule 20(3). No prisoner shall be put under restraint as a punishment.

(7)   Any means of restraint shall be of a pattern authorised by the Secretary of State, and shall be used in such manner and under such conditions as the Secretary of State may direct.

50 Compulsory testing for controlled drugs

(1)   This rule applies where an officer, acting under the powers conferred by section 16A of the Prison Act 1952 (power to test prisoners for drugs), requires a prisoner to provide a sample for the purpose of ascertaining whether he has any controlled drug in his body.

(2)   In this rule 'sample' means a sample of urine or any other description of sample specified in the authorisation by the governor for the purposes of section 16A of the Prison Act 1952.

(3)   When requiring a prisoner to provide a sample, an officer shall, so far as is reasonably practicable, inform the prisoner:

   (a)   that he is being required to provide a sample in accordance with section 16A of the Prison Act 1952; and

   (b)   that a refusal to provide a sample may lead to disciplinary proceedings being brought against him.

(4)   An officer shall require a prisoner to provide a fresh sample, free from any adulteration.

(5)   An officer requiring a sample shall make such arrangements and give the prisoner such instructions for its provision as may be reasonably necessary in order to prevent or detect its adulteration or falsification.

(6)   A prisoner who is required to provide a sample may be kept apart from other prisoners for a period not exceeding one hour to enable arrangements to be made for the provision of the sample.

(7)   A prisoner who is unable to provide a sample of urine when required to do so may be kept apart from other prisoners until he has provided the required sample, save that a prisoner may not be kept apart under this paragraph for a period of more than 5 hours.

(8)   A prisoner required to provide a sample of urine shall be afforded such degree of privacy for the purposes of providing the sample as may be compatible with the need to prevent or detect any adulteration or falsification of the sample; in particular a prisoner shall not be required to provide such a sample in the sight of a person of the opposite sex.

Offences against discipline

51 Offences against discipline

A prisoner is guilty of an offence against discipline if he—

(1)   commits any assault;

(2)   detains any person against his will;

(3)   denies access to any part of the prison to any officer or any person (other than a prisoner) who is at the prison for the purpose of working there;

(4)   fights with any person;

(5)   intentionally endangers the health or personal safety of others or, by his conduct, is reckless whether such health or personal safety is endangered;

(6)   intentionally obstructs an officer in the execution of his duty, or any person (other than a prisoner) who is at the prison for the purpose of working there, in the performance of his work;

(7)   escapes or absconds from prison or from legal custody;

(8)   fails to comply with any condition upon which he is temporarily released under rule 9;

(9)   administers a controlled drug to himself or fails to prevent the administration of a controlled drug to him by another person (but subject to rule 52);

(10) is intoxicated as a consequence of knowingly consuming any alcoholic beverage;

(11) knowingly consumes any alcoholic beverage other than that provided to him pursuant to a written order under rule 25(1);

(12) has in his possession—

(a)   any unauthorised article, or

(b)   a greater quantity of any article than he is authorised to have;

(13) sells or delivers to any person any unauthorised article;

(14) sells or, without permission, delivers to any person any article which he is allowed to have only for his own use;

(15) takes improperly any article belonging to another person or to a prison;

(16) intentionally or recklessly sets fire to any part of a prison or any other property, whether or not his own;

(17) destroys or damages any part of a prison or any other property, other than his own;

(18) absents himself from any place he is required to be or is present at any place where he is not authorised to be;

(19) is disrespectful to any officer, or any person (other than a prisoner) who is at the prison for the purpose of working there, or any person visiting a prison;

(20) uses threatening, abusive or insulting words or behaviour;

(21) intentionally fails to work properly or, being required to work, refuses to do so;

(22) disobeys any lawful order;

(23) disobeys or fails to comply with any rule or regulation applying to him;

(24) receives any controlled drug, or, without the consent of an officer, any other article, during the course of a visit (not being an interview such as is mentioned in rule 38);

(25)

(a)   attempts to commit,

(b)   incites another prisoner to commit, or

(c)   assists another prisoner to commit or to attempt to commit, any of the foregoing offences.

52 Defences to rule 51(9)

It shall be a defence for a prisoner charged with an offence under rule 51(9) to show that:

(a)   the controlled drug had been, prior to its administration, lawfully in his possession for his use or was administered to him in the course of a lawful supply of the drug to him by another person;

(b)   the controlled drug was administered by or to him in circumstances in which he did not know and had no reason to suspect that such a drug was being administered; or

(c)   the controlled drug was administered by or to him under duress or to him without his consent in circumstances where it was not reasonable for him to have resisted.

53 Disciplinary charges

(1)   Where a prisoner is to be charged with an offence against discipline, the charge shall be laid as soon as possible and, save in exceptional circumstances, within 48 hours of the discovery of the offence.

(2)   Every charge shall be inquired into by the governor.

(3)   Every charge shall be first inquired into not later, save in exceptional circumstances, than the next day, not being a Sunday or public holiday, after it is laid.

(4)   A prisoner who is to be charged with an offence against discipline may be kept apart from other prisoners pending the governor's first inquiry.

54 Rights of prisoners charged

(1)   Where a prisoner is charged with an offence against discipline, he shall be informed of the charge as soon as possible and, in any case, before the time when it is inquired into by the governor.

(2)   At an inquiry into a charge against a prisoner he shall be given a full opportunity of hearing what is alleged against him and of presenting his own case.

55 Governor's punishments

(1)   If he finds a prisoner guilty of an offence against discipline the governor may, subject to paragraph (2) and to rule 57, impose one or more of the following punishments:

(a)   caution;

(b)   forfeiture for a period not exceeding 42 days of any of the privileges under rule 8;

(c)   exclusion from associated work for a period not exceeding 21 days;

(d) stoppage of or deduction from earnings for a period not exceeding 84 days and of an amount not exceeding 42 days earnings;

(e) cellular confinement for a period not exceeding 14 days;

(f) in the case of a short-term or long-term prisoner, an award of additional days not exceeding 42 days;

(g) in the case of a prisoner otherwise entitled to them, forfeiture for any period of the right, under rule 43(1), to have the articles there mentioned.

(2) An award of a caution shall not be combined with any other punishment for the same charge.

(3) If a prisoner is found guilty of more than one charge arising out of an incident, punishments under this rule may be ordered to run consecutively but, in the case of an award of additional days, the total period added shall not exceed 42 days and, in the case of an award of cellular confinement, the total period shall not exceed 14 days.

(4) In imposing a punishment under this rule, the governor shall take into account any guidelines that the Secretary of State may from time to time issue as to the level of punishment that should normally be imposed for a particular offence against discipline.

56 Forfeiture of remission to be treated as an award of additional days

(1) In this rule, 'existing prisoner' and 'existing licensee' have the meanings assigned to them by paragraph 8(1) of Schedule 12 to the Criminal Justice Act 1991.

(2) In relation to any existing prisoner or existing licensee who has forfeited any remission of his sentence, the provisions of Part II of the Criminal Justice Act 1991 shall apply as if he had been awarded such number of additional days as equals the numbers of days of remission which he has forfeited.

57 Offences committed by young persons

(1)

(a) the maximum period of forfeiture of privileges under rule 8 shall be 21 days;

(b) the maximum period of stoppage of or deduction from earnings shall be 42 days and the maximum amount shall be 21 days;

(c) the maximum period of cellular confinement shall be 7 days.

(2) In the case of an inmate who has been sentenced to a term of youth custody or detention in a young offender institution, and by virtue of a direction of the Secretary of State under section 13 of the Criminal Justice Act 1982, is treated as if he had been sentenced to imprisonment for that term, any punishment imposed on him for an offence against discipline before the said direction was given shall, if it has not been exhausted or remitted, continue to have effect as if made pursuant to rule 55.

58 Cellular confinement

When it is proposed to impose a punishment of cellular confinement, the medical officer, or a medical practitioner such as is mentioned in rule 20(3), shall inform the governor whether there are any medical reasons why the prisoner should not be so dealt with. The governor shall give effect to any recommendation which may be made under this rule.

59 Prospective award of additional days

(1) Subject to paragraph (2), where an offence against discipline is committed by a prisoner who is detained only on remand, additional days may be awarded notwithstanding that the prisoner has not (or had not at the time of the offence) been sentenced.

(2) An award of additional days under paragraph (1) shall have effect only if the prisoner in question subsequently becomes a short-term or long-term prisoner whose sentence is reduced, under section 67 of the Criminal Justice Act 1967, by a period which includes the time when the offence against discipline was committed.

60 Suspended punishments

(1) Subject to any directions given by the Secretary of State, the power to impose a disciplinary punishment (other than a caution) shall include power to direct that the punishment is not to take effect unless, during a period specified in the direction (not being more than six months from the date of the direction), the prisoner commits another offence against discipline and a direction is given under paragraph (2).

(2) Where a prisoner commits an offence against discipline during the period specified in a direction given under paragraph (1) the person dealing with that offence may—

  (a) direct that the suspended punishment shall take effect;

  (b) reduce the period or amount of the suspended punishment and direct that it shall take effect as so reduced;

  (c) vary the original direction by substituting for the period specified a period expiring not later than six months from the date of variation; or

  (d) give no direction with respect to the suspended punishment.

61 Remission and mitigation of punishments and quashing of findings of guilt

(1) The Secretary of State may quash any finding of guilt and may remit any punishment or mitigate it either by reducing it or by substituting another award which is, in his opinion, less severe.

(2) Subject to any directions given by the Secretary of State, the governor may remit or mitigate any punishment imposed by a governor or the board of visitors.

PART III

OFFICERS OF PRISONS

62 General duty of officers

(1)   It shall be the duty of every officer to conform to these Rules and the rules and regulations of the prison, to assist and support the governor in their maintenance and to obey his lawful instructions.

(2)   An officer shall inform the governor promptly of any abuse or impropriety which comes to his knowledge.

63 Gratuities forbidden

No officer shall receive any unauthorised fee, gratuity or other consideration in connection with his office.

64 Search of officers

An officer shall submit himself to be searched in the prison if the governor so directs. Any such search shall be conducted in as seemly a manner as is consistent with discovering anything concealed.

65 Transactions with prisoners

(1)   No officer shall take part in any business or pecuniary transaction with or on behalf of a prisoner without the leave of the Secretary of State.

(2)   No officer shall without authority bring in or take out, or attempt to bring in or take out, or knowingly allow to be brought in or taken out, to or for a prisoner, or deposit in any place with intent that it shall come into the possession of a prisoner, any article whatsoever.

66 Contact with former prisoners

No officer shall, without the knowledge of the governor, communicate with any person whom he knows to be a former prisoner or a relative or friend of a prisoner or former prisoner.

67 Communications to the press

(1)   No officer shall make, directly or indirectly, any unauthorised communication to a representative of the press or any other person concerning matters which have become known to him in the course of his duty.

(2)   No officer shall, without authority, publish any matter or make any public pronouncement relating to the administration of any institution to which the Prison Act 1952 applies or to any of its inmates.

68 Code of discipline

The Secretary of State may approve a code of discipline to have effect in relation to officers, or such classes of officers as it may specify, setting out the offences against discipline, the awards which may be made in respect of them and the procedure for dealing with charges.

69 Emergencies

Where any constable or member of the armed forces of the Crown is employed by reason of any emergency to assist the governor of a prison by performing duties ordinarily performed by an officer of a prison, any reference in Part II of these Rules to such an officer (other than a governor) shall be construed as including a reference to a constable or a member of the armed forces of the Crown so employed.

PART IV

PERSONS HAVING ACCESS TO A PRISON

70 Prohibited articles

No person shall, without authority, convey into or throw into or deposit in a prison, or convey or throw out of a prison, or convey to a prisoner, or deposit in any place with intent that it shall come into the possession of a prisoner, any money, clothing, food, drink, tobacco, letter, paper, book, tool, controlled drug, firearm, explosive, weapon or other article whatever. Anything so conveyed, thrown or deposited may be confiscated by the governor.

71 Control of persons and vehicles

(1)   Any person or vehicle entering or leaving a prison may be stopped, examined and searched. Any such search of a person shall be carried out in as seemly a manner as is consistent with discovering anything concealed.

(2)   The governor may direct the removal from a prison of any person who does not leave on being required to do so.

72 Viewing of prisons

(1)   No outside person shall be permitted to view a prison unless authorised by statute or the Secretary of State.

(2)   No person viewing the prison shall be permitted to take a photograph, make a sketch or communicate with a prisoner unless authorised by statute or the Secretary of State.

73 Visitors

(1)   Without prejudice to any other powers to prohibit or restrict entry to prisons, and to his powers under rules 34 and 35, the Secretary of State may, with a view to securing discipline and good order or the prevention of crime or in the interests of any persons, impose prohibitions on visits by a person to a prison or to a prisoner in a prison for such periods of time as he considers necessary.

(2)   Paragraph (1) shall not apply in relation to any visit to a prison or prisoner by a member of the board of visitors of the prison, or justice of the peace, or to prevent any visit by a legal adviser for the purposes of an interview under rule 38 or visit allowed by the board of visitors under rule 35(6).

PART V
BOARDS OF VISITORS

74 Disqualification for membership

Any person, directly or indirectly interested in any contract for the supply of goods and services to a prison, shall not be a member of the board of visitors for that prison and any member who becomes so interested in such a contract shall vacate office as a member.

75 Board of visitors

(1) A member of the board of visitors for a prison appointed by the Secretary of State under section 6(2) of the Prison Act 1952 shall subject to paragraphs (3) and (4) hold office for three years, or such lesser period as the Secretary of State may appoint.

(2) A member—

    (a) appointed for the first time to the board of visitors for a particular prison; or

    (b) reappointed to the board following a gap of a year or more in his membership of it,

shall, during the period of 12 months following the date on which he is so appointed or (as the case may be) reappointed, undertake such training as may reasonably be required by the Secretary of State.

(3) The Secretary of State may terminate the appointment of a member if he is satisfied that—

    (a) he has failed satisfactorily to perform his duties;

    (b) he has failed to undertake training he has been required to undertake under paragraph (2), by the end of the period specified in that paragraph;

    (c) he is by reason of physical or mental illness, or for any other reason, incapable of carrying out his duties;

    (d) he has been convicted of such a criminal offence, or his conduct has been such, that it is not in the Secretary of State's opinion fitting that he should remain a member; or

    (e) there is, or appears to be or could appear to be, any conflict of interest between the member performing his duties as a member and any interest of that member, whether personal, financial or otherwise.

(4) Where the Secretary of State:

    (a) has reason to suspect that a member of the board of visitors for a prison may have so conducted himself that his appointment may be liable to be terminated under paragraph (3)(a) or (d); and

    (b) is of the opinion that the suspected conduct is of such a serious nature that the member cannot be permitted to continue to perform his functions as a member of the board pending the completion of the

Secretary of State's investigations into the matter and any decision as to whether the member's appointment should be terminated,

he may suspend the member from office for such period or periods as he may reasonably require in order to complete his investigations and determine whether or not the appointment of the member should be so terminated; and a member so suspended shall not, during the period of his suspension, be regarded as being a member of the board, other than for the purposes of this paragraph and paragraphs (1) and (3).

(5)   A board shall have a chairman and a vice chairman who shall be members of the board.

(6)   The Secretary of State shall—

(a)   upon the constitution of a board for the first time, appoint a chairman and a vice chairman to hold office for a period not exceeding twelve months;

(b)   thereafter appoint, before the date of the first meeting of the board in any year of office of the board, a chairman and vice chairman for that year, having first consulted the board; and

(c)   promptly fill, after first having consulted the board, any casual vacancy in the office of chairman or vice chairman.

(7)   The Secretary of State may terminate the appointment of a member as chairman or vice chairman of the board if he is satisfied that the member has—

(a)   failed satisfactorily to perform his functions as chairman (or as the case may be) vice chairman;

(b)   has grossly misconducted himself while performing those functions.

76 Proceedings of boards

(1)   The board of visitors for a prison shall meet at the prison once a month or, if they resolve for reasons specified in the resolution that less frequent meetings are sufficient, not fewer than eight times in twelve months.

(2)   The board may fix a quorum of not fewer than three members for proceedings.

(3)   The board shall keep minutes of their proceedings.

(4)   The proceedings of the board shall not be invalidated by any vacancy in the membership or any defect in the appointment of a member.

77 General duties of boards

(1)   The board of visitors for a prison shall satisfy themselves as to the state of the prison premises, the administration of the prison and the treatment of the prisoners.

(2)   The board shall inquire into and report upon any matter into which the Secretary of State asks them to inquire.

(3)   The board shall direct the attention of the governor to any matter which calls for his attention, and shall report to the Secretary of State any matter which they consider it expedient to report.

(4)   The board shall inform the Secretary of State immediately of any abuse which comes to their knowledge.

(5)   Before exercising any power under these Rules the board and any member of the board shall consult the governor in relation to any matter which may affect discipline.

78 Particular duties

(1)   The board of visitors for a prison and any member of the board shall hear any complaint or request which a prisoner wishes to make to them or him.

(2)   The board shall arrange for the food of the prisoners to be inspected by a member of the board at frequent intervals.

(3)   The board shall inquire into any report made to them, whether or not by a member of the board, that a prisoner's health, mental or physical, is likely to be injuriously affected by any conditions of his imprisonment.

79 Members visiting prisons

(1)   The members of the board of visitors for a prison shall visit the prison frequently, and the board shall arrange a rota whereby at least one of its members visits the prison between meetings of the board.

(2)   A member of the board shall have access at any time to every part of the prison and to every prisoner, and he may interview any prisoner out of the sight and hearing of officers.

(3)   A member of the board shall have access to the records of the prison.

80 Annual report

(1)   The board of visitors for a prison shall, in accordance with paragraphs (2) and (3) below, from time to time make a report to the Secretary of State concerning the state of the prison and its administration, including in it any advice and suggestions they consider appropriate.

(2)   The board shall comply with any directions given to them from time to time by the Secretary of State as to the following matters:

(a)   the period to be covered by a report under paragraph (1);

(b)   the frequency with which such a report is to be made; and

(c)   the length of time from the end of the period covered by such a report within which it is to be made;

either in respect of a particular report or generally; providing that no directions may be issued under this paragraph if they would have the effect of requiring a board to make or deliver a report less frequently than once in every 12 months.

(3)   Subject to any directions given to them under paragraph (2), the board

shall, under paragraph (1), make an annual report to the Secretary of State as soon as reasonably possible after 31st December each year, which shall cover the period of 12 months ending on that date or, in the case of a board constituted for the first time during that period, such part of that period during which the board has been in existence.

PART VI

SUPPLEMENTAL

81 Delegation by governor

The governor of a prison may, with the leave of the Secretary of State, delegate any of his powers and duties under these Rules to another officer of that prison.

82 Contracted out prisons

(1)   Where the Secretary of State has entered into a contract for the running of a prison under section 84 of the Criminal Justice Act 1991 ('the 1991 Act') these Rules shall have effect in relation to that prison with the following modifications—

    (a)   references to an officer in the Rules shall include references to a prisoner custody officer certified as such under section 89(1) of the 1991 Act and performing custodial duties;

    (b)   references to a governor in the Rules shall include references to a director approved by the Secretary of State for the purposes of section 85(1)(a) of the 1991 Act except—

        (i)   in rules 45, 48, 49, 53, 54, 55, 61 and 81 where references to a governor shall include references to a controller appointed by the Secretary of State under section 85(1)(b) of the 1991 Act, and

        (ii)   in rules 62(1), 66 and 77 where references to a governor shall include references to the director and the controller;

    (c)   rule 68 shall not apply in relation to a prisoner custody officer certified as such under section 89(1) of the 1991 Act and performing custodial duties.

(2)   Where a director exercises the powers set out in section 85(3)(b) of the 1991 Act (removal from association, temporary confinement and restraints) in cases of urgency, he shall notify the controller of that fact forthwith.

83 Contracted out parts of prisons

Where the Secretary of State has entered into a contract for the running of part of a prison under section 84(1) of the Criminal Justice Act 1991, that part and the remaining part shall each be treated for the purposes of Parts II to IV and Part VI of these Rules as if they were separate prisons.

84 Contracted out functions at directly managed prisons

(1)   Where the Secretary of State has entered into a contract under section 88A(1) of the Criminal Justice Act 1991 ('the 1991 Act') for any functions

at a directly managed prison to be performed by prisoner custody officers who are authorised to perform custodial duties under section 89(1) of the 1991 Act, references to an officer in these Rules shall, subject to paragraph (2), include references to a prisoner custody officer who is so authorised and who is performing contracted out functions for the purposes of, or for purposes connected with, the prison.

(2)   Paragraph (1) shall not apply to references to an officer in rule 68.

(3)   In this rule, 'directly managed prison' has the meaning assigned to it by section 88A(5) of the 1991 Act.

85 Revocations and savings

(1)   Subject to paragraphs (2) and (3) below, the Rules specified in the Schedule to these Rules are hereby revoked.

(2)   Without prejudice to the Interpretation Act 1978, where a prisoner committed an offence against discipline contrary to rule 47 of the Prison Rules 1964 prior to the coming into force of these Rules, those rules shall continue to have effect to permit the prisoner to be charged with such an offence, disciplinary proceedings in relation to such an offence to be continued, and the governor to impose punishment for such an offence.

(3)   Without prejudice to the Interpretation Act 1978, any award of additional days or other punishment or suspended punishment for an offence against discipline awarded or imposed under any provision of the rules revoked by this rule, or those rules as saved by paragraph (2), or treated by any such provision as having been awarded or imposed under the rules revoked by this rule, shall have effect as if awarded or imposed under the corresponding provision of these Rules

SCHEDULE

rule 85

Rules Revoked	SI number
The Prison Rules 1964	1964/388
The Prison (Amendment) Rules 1968	1968/440
The Prison (Amendment) Rules 1971	1971/2019
The Prison (Amendment) Rules 1972	1972/1860
The Prison (Amendment) Rules 1974	1974/713
The Prison (Amendment) Rules 1976	1976/503
The Prison (Amendment) Rules 1981	1981/70
The Prison (Amendment) Rules 1982	1982/260
The Prison (Amendment) Rules 1983	1983/568
The Prison (Amendment) Rules 1987	1987/1256
The Prison (Amendment) Rules 1988	1988/89
The Prison (Amendment) (No 2) Rules 1988	1988/747

The Prison (Amendment) (No 3) Rules 1988	1988/1421
The Prison (Amendment) Rules 1989	1989/330
The Prison (Amendment) (No 2) Rules 1989	1989/2141
The Prison (Amendment) Rules 1990	1990/1762
The Prison (Amendment) Rules 1992	1992/514
The Prison (Amendment) (No 2) Rules 1992	1992/2080
The Prison (Amendment) Rules 1993	1993/516
The Prison (Amendment) (No 2) Rules 1993	1993/3075
The Prison (Amendment) Rules 1994	1994/3195
The Prison (Amendment) Rules 1995	1995/983
The Prison (Amendment) (No 2) Rules 1995	1995/1598
The Prison (Amendment) Rules 1996	1996/1663
The Prison (Amendment) Rules 1998	1998/23
The Prison (Amendment) (No 2) Rules 1998	1998/1544

YOUNG OFFENDER INSTITUTION RULES 1988

SI 1988/1422

5th August 1988

Part I
Preliminary

1 Citation and commencement

These Rules may be cited as the Young Offender Institution Rules 1988 and shall come into force on 1st October 1988.

2 Interpretation

(1)   In these Rules, where the context so admits, the expression:—

'compulsory school age' has the same meaning as in the Education Act 1944;

['controlled drug' means any drug which is a controlled drug for the purposes of the Misuse of Drugs Act 1971]

'governor' includes an officer for the time being in charge of a young offender institution;

['inmate' means a person who is required to be detained in a young offender institution;]

'legal adviser' means, in relation to an inmate, his counsel or solicitor, and includes a clerk acting on behalf of his solicitor;

'minister appointed to a young offender institution' means a minister so appointed under section 10 of the Prison Act 1952;

'officer' means an officer of a young offender institution.

['short-term prisoner' and 'long-term prisoner' have the meanings assigned to them by section 33(5) of the Criminal Justice Act 1991, as extended by sections 43(1) and 45(1) of that Act.]

(2)   In these Rules a reference to the Church of England includes a reference to

[(a)   an award of additional days means additional days awarded under these Rules by virtue of section 42 of the Criminal Justice Act 1991; and

(b)]   the Church in Wales.

(3)   The Rules set out in the Schedule to this Order are hereby revoked.

Annotations

Para (1): definition 'controlled drug' added by SI 1994/3194, r 2, Schedule, para 1; definition 'inmate' substituted by SI 1996/1662, r 2, Schedule, para 1; definitions 'short-term prisoner' and 'long-term prisoner' added by SI 1992/2081, r 2, Schedule, para 1(a).

Para (2): words in square brackets added by SI 1992/2081, r 2, Schedule, para 1(b).

PART II
INMATES

General

3 Aims and general principles of young offender institutions

(1)   The aim of a young offender institution shall be to help offenders to prepare for their return to the outside community.

(2)   The aim mentioned in paragraph (1) above shall be achieved, in particular, by—

(a)   providing a programme of activities, including education, training and work designed to assist offenders to acquire or develop personal responsibility, self-discipline, physical fitness, interests and skills and to obtain suitable employment after release;

(b)   fostering links between the offender and the outside community;

(c)   co-operating with the services responsible for the offender's supervision after release.

4 Classification of inmates

Inmates may be classified, in accordance with any directions of the Secretary of State, taking into account their ages, characters and circumstances.

Release

[6 Temporary release

(1)   The Secretary of State may, in accordance with the other provisions of this rule, release temporarily an inmate to whom this rule applies.

(2)   An inmate may be released under this rule for any period or periods and subject to any conditions.

(3)   An inmate may only be released under this rule:

(a)   on compassionate grounds or for the purpose of receiving medical treatment;

(b)   to engage in employment or voluntary work;

(c)   to receive instruction or training which cannot reasonably be provided in the young offender institution;

(d)   to enable him to participate in any proceedings before any court, tribunal or inquiry;

(e)   to enable him to consult with his legal adviser in circumstances where it is not reasonably practicable for the consultation to take place in the young offender institution;

(f)   to assist any police officer in any enquiries;

(g)   to facilitate the inmate's transfer between the young offender institution and another penal establishment;

(h)   to assist him in maintaining family ties or in his transition from life in the young offender institution to freedom; or

(i)   to enable him to make a visit in the locality of the young offender institution, [as a privilege under rule 4 of these Rules].

(4)   An inmate shall not be released under this rule unless the Secretary of State is satisfied that there would not be an unacceptable risk of his committing offences whilst released or otherwise of his failing to comply with any condition upon which he is released.

[(4A) Where at any time an offender is subject concurrently—

(a)   to a detention and training order; and

(b)   to a sentence of detention in a young offender institution,

he shall be treated for the purposes of paragraphs (5) and (6) of this rule as if he were subject only to the one of them that was imposed on the later occasion.]

(5)   The Secretary of State shall not release under this rule an inmate if, having regard to:

(a)   the period or proportion of his sentence which the inmate has served; and

(b)   the frequency with which the inmate has been granted temporary release under this rule,

the Secretary of State is of the opinion that the release of the inmate would be likely to undermine public confidence in the administration of justice.

(6)   If an inmate has been temporarily released under this rule during the relevant period and has been sentenced to any period of detention, custody or imprisonment for a criminal offence committed whilst at large following that release, he shall not be released under this rule unless his release, having regard to the circumstances of his conviction, would not, in the opinion of the Secretary of State, be likely to undermine public confidence in the administration of justice; and for this purpose 'the relevant period':

[(a) in the case of an inmate serving a determinate sentence of imprisonment, detention or custody, is the period he has served in respect of that sentence, unless, notwithstanding paragraph (9), the sentences he is serving do not fall to be treated as a single term, in which case it is the period since he was last released in relation to one of those sentences under Part II of the Criminal Justice Act 1991 ('the 1991 Act') [or section 75 of the Crime and Disorder Act 1998 ('the 1998 Act')]; or]

(b) in the case of an inmate serving an indeterminate sentence of imprisonment, detention or custody, is, if the inmate has previously been released on licence under Part II of the Criminal Justice Act 1991, the period since the date of his last recall to a penal establishment in respect of that sentence or, where the inmate has not been so released, the period he has served in respect of that sentence,

save that where an inmate falls within both of sub-paragraphs (a) and (b) above, the 'relevant period', in the case of that inmate, shall be determined by whichever of the applicable sub-paragraphs that produces the longer period.

(7) An inmate released under this rule may be recalled at any time whether the conditions of his release have been broken or not.

(8) This rule applies to inmates other than persons committed in custody for trial or to be sentenced or otherwise dealt with before or by the Crown Court or remanded in custody by any court.

[(9) For the purposes of any reference in this rule to an inmate's sentence consecutive terms and terms which are wholly or partly concurrent shall be treated as a single term if they would fall to be treated as a single term for the purposes of any reference to the term of imprisonment, detention or custody to which a person has been sentenced in Part II of the 1991 Act [or to the term of a detention and training order in sections 75 to 78 of the 1998 Act].

(10) In this rule, any reference to release on licence under Part II of the 1991 Act includes any release on licence under any earlier legislation providing for early release on licence.]]

Annotations

Substituted by SI 1995/984, r 2, Schedule, para 1.

Para (3): in sub-para (i) words in square brackets substituted by SI 1995/1599, r 2, Schedule, para 1; in sub-para (i) words in square brackets beginning with the words 'as a privilege under' substituted by SI 1995/1599, r 2, Schedule, para 1; in sub-para (i) words 'rule 7 of these Rules' in square brackets subsituted by SI 1996/1662, r 2, Schedule, para 2.

Para (4A): inserted by SI 2000/700, r 2, Schedule, para 1(a).

Para (5): words from 'or, in a case' to 'he has served' in square brackets inserted by SI 1999/962, r 3, Schedule, para 1(a).

Para (6): sub-para (a) substituted by SI 1999/962, r 3, Schedule, para 1(b); in sub-para (a) words from 'or section 75' to '(the 1998 Act)' in square brackets inserted by SI 2000/700, r 2, Schedule, para 1(b); in sub-para (b) words 'Part II of the 1991 Act or Part II of the Crime (Sentences) Act 1997' in square brackets substituted by SI 1999/962, r 3, Schedule, para 1(c).

Paras (9), (10): substituted, for para (9) as originally enacted, by SI 1999/962, r 3, Schedule, para 1(d).

Para (9): words from 'or to the' to 'the 1998 Act' in square brackets inserted by SI 2000/700, r 2, Schedule, para 1(c).

See further, for provision as to the interpretation of references herein to rule 6: the Young Offender Institution (Amendment) Rules 1995, SI 1995/984, r 3(2).

Conditions

[7 Privileges

(1)   There shall be established at every young offender institution systems of privileges approved by the Secretary of State and appropriate to the classes of inmates thereof and their ages, characters and circumstances, which shall include arrangements under which money earned by inmates may be spent by them within the young offender institution.

(2)   Systems of privileges approved under paragraph (1) may include arrangements under which inmates may be allowed time outside the cells and in association with one another, in excess of the minimum time which, subject to the other provisions of these Rules apart from this rule, is otherwise allowed to inmates at the young offender institution for this purpose.

(3)   Systems of privileges approved under paragraph (1) may include arrangements under which privileges may be granted to inmates only in so far as they have met, and for so long as they continue to meet, specified standards in their behaviour and their performance in work or other activities.

(4)   Systems of privileges which include arrangements of the kind referred to in paragraph (3) shall include procedures to be followed in determining whether or not any of the privileges concerned shall be granted, or shall continue to be granted, to an inmate; such procedures shall include a requirement that the inmate be given reasons for any decision adverse to him together with a statement of the means by which he may appeal against it.

(5)   Nothing in this rule shall be taken to confer on an inmate any entitlement to any privilege or to affect any provision in these Rules other than this rule as a result of which any privilege may be forfeited or otherwise lost or an inmate deprived of association with other inmates.]

Annotations

Substituted by SI 1995/1599, r 2, Schedule, para 2.

8 Information to inmates

(1)   Every inmate shall be provided, as soon as possible after his reception into the young offender institution, and in any case within 24 hours, with information in writing about those provisions of these Rules and other

matters which it is necessary that he should know, including earnings and privileges, and the proper method of making requests and complaints . . . .

(2)   In the case of an inmate aged less than 18, or an inmate aged 18 or over who cannot read or appears to have difficulty in understanding the information so provided, the governor, or an officer deputed by him, shall so explain it to him that he can understand his rights and obligations.

(3)   A copy of these Rules shall be made available to any inmate who requests it.

Annotations

Para (1): words omitted revoked by SI 1990/1763, r 2(a).

[9 Requests and complaints

(1)   A request or complaint to the governor or Board of Visitors relating to an inmate's detention shall be made orally or in writing by that inmate.

(2)   On every day the governor shall hear any oral requests and complaints that are made to him under paragraph (1) above.

(3)   A written request or complaint under paragraph (1) above may be made in confidence.]

Annotations

Substituted by SI 1990/1763, r 2(b).

10 [Communications generally]

(1)   The Secretary of State may, with a view to securing discipline and good order or the prevention of crime or in the interests of any persons, impose restrictions, either generally or in a particular case, upon the communications to be permitted between an inmate and other persons.

[(1A) Without prejudice to the generality of paragraph (1), the Secretary of State may require that any visit, or class of visits, shall be held in facilities which include special features restricting or preventing physical contact between an inmate and a visitor.]

(2)   [Without prejudice to sections 6 and 19 of the Prison Act 1952, and] except as provided by . . . these Rules, an inmate shall not be permitted to communicate with any outside person, or that person with him, without the leave of the Secretary of State [or as a privilege under rule 7 of these Rules].

(3)   Except as provided by these Rules, every letter or [other] communication to or from an inmate may be read, [listened to, logged, recorded] or examined by the governor or an officer deputed by him, and the governor may, at his discretion, stop any [letter or other] communication on the ground that its contents are objectionable or that it is of inordinate length.

(4)   Subject to the provisions of these Rules, the governor may give such directions as he thinks fit for the supervision of visits to inmates, either generally or in a particular case.

[(5)   In this rule 'communications' includes communications during or by means of visits or by means of a telecommunications system or telecommunications apparatus, and 'telecommunications apparatus' has the meaning assigned by paragraph 1 of Schedule 2 to the Telecommunications Act 1984.]

Annotations

Provision heading: substituted by SI 1999/962, r 3, Schedule, para 2(a).

Para (1): words 'letters or other' in square brackets inserted by SI 1999/962, r 3, Schedule, para 2(b).

Para (1A): inserted by SI 1999/962, r 3, Schedule, para 2(c).

Para (2): words 'Without prejudice to sections 6 and 19 of the Prison Act 1952, and' in square brackets inserted and words omitted revoked by SI 1999/962, r 3, Schedule, para 2(d); words 'or as a privilege under rule 7 of these Rules' in square brackets inserted by SI 1995/1599, r 2, Schedule, para 3

Para (3): words in square brackets inserted by SI 1999/962, r 3, Schedule, para 2(e).

Para (5): inserted by SI 1999/962, r 3, Schedule, para 2(f).

11 Personal letters and visits

(1)   [Subject to paragraph (7)] an inmate shall be entitled—

    (a)   to send and to receive a letter on his reception into a young offender institution and thereafter once a week; and

    (b)   to receive a visit [twice in every period of four weeks, but only once in every such period if the Secretary of State so directs].

(2)   The governor may allow an inmate an additional letter or visit [as a privilege under rule 7 of these Rules or] when necessary for his welfare or that of his family.

(3)   The governor may allow an inmate entitled to a visit to send and to receive a letter instead.

(4)   The governor may defer the right of an inmate to a visit until the expiration of any period of confinement to a cell or room.

(5)   The board of visitors may allow an inmate an additional letter or visit in special circumstances, and may direct that a visit may extend beyond the normal duration.

(6)   The Secretary of State may allow additional letters and visits in relation to any inmate or class of inmates.

[(7)   An inmate shall not be entitled under this rule to receive a visit from—

    (a)   any person, whether or not a relative or friend, during any period of time that person is the subject of a prohibition imposed under rule 71A; or

    (b)   any other person, other than a relative or friend, except with the leave of the Secretary of State.]

(8)   Any letter or visit under the succeeding provisions of these Rules shall not be counted as a letter or visit for the purposes of this rule.

Annotations

Para (1): words 'Subject to paragraph (7)' in square brackets inserted by SI 1999/962, r 3, Schedule, para 3(a); words from 'twice in every period' to 'so directs' in square brackets substituted by SI 1992/513, r 2(1), Schedule, para 1.

Para (2): words in square brackets inserted by SI 1995/1599, r 2, Schedule, para 4.

Para (7): substituted by SI 1999/962, r 3, Schedule, para 3(b).

12 Police interviews

A police officer may, on production of an order issued by or on behalf of a chief officer of police, interview any inmate willing to see him.

13 Legal advisers

(1) The legal adviser of an inmate in any legal proceedings, civil or criminal, to which the inmate is a party shall be afforded reasonable facilities for interviewing him in connection with those proceedings, and may do so out of hearing of an officer.

(2) An inmate's legal adviser may, with the leave of the Secretary of State, interview the inmate in connection with any other legal business.

[14 Correspondence with legal advisers and courts

(1) An inmate may correspond with his legal adviser and any court and such correspondence may only be opened, read or stopped by the governor in accordance with the provisions of this rule.

(2) Correspondence to which this rule applies may be opened if the governor has reasonable cause to believe that it contains an illicit enclosure and any such enclosure shall be dealt with in accordance with the other provisions of these Rules.

(3) Correspondence to which this rule applies may be opened, read and stopped if the governor has reasonable cause to believe its contents endanger prison or young offender institution security or the safety of others or are otherwise of a criminal nature.

(4) An inmate shall be given the opportunity to be present when any correspondence to which this rule applies is opened and shall be informed if it or any enclosure is to be read or stopped.

(5) An inmate shall on request be provided with any writing materials necessary for the purposes of paragraph (1) of this rule.

(6) In this rule, 'court' includes the European Commission of Human Rights, the European Court of Human Rights and the European Court of Justice; and 'illicit enclosure' includes any article possession of which has not been authorised in accordance with the other provisions of these Rules and any correspondence to or from a person other than the inmate concerned, his legal adviser or a court.]

Annotations

Substituted by SI 1993/3076, r 2, Schedule, para 1.

15 Securing release of defaulters

An inmate detained in a young offender institution in default of payment of a fine or any other sum of money may communicate with, and be visited at any reasonable time on a weekday by, any relative or friend to arrange for payment in order to secure his release.

16 Clothing

(1) An inmate shall be provided with clothing adequate for warmth and health in accordance with a scale approved by the Secretary of State.

(2) The clothing provided under this rule shall include suitable protective clothing for use at work, where this is needed.

(3) Subject to the provisions of rule 42(3) of these Rules, an inmate shall wear clothing provided under this rule and/other, except on the directions of the Secretary of State [or as a privilege under rule 7 of these Rules].

(4) An inmate shall where necessary be provided with suitable and adequate clothing on his release.

Annotations

Para (3): words in square brackets added by SI 1995/1599, r 2, Schedule, para 5.

17 Food

(1) Subject to any directions of the Secretary of State, no inmate shall be allowed, except as authorised by the medical officer [or a medical practitioner such as is mentioned in rule 24(3)], to have any food other than that ordinarily provided.

(2) The food provided shall be wholesome, nutritious, well prepared and served, reasonably varied and sufficient in quantity.

[(3) The medical officer, a medical practitioner such as is mentioned in rule 24(3) or any person deemed by the governor to be competent, shall from time to time inspect the food both before and after it is cooked, and shall report any deficiency or defect to the governor.]

(4) In this rule, 'food' includes drink.

Annotations

Para (1): words 'or a medical practitioner such as is mentioned in rule 24(3)' in square brackets inserted by SI 1998/1545, r 2, Schedule, para 1(2).

Para (3): substituted by SI 1998/1545, r 2, Schedule, para 1(3).

18 Alcohol and tobacco

(1) No inmate shall be allowed to have any intoxicating liquor except under a written order of the medical officer [or a medical practitioner such as is mentioned in rule 24(3)] specifying the quantity and the name of the inmate.

[(2)   No inmate shall be allowed to smoke or to have any tobacco except in accordance with any directions of the Secretary of State.]

Annotations

Para (1): words 'or a medical practitioner such as is mentioned in rule 24(3)' in square brackets inserted by SI 1998/1545, r 2, Schedule, para 2.

Para (2): substituted by SI 1992/2081, r 2, Schedule, para 3.

19 Sleeping accommodation

(1)   No room or cell shall be used as sleeping accommodation for an inmate unless it has been certified by an officer of the Secretary of State (not being an officer of a young offender institution) that its size, lighting, heating, ventilation and fittings are adequate for health, and that it allows the inmate to communicate at any time with an officer.

(2)   A certificate given under this rule shall specify the maximum number of inmates who may sleep in the room or cell at one time, and the number so specified shall not be exceeded without the leave of the Secretary of State.

20 Beds and bedding

Each inmate shall be provided with a separate bed and with separate bedding adequate for warmth and health.

21 Hygiene

(1)   Every inmate shall be provided with toilet articles necessary for his health and cleanliness, which shall be replaced as necessary.

(2)   Every inmate shall be required to wash at proper times, have a hot bath or shower on reception and thereafter at least once a week.

[(3)   An inmate's hair shall not be cut without his consent.]

Annotations

Para (3): substituted, for paras (3), (4) as originally enacted, by SI 1999/962, r 3, Schedule, para 4.

22 Female inmates

The Secretary of State may, subject to any conditions he thinks fit, permit a female inmate to have her baby with her in a young offender institution, and everything necessary for the baby's maintenance and care may be provided there.

23 Library books

A library shall be provided in every young offender institution and, subject to any directions of the Secretary of State, every inmate shall be allowed to have library books and to exchange them.

Medical attention

24 Medical attendance

(1) The medical officer of a young offender institution shall have the care of the health, mental and physical, of the inmates of that institution.

(2) Every request by an inmate to see the medical officer shall be recorded by the officer to whom it is made and promptly passed on to the medical officer.

[(3) The medical officer may consult a medical practitioner who is a fully registered person within the meaning of the Medical Act 1983. Such a practitioner may work within the prison under the general supervision of the medical officer.

(3A) The medical officer shall consult another medical practitioner, if time permits, before performing any serious operation.]

[(4) Subject to any directions given in the particular case by the Secretary of State, a registered medical practitioner selected by or on behalf of an inmate who is a party to any legal proceedings shall be afforded reasonable facilities for examining him in connection with the proceedings, and may do so out of hearing but in the sight of an officer.]

Annotations

Paras (3), (3A): substituted, for para (3) as originally enacted, by SI 1998/1545, r 2, Schedule, para 4.

Para 4: inserted by SI 1993/3076, r 2, Schedule, para 2.

25 Special illnesses and conditions

(1) The medical officer [or a medical practitioner such as is mentioned in rule 24(3)] shall report to the governor on the case of any inmate whose health is likely to be injuriously affected by continued detention or any conditions of detention. The governor shall send the report to the Secretary of State without delay, together with his own recommendations.

(2) The medical officer [or a medical practitioner such as is mentioned in rule 24(3)] shall pay special attention to any inmate whose mental condition appears to require it, and make any special arrangements which appear necessary for his supervision or care.

(3) . . .

Annotations

Para (1): words 'or a medical practitioner such as is mentioned in rule 24(3)' in square brackets inserted by SI 1998/1545, r 2, Schedule, para 5(2).

Para (2): words 'or a medical practitioner such as is mentioned in rule 24(3)' in square brackets inserted by SI 1998/1545, r 2, Schedule, para 5(3).

Para (3): revoked by SI 1998/1545, r 2, Schedule, para 5(4).

26 Notification of illness or death

(1) If an inmate dies, becomes seriously ill, sustains any severe injury or is removed to hospital on account of mental disorder, the governor shall, if he knows his or her address, at once inform the inmate's spouse or next of kin, and also any person who the inmate may reasonably have asked should be informed.

(2) If an inmate dies, the governor shall give notice immediately to the coroner having jurisdiction, to the board of visitors and to the Secretary of State.

Religion

27 Religious denomination

An inmate shall be treated as being of the religious denomination stated in the record made in pursuance of section 10(5) of the Prison Act 1952, but the governor may, in a proper case after due inquiry, direct that record to be amended.

28 Special duties of chaplains and appointed ministers

(1) The chaplain or a minister appointed to a young offender institution shall—

    (a) interview every inmate of his denomination individually as soon as he reasonably can after the inmate's reception into that institution and shortly before his release; and

    (b) if no other arrangements are made, read the burial service at the funeral of any inmate of his denomination who dies in that institution.

(2) The chaplain shall visit daily all inmates belonging to the Church of England who are sick, under restraint or confined to a room or cell; and a minister appointed to a young offender institution shall do the same, as far as he reasonably can, for inmates of his own denomination.

(3) If the inmate is willing, the chaplain shall visit any inmate not of the Church of England who is sick, under restraint or confined to a room or cell, and is not regularly visited by a minister of his own denomination.

29 Regular visits by ministers of religion, etc

(1) The chaplain shall visit regularly the inmates belonging to the Church of England.

(2) A minister appointed to a young offender institution shall visit the inmates of his denomination as regularly as he reasonably can.

(3) The governor shall, if so requested by an inmate belonging to a denomination for which no minister has been appointed to a young offender institution do what he reasonably can to arrange for that inmate to be visited regularly by a minister of that denomination.

(4) Every request by an inmate to see the chaplain or a minister appointed to a young offender institution shall be promptly passed on to the chaplain or minister.

30 Religious services

(1) The chaplain shall conduct Divine Service for inmates belonging to the Church of England at least once every Sunday, Christmas Day and Good Friday, and such celebrations of Holy Communion and weekday services as may be arranged.

(2) A minister appointed to a young offender institution shall conduct Divine Service for inmates of his denomination at such times as may be arranged.

31 Substitute for chaplain or appointed minister

(1) A person approved by the Secretary of State may act for the chaplain in his absence.

(2) A minister appointed to a young offender institution may, with the leave of the Secretary of State, appoint a substitute to act for him in his absence.

32 Sunday work

Arrangements shall be made so as not to require inmates to do any unnecessary work on Sunday, Christmas Day or Good Friday nor inmates of religions other than the Christian religion to do any unnecessary work on their recognised days of religious observance (as an alternative, but not in addition, to those days).

33 Religious books

There shall, so far as reasonably practicable, be available for the personal use of every inmate such religious books recognised by his denomination as are approved by the Secretary of State for use in young offender institutions.

Occupation and links with the community

34 Regime activities

[(1) An inmate shall be occupied in a programme of activities provided in accordance with rule 3 of these Rules which shall include education, training courses, work and physical education.]

(2) In all such activities regard shall be paid to individual assessment and personal development.

(3) The medical officer may excuse an inmate from work or any other activity on medical grounds; and no inmate shall be set to participate in work or any other activity of a kind for which he is considered by the medical officer to be unfit.

[(4) An inmate may be required to participate in regime activities for no longer than the relevant period in a day, 'the relevant period' for this purpose being—

   (a) on a day in which an hour or more of physical education is provided for the inmate, 11 hours;

(b)   on a day in which no such education is provided for the inmate, 10 hours; or

(c)   on a day in which a period of less than an hour of such education is provided for the inmate, the sum of 10 hours and the period of such education provided,

provided that he may not be required to participate in any one regime activity for more than 8 hours in a day.]

(5)   Inmates may be paid for their work or participation in other activities at rates approved by the Secretary of State, either generally or in relation to particular cases.

Annotations

Para (1): substituted by SI 1996/1662, r 2, Schedule, para 3.

Para (3): words 'or a medical practitioner such as is mentioned in rule 24(3)' in square brackets in both places they occur inserted by SI 1998/1545, r 2, Schedule, para 6.

Para (4): substituted by SI 1996/1662, r 2, Schedule, para 3.

Occupation and links with the community

35 Education

(1)   Provision shall be made at a young offender institution for the education of inmates by means of programmes of class teaching or private study within the normal working week and, so far as practicable, programmes of evening and weekend educational classes or priave study. The educational activities shall, so far as practicable, be such as will foster personal responsibility and an inmate's interests and skills and help him to prepare for his return to the community.

(2)   In the case of [an inmate of compulsory school age as defined in section 8 of the Education Act 1996], arrangements shall be made for his participation in education or training courses for at least 15 hours a week within the normal working week.

(3)   In the case of an inmate aged 17 or over who [has special educational needs], arrangements shall be made for education appropriate to his needs, if necessary within the normal working week.

(4)   In the case of a female inmate aged 21 or over who is serving a sentence of imprisonment or who has been committed to prison for default and who is detained in a young offender institution instead of a prison, reasonable facilities shall be afforded if she wishes to improve her education, by class teaching or private study.

Annotations

Para (2): words from 'an inmate' to 'Education Act 1996' in square brackets substituted by SI 1999/962, r 3, Schedule, para 5(1), (2).

Para (3): words 'has special educational needs' in square brackets substituted by SI 1999/962, r 3, Schedule, para 5(1), (3).

36 Training courses

(1) Provision shall be made at a young offender institution for the training of inmates by means of training courses, in acccordance with directions of the Secretary of State.

(2) Training courses shall be such as will foster personal responsibility and an inmate's interests and skills and improve his prospects of finding suitable employment after release.

(3) Training courses shall, so far as practicable, be such as to enable inmates to acquire suitable qualifications.

37 Work

(1) Work shall, so far as practicable, be such as will foster personal responsibility and an inmate's interests and skills and help him to prepare for his return to the community.

(2) No inmate shall be set to do work of a kind not authorised by the Secretary of State.

38 Physical education

(1) Provision shall be made at a young offender institution for the physical education of inmates within the normal working week, as well as evening and weekend physical recreation. The physical education activities shall be such as will foster personal responsibility and an inmate's interests and skills and encourage him to make good use of his leisure on release.

(2) Arrangements shall be made for each inmate, other than one to whom [paragraphs (2A) and (4)] of this rule applies, to participate in physical education for at least two hours a week on average or, in the case of inmates detained in such institutions or parts of institutions as the Secretary of State may direct, for at least 1 hour each weekday on average, but outside the hours allotted to education under rule 35(2) in the case of an inmate of compulsory school age.

[(2A) If circumstances reasonably permit, a female inmate aged 21 years or over shall be given the opportunity to participate in physical education for at least one hour a week.]

(3) In the case of an inmate with a need for remedial physical activity, appropriate facilities shall be provided.

[(4) If the weather permits and subject to the need to maintain good order and discipline, a female inmate aged 21 years or over shall be given the opportunity to spend time in the open air at least once every day, for such period as may be reasonable in the circumstances.]

Annotations

Para (2): words in square brackets substituted by SI 1996/1662, r 2, Schedule, para 4(a).

Para (2A): inserted by SI 1996/1662, r 2, Schedule, para 4(b).

Para (4): substituted by SI 1996/1662, r 2, Schedule, para 4(c).

39 Outside contacts

(1)   The governor shall encourage links between the young offender institution and the community by taking steps to establish and maintain relations with suitable persons and agencies outside the institution.

(2)   The governor shall ensure that special attention is paid to the maintenance of such relations between an inmate and his family as seem desirable in the best interests of both.

(3)   Subject to any directions of the Secretary of State, an inmate shall be encouraged, as far as practicable, to participate in activities outside the young offender institution which will be of benefit to the community or of benefit to the inmate in helping him to prepare for his return to the community.

40 After-care

(1)   From the beginning of his sentence, consideration shall be given, in consultation with the appropriate supervising service, to an inmate's future and the help to be given to him in preparation for and after his return to the community.

(2)   Every inmate who is liable to supervision after release shall be given a careful explanation of his liability and the requirements to which he will be subject while under supervision.

Discipline and control

41 Maintenance of order and discipline

(1)   Order and discipline shall be maintained, but with no more restriction than is required in the interests of security and well-ordered community life.

[(1A) Notwithstanding paragraph (1), regimes may be established at young offender institutions under which stricter order and discipline are maintained and which emphasise strict standards of dress, appearance and conduct; provided that no inmate shall be required to participate in such a regime unless he has been first assessed as being suitable for it and no inmate shall be required to continue with such a regime if at any time it appears that he is no longer suitable for it.

(1B) For the purposes of paragraph (1A), whether an inmate is suitable for a stricter regime is to be assessed by reference to whether he is sufficiently fit in mind and body to undertake it and whether, in the opinion of the Secretary of State, experience of the regime will further his rehabilitation.]

(2)   In the control of inmates, officers shall seek to influence them through their own example and leadership, and to enlist their willing co-operation.

Annotations

Paras (1A), (1B): inserted by SI 1996/1662, r 2, Schedule, para 5.

42 Custody outside a young offender institution

(1)   A person being taken to or from a young offender institution in custody shall be exposed as little as possible to public observation and proper care shall be taken to protect him from curiosity and insult.

(2)   An inmate required to be taken in custody anywhere outside a young offender institution shall be kept in the custody of an officer appointed under section 3 of the Prison Act 1952 or of a police officer.

[(3)   An inmate required to be taken in custody to any court shall, when he appears before the court, wear his own clothing or ordinary civilian clothing provided by the governor.]

Annotations

Para (3): substituted by SI 1995/1599, r 2, Schedule, para 6.

43 Search

(1)   Every inmate shall be searched when taken into custody by an officer, on his reception into a young offender institution and subsequently as the governor thinks necessary [or as the Secretary of State may direct].

(2)   An inmate shall be searched in as seemly a manner as is consistent with discovering anything concealed.

[(3)   No inmate shall be stripped and searched in the sight of another inmate or in the sight of a person of the opposite sex.]

(4)   . . .

Annotations

Para (1): words in square brackets inserted by SI 1996/1662, r 2, Schedule, para 6.
Para (3): substituted by SI 1999/962, r 3, Schedule, para 6.
Para (4): revoked by SI 1992/2081, r 2, Schedule, para 4.

44 Record and photograph

(1)   A personal record of each inmate shall be prepared and maintained in such manner as the Secretary of State may direct, but no part of the record shall be disclosed to any person not authorised to receive it.

(2)   Every inmate may be photographed on reception and subsequently, but no copy of the photograph shall be given to any person not authorised to receive it.

45 Inmates' property

(1)   Anything, other than cash, which an inmate has at a young offender institution and which he is not allowed to retain for his own use shall be taken into the governor's custody.

(2)   Any cash which an inmate has at a young offender institution shall be paid into an account under the control of the governor and the inmate shall be credited with the amount in the books of the institution.

(3)   Any article belonging to an inmate which remains unclaimed for a period of more than 3 years after he is released, or dies, may be sold or otherwise disposed of; and the net proceeds of any sale shall be paid to the National Association for the Care and Resettlement of Offenders, for its general purposes.

(4)   The governor may confiscate any unauthorised article found in the possession of an inmate after his reception into a young offender institution, or concealed or deposited within a young offender institution.

46 Removal from association

(1)   Where it appears desirable, for the maintenance of good order or discipline or in his own interests, that an inmate should not associate with other inmates, either generally or for particular purposes, the governor may arrange for the inmate's removal from association accordingly.

(2)   An inmate shall not be removed under this rule for a period of more than [3 days] without the authority of a member of the board of visitors or of the Secretary of State. An authority given under this paragraph shall in the case of a female inmate aged 21 years or over, be for a period not exceeding one month and, in the case of any other inmate, be for a period not exceeding 14 days, but may be renewed from time to time for a like period.

(3)   The governor may arrange at his discretion for such an inmate as aforesaid to resume association with other inmates, and shall do so if in any case the medical officer [or a medical practitioner such as is mentioned in rule 24(3)] so advises on medical grounds.

Annotations

Para (2): words in square brackets substituted by SI 1989/2142, r 2(a).

Para (3): words 'or a medical practitioner such as is mentioned in rule 24(3)' in square brackets inserted by SI 1998/1545, r 2, Schedule, para 7.

47 Use of force

(1)   An officer in dealing with an inmate shall not use force unnecessarily and, when the application of force to an inmate is necessary, no more force than is necessary shall be used.

(2)   No officer shall act deliberately in a manner calculated to provoke an inmate.

48 Temporary confinement

(1)   The governor may order an inmate who is refractory or violent to be confined temporarily in a special cell or room, but an inmate shall not be so confined as a punishment, or after he has ceased to be refractory or violent.

(2)   A cell or room shall not be used for the purpose of this rule unless it has been certified by an officer of the Secretary of State (not being an officer of a young offender institution) that it is suitable for the purpose, that its size, lighting, heating, ventilation and fittings are adequate for health, and that it allows the inmate to communicate at any time with an officer.

(3)   In relation to any young offender institution, section 14(6) of the Prison Act 1952 shall have effect so as to enable the provision of special rooms instead of special cells for the temporary confinement of refractory or violent inmates.

[(4)   An inmate shall not be confined under this rule for longer than 24 hours without a direction in writing given by a member of a board of visitors or by an officer of the Secretary of State not being an officer of the young offender institution.]

Annotations

Para (4): inserted by SI 1999/962, r 3, Schedule, para 7.

49 Restraints

(1)   The governor may order an inmate . . . to be put under restraint where this is necessary to prevent the inmate from injuring himself or others, damaging property or creating a disturbance.

[(1A) The governor may not order an inmate aged less than 17 to be put under restraint, except that he may order such an inmate be placed in handcuffs where this is necessary to prevent the inmate from injuring himself or others, damaging property or creating a disturbance.]

(2)   Notice of such an order shall be given without delay to a member of the board of visitors and to the medical officer [or a medical practitioner such as is mentioned in rule 24(3)].

[(3)   On receipt of the notice, the medical officer, or the medical practitioner referred to in paragraph (2) above, shall inform the governor whether there are any reasons why the inmate should not be put under restraint. The governor shall give effect to any recommendation which may be made under this paragraph.]

(4)   An inmate shall not be kept under restraint longer than necessary, nor shall he be so kept for longer than 24 hours without a direction in writing given by a member of the board of visitors or by an officer of the Secretary of State (not being an officer of a young offender institution). Such a direction shall state the grounds for the restraint and the time during which it may continue.

(5)   Particulars of every case of restraint under the foregoing provisions of this rule shall be forthwith recorded.

(6)   Except as provided by this rule no inmate shall be put under restraint otherwise than for safe custody during removal, or on medical grounds by direction of the medical officer [or of a medical practitioner such as is mentioned in rule 24(3)]. No inmate shall be put under restraint as a punishment.

(7)   Any means of restraint shall be of a pattern authorised by the Secretary of State, and shall be used in such manner and under such conditions as the Secretary of State may direct.

Annotations

Para (1): words omitted revoked by SI 1999/962, r 3, Schedule, para 8(1), (2).

Para (1A): inserted by SI 1999/962, r 3, Schedule, para 8(1), (3).

Para (2): words 'or a medical practitioner such as is mentioned in rule 24(3)' in square brackets inserted by SI 1998/1545, r 2, Schedule, para 8(2).

Para (3): substituted by SI 1998/1545, r 2, Schedule, para 8(3).

Para (6): words 'or of a medical practitioner such as is mentioned in rule 24(3)' in square brackets inserted by SI 1998/1545, r 2, Schedule, para 8(4).

[49A Compulsory testing for controlled drugs

(1)   This rule applies where an officer, acting under the powers conferred by section 16A of the Prison Act 1952 (power to test inmates for drugs), requires an inmate to provide a sample for the purpose of ascertaining whether he has any controlled drug in his body.

(2)   In this rule 'sample' means a sample of urine or any other description of sample specified in the authorisation by the governor for the purposes of section 16A.

(3)   When requiring an inmate to provide a sample, an officer shall, so far as is reasonably practicable, inform the inmate:

(a)   that he is being required to provide a sample in accordance with section 16A of the Prison Act 1952; and

(b)   that a refusal to provide a sample may lead to disciplinary proceedings being brought against him.

(4)   An officer shall require an inmate to provide a fresh sample, free from any adulteration.

(5)   An officer requiring a sample shall make such arrangements and give the inmate such instructions for its provision as may be reasonably necessary in order to prevent or detect its adulteration or falsification.

(6)   An inmate who is required to provide a sample may be kept apart from other inmates for a period not exceeding one hour to enable arrangements to be made for the provision of the sample.

(7)   An inmate who is unable to provide a sample of urine when required to do so may be kept apart from other inmates until he has provided the required sample, save that an inmate may not be kept apart under this paragraph for a period of more than 5 hours.

(8)   An inmate required to provide a sample of urine shall be afforded such degree of privacy for the purposes of providing the sample as may be compatible with the need to prevent or detect any adulteration or falsification of the sample; in particular an inmate shall not be required to provide such a sample in the sight of a person of the opposite sex.]

Annotations

This rule was added by SI 1994/3194, r 2, Schedule, para 2.

[50 Offences against discipline

An inmate is guilty of an offence against discipline if he—

    (1)   commits any assault;

    (2)   detains any person against his will;

    [(3) denies access to any part of the young offender institution to any officer or any person (other than an inmate) who is at the young offender institution for the purpose of working there;]

    (4)   fights with any person;

    (5)   internationally endangers the health or personal safety of others or, by his conduct, is reckless whether such health or personal safety is endangered;

    [(6) intentionally obstructs an officer in the execution of his duty, or any person (other than an inmate) who is at the young offender institution for the purpose of working there, in the performance of his work;]

    (7)   escapes or absconds from a young offender institution or from legal custody;

    (8)   fails—

        (a) . . .

        (b) to comply with any condition upon which he was [temporarily released under rule 6 of these rules];

    [(8A)administers a controlled drug to himself or fails to prevent the administration of a controlled drug to him by another person (but subject to rule 50A below);]

    [(8B) is intoxicated as a consequence of knowingly consuming any alcoholic beverage;

    (8C) knowingly consumes any alcoholic beverage, other than any provided to him pursuant to a written order of the medical officer under rule 18(1);]

    (9)   has in his possession—

        (a) any unauthorised article, or

        (b) a greater quantity of any article than he is authorised to have;

    (10) sells or delivers to any person any unauthorised article;

    (11) sells or, without permission, delivers to any person any article which he is allowed to have only for his own use;

    (12) takes improperly any article belonging to another person or to a young offender institution;

    (13) intentionally or recklessly sets fire to any part of a young offender institution or any other property, whether or not his own;

    (14) destroys or damages any part of a young offender institution or any other property other than his own;

(15) absents himself from any place where he is required to be or is present at any place where he is not authorised to be;

[(16) is disrespectful to any officer, or any person (other than an inmate) who is at the young offender institution for the purpose of working there, or any person visiting a young offender institution;]

(17) uses threatening, abusive or insulting words or behaviour;

(18) intentionally fails to work properly or, being required to work, refuses to do so;

(19) disobeys any lawful order;

(20) disobeys or fails to comply with any rule or regulation applying to him;

[(21) receives any controlled drug or, without the consent of an officer, any other article, during the course of a visit (not being an interview such as is mentioned in rule 13);]

(22)

    (a)   attempts to commit,

    (b)   incites another inmate to commit, or

    (c)   assists another inmate to commit or to attempt to commit any of the foregoing offences.]

Annotations

Substituted by SI 1989/331, r 2(a).

Paras (3), (6), (16): substituted by SI 1994/3194, r 2, Schedule, paras 3, 4, 6.

Para (8): sub-para (a) revoked, and words in square brackets in sub-para (b) substituted, by SI 1992/513, r 2(1), Schedule, paras 2, 3.

Para (8A): inserted by SI 1994/3194, r 2, Schedule, para 5.

Paras (8B), (8C): inserted by SI 1996/1662, r 2, Schedule, para 7.

Para (21): substituted by SI 1999/962, r 3, Schedule, para 9.

See further, in relation to the interpretation of references in para (8) above to rule 6: the Young Offender Institution (Amendment) Rules 1995, SI 1995/984, r 3(2).

[50A

It shall be a defence for an inmate charged with an offence under rule 50(8A) to show that—

    (a)   the controlled drug had been, prior to its administration, lawfully in his possession for his use or was administered to him in the course of a lawful supply of the drug to him by another person;

    (b)   the controlled drug was administered by or to him in circumstances in which he did not know and had no reason to suspect that such a drug was being administered; or

    (c)   the controlled drug was administered by or to him under duress or to him without his consent in circumstances where it was not reasonable for him to have resisted.]

Annotations

Inserted by SI 1994/3194, r 2, Schedule, para 7.

[51 Disciplinary charges

(1)   Where an inmate is to be charged with an offence against discipline, the charge shall be laid as soon as possible and, save in exceptional circumstances, within 48 hours of the discovery of the offence.

(2)   . . .

(3)   Every charge shall be inquired into . . . by the governor.

(4)   Every charge shall be first inquired into not later, save in exceptional circumstances, than the next day, not being a Sunday or public holiday, after it is laid.]

[(5)   An inmate who is to be charged with an offence against discipline may be kept apart from other inmates pending the governor's first inquiry.]

Annotations

Substituted by SI 1989/331, r 2(a).
Para (2): revoked by SI 1992/513, r 2(1), Schedule, para 4.
Para (3): words omitted revoked by SI 1992/513, r 2(1), Schedule, para 5.
Para (5): inserted by SI 1992/513, r 2(1), Schedule, para 6.

[52 Rights of inmates charged

(1)   Where an inmate is charged with an offence against discipline, he shall be informed of the charge as soon as possible and, in any case, before the time when it is inquired into by the governor.

(2)   At any inquiry into a charge against an inmate he shall be given a full opportunity of hearing what is alleged against him and of presenting his own case.]

Annotations

Substituted by SI 1989/331, r 2(a).

[53 Governor's punishments

(1)   If he finds an inmate guilty of an offence against discipline the governor may, subject to [paragraph (3) below and] rule 60 of these Rules, impose one or more of the following punishments:

   (a)   caution;

   (b)   forfeiture for a period not exceeding [21 days] of any of the privileges under rule 7 of these Rules;

   (c)   removal for a period not exceeding [21 days] from any particular activity or activities of the young offender institution, other than education, training courses, work and physical education in accordance with rules 34, 35, 36, 37 and 38 of these Rules;

(d)   extra work outside the normal working week for a period not exceeding [21 days] and for not more than 2 hours on any day;

(e)   [stoppage of or deduction from earnings for a period not exceeding [42 days] of an amount not exceeding [21 days' earnings]];

(f)   [in the case of an offence against discipline committed by an inmate who was aged 18 or over at the time of commission of the offence, other than an inmate who is serving the period of detention and training under a detention and training order pursuant to section 75(1) of the Crime and Disorder Act 1998,] confinement to a cell or room for a period not exceeding [7 days];

(g)   removal from his wing or living unit for a period not exceeding [21 days];

(h)   [in the case of an inmate who is a short-term or long-term prisoner, an award of additional days not exceeding [42 days].]

(2)   If an inmate is found guilty of more than one charge arising out of an incident punishments under this rule may be ordered to run consecutively[, but, [in the case of an award of additional days, the total period added] shall not exceed [42 days]][and in the case of an award of cellular confinement the total period shall not exceed 7 days].

[(3)   An award of a caution shall not be combined with any other punishment for the same charge.

(4)   In imposing a punishment under this rule, the governor shall take into account any guidelines that the Secretary of State may from time to time issue as to the level of punishment that should normally be imposed for a particular offence against discipline.]]

Annotations

This rule was substituted by SI 1989/331, r 2(a).

Para (1): words 'paragraph (3) below and' in square brackets inserted by SI 1999/962, r 3, Schedule, para 10(1), (2); in sub-paras (b)–(d), (g) words in square brackets substituted by SI 1995/984, r 2, Schedule, para 2(a)(i)–(iii), (v); sub-para (e) substituted by SI 1992/513, r 2(1), Schedule, para 7, words in square brackets substituted by SI 1995/984, r 2, Schedule, para 2(a)(iv); in sub-para (f) words in square brackets substituted by SI 1993/3076, r 2, Schedule, para 3; in sub-para (f) words from 'in the case' to 'Disorder Act 1998,' in square brackets inserted by SI 2000/700, r 2, Schedule, para 2; sub-para (h) substituted by SI 1992/2081, r 2, Schedule, para 5, words in square brackets substituted by SI 1995/984, r 2, Schedule, para 2(a)(vi).

Para (2): first words in square brackets added by SI 1989/2142, r 2(b), first words in square brackets therein substituted by SI 1992/2081, r 2, Schedule, para 5, second words in square brackets therein substituted by SI 1995/984, r 2, Schedule, para 2(b); words from 'and in the case' to '7 days' in square brackets inserted by SI 1999/962, r 3, Schedule, para 10(1), (3).

Paras (3), (4): inserted by SI 1999/962, r 3, Schedule, para 10(1), (4).

[**56 Confinement to a cell or room**

[(1)   When it is proposed to impose a punishment of confinement in a cell or room, the medical officer, or a medical practitioner such as is mentioned in rule 24(3), shall inform the governor whether there are any medical reasons why the inmate should not be so dealt with. The governor shall give effect to any recommendation which may be made under this paragraph.]

(2)   No cell or room shall be used as a detention cell or room for the purpose of a punishment of confinement to a cell or room unless it has been certified by an officer of the Secretary of State (not being an officer of a young offender institution) that it is suitable for the purpose; that its size, lighting, heating, ventilation and fittings are adequate for health; and that it allows the inmate to communicate at any time with an officer.]

Annotations

Substituted by SI 1989/331, r 2(a).

Para (1): substituted by SI 1998/1545, r 2, Schedule, para 9.

57 Removal from wing or living unit

[Following the imposition of a punishment of removal from his wing or living unit, an inmate shall be accommodated in a separate part of the young offender institution under such restrictions of earnings and activities as the Secretary of State may direct.]

Annotations

Substituted by SI 1989/331, r 2(a).

[58 Suspended punishments

(1)   Subject to any directions of the Secretary of State, the power to impose a disciplinary punishment (other than a caution) shall include a power to direct that the punishment is not to take effect unless, during a period specified in the direction (not being more than 6 months from the date of the direction), the inmate commits another offence against disicpline and a direction is given under paragraph (2) below.

(2)   Where an inmate commits an offence against discipline during the period specified in a direction given under paragraph (1) above, the person . . . dealing with that offence may—

    (a)   direct that the suspended punishment shall take effect; or

    (b)   reduce the period or amount of the suspended punishment and direct that it shall take effect as so reduced; or

    (c)   vary the original direction by substituting for the period specified therein a period expiring not later than 6 months from the date of variation; or

    (d)   give no direction with respect to the suspended punishment.]

Annotations

Substituted by SI 1989/331, r 2(a).

Para (2): words omitted revoked by SI 1992/513, r 2(1), Schedule, para 10.

[59 Remission and mitigation of punishments and quashing of findings of guilt

(1)   The Secretary of State may quash any finding of guilt and may remit a disciplinary punishment or mitigate it either by reducing it or by substituting a punishment which is, in his opinion, less severe.

(2)   Subject to any directions of the Secretary of State, the governor may remit or mitigate any punishment imposed by a governor [or the board of visitors].]

Annotations

Substituted by SI 1989/331, r 2(a).

Para (2): words in square brackets substituted by SI 1992/513, r 2(1), Schedule, para 11.

[60 Adult female inmates: disciplinary punishments

[(1)   In the case of a female inmate aged 21 years or over who is serving a sentence of imprisonment or who has been committed to prison for default [and who is detained in a young offender institution pursuant to a direction of the Secretary of State under section 43(2)(a) of the Prison Act 1952]—

    (i)   rule 53 of these Rules shall not apply, but the governor may, if he finds the inmate guilty of an offence against discipline, impose one or more of the following punishments:

        (a)   caution;

        (b)   forfeiture for a period not exceeding [42 days] of any of the privileges under rule 7 of these Rules;

        (c)   removal for a period not exceeding [21 days] from any particular activity or activities of the young offender institution, other than education, training courses, work and physical education in accordance with rules 34, 35, 36, 37 and 38 of these Rules;

        (d)   . . .

        (e)   [stoppage of or deduction from earnings for a period not exceeding [84 days] of an amount not exceeding [42 days' earnings]];

        (f)   confinement to a cell or room for a period not exceeding [14 days];

        (g)   [in the case of an inmate who is a short-term or long-term prisoner, an award of additional days not exceeding [42 days];]

    (ii)   . . .

(2)   . . .

(3)   If an inmate is found guilty of more than one charge arising out of an incident, punishments under this rule may be ordered to run consecutively, but [in the case of an award of additional days, the total period added] shall not exceed [42 days].]

Annotations

Substituted by SI 1989/331, r 2(a).

Para (1): words from 'and who is' to 'Prison Act 1952' in square brackets inserted by SI 1999/962, r 3, Schedule, para 11(1), (2)(a); in sub-paras (i)(b)–(d) words in square brackets substituted by SI 1995/984, r 2, Schedule, para 3(a)(i)–(iii); sub-para (i)(e) substituted by SI 1992/513, r 2(1), Schedule, para 12, words in square brackets substituted by SI 1995/984, r 2, Schedule, para 3(a)(iv); in sub-para (i)(f) words in square brackets substituted by SI 1993/3076, r 2, Schedule, para 4; sub-para (i)(g) substituted by SI 1992/2081, r 2, Schedule, para 6, words in square brackets substituted by SI 1995/984, r 2, Schedule, para 3(a)(v); sub-para (ii) revoked by SI 1992/513, r 2(1), Schedule, para 13.

Para (2): revoked by SI 1992/513, r 2(1), Schedule, para 13.

Para (3): first words in square brackets substituted by SI 1992/2081, r 2, Schedule, para 6; second words in square brackets substituted by SI 1995/984, r 2, Schedule, para 3(b).

[60A Forfeiture of remission to be treated as an award of additional days

(1)   In this rule, 'existing prisoner' and 'existing licensee' have the meanings assigned to them by paragraph 8(1) of Schedule 12 to the Criminal Justice Act 1991.

(2)   In relation to any existing prisoner or existing licensee who has forfeited any remission of his sentence, the provisions of Part II of the Criminal Justice Act 1991 shall apply as if he had been awarded such number of additional days as equals the number of days of remission which he has forfeited.]

Annotations

Inserted by SI 1992/2081, r 2, Schedule, para 7.

PART III

OFFICERS OF YOUNG OFFENDER INSTITUTIONS

61 General duty of officers

(1)   It shall be the duty of every officer to conform to these Rules and the rules and regulations of the young offender institution, to assist and support the governor in their maintenance and to obey his lawful instructions.

(2)   An officer shall inform the governor promptly of any abuse or impropriety which comes to his knowledge.

62 Gratuities forbidden

No officer shall receive any unauthorised fee, gratuity or other consideration in connection with his office.

63 Search of officers

An officer shall submit himself to be searched in a young offender institution if the governor so directs. [Any such search shall be conducted in as seemly a manner as is consistent with discovering anything concealed.]

Annotations

Words in square brackets inserted by SI 1999/962, r 3, Schedule, para 12.

64 Transactions with inmates

(1)   No officer shall take part in any business or pecuniary transaction with or on behalf of an inmate without the leave of the Secretary of State.

(2)   No officer shall, without authority, bring in or take out, or attempt to bring in or take out, or knowingly allow to be brought in or taken out, to or for an inmate, or deposit in any place with intent that it shall come into the possession of an inmate, any article whatsoever.

65 Contact with former inmates, etc

No officer shall, without the knowledge of the governor, communicate with any person who he knows to be a former inmate or a relative or friend of an inmate or former inmate.

66 Communications to the press, etc

(1)   No officer shall make, directly or indirectly, any unauthorised communication to a representative of the press or any other person concerning matters which have become known to him in the course of his duty.

(2)   No officer shall, without authority, publish any matter or make any public pronouncement relating to the administration of any institution to which the Prison Act 1952 applies or to any of its inmates.

67 Quarters

. . .

Annotations

Revoked by SI 1999/962, r 3, Schedule, para 13.

68 Code of discipline

The Secretary of State may approve a code of discipline to have effect in relation to officers, or such classes of officers as it may specify, setting out the offences against discipline, the awards which may be made in respect of them and the procedure for dealing with charges.

Part IV
Persons having Access to a Young Offender Institution

69 Prohibited articles

No person shall, without authority, convey into or throw into or deposit in a young offender institution, or convey to an inmate, or deposit in any place with intent that it shall come into the possession of an inmate, any article whatsoever. Anything so conveyed, thrown or deposited may be confiscated by the governor.

70 Control of persons and vehicles

(1)   Any person or vehicle entering or leaving a young offender institution may be stopped, examined and searched.[Any such search of a person shall be carried out in as seemly a manner as is consistent with discovering anything concealed.]

(2)   The governor may direct the removal from a young offender institution of any person who does not leave on being required to do so.

Annotations

Para (1): words from 'Any such' to 'anything concealed.' in square brackets inserted by SI 1999/962, r 3, Schedule, para 14.

71 Viewing of young offender institutions

(1)   No outside person shall be permitted to view a young offender institution unless authorised by statute or the Secretary of State.

(2)   No person viewing a young offender institution shall be permitted to take a photograph, make a sketch or communicate with an inmate unless authorised by statute or the Secretary of State.

[71A Visitors

(1)   Without prejudice to any other powers to prohibit or restrict entry to young offender institutions, and to his powers under rules 10 and 11, the Secretary of State may, with a view to securing discipline and good order or the prevention of crime or in the interests of any persons, impose prohibitions on visits by a person to a young offender institution or to an inmate in a young offender institution for such periods of time as he considers necessary.

(2)   Paragraph (1) shall not apply in relation to any visit to a young offender institution or inmate by a member of the board of visitors of the young offender institution, or justice of the peace, or to prevent any visit by a legal adviser for the purposes of an interview under rule 13 or visit allowed by the board of visitors under rule 11(5).]

Annotations

Inserted by SI 1999/962, r 3, Schedule, para 15.

PART V
BOARDS OF VISITORS

[72 Disqualification for membership

Any person directly or indirectly interested in any contract for the supply of goods or services to a young offender institution shall not be a member of the board of visitors for that institution and any member who becomes so interested in such a contract shall vacate office as a member.]

Annotations

Substituted by SI 1999/962, r 3, Schedule, para 16.

73 Appointment

(1)   A member of the board of visitors for a young offender institution appointed by the Secretary of State under section 6(2) of the Prison Act 1952 [subject to [paragraphs (1A) and (1B)] below], shall hold office for 3 years or such less period as the Secretary of State may appoint.

[(1ZA) A member—

    (a)   appointed for the first time to the board of visitors for a particular young offender institution; or

    (b)   reappointed to the board following a gap of a year or more in his membership of it, shall, during the prior of 12 months following the date on which he is so appointed or (as the case may be) reappointed, undertake such training as may reasonably be required by the Secretary of State.]

[(1A) The Secretary of State may terminate the appointment of a member if satisfied that—

    (a)   he has failed satisfactorily to perform his duties,

    [(aa) he has failed to undertake training he has been required to undertake under paragraph (1ZA) of this rule, by the end of the period specified in that paragraph;]

    (b)   he is by reason of physical or mental illness, or for any other reason, incapable of carrying out his duties, or

    (c)   he has been convicted of such a criminal offence, or his conduct has been such, that it is not in the Secretary of State's opinion fitting that he should remain a member[; or

    (d)   there is, or appears to be, or could appear to be, any conflict of interest between the member performing his duties as a member and any interest of that member, whether personal, financial or otherwise].]

[(1B) Where the Secretary of State:

    (a)   has reason to suspect that a member of the board of visitors for a young offender institution may have so conducted himself that his appointment may be liable to be terminated under paragraph (1A)(a) or (c) above; and

(b)   is of the opinion that the suspected conduct is of such a serious nature that the member cannot be permitted to continue to perform his functions as a member of the board pending the completion of the Secretary of State's investigations into the matter and any decision as to whether the member's appointment should be terminated,

he may suspend the member from office for such period or periods as he may reasonably require in order to complete his investigations and determine whether or not the appointment of the member should be so terminated; and a member so suspended shall not, during the period of the suspension, be regarded as being a member of the board, other than for the purposes of this paragraph and paragraphs (1) and (1A) above.

[2]   A board shall have a chairman and a vice chairman, who shall be members of the board.

(3)   The Secretary of State shall—

(a)   upon the constitution of a board for the first time, appoint a chairman and a vice chairman to hold office for a period not exceeding twelve months;

(b)   thereafter appoint, before the date of the first meeting of the board in any year of office of the board, a chairman and a vice chairman for that year, having first consulted the board; and

(c)   promptly fill, after having first consulted the board, any casual vacancy in the office of chairman or vice chairman.

(4)   The Secretary of State may terminate the appointment of a member as chairman or vice chairman of the board if he is satisfied that the member has—

(a)   failed satisfactorily to perform his functions as chairman or (as the case may be) vice-chairman; or

(b)   has grossly misconducted himself whilst performing those functions.]

Annotations

Para (1): first words in square brackets inserted by SI 1989/331, r 2(b), words in square brackets therein substituted by SI 1996/1662, r 2, Schedule, para 8(2).

Para (1ZA): inserted by SI 1996/1662, r 2, Schedule, para 8(3).

Para (1A): substituted by SI 1989/331, r 2(b); sub-para (aa) inserted by SI 1996/1662, r 2, Schedule, para 8(4); sub-para (d) inserted by SI 1999/962, r 3, Schedule, para 17.

Para (1B): inserted by SI 1996/1662, r 2, Schedule, para 8(5).

Paras (2)–(4): substituted by SI 1996/1662, r 2, Schedule, para 8(6).

74 Proceedings of boards

(1)   The board of visitors for a young offender institution shall meet at the institution at least once a month.

(2)   The board may fix a quorum of not fewer than 3 members for proceedings . . . .

(3)   The board shall keep minutes of their proceedings.

(4)   The proceedings of the board shall not be invalidated by any vacancy in the membership or any defect in the appointment of a member.

Annotations

Para (2): words omitted revoked by SI 1992/513, r 2(1), Schedule, para 15.

75 General duties of boards

(1)   The board of visitors for a young offender institution shall satisfy themselves as to the state of the premises, the administration of the institution and the treatment of the inmates.

(2)   The board shall inquire into and report upon any matter into which the Secretary of State asks them to inquire.

(3)   The board shall direct the attention of the governor to any matter which calls for his attention, and shall report to the Secretary of State any matters which they consider it expedient to report.

(4)   The board shall inform the Secretary of State immediately of any abuse which comes to their knowledge . . . .

(5)   Before exercising any power under these Rules . . . the board and any member of the board shall consult the governor in relation to any matter which may affect discipline.

Annotations

Para (4): words omitted revoked by SI 1989/331, r 2(c).
Para (5): words omitted revoked by SI 1992/513, r 2(1), Schedule, para 16.

76 Particular duties

(1)   The board of visitors for a young offender institution and any member of the board shall hear any complaint or request which an inmate wishes to make to them or him.

(2)   The board shall arrange for the food of the inmates to be inspected by a member of the board at frequent intervals.

(3)   The board shall inquire into any report made to them, whether or not by a member of the board, that an inmate's health, mental or physical, is likely to be injuriously affected by any conditions of his detention.

77 Members visiting young offender institutions

(1) The members of the board of visitors for a young offender institution shall visit the institution frequently, and the board shall arrange a rota for the purpose.

(2) A member of the board shall have access at any time to every part of the institution and to every inmate, and he may interview any inmate out of the sight and hearing of officers.

(3) A member of the board shall have access to the records of the young offender institution.

[78 Annual report

(1) The board of visitors for a young offender institution shall, in accordance with paragraphs (2) and (3) below, from time to time make a report to the Secretary of State concerning the state of the institution and its administration, including in it any advice and suggestions they consider appropriate.

(2) The board shall comply with any directions given to them from time to time by the Secretary of State as to the following matters—

   (a) the period to be covered by a report under paragraph (1);

   (b) the frequency with which such a report is to be made; and

   (c) the length of time from the end of the period covered by such a report within which it is to be made,

either in respect of a particular report or generally; provided that no directions may be issued under this paragraph if they would have the effect of requiring a board to make or deliver a report less frequently than once in every 12 months.

(3) Subject to any directions given to them under paragraph (2), the board shall, under paragraph (1), make an annual report to the Secretary of State as soon as reasonably possible after 31st December each year, which shall cover the period of 12 months ending on that date or, in the case of a board constituted for the first time during that period, such part of that period during which the board has been in existence.]

Annotations

Substituted by SI 1996/1662, r 2, Schedule, para 9.

PART VI
SUPPLEMENTAL

79 Delegation by governor

The governor of a young offender institution may, with the leave of the Secretary of State, delegate any of his powers and duties under these Rules to another officer of that institution.

[79A Contracted out young offender institutions

1) Where the Secretary of State has entered into a contract for the running of a young offender institution under section 84 of the Criminal Justice Act 1991 (in this rule 'the 1991 Act') these Rules shall have effect in relation to that young offender institution with the following modifications—

   (a) references to an officer shall include references to a prisoner custody officer certified as such under section 89(1) of the 1991 Act;

   (b) references to a governor shall include references to a director approved by the Secretary of State for the purposes of section 85(1)(a) of the 1991 Act except—

      (i) in rules 46, 48, 49, 51, 52, 53, 59, 60 and 79 where references to a governor shall include references to a controller appointed by the Secretary of State under section 85(1)(b) of the 1991 Act; and

      (ii) in rules 61(1), 65 and 75 where references to a governor shall include references to a director and a controller;

   (c) rule 68 shall not apply in relation to a prisoner custody officer certified as such under section 89(1) of the 1991 Act and performing custodial duties.

(2) Where a director exercises the powers set out in section 85(3)(b) of the 1991 Act (removal from association, temporary confinement and restraints) in cases of urgency, he shall notify the controller of that fact forthwith.]

Annotations

Inserted by SI 1997/789, r 2.

[79B Contracted out parts of young offender institutions

Where the Secretary of State has entered into a contract for the running of part of a young offender institution under section 84(1) of the Criminal Justice Act 1991, that part and the remaining part shall each be treated for the purposes of Parts I to IV and Part VI of these Rules as if they were separate young offender institutions.]

Annotations

Inserted by SI 1997/789, rule 2.

[79C Contracted out functions at directly managed young offender institutions

(1) Where the Secretary of State has entered into a contract under section 88A(1) of the Criminal Justice Act 1991 for any functions at a directly managed young offender institution to be performed by prisoner custody officers who are authorised to perform custodial duties under section 89(1) of that Act, references to an officer in these Rules shall, subject to paragraph (2) below, include references to a prisoner custody officer who is so authorised and who is performing contracted out functions for the purposes of, or for purposes connected with, the young offender institution.

(2) Paragraph (1) above shall not apply to references to an officer in rule 68.

(3) In this rule 'directly managed young offender institution' means a young offender institution which is not a contracted out young offender institution.]

Annotations

Inserted by SI 1997/789, r 2.

80 Transitional

In the case of an inmate who, by virtue of paragraph 12 of Schedule 8 to the Criminal Justice Act 1988, falls to be treated for all purposes of detention, release and supervision as if he had been sentenced to detention in a young offender institution or who, under paragraph 13 of the said Schedule 8, is detained in such an institution, any award for an offence against discipline made in respect of him under rule 53 or 54 of the Detention Centre Rules 1983 or rule 53 or 54 of the Youth Custody Centre Rules 1983 shall, if it has not been exhausted or remitted, continue to have effect as if it had been made under rule 53 or 54, respectively, of those Rules.

SCHEDULE

INSTRUMENTS REVOKED

Rule 2(3)

. . .

Annotations

This Schedule revokes SI 1983/569, SI 1983/570, SI 1987/1255, SI 1987/1257.

HUMAN RIGHTS ACT 1998

1998 Chapter 42

9th November 1998

An Act to give further effect to rights and freedoms guaranteed under the European Convention on Human Rights; to make provision with respect to holders of certain judicial offices who become judges of the European Court of Human Rights; and for connected purposes.

BE IT ENACTED by the Queen's most Excellent Majesty, by and with the advice and consent of the Lords Spiritual and Temporal, and Commons, in this present Parliament assembled, and by the authority of the same, as follows:—

Introduction

1 The Convention Rights

(1) In this Act 'the Convention rights' means the rights and fundamental freedoms set out in—

    (a) Articles 2 to 12 and 14 of the Convention,

    (b) Articles 1 to 3 of the First Protocol, and

    (c) Articles 1 and 2 of the Sixth Protocol,

as read with Articles 16 to 18 of the Convention.

(2) Those Articles are to have effect for the purposes of this Act subject to any designated derogation or reservation (as to which see sections 14 and 15).

(3) The Articles are set out in Schedule 1.

(4) The Secretary of State may by order make such amendments to this Act as he considers appropriate to reflect the effect, in relation to the United Kingdom, of a protocol.

(5) In subsection (4) 'protocol' means a protocol to the Convention—

    (a) which the United Kingdom has ratified; or

    (b) which the United Kingdom has signed with a view to ratification.

(6)   No amendment may be made by an order under subsection (4) so as to come into force before the protocol concerned is in force in relation to the United Kingdom.

2 Interpretation of Convention rights

(1)   A court or tribunal determining a question which has arisen in connection with a Convention right must take into account any—

(a)   judgment, decision, declaration or advisory opinion of the European Court of Human Rights,

(b)   opinion of the Commission given in a report adopted under Article 31 of the Convention,

(c)   decision of the Commission in connection with Article 26 or 27(2) of the Convention, or

(d)   decision of the Committee of Ministers taken under Article 46 of the Convention,

whenever made or given, so far as, in the opinion of the court or tribunal, it is relevant to the proceedings in which that question has arisen.

(2)   Evidence of any judgment, decision, declaration or opinion of which account may have to be taken under this section is to be given in proceedings before any court or tribunal in such manner as may be provided by rules.

(3)   In this section 'rules' means rules of court or, in the case of proceedings before a tribunal, rules made for the purposes of this section—

(a)   by the Lord Chancellor or the Secretary of State, in relation to any proceedings outside Scotland;

(b)   by the Secretary of State, in relation to proceedings in Scotland; or

(c)   by a Northern Ireland department, in relation to proceedings before a tribunal in Northern Ireland—

(i)   which deals with transferred matters; and

(ii)   for which no rules made under paragraph (a) are in force.

Legislation

3 Interpretation of legislation

(1)   So far as it is possible to do so, primary legislation and subordinate legislation must be read and given effect in a way which is compatible with the Convention rights.

(2)   This section—

(a)   applies to primary legislation and subordinate legislation whenever enacted;

(b)   does not affect the validity, continuing operation or enforcement of any incompatible primary legislation; and

(c)   does not affect the validity, continuing operation or enforcement of any incompatible subordinate legislation if (disregarding any possibility of revocation) primary legislation prevents removal of the incompatibility.

4 Declaration of incompatibility

(1) Subsection (2) applies in any proceedings in which a court determines whether a provision of primary legislation is compatible with a Convention right.

(2) If the court is satisfied that the provision is incompatible with a Convention right, it may make a declaration of that incompatibility.

(3) Subsection (4) applies in any proceedings in which a court determines whether a provision of subordinate legislation, made in the exercise of a power conferred by primary legislation, is compatible with a Convention right.

(4) If the court is satisfied—

    (a) that the provision is incompatible with a Convention right, and

    (b) that (disregarding any possibility of revocation) the primary legislation concerned prevents removal of the incompatibility,

it may make a declaration of that incompatibility.

(5) In this section 'court' means—

    (a) the House of Lords;

    (b) the Judicial Committee of the Privy Council;

    (c) the Courts-Martial Appeal Court;

    (d) in Scotland, the High Court of Justiciary sitting otherwise than as a trial court or the Court of Session;

    (e) in England and Wales or Northern Ireland, the High Court or the Court of Appeal.

(6) A declaration under this section ('a declaration of incompatibility')—

    (a) does not affect the validity, continuing operation or enforcement of the provision in respect of which it is given; and

    (b) is not binding on the parties to the proceedings in which it is made.

5 Right of Crown to intervene

(1) Where a court is considering whether to make a declaration of incompatibility, the Crown is entitled to notice in accordance with rules of court.

(2) In any case to which subsection (1) applies—

    (a) a Minister of the Crown (or a person nominated by him),

    (b) a member of the Scottish Executive,

    (c) a Northern Ireland Minister,

    (d) a Northern Ireland department,

is entitled, on giving notice in accordance with rules of court, to be joined as a party to the proceedings.

(3)   Notice under subsection (2) may be given at any time during the proceedings.

(4)   A person who has been made a party to criminal proceedings (other than in Scotland) as the result of a notice under subsection (2) may, with leave, appeal to the House of Lords against any declaration of incompatibility made in the proceedings.

(5)   In subsection (4)—

'criminal proceedings' includes all proceedings before the Courts-Martial Appeal Court; and

'leave' means leave granted by the court making the declaration of incompatibility or by the House of Lords.

Public authorities

6 Acts of public authorities

(1)   It is unlawful for a public authority to act in a way which is incompatible with a Convention right.

(2)   Subsection (1) does not apply to an act if—

(a)   as the result of one or more provisions of primary legislation, the authority could not have acted differently; or

(b)   in the case of one or more provisions of, or made under, primary legislation which cannot be read or given effect in a way which is compatible with the Convention rights, the authority was acting so as to give effect to or enforce those provisions.

(3)   In this section 'public authority' includes—

(a)   a court or tribunal, and

(b)   any person certain of whose functions are functions of a public nature,

but does not include either House of Parliament or a person exercising functions in connection with proceedings in Parliament.

(4)   In subsection (3) 'Parliament' does not include the House of Lords in its judicial capacity.

(5)   In relation to a particular act, a person is not a public authority by virtue only of sub-section (3)(b) if the nature of the act is private.

(6)   'An act' includes a failure to act but does not include a failure to—

(a)   introduce in, or lay before, Parliament a proposal for legislation; or

(b)   make any primary legislation or remedial order.

7 Proceedings

(1)   A person who claims that a public authority has acted (or proposes to act) in a way which is made unlawful by section 6(1) may—

(a) bring proceedings against the authority under this Act in the appropriate court or tribunal, or

(b) rely on the Convention right or rights concerned in any legal proceedings,

but only if he is (or would be) a victim of the unlawful act.

(2) In subsection (1)(a) 'appropriate court or tribunal' means such court or tribunal as may be determined in accordance with rules; and proceedings against an authority include a counterclaim or similar proceeding.

(3) If the proceedings are brought on an application for judicial review, the applicant is to be taken to have a sufficient interest in relation to the unlawful act only if he is, or would be, a victim of that act.

(4) If the proceedings are made by way of a petition for judicial review in Scotland, the applicant shall be taken to have title and interest to sue in relation to the unlawful act only if he is, or would be, a victim of that act.

(5) Proceedings under subsection (1)(a) must be brought before the end of—

(a) the period of one year beginning with the date on which the act complained of took place; or

(b) such longer period as the court or tribunal considers equitable having regard to all the circumstances,

but that is subject to any rule imposing a stricter time limit in relation to the procedure in question.

(6) In subsection (1)(b) 'legal proceedings' includes—

(a) proceedings brought by or at the instigation of a public authority; and

(b) an appeal against the decision of a court or tribunal.

(7) For the purposes of this section, a person is a victim of an unlawful act only if he would be a victim for the purposes of Article 34 of the Convention if proceedings were brought in the European Court of Human Rights in respect of that act.

(8) Nothing in this Act creates a criminal offence.

(9) In this section 'rules' means—

(a) in relation to proceedings before a court or tribunal outside Scotland, rules made by the Lord Chancellor or the Secretary of State for the purposes of this section or rules of court,

(b) in relation to proceedings before a court or tribunal in Scotland, rules made by the Secretary of State for those purposes,

(c) in relation to proceedings before a tribunal in Northern Ireland—

(i) which deals with transferred matters; and

(ii) for which no rules made under paragraph (a) are in force,

rules made by a Northern Ireland department for those purposes, and includes provision made by order under section 1 of the Courts and Legal Services Act 1990.

(10)   In making rules, regard must be had to section 9.

(11)   The Minister who has power to make rules in relation to a particular tribunal may, to the extent he considers it necessary to ensure that the tribunal can provide an appropriate remedy in relation to an act (or proposed act) of a public authority which is (or would be) unlawful as a result of section 6(1), by order add to—

(a)   the relief or remedies which the tribunal may grant; or

(b)   the grounds on which it may grant any of them.

(12)   An order made under subsection (11) may contain such incidental, supplemental, consequential or transitional provision as the Minister making it considers appropriate.

(13)   'The Minister' includes the Northern Ireland department concerned.

8 Judicial remedies

(1)   In relation to any act (or proposed act) of a public authority which the court finds is (or would be) unlawful, it may grant such relief or remedy, or make such order, within its powers as it considers just and appropriate.

(2)   But damages may be awarded only by a court which has power to award damages, or to order the payment of compensation, in civil proceedings.

(3)   No award of damages is to be made unless, taking account of all the circumstances of the case, including—

(a)   any other relief or remedy granted, or order made, in relation to the act in question (by that or any other court), and

(b)   the consequences of any decision (of that or any other court) in respect of that act,

the court is satisfied that the award is necessary to afford just satisfaction to the person in whose favour it is made.

(4)   In determining—

(a)   whether to award damages, or

(b)   the amount of an award,

the court must take into account the principles applied by the European Court of Human Rights in relation to the award of compensation under Article 41 of the Convention.

(5)   A public authority against which damages are awarded is to be treated—

(a)   in Scotland, for the purposes of section 3 of the Law Reform (Miscellaneous Provisions) (Scotland) Act 1940 as if the award were made in an action of damages in which the authority has been found liable in respect of loss or damage to the person to whom the award is made;

(b)   for the purposes of the Civil Liability (Contribution) Act 1978 as liable in respect of damage suffered by the person to whom the award is made.

(6)   In this section—

'court' includes a tribunal;

'damages' means damages for an unlawful act of a public authority; and

'unlawful' means unlawful under section 6(1).

9 Judicial acts

(1)   Proceedings under section 7(1)(a) in respect of a judicial act may be brought only—

(a)   by exercising a right of appeal;

(b)   on an application (in Scotland a petition) for judicial review; or

(c)   in such other forum as may be prescribed by rules.

(2)   That does not affect any rule of law which prevents a court from being the subject of judicial review.

(3)   In proceedings under this Act in respect of a judicial act done in good faith, damages may not be awarded otherwise than to compensate a person to the extent required by Article 5(5) of the Convention.

(4)   An award of damages permitted by subsection (3) is to be made against the Crown; but no award may be made unless the appropriate person, if not a party to the proceedings, is joined.

(5)   In this section—

'appropriate person' means the Minister responsible for the court concerned, or a person or government department nominated by him;

'court' includes a tribunal;

'judge' includes a member of a tribunal, a justice of the peace and a clerk or other officer entitled to exercise the jurisdiction of a court;

'judicial act' means a judicial act of a court and includes an act done on the instructions, or on behalf, of a judge; and

'rules' has the same meaning as in section 7(9).

Remedial action

10 Power to take remedial action

(1)   This section applies if—

(a)   a provision of legislation has been declared under section 4 to be incompatible with a Convention right and, if an appeal lies—

(i)   all persons who may appeal have stated in writing that they do not intend to do so;

389

(ii) the time for bringing an appeal has expired and no appeal has been brought within that time; or

(iii) an appeal brought within that time has been determined or abandoned; or

(b) it appears to a Minister of the Crown or Her Majesty in Council that, having regard to a finding of the European Court of Human Rights made after the coming into force of this section in proceedings against the United Kingdom, a provision of legislation is incompatible with an obligation of the United Kingdom arising from the Convention.

(2) If a Minister of the Crown considers that there are compelling reasons for proceeding under this section, he may by order make such amendments to the legislation as he considers necessary to remove the incompatibility.

(3) If, in the case of subordinate legislation, a Minister of the Crown considers—

(a) that it is necessary to amend the primary legislation under which the subordinate legislation in question was made, in order to enable the incompatibility to be removed, and

(b) that there are compelling reasons for proceeding under this section,

he may by order make such amendments to the primary legislation as he considers necessary.

(4) This section also applies where the provision in question is in subordinate legislation and has been quashed, or declared invalid, by reason of incompatibility with a Convention right and the Minister proposes to proceed under paragraph 2(b) of Schedule 2.

(5) If the legislation is an Order in Council, the power conferred by subsection (2) or (3) is exercisable by Her Majesty in Council.

(6) In this section 'legislation' does not include a Measure of the Church Assembly or of the General Synod of the Church of England.

(7) Schedule 2 makes further provision about remedial orders.

Other rights and proceedings

11 Safeguard for existing human rights

A person's reliance on a Convention right does not restrict—

(a) any other right or freedom conferred on him by or under any law having effect in any part of the United Kingdom; or

(b) his right to make any claim or bring any proceedings which he could make or bring apart from sections 7 to 9.

12 Freedom of expression

(1) This section applies if a court is considering whether to grant any relief which, if granted, might affect the exercise of the Convention right to freedom of expression.

(2) If the person against whom the application for relief is made ('the respondent') is neither present nor represented, no such relief is to be granted unless the court is satisfied—

   (a) that the applicant has taken all practicable steps to notify the respondent; or

   (b) that there are compelling reasons why the respondent should not be notified.

(3) No such relief is to be granted so as to restrain publication before trial unless the court is satisfied that the applicant is likely to establish that publication should not be allowed.

(4) The court must have particular regard to the importance of the Convention right to freedom of expression and, where the proceedings relate to material which the respondent claims, or which appears to the court, to be journalistic, literary or artistic material (or to conduct connected with such material), to—

   (a) the extent to which—

      (i) the material has, or is about to, become available to the public; or

      (ii) it is, or would be, in the public interest for the material to be published;

   (b) any relevant privacy code.

(5) In this section—

   'court' includes a tribunal; and

   'relief' includes any remedy or order (other than in criminal proceedings).

13 Freedom of thought, conscience and religion

(1) If a court's determination of any question arising under this Act might affect the exercise by a religious organisation (itself or its members collectively) of the Convention right to freedom of thought, conscience and religion, it must have particular regard to the importance of that right.

(2) In this section 'court' includes a tribunal.

Derogations and reservations

14 Derogations

(1) In this Act 'designated derogation' means—

   (a) the United Kingdom's derogation from Article 5(3) of the Convention; and

   (b) any derogation by the United Kingdom from an Article of the Convention, or of any protocol to the Convention, which is designated for the purposes of this Act in an order made by the Secretary of State.

(2) The derogation referred to in subsection (1)(a) is set out in Part I of Schedule 3.

(3) If a designated derogation is amended or replaced it ceases to be a designated derogation.

(4) But subsection (3) does not prevent the Secretary of State from exercising his power under subsection (1)(b) to make a fresh designation order in respect of the Article concerned.

(5) The Secretary of State must by order make such amendments to Schedule 3 as he considers appropriate to reflect—

(a) any designation order; or

(b) the effect of subsection (3).

(6) A designation order may be made in anticipation of the making by the United Kingdom of a proposed derogation.

15 Reservations

(1) In this Act 'designated reservation' means—

(a) the United Kingdom's reservation to Article 2 of the First Protocol to the Convention; and

(b) any other reservation by the United Kingdom to an Article of the Convention, or of any protocol to the Convention, which is designated for the purposes of this Act in an order made by the Secretary of State.

(2) The text of the reservation referred to in subsection (1)(*a*) is set out in Part II of Schedule 3.

(3) If a designated reservation is withdrawn wholly or in part it ceases to be a designated reservation.

(4) But subsection (3) does not prevent the Secretary of State from exercising his power under subsection (1)(*b*) to make a fresh designation order in respect of the Article concerned.

(5) The Secretary of State must by order make such amendments to this Act as he considers appropriate to reflect—

(a) any designation order; or

(b) the effect of subsection (3).

16 Period for which designated derogations have effect

(1) If it has not already been withdrawn by the United Kingdom, a designated derogation ceases to have effect for the purposes of this Act—

(a) in the case of the derogation referred to in section 14(1)(a), at the end of the period of five years beginning with the date on which section 1(2) came into force;

(b) in the case of any other derogation, at the end of the period of five years beginning with the date on which the order designating it was made.

(2)   At any time before the period—

    (a)   fixed by subsection (1)(a) or (b), or

    (b)   extended by an order under this subsection,

comes to an end, the Secretary of State may by order extend it by a further period of five years.

(3)   An order under section 14(1)(b) ceases to have effect at the end of the period for consideration, unless a resolution has been passed by each House approving the order.

(4)   Subsection (3) does not affect—

    (a)   anything done in reliance on the order; or

    (b)   the power to make a fresh order under section 14(1)(b).

(5)   In subsection (3) 'period for consideration' means the period of forty days beginning with the day on which the order was made.

(6)   In calculating the period for consideration, no account is to be taken of any time during which—

    (a)   Parliament is dissolved or prorogued; or

    (b)   both Houses are adjourned for more than four days.

(7)   If a designated derogation is withdrawn by the United Kingdom, the Secretary of State must by order make such amendments to this Act as he considers are required to reflect that withdrawal.

17 Periodic review of designated reservations

(1)   The appropriate Minister must review the designated reservation referred to in section 15(1)(a)—

    (a)   before the end of the period of five years beginning with the date on which section 1(2) came into force; and

    (b)   if that designation is still in force, before the end of the period of five years beginning with the date on which the last report relating to it was laid under subsection (3).

(2)   The appropriate Minister must review each of the other designated reservations (if any)—

    (a)   before the end of the period of five years beginning with the date on which the order designating the reservation first came into force; and

    (b)   if the designation is still in force, before the end of the period of five years beginning with the date on which the last report relating to it was laid under subsection (3).

(3)   The Minister conducting a review under this section must prepare a report on the result of the review and lay a copy of it before each House of Parliament.

Judges of the European Court of Human Rights

18 Appointment to European Court of Human Rights

(1)   In this section 'judicial office' means the office of—

    (a)   Lord Justice of Appeal, Justice of the High Court or Circuit judge, in England and Wales;

    (b)   judge of the Court of Session or sheriff, in Scotland;

    (c)   Lord Justice of Appeal, judge of the High Court or county court judge, in Northern Ireland.

(2)   The holder of a judicial office may become a judge of the European Court of Human Rights ('the Court') without being required to relinquish his office.

(3)   But he is not required to perform the duties of his judicial office while he is a judge of the Court.

(4)   In respect of any period during which he is a judge of the Court—

    (a)   a Lord Justice of Appeal or Justice of the High Court is not to count as a judge of the relevant court for the purposes of section 2(1) or 4(1) of the Supreme Court Act 1981 (maximum number of judges) nor as a judge of the Supreme Court for the purposes of section 12(1) to (6) of that Act (salaries etc);

    (b)   a judge of the Court of Session is not to count as a judge of that court for the purposes of section 1(1) of the Court of Session Act 1988 (maximum number of judges) or of section 9(1)(c) of the Administration of Justice Act 1973 ('the 1973 Act') (salaries etc);

    (c)   a Lord Justice of Appeal or judge of the High Court in Northern Ireland is not to count as a judge of the relevant court for the purposes of section 2(1) or 3(1) of the Judicature (Northern Ireland) Act 1978 (maximum number of judges) nor as a judge of the Supreme Court of Northern Ireland for the purposes of section 9(1)(d) of the 1973 Act (salaries etc);

    (d)   a Circuit judge is not to count as such for the purposes of section 18 of the Courts Act 1971 (salaries etc);

    (e)   a sheriff is not to count as such for the purposes of section 14 of the Sheriff Courts (Scotland) Act 1907 (salaries etc);

    (f)   a county court judge of Northern Ireland is not to count as such for the purposes of section 106 of the County Courts Act (Northern Ireland) 1959 (salaries etc).

(5)   If a sheriff principal is appointed a judge of the Court, section 11(1) of the Sheriff Courts (Scotland) Act 1971 (temporary appointment of sheriff principal) applies, while he holds that appointment, as if his office is vacant.

(6)   Schedule 4 makes provision about judicial pensions in relation to the holder of a judicial office who serves as a judge of the Court.

(7)   The Lord Chancellor or the Secretary of State may by order make such transitional provision (including, in particular, provision for a temporary

increase in the maximum number of judges) as he considers appropriate in relation to any holder of a judicial office who has completed his service as a judge of the Court.

Parliamentary procedure

19 Statements of compatibility

(1) A Minister of the Crown in charge of a Bill in either House of Parliament must, before Second Reading of the Bill—

 (a) make a statement to the effect that in his view the provisions of the Bill are compatible with the Convention rights ('a statement of compatibility'); or

 (b) make a statement to the effect that although he is unable to make a statement of compatibility the government nevertheless wishes the House to proceed with the Bill.

(2) The statement must be in writing and be published in such manner as the Minister making it considers appropriate.

Supplemental

20 Orders etc under this Act

(1) Any power of a Minister of the Crown to make an order under this Act is exercisable by statutory instrument.

(2) The power of the Lord Chancellor or the Secretary of State to make rules (other than rules of court) under section 2(3) or 7(9) is exercisable by statutory instrument.

(3) Any statutory instrument made under section 14, 15 or 16(7) must be laid before Parliament.

(4) No order may be made by the Lord Chancellor or the Secretary of State under section 1(4), 7(11) or 16(2) unless a draft of the order has been laid before, and approved by, each House of Parliament.

(5) Any statutory instrument made under section 18(7) or Schedule 4, or to which sub-section (2) applies, shall be subject to annulment in pursuance of a resolution of either House of Parliament.

(6) The power of a Northern Ireland department to make—

 (a) rules under section 2(3)(c) or 7(9)(c), or

 (b) an order under section 7(11),

is exercisable by statutory rule for the purposes of the Statutory Rules (Northern Ireland) Order 1979.

(7) Any rules made under section 2(3)(c) or 7(9)(c) shall be subject to negative resolution; and section 41(6) of the Interpretation Act (Northern Ireland) 1954 (meaning of 'subject to negative resolution') shall apply as if the power to make the rules were conferred by an Act of the Northern Ireland Assembly.

(8)   No order may be made by a Northern Ireland department under section 7(11) unless a draft of the order has been laid before, and approved by, the Northern Ireland Assembly.

21 Interpretation, etc

(1)   In this Act—

'amend' includes repeal and apply (with or without modifications);

'the appropriate Minister' means the Minister of the Crown having charge of the appropriate authorised government department (within the meaning of the Crown Proceedings Act 1947);

'the Commission' means the European Commission of Human Rights;

'the Convention' means the Convention for the Protection of Human Rights and Fundamental Freedoms, agreed by the Council of Europe at Rome on 4th November 1950 as it has effect for the time being in relation to the United Kingdom;

'declaration of incompatibility' means a declaration under section 4;

'Minister of the Crown' has the same meaning as in the Ministers of the Crown Act 1975;

'Northern Ireland Minister' includes the First Minister and the deputy First Minister in Northern Ireland;

'primary legislation' means any—

(a)   public general Act;

(b)   local and personal Act;

(c)   private Act;

(d)   Measure of the Church Assembly;

(e)   Measure of the General Synod of the Church of England;

(f)   Order in Council—

(i)   made in exercise of Her Majesty's Royal Prerogative;

(ii)   made under section 38(1)(a) of the Northern Ireland Constitution Act 1973 or the corresponding provision of the Northern Ireland Act 1998; or

(iii)   amending an Act of a kind mentioned in paragraph (a), (b) or (c);

and includes an order or other instrument made under primary legislation (otherwise than by the National Assembly for Wales, a member of the Scottish Executive, a Northern Ireland Minister or a Northern Ireland department) to the extent to which it operates to bring one or more provisions of that legislation into force or amends any primary legislation;

'the First Protocol' means the protocol to the Convention agreed at Paris on 20th March 1952;

'the Sixth Protocol' means the protocol to the Convention agreed at Strasbourg on 28th April 1983;

'the Eleventh Protocol' means the protocol to the Convention (restructuring the control machinery established by the Convention) agreed at Strasbourg on 11th May 1994;

'remedial order' means an order under section 10;

'subordinate legislation' means any—

   (a) Order in Council other than one—

      (i)   made in exercise of Her Majesty's Royal Prerogative;

      (ii) made under section 38(1)(a) of the Northern Ireland Constitution Act 1973 or the corresponding provision of the Northern Ireland Act 1998; or

      (iii) amending an Act of a kind mentioned in the definition of primary legislation;

   (b) Act of the Scottish Parliament;

   (c) Act of the Parliament of Northern Ireland;

   (d   Measure of the Assembly established under section 1 of the Northern Ireland Assembly Act 1973;

   (e) Act of the Northern Ireland Assembly;

   (f) order, rules, regulations, scheme, warrant, byelaw or other instrument made under primary legislation (except to the extent to which it operates to bring one or more provisions of that legislation into force or amends any primary legislation);

   (g) order, rules, regulations, scheme, warrant, byelaw or other instrument made under legislation mentioned in paragraph (b), (c), (d) or (e) or made under an Order in Council applying only to Northern Ireland;

   (h) order, rules, regulations, scheme, warrant, byelaw or other instrument made by a member of the Scottish Executive, a Northern Ireland Minister or a Northern Ireland department in exercise of prerogative or other executive functions of Her Majesty which are exercisable by such a person on behalf of Her Majesty;

'transferred matters' has the same meaning as in the Northern Ireland Act 1998; and

'tribunal' means any tribunal in which legal proceedings may be brought.

(2) The references in paragraphs (b) and (c) of section 2(1) to Articles are to Articles of the Convention as they had effect immediately before the coming into force of the Eleventh Protocol.

(3) The reference in paragraph (d) of section 2(1) to Article 46 includes a reference to Articles 32 and 54 of the Convention as they had effect immediately before the coming into force of the Eleventh Protocol.

(4)   The references in section 2(1) to a report or decision of the Commission or a decision of the Committee of Ministers include references to a report or decision made as provided by paragraphs 3, 4 and 6 of Article 5 of the Eleventh Protocol (transitional provisions).

(5)   Any liability under the Army Act 1955, the Air Force Act 1955 or the Naval Discipline Act 1957 to suffer death for an offence is replaced by a liability to imprisonment for life or any less punishment authorised by those Acts; and those Acts shall accordingly have effect with the necessary modifications.

22 Short title, commencement, application and extent

(1)   This Act may be cited as the Human Rights Act 1998.

(2)   Sections 18, 20 and 21(5) and this section come into force on the passing of this Act.

(3)   The other provisions of this Act come into force on such day as the Secretary of State may by order appoint; and different days may be appointed for different purposes.

(4)   Paragraph (b) of subsection (1) of section 7 applies to proceedings brought by or at the instigation of a public authority whenever the act in question took place; but otherwise that subsection does not apply to an act taking place before the coming into force of that section.

(5)   This Act binds the Crown.

(6)   This Act extends to Northern Ireland.

(7)   Section 21(5), so far as it relates to any provision contained in the Army Act 1955, the Air Force Act 1955 or the Naval Discipline Act 1957, extends to any place to which that provision extends.

SCHEDULE 1
THE ARTICLES

Section 1(3)

PART I
THE CONVENTION

Rights and Freedoms

Article 2
Right to life

1 Everyone's right to life shall be protected by law. No one shall be deprived of his life intentionally save in the execution of a sentence of a court following his conviction of a crime for which this penalty is provided by law.

2 Deprivation of life shall not be regarded as inflicted in contravention of this Article when it results from the use of force which is no more than absolutely necessary:

(a)   in defence of any person from unlawful violence;

(b)   in order to effect a lawful arrest or to prevent the escape of a person lawfully detained;

(c)   in action lawfully taken for the purpose of quelling a riot or insurrection.

Article 3
Prohibition of torture

No one shall be subjected to torture or to inhuman or degrading treatment or punishment.

Article 4
Prohibition of slavery and forced labour

1 No one shall be held in slavery or servitude.

2 No one shall be required to perform forced or compulsory labour.

3 For the purpose of this Article the term 'forced or compulsory labour' shall not include:

(a)   any work required to be done in the ordinary course of detention imposed according to the provisions of Article 5 of this Convention or during conditional release from such detention;

(b)   any service of a military character or, in case of conscientious objectors in countries where they are recognised, service exacted instead of compulsory military service;

(c)   any service exacted in case of an emergency or calamity threatening the life or well-being of the community;

(d)   any work or service which forms part of normal civic obligations.

Article 5
Right to liberty and security

1 Everyone has the right to liberty and security of person. No one shall be deprived of his liberty save in the following cases and in accordance with a procedure prescribed by law:

(a)   the lawful detention of a person after conviction by a competent court;

(b)   the lawful arrest or detention of a person for non-compliance with the lawful order of a court or in order to secure the fulfilment of any obligation prescribed by law;

(c)   the lawful arrest or detention of a person effected for the purpose of bringing him before the competent legal authority on reasonable suspicion of having committed an offence or when it is reasonably considered necessary to prevent his committing an offence or fleeing after having done so;

(d)   the detention of a minor by lawful order for the purpose of educational supervision or his lawful detention for the purpose of bringing him before the competent legal authority;

(e)   the lawful detention of persons for the prevention of the spreading of infectious diseases, of persons of unsound mind, alcoholics or drug addicts or vagrants;

(f)   the lawful arrest or detention of a person to prevent his effecting an unauthorised entry into the country or of a person against whom action is being taken with a view to deportation or extradition.

2 Everyone who is arrested shall be informed promptly, in a language which he understands, of the reasons for his arrest and of any charge against him.

3 Everyone arrested or detained in accordance with the provisions of paragraph 1(*c*) of this Article shall be brought promptly before a judge or other officer authorised by law to exercise judicial power and shall be entitled to trial within a reasonable time or to release pending trial. Release may be conditioned by guarantees to appear for trial.

4 Everyone who is deprived of his liberty by arrest or detention shall be entitled to take proceedings by which the lawfulness of his detention shall be decided speedily by a court and his release ordered if the detention is not lawful.

5 Everyone who has been the victim of arrest or detention in contravention of the provisions of this Article shall have an enforceable right to compensation.

Article 6
Right to a fair trial

1 In the determination of his civil rights and obligations or of any criminal charge against him, everyone is entitled to a fair and public hearing within a reasonable time by an independent and impartial tribunal established by law. Judgment shall be pronounced publicly but the press and public may be excluded from all or part of the trial in the interest of morals, public order or national security in a democratic society, where the interests of juveniles or the protection of the private life of the parties so require, or to the extent strictly necessary in the opinion of the court in special circumstances where publicity would prejudice the interests of justice.

2 Everyone charged with a criminal offence shall be presumed innocent until proved guilty according to law.

3 Everyone charged with a criminal offence has the following minimum rights:

(a)   to be informed promptly, in a language which he understands and in detail, of the nature and cause of the accusation against him;

(b)   to have adequate time and facilities for the preparation of his defence;

(c)   to defend himself in person or through legal assistance of his own choosing or, if he has not sufficient means to pay for legal assistance, to be given it free when the interests of justice so require;

(d)   to examine or have examined witnesses against him and to obtain the attendance and examination of witnesses on his behalf under the same conditions as witnesses against him;

(e)   to have the free assistance of an interpreter if he cannot understand or speak the language used in court.

Article 7
No punishment without law

1 No one shall be held guilty of any criminal offence on account of any act or omission which did not constitute a criminal offence under national or international law at the time when it was committed. Nor shall a heavier penalty be imposed than the one that was applicable at the time the criminal offence was committed.

2 This Article shall not prejudice the trial and punishment of any person for any act or omission which, at the time when it was committed, was criminal according to the general principles of law recognised by civilised nations.

Article 8
Right to respect for private and family life

1 Everyone has the right to respect for his private and family life, his home and his correspondence.

2 There shall be no interference by a public authority with the exercise of this right except such as is in accordance with the law and is necessary in a democratic society in the interests of national security, public safety or the economic well-being of the country, for the prevention of disorder or crime, for the protection of health or morals, or for the protection of the rights and freedoms of others.

Article 9
Freedom of thought, conscience and religion

1 Everyone has the right to freedom of thought, conscience and religion; this right includes freedom to change his religion or belief and freedom, either alone or in community with others and in public or private, to manifest his religion or belief, in worship, teaching, practice and observance.

2 Freedom to manifest one's religion or beliefs shall be subject only to such limitations as are prescribed by law and are necessary in a democratic society in the interests of public safety, for the protection of public order, health or morals, or for the protection of the rights and freedoms of others.

Article 10
Freedom of expression

1 Everyone has the right to freedom of expression. This right shall include freedom to hold opinions and to receive and impart information and ideas without interference by public authority and regardless of frontiers. This Article shall not prevent States from requiring the licensing of broadcasting, television or cinema enterprises.

2 The exercise of these freedoms, since it carries with it duties and responsibilities, may be subject to such formalities, conditions, restrictions or penalties as are prescribed by law and are necessary in a democratic society, in the interests of national security, territorial integrity or public safety, for the prevention of disorder or crime, for the protection of health or morals, for the protection of the reputation or rights of others, for preventing the disclosure of information received in confidence, or for maintaining the authority and impartiality of the judiciary.

Article 11
Freedom of assembly and association

1 Everyone has the right to freedom of peaceful assembly and to freedom of association with others, including the right to form and to join trade unions for the protection of his interests.

2 No restrictions shall be placed on the exercise of these rights other than such as are prescribed by law and are necessary in a democratic society in the interests of national security or public safety, for the prevention of disorder or crime, for the protection of health or morals or for the protection of the rights and freedoms of others. This Article shall not prevent the imposition of lawful restrictions on the exercise of these rights by members of the armed forces, of the police or of the administration of the State.

Article 12
Right to marry

Men and women of marriageable age have the right to marry and to found a family, according to the national laws governing the exercise of this right.

Article 14
Prohibition of discrimination

The enjoyment of the rights and freedoms set forth in this Convention shall be secured without discrimination on any ground such as sex, race, colour, language, religion, political or other opinion, national or social origin, association with a national minority, property, birth or other status.

Article 16
Restrictions on political activity of aliens

Nothing in Articles 10, 11 and 14 shall be regarded as preventing the High Contracting Parties from imposing restrictions on the political activity of aliens.

Article 17
Prohibition of abuse of rights

Nothing in this Convention may be interpreted as implying for any State, group or person any right to engage in any activity or perform any act aimed at the destruction of any of the rights and freedoms set forth herein or at their limitation to a greater extent than is provided for in the Convention.

Article 18
Limitation on use of restrictions on rights

The restrictions permitted under this Convention to the said rights and freedoms shall not be applied for any purpose other than those for which they have been prescribed.

PART II
THE FIRST PROTOCOL

Article 1
Protection of property

Every natural or legal person is entitled to the peaceful enjoyment of his possessions. No one shall be deprived of his possessions except in the public interest and subject to the conditions provided for by law and by the general principles of international law.

The preceding provisions shall not, however, in any way impair the right of a State to enforce such laws as it deems necessary to control the use of property in accordance with the general interest or to secure the payment of taxes or other contributions or penalties.

Article 2
Right to education

No person shall be denied the right to education. In the exercise of any functions which it assumes in relation to education and to teaching, the State shall respect the right of parents to ensure such education and teaching in conformity with their own religious and philosophical convictions.

Article 3
Right to free elections

The High Contracting Parties undertake to hold free elections at reasonable intervals by secret ballot, under conditions which will ensure the free expression of the opinion of the people in the choice of the legislature.

PART III
THE SIXTH PROTOCOL

Article 1
Abolition of the death penalty

The death penalty shall be abolished. No one shall be condemned to such penalty or executed.

Article 2
Death penalty in time of war

A State may make provision in its law for the death penalty in respect of acts committed in time of war or of imminent threat of war; such penalty shall be applied only in the instances laid down in the law and in accordance with its provisions. The State shall communicate to the Secretary General of the Council of Europe the relevant provisions of that law.

SCHEDULE 2
REMEDIAL ORDERS

Section 10

Orders

1 (1)   A remedial order may—

    (a)   contain such incidental, supplemental, consequential or transitional provision as the person making it considers appropriate;

    (b)   be made so as to have effect from a date earlier than that on which it is made;

    (c)   make provision for the delegation of specific functions;

    (d)   make different provision for different cases.

(2)   The power conferred by sub-paragraph (1)(a) includes—

    (a)   power to amend primary legislation (including primary legislation other than that which contains the incompatible provision); and

    (b)   power to amend or revoke subordinate legislation (including subordinate legislation other than that which contains the incompatible provision).

(3)   A remedial order may be made so as to have the same extent as the legislation which it affects.

(4)   No person is to be guilty of an offence solely as a result of the retrospective effect of a remedial order.

Procedure

2 No remedial order may be made unless—

    (a)   a draft of the order has been approved by a resolution of each House of Parliament made after the end of the period of 60 days beginning with the day on which the draft was laid; or

    (b)   it is declared in the order that it appears to the person making it that, because of the urgency of the matter, it is necessary to make the order without a draft being so approved.

Orders laid in draft

3 (1)   No draft may be laid under paragraph 2(a) unless—

    (a)   the person proposing to make the order has laid before Parliament a document which contains a draft of the proposed order and the required information; and

    (b)   the period of 60 days, beginning with the day on which the document required by this sub-paragraph was laid, has ended.

(2)   If representations have been made during that period, the draft laid under paragraph 2(*a*) must be accompanied by a statement containing—

(a)   a summary of the representations; and

(b)   if, as a result of the representations, the proposed order has been changed, details of the changes.

Urgent cases

4 (1)   If a remedial order ('the original order') is made without being approved in draft, the person making it must lay it before Parliament, accompanied by the required information, after it is made.

(2)   If representations have been made during the period of 60 days beginning with the day on which the original order was made, the person making it must (after the end of that period) lay before Parliament a statement containing—

(a)   a summary of the representations; and

(b)   if, as a result of the representations, he considers it appropriate to make changes to the original order, details of the changes.

(3)   If sub-paragraph (2)(b) applies, the person making the statement must—

(a)   make a further remedial order replacing the original order; and

(b)   lay the replacement order before Parliament.

(4)   If, at the end of the period of 120 days beginning with the day on which the original order was made, a resolution has not been passed by each House approving the original or replacement order, the order ceases to have effect (but without that affecting anything previously done under either order or the power to make a fresh remedial order).

Definitions

5 In this Schedule—

'representations' means representations about a remedial order (or proposed remedial order) made to the person making (or proposing to make) it and includes any relevant Parliamentary report or resolution; and

'required information' means—

(a)   an explanation of the incompatibility which the order (or proposed order) seeks to remove, including particulars of the relevant declaration, finding or order; and

(b)   a statement of the reasons for proceeding under section 10 and for making an order in those terms.

Calculating periods

6 In calculating any period for the purposes of this Schedule, no account is to be taken of any time during which—

(a)   Parliament is dissolved or prorogued; or

(b)   both Houses are adjourned for more than four days.

SCHEDULE 3
Derogation and Reservation

Sections 14 and 15

Part I
Derogation

The 1988 notification

The United Kingdom Permanent Representative to the Council of Europe presents his compliments to the Secretary General of the Council, and has the honour to convey the following information in order to ensure compliance with the obligations of Her Majesty's Government in the United Kingdom under Article 15(3) of the Convention for the Protection of Human Rights and Fundamental Freedoms signed at Rome on 4 November 1950.

There have been in the United Kingdom in recent years campaigns of organised terrorism connected with the affairs of Northern Ireland which have manifested themselves in activities which have included repeated murder, attempted murder, maiming, intimidation and violent civil disturbance and in bombing and fire raising which have resulted in death, injury and widespread destruction of property. As a result, a public emergency within the meaning of Article 15(1) of the Convention exists in the United Kingdom.

The Government found it necessary in 1974 to introduce and since then, in cases concerning persons reasonably suspected of involvement in terrorism connected with the affairs of Northern Ireland, or of certain offences under the legislation, who have been detained for 48 hours, to exercise powers enabling further detention without charge, for periods of up to five days, on the authority of the Secretary of State. These powers are at present to be found in Section 12 of the Prevention of Terrorism (Temporary Provisions) Act 1984, Article 9 of the Prevention of Terrorism (Supplemental Temporary Provisions) Order 1984 and Article 10 of the Prevention of Terrorism (Supplemental Temporary Provisions) (Northern Ireland) Order 1984.

Section 12 of the Prevention of Terrorism (Temporary Provisions) Act 1984 provides for a person whom a constable has arrested on reasonable grounds of suspecting him to be guilty of an offence under Section 1, 9 or 10 of the Act, or to be or to have been involved in terrorism connected with the affairs of Northern Ireland, to be detained in right of the arrest for up to 48 hours and thereafter, where the Secretary of State extends the detention period, for up to a further five days. Section 12 substantially re-enacted Section 12 of the Prevention of Terrorism (Temporary Provisions) Act 1976 which, in turn, substantially re-enacted Section 7 of the Prevention of Terrorism (Temporary Provisions) Act 1974.

Article 10 of the Prevention of Terrorism (Supplemental Temporary Provisions) (Northern Ireland) Order 1984 (SI 1984/417) and Article 9 of the Prevention of Terrorism (Supplemental Temporary Provisions) Order 1984 (SI 1984/418) were both made under Sections 13 and 14 of and Schedule 3 to the 1984 Act and substantially re-enacted powers of detention in Orders made under the 1974 and 1976 Acts. A person who is being examined under Article 4 of either Order on his arrival in, or on seeking to leave, Northern Ireland or Great Britain for the purpose of determining whether he is or has been involved in terrorism connected with the affairs of Northern Ireland, or whether there are grounds for suspecting that he has committed an offence under Section 9 of the 1984 Act, may be detained under Article 9 or 10, as appropriate, pending the conclusion of his examination. The period of this examination may exceed 12 hours if an examining officer has reasonable grounds for suspecting him to be or to have been involved in acts of terrorism connected with the affairs of Northern Ireland.

Where such a person is detained under the said Article 9 or 10 he may be detained for up to 48 hours on the authority of an examining officer and thereafter, where the Secretary of State extends the detention period, for up to a further five days.

In its judgment of 29 November 1988 in the Case of *Brogan and Others*, the European Court of Human Rights held that there had been a violation of Article 5(3) in respect of each of the applicants, all of whom had been detained under Section 12 of the 1984 Act. The Court held that even the shortest of the four periods of detention concerned, namely four days and six hours, fell outside the constraints as to time permitted by the first part of Article 5(3). In addition, the Court held that there had been a violation of Article 5(5) in the case of each applicant.

Following this judgment, the Secretary of State for the Home Department informed Parliament on 6 December 1988 that, against the background of the terrorist campaign, and the over-riding need to bring terrorists to justice, the Government did not believe that the maximum period of detention should be reduced. He informed Parliament that the Government were examining the matter with a view to responding to the judgment. On 22 December 1988, the Secretary of State further informed Parliament that it remained the Government's wish, if it could be achieved, to find a judicial process under which extended detention might be reviewed and where appropriate authorised by a judge or other judicial officer. But a further period of reflection and consultation was necessary before the Government could bring forward a firm and final view.

Since the judgment of 29 November 1988 as well as previously, the Government have found it necessary to continue to exercise, in relation to terrorism connected with the affairs of Northern Ireland, the powers described above enabling further detention without charge for periods of up to 5 days, on the authority of the Secretary of State, to the extent strictly required by the exigencies of the situation to enable necessary enquiries and investigations properly to be completed in order to decide whether criminal proceedings should be instituted. To the extent that the exercise of these powers may be inconsistent with the obligations imposed by the Convention the Government has availed itself of the right of derogation conferred by Article 15(1) of the Convention and will continue to do so until further notice.

Dated 23 December 1988.

The 1989 notification

The United Kingdom Permanent Representative to the Council of Europe presents his compliments to the Secretary General of the Council, and has the honour to convey the following information.

In his communication to the Secretary General of 23 December 1988, reference was made to the introduction and exercise of certain powers under section 12 of the Prevention of Terrorism (Temporary Provisions) Act 1984, Article 9 of the

Prevention of Terrorism (Supplemental Temporary Provisions) Order 1984 and Article 10 of the Prevention of Terrorism (Supplemental Temporary Provisions) (Northern Ireland) Order 1984.

These provisions have been replaced by section 14 of and paragraph 6 of Schedule 5 to the Prevention of Terrorism (Temporary Provisions) Act 1989, which make comparable provision. They came into force on 22 March 1989. A copy of these provisions is enclosed.

The United Kingdom Permanent Representative avails himself of this opportunity to renew to the Secretary General the assurance of his highest consideration.

23 March 1989.

PART II
RESERVATION

At the time of signing the present (First) Protocol, I declare that, in view of certain provisions of the Education Acts in the United Kingdom, the principle affirmed in the second sentence of Article 2 is accepted by the United Kingdom only so far as it is compatible with the provision of efficient instruction and training, and the avoidance of unreasonable public expenditure.

Dated 20 March 1952. Made by the United Kingdom Permanent Representative to the Council of Europe.

SCHEDULE 4
JUDICIAL PENSIONS

Section 18(6)

Duty to make orders about pensions

1 (1)   The appropriate Minister must by order make provision with respect to pensions payable to or in respect of any holder of a judicial office who serves as an ECHR judge.

(2)   A pensions order must include such provision as the Minister making it considers is necessary to secure that—

(a)   an ECHR judge who was, immediately before his appointment as an ECHR judge, a member of a judicial pension scheme is entitled to remain as a member of that scheme;

(b)   the terms on which he remains a member of the scheme are those which would have been applicable had he not been appointed as an ECHR judge; and

(c)   entitlement to benefits payable in accordance with the scheme continues to be determined as if, while serving as an ECHR judge, his salary was that which would (but for section 18(4)) have been payable to him in respect of his continuing service as the holder of his judicial office.

Contributions

2 A pensions order may, in particular, make provision—

(a) for any contributions which are payable by a person who remains a member of a scheme as a result of the order, and which would otherwise be payable by deduction from his salary, to be made otherwise than by deduction from his salary as an ECHR judge; and

(b) for such contributions to be collected in such manner as may be determined by the administrators of the scheme.

Amendments of other enactments

3 A pensions order may amend any provision of, or made under, a pensions Act in such manner and to such extent as the Minister making the order considers necessary or expedient to ensure the proper administration of any scheme to which it relates.

Definitions

4 In this Schedule—

'appropriate Minister' means—

(a) in relation to any judicial office whose jurisdiction is exercisable exclusively in relation to Scotland, the Secretary of State; and

(b) otherwise, the Lord Chancellor;

'ECHR judge' means the holder of a judicial office who is serving as a judge of the Court;

'judicial pension scheme' means a scheme established by and in accordance with a pensions Act;

'pensions Act' means—

(a) the County Courts Act (Northern Ireland) 1959;

(b) the Sheriffs' Pensions (Scotland) Act 1961;

(c) the Judicial Pensions Act 1981; or

(d) the Judicial Pensions and Retirement Act 1993; and

'pensions order' means an order made under paragraph 1.

INDEX

Absence, unauthorised
offence of, 8.50–8.51
Access to any part of prison
denying, offence of, 8.20
Accommodation
certification of, 2.17
searches of. *See* Searches of
accommodation
Additional days
punishment, as, 8.84, 8.88
remission of, applications for, 8.95–8.100
Adjudications
adjournment of—
generally, 8.9, 8.76
police investigations and, 17.5
appeals against finding of guilt. *See*
review *below*
conduct of, 8.71–8.81
contracted out prisons and, 2.42
defence, prisoner's—
assistance in putting forward, 8.10
copies of statements, access to, 8.8
legal aid and, 8.15
time for preparing, 8.3, 8.76
witnesses, 8.3, 8.8, 8.14, 8.78
written on charge form, may be, 8.3
double jeopardy and, 17.25–17.30
evidence, 8.72, 8.77, 8.78, 8.82, 8.83
generally, 2.10
guilt of prisoner, 8.16, 8.79, 8.80, 8.82
hearsay evidence, 8.83
judicial review and, 3.34, 8.93, 8.94
legal representation and, 8.9–8.15, 8.75,
8.76
medical examination of prisoner prior to,
8.7, 8.74
mitigating evidence, 8.80
model procedure, 8.71–8.81
Prisons Ombudsman and, 3.19, 8.92
reduction of charge, 8.4, 8.79
review of, 3.9, 7.15, 7.32, 8.89–8.91
standard of proof, 8.82, 8.83
witnesses, 8.3, 8.8, 8.14, 8.78, 8.81
AIDS/HIV
condoms, issue of, 10.85

AIDS/HIV—*contd*
educating prisoners about, 10.85
HIV infected prisoners, 10.86, 10.87
policy on, 10.85
syringes, 10.85
tests, 10.86
Alcohol offences
being intoxicated, 8.35, 8.36
bringing into prison, 2.18
knowingly consuming, 8.37, 8.38
Allocation of prisoners
adult female prisoners, 6.54–6.60
adult male prisoners, 6.35–6.40
availability of places and, 6.38, 6.39
categorisation process distinguished, 6.35
categorisation, effect of, 6.10
category A prisoners, 6.45
category C prisoners, 6.46–6.48
higher security category prison, to, 6.38,
6.39
lower security category prison, to, 6.39
mandatory life sentence prisoners, 6.44,
11.26–11.29, 11.31, 11.32
nature of offence and, 6.38
procedure for initial allocation, 6.40
reallocation, 6.41–6.43
young female offenders, 6.61–6.63
young male offenders, 6.49–6.53
Arson
offence of, 8.47
Artificial insemination
applications for, 7.15, 7.40
Assault
claims. *See* Assault claims
fear of, procedures to be followed, 15.17,
15.18
offence of, 8.17
offences generally, 17.15
recording of incidents by prisoners, 15.19
restraint constituting, 3.51, 3.52
Assault claims
death in custody, following, 10.152
prisoners, by—
access to medical records and,
15.7–15.10

411

Index

Index